Howard Kohn

WE HAD A DREAM

A Tale of the Struggle for Integration in America

Simon & Schuster

SIMON & SCHUSTER
Rockefeller Center
1230 Avenue of the Americas
New York, NY 10020
Copyright © 1998 by Howard Kohn

Simon & Schuster and colophon are registered trademarks of Simon & Schuster Inc.
Designed by Karolina Harris
Manufactured in the United States of America
10 9 8 7 6 5 4 3 2 1

Library of Congress Cataloging-in-Publication Data
Kohn, Howard
We had a dream: a tale of the struggle for integration in America/Howard Kohn
     p.   cm.
1. Prince George's County (Md.)—Race relations. 2. Prince George's County (Md.)—Biography
3. Afro-Americans—Civil rights—Maryland—Prince George's County—History—20th century
4. Interracial dating—Maryland—Prince George's County
5. Interracial marriage—Maryland—Prince George's County
6. United States—Race relations—Case studies   I. Title
F187.P9K64   1998
305.8'009752'51—dc21   98-23808
                                                   CIP

ISBN 0-684-80874-9

For my children, Jennifer and Gregory

Introduction

It is almost always wrong to believe we were a better people when we were younger, but sometimes it can't be helped. Call it what you will, an exhilaration that ran through us, the stone rolled back, a glimpse of the Promised Land. There was a time, one decade removed from the armistice with the Axis powers, when a significant number of us got up our nerve and attempted to set aside the nonsense of racial divisions in America. The period that became known as the modern civil rights movement began in 1957 (to pick a date) with the Little Rock Four, heads held high against a street church of stone-throwers, and ended in 1972 (to pick another) with a gunshot that crippled for good the other side's messiah, George Wallace, who at the onset of the movement was a consistently high finisher in the standings of Most Admired Americans. For those of us who lived through the period, the temptation can be overwhelming to look back and see a grand transforming of the American mission. This is not just a trick of memory either, nor mad dreaming. Read the periodicals of the time; there are *Time* and *Newsweek* passages in which it appears a racial oneness has replaced all other social goals. Sit-ins, jail time, the shedding of some blood, these were on the highlight films, but the underlying reality was even more powerful. On the roadsides there were billboard posters of a black hand and white hand clasped together. What a sign to guide us in our private lives! Thousands upon thousands of us acted on a renunciation of the status quo, that horrid society. We made personal statements against bosses, against parents, against the elders of the racial order. The desire to obtain bona fides, or just to do the right thing, was high.

Toward the end of the civil rights movement I was a chronicler at a couple of newspapers and then for *Rolling Stone*. From the cold months of 1967 I can recall for you one little test of conscience that perhaps signified the times. Two friends, a white man and a black man, broke from college studies to take jobs in the Michigan town where the two had attended high school. The two were nineteen years old, both of them married, both about to become fathers. The white man took a news job at the local daily, the black man a job with the local office of a federal poverty program. A situation arose: The black man, the most popular kid in his high school class, an outstanding drum major, president of the student body—and who, by the way, was married to a white woman—could find no dwelling for his family to rent. With a host of excuses landlords gave them the bum's rush. The black man approached his friend at the newspaper. *You got to, man! You got to write a story!* Was there equivocation on the white man's part? Of course there was. Friendship had to be measured against the track of a career. There was certain to be trouble with the white man's editors, older men of the same color who wished for a world ignorant of such a thing as miscegenation. The white man went forward with the story anyway, a triumph over himself. The element of race was decisive. He was elevated to do good because he could live out his beliefs. (Who knows if he would have put his young career on the line for a white friend?) The newsman fought with his editors and lost his job. Probably he would have been disappointed had the drama been less eventful. For a spell thereafter he paid his bills with a job at Prestolite, yanking an assembly-line lever twelve times a minute to fire pins into auto generators. He felt virtuous.

Out of such experiences (this one happens to be my own) a common vision of the future grew. Most of us came onto the scene some years after those who pioneered the special enterprise of unifying the races, and, as latecomers, we may have held an exaggerated esteem for the concept. Nonetheless, millions of us seemed committed to it. I remember thinking my children would automatically have sleepovers with their black friends. Integration was to be our way of life; integration would hit it big. I moved around the country—California, Oklahoma, Florida, New York—and found people everywhere who believed as I did.

A quarter century or more has passed. What is our legacy? You may think you know the punch line. You have read that King is dead, the civil rights movement scattered, and those awaiting a new crusade are looking for a hustle, not for work. Integration years ago ceased being the point of just about everybody's life. Same as always, America remains two separate communities, one a place of tenements and a dispiriting city life, the other a place of comfort, far from the cities and the rumpus—Black America and White America, in other words. But on instinct you have to know this is too pat an answer. When people live in conditions so disparate that the conditions keep them apart, the issue of race is almost a false issue. Anyway, not all of America is limited to white people driving to work on highrise thruways above the dire straits of black people. To get a much better handle on the state of race relations in the 1990s, why not go to a place where white people and black people meet every day on terms of regular engagement, a place where, on paper at least, there is equality between the two races?

The boundary of one such place begins about two miles from where I live in suburban Washington, D.C. It is located on the Yankee side of the Potomac River and is adjacent to the nation's capital on the northeastern perimeter. This is Prince George's County, and life here, arguably as good as it gets, is reflected on deliberately crooked streets of such recent history they lack corner signs. In these subdivisions the houses feature an attempt at flamboyant beauty—cathedral ceilings, gables, even turrets. Aluminum siding is banned. Curbsides are planted with nursery saplings. The extravagant entranceways of brick columns and wrought-iron gates with names inscribed in brick facings or on brass plates or set out in arcs of metal lettering—Enterprise Estates and Paradise Acres—sharpen the most characteristic effect, the air of fast money and the earnest striving that suggests the place is being built as an illustration of the American dream. What is less obvious, until one chances to drive through the gates and enter the enclaves of cul-de-sacs and catches the children at play, is that a vast number of the people living life to the limit here are African-Americans.

Prince George's County is within the state of Maryland, the "Free State," but for nearly three hundred years the white people of Prince George's were said to have a southern attitude with a northern address. Toward the end of the seventeenth century, English colonists had established a settlement here on the upriver flatlands of the Potomac that seemed, through the steadfastness of one generation of European descendants after another, as if it would be forever rural, forever the province of tobacco growers and other landholders engaged in local customs of racial separatism. Slaves were once auctioned off in the marketplace of Upper Marlboro, the county seat. The near-assassination of George Wallace took place at a Prince George's shopping mall in 1972 during his second presidential campaign. The shooter aside, many Prince Georgians were Wallace people. Twice, Prince Georgian voters wished a Wallace presidency on the country. Even so, by 1972, this was a territory on the eve of a historic turn. If the modern civil rights movement changed all of America, perhaps no place experienced a changeover as dramatic as in Prince George's County. For so long the capital of nothing, for so long a "backwater" and an "ugly sister" in the pages of the *Washington Post,* Prince George's County has become a capital of the Civil Rights Dream. Certain people departed the county, people associated with the terms "lunch bucket" and "redneck." But more people arrived. From 1970 to 1990 the population tripled, up to 730,000. Between 1980 and 1990 the average family income nearly doubled, from $25,000 to $48,000, due in the main to the addition of black couples who worked in the computer industry or the law or the media or in a civil-service role with the federal government. Overall, by 1990, black and white adult residents had reached essential equality in levels of education, percentages of homeownership, the size of personal income, and in total numbers. I first took an active interest in Prince George's County in 1992, the same year the *New York Times Sunday Magazine* referred to it as a place "fast becoming the closest thing to utopia." A high percentage of the black newcomers, from all appearances, wanted to show the world what professionalism and a civil rights self-identity can do. In combination with white people of a like mind they were attempting to create a crucible of racial integration.

On the following pages is the collected story of a handful of these Prince Georgians, whose lives, if not extraordinary, are at least indicative of what has happened to the spirit of a generation ago. They wanted to be good integrationists, and for these intentions they ought to be admired. Even more, they ought to be admired for their forthrightness. They were honest about their failings, which, speaking for myself anyway, are failings that strike close to home. As for their triumphs, well, you will see for yourself.

Just so you know, I began this book with two biases. One is that good people matter. Fever and adrenaline aren't always on the side of people with guns. Enough has been written, I believe, about the violent nature of American race relations. Having said that, it is fair to report that the intertwined influences of violence and race are once again important to the people in this story, the link between violence and race being on some level unavoidable anywhere in America. My second bias is that individual actions coalesce into social change. A romance between a white man and a black woman—the reference here is to Bruce Gordon and Camilla Brown, whose acquaintance you are about to make—was a challenge to the order of things in Prince George's County. Under the weight of all manner of challenges—sexual, legal, political—the old order of Prince George's collapsed, although not absolutely.

There are no absolutes in the real world.

Prologue

Bruce Gordon and Camilla Brown were infatuated with each other but not so infatuated that they were able to forget that the mere act of holding hands might be a provocation to many people. So on their first date, a Saturday night near the start of the 1973–74 school year, Bruce borrowed his father's three-tone Cadillac and drove Camilla across the border into Washington, D.C. He squired her down Wisconsin Avenue, in a benevolent neighborhood where lived Georgetown professors. At a movie house they watched *The Groove Tube,* not quite pornographic but you get the picture. He wanted to show her how adult he was, and among purveyors of avant-gardism they would be safe. Afterward, walking the avenue, hands touching, they saw many other boldly paired-up people, and yet they grew ever more self-conscious. At Maison de Crepe they ordered onion soup. They kept eyeing the room. Was everyone staring at them? Back in Prince George's County, saying good-night, they exchanged their first kiss. Bruce was quite impressed with the effect it had on him; it was probably all the tension of the evening whooshing out of him, but he thought the kiss possessed "a supernatural quality." He went reeling, jiggidy-jig, into the house.

At Potomac High School, where Bruce Gordon and Camilla Brown were seniors, a romance then developed between the two of them, a romance across the color line. As far as can be determined, there had never before been an instance at Potomac High of a young white man and a young black woman becoming sweethearts. For that matter, there had been very few such romances at any locality or at any time in the English-speaking history of Prince George's County.

Bruce and Camilla had begun paying notice to each other during lunchtime in the school cafeteria. He was amazed and beguiled by her forthrightness. ("It was chemistry, plain and simple. Every day the air was getting thick with this interesting kind of attention.") Bruce flirted by sitting next to her, and Camilla flirted back by playing with his hair. "You need to pick it, you need a pick comb," she told him, fluffing it out for him. Bruce's hair was growing into a mound of hyperextended curlicues, an "Isro" in the vernacular of the time. In the eyes of his fellow students Bruce's hairdo would constitute in later years one of the bases for remembering him. *Oh, yeah, he had the big Jewish Afro.* This was during a period when Afros were all the rage for black kids and for the ultrahip white kids. But for Bruce, who once upon a time had wished for straight "American" hair, who as a boy would sit for hours on a stool in front of the bathroom sink while his sister tried various tricks to straighten his kinks—and who, furthermore, had hated his lips, which Camilla later found "big and wonderful," who had thought of saving money and hiring a surgeon to alter them, and who, whenever anyone snapped pictures, would suck in those lips so they would look thinner, who had exuded so much shame about the uncool face God had given him—for this white kid to grow on purpose a full head of frizzed-out hair amounted to a conscious linkage with the opposite race. Ultrahip—to see Bruce at Potomac High presenting a showoff, aggressive alter ego that reveled now in Semitic features that could be taken for African. He was making a statement. *Oh yeah, the white kid who tried to look black.* And he cultivated his reverse electric image with élan, the better to go courting girls of color.

Bruce and Camilla had known each other since sixth grade, when she transferred into the public schools from Georgetown Day. She had skipped the fifth grade. Immediately they became rivals for the title of brightest kid in the class. ("Right from the start she was this legend. I remember very clearly thinking, 'Oh, my God, she's smarter than me, and she'll make me look bad.' She was my biggest threat.") Long ago Camilla had won the competition. At Potomac High, she was about to graduate number two in the Class of 1974—Bruce would finish a few rungs below—and if not for school politics Bruce thought she might have been number one. ("Camilla deserved to be valedictorian. But she was starting to flex her political muscles a bit and did some things that were considered rebellious, such as dating me, and she got in a dispute with the sponsor of the awards program. So for political reasons she was bumped down to salutatorian. I can't swear to you it was racial, but give me a break!") Charming her way up was not Camilla's specialty, and yet she was a dream student for an integrated school—a black girl who could dance and could act and who was book smart and who never got in trouble. On the introductory page of the school yearbook, *The Powhatan,* she is posed, hair in a modest Afro, with the white principal. Camilla deplored drugs and had no interest in alcohol, and was to Bruce's mind "a goody-goody." Her good citizenship, her high achievements, her beauty: they all contributed to her sexiness, the ultimately attractive opposite for Bruce. At the Potomac High football games she was a cheerleader. Bruce cared little for the action on the field—his only foray into the jock world had been with the tennis team—but he loved to watch Camilla jumping for touchdowns. He would stare at her while the overhead stadium strobes bore down in a glory of light that everywhere means Friday night in America. Bruce's vantage point was a hill behind the rickety wood bleachers. He would climb up there to be among a group of misfits and academic fugitives and practitioners of independent thinking whose principal activity during the games was to sit powwow style and toke up. Rebel though Bruce was, he remained mindful that an arrest involving marijuana might ruin his chances for medical school, and he never ceased being on the lookout. In case of a police raid he planned on an escape route into the woods beyond the near end zone. One evening Prince George's narcotics officers afforded him a test. ("I said to myself, 'Feet, get hot!' ") Zigging through the mature sycamores and beeches and into the backyards of brick ramblers, bumping past vinyl-and-aluminum lawn furniture, he made a getaway. Afterward he sneaked back to the stadium and hooked up with Camilla.

Camilla and Bruce had the same career ambition, to become physicians like his father, Dr. David S. Gordon, a family-practice doctor. Car-crazy and a gallant lover of fast horses, Bruce's father was an all-around good fellow known as Doc. Everyone in the community—black people, white people—went to see Dr. Gordon. In the realm of race relations in Prince George's County, the liberalizing influence of such figures as Bruce's father cannot be overestimated. Otherwise an interracial love affair would have been next to impossible. Yet for Dr. Gordon to like and accept Bruce's involvement with a black girl was asking "too much." It was disrespect of the father by the son. Camilla learned of Dr. Gordon's attitude when Bruce brought her to meet his parents. Bruce's mother, with her poodle, was welcoming, but not Doc. Eventually, Camilla would come to see that the relationship between Bruce and his father could not be separated from her own relationship with Bruce, and that the one must inevitably undo the other, but that was later, after her heart had been broken.

Leaving for college, Bruce and Camilla's romance was unconsummated—not for the lack of trying, just nerves getting the better of them—

but they were as passionate about each other as virgins can be. They selected schools near Boston—Brandeis for him, Mount Holyoke for her—separated by less than an hour's drive. On weekends they holed up together in her dormitory room; they studied and made love. Dorm life broke down all inhibitions. "Who are those two? They're intense!" a dorm counselor once remarked. It was a line that could have served as their slogan. During the week, parted by their school schedules, they rang up long-distance bills, hanging on to the phone even after talk was exhausted, just listening to each other breathe. On Sunday nights, before Bruce headed back to Brandeis, they would talk of the pact between them. Every indication pointed toward wedded bliss. They wanted to have it all, the quality things their parents had, a stable income, a double-lot house, a luxury car, and also a home ruled by heart and conscience. They thought they had their minds made up, but then desperation began to creep into their grandiose plans. Just when it appeared Bruce would propose to Camilla, the opposite happened. Suddenly the Pink Floyd in him sprang out full grown—a wild, party-boy disdain for the settled life. He stopped his weekend trips to Mount Holyoke and cut off the phone calls. Camilla never understood why, notwithstanding the letter Bruce sent quoting his father's fears that a mixed marriage would undermine their medical careers. The letter made no sense because, at the same time, Bruce gave up on medical school. He transferred to the University of Florida and switched his major to sociology. He read the Great Philosophers. He announced to a friend, "I am going to fuck blond women and get straight A's and party all year. It'll be perfect, especially the blond women." The first few days after the transfer were the roughest; he thought constantly of Camilla; and, in the end, Florida was a big letdown. No blond women materialized for him, no women at all. It was only after graduation, returning for a while to Prince George's County, that he launched into several affairs, all of them ill-advised, even as they fulfilled his bohemian self-image and secured his bad-boy reputation. Bruce became for a time a boastful, exhibitionistic, get-lucky admirer of the here and now, a man who moved from woman to woman. He paid nothing for this thrill ride and did not get anything either. There was no one special until, on a trip to Mexico City, he met a native beauty. After six weeks of courtship he married her, but by 1992 their marriage was falling apart. Bruce was then thirty-six years old, a loan financier living in Denver, and once again he found himself being ineluctably drawn into dreams about Camilla. Setting out to find her, Bruce contacted his mother, now divorced from his father, and asked if she knew Camilla's whereabouts. As it had happened, just a short time earlier, Camilla had phoned Bruce's mother to inquire about him. The two phone calls, occurring out of the blue and within weeks of each other, threw Mrs. Gordon for a loop. She reported to Camilla only that Bruce was doing something with banks. Municipal loans, was it? She would not pass on his phone number. And despite Bruce's wheedling, she would impart to him only the knowledge that Camilla was a doctor in the Massachusetts town of Cambridge, outside Boston. For their own good she would not give out more information. What but misery could come of Bruce horning in on Camilla's life?

As far as Mrs. Gordon knew, Camilla and Bruce were content in their marriages. In point of fact, however, Camilla had just finalized a divorce from her husband, and Bruce had entered into proceedings to end his marriage. Bruce tried locating Camilla through directory assistance, but her phone number was unlisted, and, for a while, he gave his scheme a rest. Then, on impulse, he checked again with the phone company. For some reason, Camilla had decided to list her number. A sensation of Eureka! came over him. He phoned immediately, not knowing if Camilla was married or not, not knowing even if he had the right number, and got tongue-tied when her answering machine clicked on. The message he left was filled with coughing—he had a bad cold—plus a few mumbled words. He signed off without leaving his name.

Bruce had disappeared from Camilla's life for nearly fifteen years, and then there arrived an obtuse message in an unrecognizably hoarse voice. Might it really be her teenage boyfriend? She shrugged off the notion.

A few days later Bruce succumbed to "an uncontrollable urge" and called again. "Hi, this is Bruce Gordon."

"Bruce? *My* Bruce Gordon?!"

"The very same!"

Bruce finagled a business trip to Boston, and he and Camilla were re-united for a weekend. Some things had not changed. Bruce still had pale watery eyes and a high forehead that turns red in the sun. Camilla still had a soulful smile and two small moles on elegantly arched cheekbones. She still had her preternaturally girlish face, and, with a city girl's taste in clothes, she looked jazzy in the flowing folds of a gypsylike, color-splashed dress. But some things were also different. Camilla now had her dark tendrills done in dreads. Bruce's hair was a prematurely graying thatch of curls, combed in a banker's style. He was wearing wraparound sunglasses and a cottonblend shirt. ("He had a corporate look, which was new. More interestingly, he had a macho look, which was new, too.") Bruce was now a fitness nut and a devotee of tai kwon do. He was appreciably more muscular; he could throw Camilla into the air and catch her. He seemed to her like a "super-action hero." She seemed to him like "Paris in June." Camilla was "the same vital presence she'd always been. She looked a little softer, but she still had that sultry, athletic body, a dancer's body. She looked perfect."

As Bruce and Camilla began to fill in the blanks about each other's adult lives, Bruce got word that his father had suffered a stroke. After a period of recovery, Dr. Gordon was to be discharged from a medical institution; someone would have to care for him at the Gordon house. It was up to Bruce—a guy who had always conceived of his life as separate from the fate of those left behind in Prince George's County.

1 **The flat,** green countryside of Prince George's County that Bruce Gordon came home to in the autumn of 1992 was still under tobacco on large parcels of land, but only in the outlying regions, out by Upper Marlboro, the county seat, where there were also grazing Holsteins in the bogs and rolling hillocks. Elsewhere the farmland had been turned into a suburban society, with shopping plazas and streetlamps. To look upon the new Prince George's County from the plane Bruce rode in on was to witness progress. Through the clouds were revealed black lines of asphalt and big, open, immature gardens and flat mall roofs with monster air-conditioning units, all the spanking work of building crews that had been laying in commercial strips and subdivisions on the old fields since the 1970s.

On the other side of the Potomac River, at National Airport, the plane touched chill ground. In a rental car Bruce crossed the river, trying to remember his way. The green signs on the I-495 Beltway were half familiar. He passed by the first turnoff in Prince George's County—Indian Head Highway. Somewhere along here a wild and panicked bunch of European colonists had slaughtered the native Piscataways and Accokeeks and hung their heads on a line of poles. In a couple of miles came Branch Avenue, the main drag into an unincorporated community that went by the post office name of Hillcrest Heights. This was Bruce's home ground. The lots were neatly spaced and the houses nearly identical, everything with an orderly look, like an architect's rendering of postwar suburbia. Before builders began building subdivisions in outer Prince George's County, they had built neighborhoods in inner Prince George's County. Many of the houses of Hillcrest Heights had been put up one after another in the fifties by an old-line Italian-American patriarch, Anthony Carozza. They are ramblers that will never win the cover of *Architectural Digest,* but they are workmanlike, made of brick and cinder block, some with an upper story, and they were ritzy for their time, among the first in the county equipped with central air and central heat. When Bruce was growing up, the fashionable area in Prince George's County was Hillcrest Heights; it had paved driveways, sodded lawns, automatic-opening garages, front yards planted with razzle-dazzle rhododendrons and costume-jewelry peonies. Teachers and engineers and doctors had snapped up the Carozza houses the minute they came on the market. There is a four-way intersection at 23rd Place and Iverson Street, and on the southwest corner is a Carozza rambler, red brick with white trim, sited on a double lot, and built extralarge, nearly twice the size of others on the block. The big front door has squares carved into it in a Spanish motif. Dr. Gordon, smelling of Mentholatum and cursing at his wheelchair, let Bruce in. Bruce had lived his first eighteen years in the upstairs half of the house but was now to occupy the huge bottom half, the warren of rooms that as a child he could not enter unless summoned. These had been his father's medical offices—a waiting room, an X-ray room of painted cinder blocks, two examining rooms, and a room for a desk and file cabinets. Although Dr. Gordon had been able to keep his practice going until shortly before his stroke, the basement was now empty, all the medical equipment removed, the walls stripped of the sunset paintings and the medical certificates. Bruce took over his father's old office desk for his own. He put his barbells and his weight bench into the X-ray room and set up his bed in the waiting room, a low, bare place. His new quarters would be sparely furnished, to the point of asceticism. The only arresting detail was the silk sheeting he put on a king-sized bed. Bruce's divorce had cost him virtually all he owned. He had received a phone call at 11:30 one morning in Denver from his lawyer, "You are to be out of your house by 2:30 this afternoon," to which Bruce had shouted, "What am I paying you for?" He had been living out of boxes and suitcases ever since. At his father's house he needed no furniture. Upstairs, Dr. Gordon had left intact the overstuffed couches and mahogany sideboards and carpeting Bruce's mother had installed before she left.

Of course, Dr. Gordon would not inquire about Bruce's divorce. Divorce was a sore subject for the two of them. The marriage of Bruce's parents had dissolved when Bruce was twenty-one, and Dr. Gordon was still unhappy about the way Bruce had seemed to root for his mother. An odd couple, two men without women in their lives, the father in his wheelchair grumping at the TV, the son puttering around with his barbells—they had been estranged for much of Bruce's adult life. In the past twelve years he had not once stepped foot in the Gordon house, and had seen his father on only one occasion in Denver. Over the next several days they exchanged mainly the details of schedule-making that might pass between two men at a boardinghouse. They had no practice in being devoted to blood kin and felt foolish about trying. "You can use my desk, but you can't have it. It's mine. I'll be needing it," Dr. Gordon said at one point, and that was probably as close as either of them came to an emotionally revealing statement.

Before Bruce's return, his father had spent the first hushed and pessimistic stage of his recuperation in a convalescent home. Everyone now knew Dr. Gordon might live another twenty years but probably would never again have full strength in his right leg and right arm. And the stroke had rendered him crankier than usual. What cheer he had came from his high-octane, leather-seated Cadillac Fleetwood Brougham, model year 1989, the Doc's pride and joy, waxed and tanked up in his garage and ready to go. The Caddy's odometer read 45,011 miles, and the vast majority of those miles had been spent in "pleasure cruising" around town. To be able to drive again Dr. Gordon would have to retrain a set of muscles and nerves on his right side. "But I aim to do it," he told Bruce. "I'm determined."

Almost as soon as Bruce was moved in, he began talking about leaving. Once his father was settled into a satisfactory routine, Bruce planned to look for work in Boston to be closer to Camilla.

That day could not come soon enough to suit Dr. Gordon, whose fearsome sense of dignity was offended by his son's taking up with this particular old flame. "I just can't take the values he has. His values are not my values," Dr. Gordon would tell anybody who cared to listen. "We've never gotten along. Bruce swore he'd never come back to this house, and that was fine with me. If he stays here, he and that girl will drive more nails in my casket, them carrying on like two love-crazed kids."

The affair Bruce had resumed with Camilla was not being carried out in the Gordon house, however. "Don't bring that girl here. She's not welcome," Dr. Gordon had told Bruce. A tall, imposing man, even in the wheelchair, Dr. Gordon did not seem an enfeebled spirit, and he did not speak with the weak voice of an old man.

"I'll do what I damn well please," Bruce said, but he had winced at his father's words.

In any event, Bruce was not anxious to invite Camilla to the house, and, the truth was, Camilla would not have come. Everything about Dr. Gordon aggravated Camilla, his sanctimonious voice, his habit of leaving the room when she entered. The interpretation Camilla placed on Doc's behavior was that of a priggish and standoffish lout. In her formal introduction to the man years ago, he had stood in his living room, red in the face, a bit toothy and horsey of features. With Bruce shifting his feet awkwardly beside her, Camilla had extended a polite hand; Dr. Gordon had recoiled from the contact.

In the current situation, there was no need for Camilla to travel to Hillcrest Heights. The Washington-to-Boston commuter line could bring Bruce to her house in Cambridge on the spur of the moment—Bruce called it an "I miss her like crazy" moment. One weekend he met Camilla's children, a ten-year-old boy and an eight-year-old girl. "I feel kind of wistful," he told her. "They could have been my children." During the week, like old times, corny correspondence passed between Bruce and Camilla, and they spoke in long drawn-out phone calls. To listen to them, they were possessors not only of an old magic but a new one as well. When they had first gotten back together they had gone off to romantic hideouts, a week at Telluride, another on Cape Cod. They had drunk champagne out of plastic throwaway glasses. He was courtly and soft-spoken. She brushed back droplets of dark, heavy hair. Bruce described her as "a sixties girl who will always be a sixties girl," by which he meant she was sassy and confident and open to the world. Twice a week, from eight in the evening until midnight, she danced barefooted at a community center, and for two weeks each August she was the resident physician at a dance camp in the Maine woods, where she fed and enlivened the mystical body with Afro-Haitian ragtime, Moroccan dance ("what is incorrectly called belly dancing"), West African street funk, the six-step Lindy, massage, yoga, sweat-lodge meditation, communal vegetarian meals, and skinny dipping at the swim hole. In Cambridge, while the wind blasted the windows, Bruce found it absurdly endearing to watch Camilla let her clothes fall to the floor and walk around the room. Hers was not a froufrou sexuality but a carefree innocence about her body. It was as though the years had never happened. *I am ga-ga about you,* he said affectionately to her.

Later, returning to Hillcrest Heights, Bruce would tell himself: Do not bank on this feeling; it will vanish, like a trick. But for now the world was perfection itself.

• • •

It did not take long for the news about Bruce's return, and the news about his second-chance romance with Camilla, to travel the eight blocks from 23rd and Iverson to a house on Foster Place, home of Merv and Dell Strickler, a white couple getting up in age. The Gordons and Stricklers had once been active in the same parent-teacher groups and the local neighborhood association, and the two wives had done volunteer hospital work together. Dell Strickler was now a silvery slip of a woman with an oval, pixieish face, and she spoke with thoroughgoing enthusiasm about her good wishes for Bruce and Camilla, "I hope they'll be happy this time around. I hope it works out. Bruce and Camilla were always the nicest couple." In reality, Dell had her doubts—what were the chances of success for two people faced not just with the prejudices of the outside world but with the recriminations and bad feelings that must be inside them from that terrible, in-the-dark-of-night parting years ago? But she did not think it appropriate to say anything aloud. As for Merv Strickler, a thick, ruddy-faced man with rippled grayish hair, he was without qualms. "I hope Camilla moves back here with Bruce. I'd like to see them living in Hillcrest Heights. It's what we need in this community," he said. "That's how integration succeeds best, on a personal level."

This discussion took place in a house furnished in a crowded, eclectic, and independent style that was pure Merv and Dell. In the kitchen was a white stand-up Nesco electric roaster, bought in 1949 when Merv was a doctoral student at Stanford and Dell was one of the rare women to be found in the technical white-coated man's world of the physics lab. Over the years she had used the Nesco roaster for dozens of holiday turkeys. It was in tip-top condition still; probably, in all of America, there were not more than a hundred others like it in working order. Next to the roaster was a Westinghouse range, bought in 1955 soon after the Stricklers settled on Hillcrest Heights for a permanent home. A black rotary dial phone occupied the same place on the kitchen wall it always had. The living room walls were hung with the casual collections of Merv's far-flung overseas trips: artists' sketches on authentic Egyptian papyrus and on Oriental rice paper. Merv had a Stanford Ph.D. in the twin majors of aviation and education, a combination unheard of until he proposed it, and he had made a career out of selling to government chieftains around the world the idea of inserting aviation into school curricula. He had been an honored guest from Moscow to Cairo. On the fireplace mantel was a Russian wooden doll brought back from Siberia. The living room floor was crowded with a piano that had seen much use and two satiny upright Troubadour harps that Dell played regularly during services at their church and also once in a while at the Kennedy Center.

Another wall was hung with a framed photograph of their daughter, Heather, best friends with Camilla since eleventh grade. Heather was a woman of striking looks—honey-red hair, freckles around eyes, pink cheeks—and a smile that radiated sweetness, wholesomeness, guilelessness. Atop the piano sat pictures of her three daughters, blond and pug-nosed and also all smiles. Heather had had only one serious romance in her life—with the man she ultimately married, a white man—but during the years at Potomac High, when Heather and Camilla used to bake cookies in the Westinghouse oven and talk girlishly about boys, it seemed not at all improbable that Heather might join Camilla in cross-racial dating. At least it seemed so to the three Hillcrest Heights women who played canasta with Dell. These friends of Dell were concerned about the foolishness of teenage love and what it might portend for the Strickler family. On evenings when the topic came up Dell would make light of it, but one evening the women pressed harder, and Dell said, yes, she had entertained thoughts of her daughter falling in love with a young black man.

"What would you do? How would you put an end to it?"

"I would not try to put an end to it."

"But what if Heather didn't come to her senses of her own accord? What then? What if she got married to a black fellow? Your grandchildren would be mulattoes."

"And I would hug them and kiss them and thank God for them."

"You can't be serious."

For the rest of the evening no canasta was played. ("There went the game. They were in such a tizzy. Didn't I realize it would ruin Heather's life? How could I be so naive? How could I be so dumb? Well, my goodness, I knew it would be difficult if something like that came to pass, if Heather really got into a mixed marriage, but I am a believer in integration. If I was going to be Christian about it, I would have to accept a black son-in-law with open arms, and I would love my grandchildren regardless. I wouldn't care what shade they were.")

The news that Camilla had taken up again with Bruce also traveled by phone to West Virginia, to a white frame house in a wilderness valley so isolated that mountain lions can be seen padding through the front yards. In this valley lived the former Heather Strickler, now Heather Holstine, who took the call from Camilla after ten o'clock one night, a point of the day when Heather was usually in her pajamas but Camilla was gearing up for a social hour. The differences between Heather and Camilla were not insignificant, and since graduating from Potomac High they had lived in places apart. Camilla had devoted herself to her career in medicine, whereas Heather had let her two careers, in dance and in linguistics, play second fiddle to homemaking. "I'm the country mouse, and Camilla is the city mouse" was Heather's description of their different lives. Yet because of dozens upon dozens of phone calls, their friendship had never waned through four colleges and universities, a pair of weddings, five children, a divorce, and all the usual ups and downs. The friendship got its start in the summer of 1972, between their tenth and eleventh grades, when Camilla and Heather visited museums and antique houses in the south of France. The girls were on separate vacations with their parents, and it was not until they were back at Potomac High and involved in the what-I-did-last-summer phase of French class that they discovered their vacation stories were one and the same. French class and then a school production of *Hello Dolly!*—Camilla in the cast, Heather the choreographer—made boon companions of them. They were the cutups on the set. As best friends sometimes do, they began to copy each other in their behavior and their dress, to the point they were good-naturedly called by their teachers "the Bobbsey twins." In the twelfth grade, when Camilla's parents moved to Baltimore, she remained in Hillcrest Heights and slept in the spare bedroom of a family friend in order to finish high school with Heather. All that year Camilla practically lived at the Strickler house.

It was the sober side of their natures that had always attracted Camilla and Heather to each other. They were viewed by their friends as possessing no-nonsense personalities. Their normal way of speaking was crisp and rapid and formal, no slang, no shortcuts, though they might perk up their heads and cut off someone in the middle of a conversation—they'd gotten the point and had a retort ready. So for Camilla to speak of her new tête-à-têtes with Bruce in a tone completely out of the ordinary, in a tone "almost gushy," set off little alarm bells inside Heather. The Camilla that Heather knew was too worldly and too prudent to swoon over a guy who years ago had caused her so much misery. Camilla would not make the same mistake twice, would she?

Still, what could Heather say? Ever since Camilla got her divorce and began living the single life there had occurred an inevitable change in the even-steven dynamic that had existed for so long between the two old friends. This change led to awkwardness. The best thing to do was to put a bright face on things, cross your fingers, and hope everything would turn out okay. At the other end of the phone line Camilla was deciding much the same thing, which perhaps meant they were still operating on their old wave length, after all.

• • •

At the stroke of seven on a morning shortly after his return Bruce awoke to the sound of a work crew joking and setting up for the day. It was a day for a T-shirt and gym shorts—a freakishly warm day. Out the front door and across 23rd Place, at the Hillcrest Heights strip mall, carpenters were tugging sheets of plywood off a truck. Yawning, rubbing the sleep from his eyes, Bruce snapped a leash on Blimpie, an old, hard-of-hearing black Labrador, and headed over.

The Hillcrest Heights strip mall was one of the first to go up in Prince George's County, fifteen stores arranged in a row along a straight sidewalk. Bruce had a childhood memory of the grand opening—the actor Gene Barry signing "Bat Masterson" autographs on anything the girls presented, salesclerks dressed in petticoats, a band playing "Bargain Days Are Here Again." Thirty years later the shopping center was showing wear and tear. The pavement was buckled; rainwater filled the depressions. Storefront lettering was banged up. The mall merchants had met and agreed to install new facades over the old signwork, but the carpentry job being done today had nothing to do with a facelift. The carpenters were eliminating a defect in the blueprints, an inadvertent mistake made a generation ago. The original architect had cut an alley into the middle of the strip mall, between a Laundromat and the Dollar Store, as a convenience for deliverymen. Soon after the grand opening, however, the alleyway had become instead a perfect staging area for assaults on two minority groups: any white teenage boy bound for college, and anyone regardless of age or sex who was of African descent. According to the shorthand directory then in use, those in the first group were "Collegiates," and those in the second group, with indelible nativism, were "niggers." Their tormentors were white teenage hoodlums who were referred to colloquially as "Grits" (or "Blocks"). The Grits were the type of young men who worked at gas stations one month and stuck them up the next. They could be identified by their haircuts, shiny and brittle with Brylcreem, and their dousings of Mennen's Skin Bracer. When loitering in the alleyway, killing time, one Grit would sometimes press his arm to the arm of another Grit in order to extinguish lit cigarettes. They had forearms scarred with burns. They carried switchblades, primarily to clean fingernails, but on occasion blood was spilled. Some of the Grits were true to classical fighting, waiting for whatever action might come their way, the quick, physical, one-on-one showdown, but some were bullies who operated in packs. In a legendary incident they stole all the baseball bats from Murphy's department store and hid out in the alleyway and whacked dozens of passersby on the head just for kicks. Someone like Bruce was courting trouble anytime he walked near the alleyway. "Oh, yeah, this was once an all-white neighborhood, and very dangerous," Bruce would explain, not sarcastically, to friends who had not known him in that period. "I never felt safe all the time I was growing up—the Grits were terrorists." Bruce had been a Collegiate, a tense kid with an ethereal face, tall for his age, top-heavy in the body; a kid who throughout his boyhood never learned to hold his ground in a fight. Just the sight of the strip mall used to evoke his vulnerability. During his long courtship of Camilla, he did not once go in her company to this shopping center directly across the street from his home.

Bruce's trepidation had been made up, he thought now, partly of fear and partly of envy. He had been a big kid, but scared. To have been as fearsome as a Grit would have meant the world to him. Finally, about ten years ago, Bruce had transformed himself physically with weights and martial arts, and established a tough-guy persona. He had lost his gawky, slightly clumsy look. Now he could back up any pugnacious act he might put on. Handling barroom rowdies did not faze him. On the other hand, he had never been tested in a street fight, and, illogically perhaps, he found himself feeling a little jittery as he now approached the alleyway.

The short-sleeved carpenters, slamming nails into plywood with air hammers, were erecting a makeshift wall, sealing up the old lair of the Grits. Bruce stood transfixed. The wall was to be ten feet high and would eliminate all access. A man with clipboard in hand was questioning whether this solution might be too drastic. "We could put a door in the wall," the head carpenter said. The clipboard man had doubts about the door. Would it not defeat the purpose of the wall? The head carpenter suggested putting a padlock on the door and restricting the keys to the store owners.

"Okay, sure."

The walk past the strip mall left Bruce in a condition of sentimental intoxication. For the next several minutes he raced with his dog through the neighborhood. Pumped-up, almost giddy from adrenaline, he exploded bare-legged through the traffic as though a runaway horse was carrying him. He felt safe in Hillcrest Heights, and not just because of the plywood. He felt as if at last he had entered his own element. The sidewalks were encroached on by BMWs, Cherokees, and Town Cars shining in the sun; gone were the Chevys with driveway paint jobs. The people making a beeline for the mall were dressed to the nines. The peak of fashion in Hillcrest Heights seemed now to be jazzy. But it was the hairdos that told the story—the dread, the weave, the wet-set, the high-top fade, the Jheri curl, the shiny shave-off, even a modest poodle-balled version of the Afro making a comeback. Many of the standard-issue brick houses that used to be home to the Grit families of hard-drinking machinists and teamsters were now home to white-collar African-American professionals, the parents of new Collegiates. The streets around his father's house looked like a vision from Bruce's adolescence when he still believed in the perfectability of society, a vision of black people and white people in a comfortable middle-class milieu.

Pulled along by his dog, his face heat-splotched, perspiring heavily, Bruce passed once more down the long runway of the strip mall. Then he headed home for breakfast. Only later did it occur to him that there was a definite question about why, with the Grits long departed from Hillcrest Heights, the owners of the shopping center felt compelled at this late date to board up the alleyway.

April 4 was a date Merv Strickler considered auspicious. On one April 4 he had been hired by the Civil Air Patrol, and on another April 4 he had started a job with the Federal Aviation Administration. In addition, April 4, 1955, was the day Merv and Dell had moved onto Foster Lane, then a rocky lane that would not be paved for months. Their house, faced with brick, was on a corner lot. A driveway sloped to a garage under the upstairs bedrooms. There was a walkway of flagstone set in cement and a walkup of cement steps. Inside everything smelled of the lumberyard. In years to come the Stricklers would plant rhododendrons and azaleas out front. They would attach a pineboard deck off the kitchen and wedge into a corner a lidded box stuffed with toys. They would install a swing set on the back lawn. Their yard would be the playground for as many as forty youngsters racing from up and down the street, hands waving, shrieking. Dell would read to the kids and serve them juice. They would have an open invitation.

One of the first neighbors to extend greetings to Merv and Dell was a white man who worked for the federal government. He let them know he was relieved to see they were white people and not Negroes. Not too many days passed before Merv and Dell, seizing on the opportunity of soft, gaudy spring weather, served up a barbecue on their lawn. They invited a visitor from Atlanta, a black man, John Somersette, chairman of the English department at Spellman University, who had been an air force pilot and intelligence officer, who had been the first of his race to receive a Ph.D. in education from Stanford, and who had gotten acquainted with

Merv and Dell at the university and had become the closest of friends. The barbecue with a tall, boom-voiced black man, his happy, backslapping affection for the white newcomers, their reciprocal affection—these things did not go unnoticed. Blinds went up and down in houses across the street. ("You could almost hear the whispers: Who is this dark-skinned guy? Of course, we had invited John on purpose.") The two Stricklers—Merv the educator–author–lecturer–world traveler–community leader, and Dell the science teacher–physics technician–medical technologist–hospital volunteer–community leader—belonged to a category of civil rights activists who never marched, never picketed, never got arrested, and never joined the NAACP but who, whenever they came across a barrier of racism, made a Gandhian effort to smash it down. They had grown up in Pennsylvania—he in a row house in York, she on a farm in the northwestern hills. He was the son of a minister; she was the daughter of a farmer and a schoolteacher. Merv and Dell both attended one-room schools with potbellied stoves and came out of Pennsylvania imprinted ineradicably by the kind of countrified church-anchored Methodist world that defines morality according to personal conduct and fairness in all things. As long ago as World War II, when Merv was an air force instructor for pilots, he made it a point to eat his lunch in mess rooms reserved for black GI's and to escort black members of the officer corps past the doormen at segregated military clubs. While with the Civilian Air Patrol in the peacetime of the 1950s, Merv helped to establish a number of racially meaningful "firsts" around the country. He was already a world-renowned expert on aviation, and, as a practical matter, most of these civil rights breakthroughs were achieved on the job merely by his inclusion of black aviators on the panels of the seminars and conferences he was regularly organizing. The other way to look at it is that Merv, at the time, was running the risk of having his own career blackballed. There was a black man who had been a flying ace during the big war, shot down over Kamchatka, who could handle the challenge of being a racial pioneer, who enjoyed the trouble it caused, who, keeping his Ph.D. perfectly in check, would conduct a hilarious Stepin Fetchit routine, scraping and bowing, telling a dumb joke on himself whenever some dolt of a janitor shooed him off a Whites-Only drinking fountain. *Ah's so sorry, captain, but ah's a poor color'd man who ain't had no readin' and writin'.* This was John Somersette. One time Merv placed Dr. Somersette in charge of advance planning for a conference at the University of Colorado, which meant he had to spend several days in Boulder. A dean at the university objected, "There's no barbershop in Boulder for coloreds. Where's he going to get his hair cut?" Merv prevailed by taking the matter directly to the president of the University of

Colorado, the father-in-law of future Supreme Court Justice Byron "Whizzer" White, but then other conference participants raised new objections. Merv would not give in. ("That's how you change people.") In 1956, John Somersette, conspiring again with Merv Strickler, became the first black man to stay overnight in a Las Vegas Strip hotel that previously had a whites-only policy. Informed at the reception desk that there was no room, Merv went straight to the mayor and then to a U.S. senator's office. ("When we got through raising hell, John had the best suite in the hotel.") John Somersette put in a call to his good friend Nat King Cole, the balladeer, living in Beverly Hills: "Nat, I've just one-upped you." Years later it would seem like a big joke, but in 1956 the Las Vegas Strip rules kept black entertainers from socializing with white patrons. A hotel manager told the actress Dorothy Dandridge he would drain the pool before he would let her have a swim. Nor could the audiences be taken for granted. Nat King Cole's show had been interrupted by white supremacists who knocked him to the stage floor.

Merv's work with the Civil Air Patrol placed him in contact with aviators from around the world, and he brought many of them home to dinner and for overnight stays in Hillcrest Heights. Heather had the impression her father worked for the United Nations ("We had guests from at least six different continents"). The Stricklers sponsored a lawn party for dignitaries from the University of Hawaii, many of them people of color. Afterward, eggs were thrown at the Stricklers' front door. Later, when an African-American couple moved onto the block, the Stricklers hosted a welcome party and were criticized by several neighbors, which only persuaded them to host more parties, one for each and every family of color that came to live on the nearby streets. Over time, as the neighborhood changed and as public thinking turned more modern, the Stricklers found greater and greater acceptance for their point of view. In 1965 there was a big shindig at the Strickler house, of which Heather had a lasting memory. ("Half the neighborhood came, plus all these international people—Africans, Asians, Hindus, Moslems. Some couldn't eat lamb, or pork, or beef, or couldn't drink alcohol or caffeine. So my mom put different food on different tables in the backyard. And we put rugs on the lawn. It was like out of a movie. I was nine years old, and I got to be the caterer and pass out desserts. Everyone was talking and laughing. It was one big happy mix.")

Many of the new black families in Hillcrest Heights made the move from the hard-lot southeastern quadrant of Washington, D.C., following on the heels of an identical migration of white families who had earlier jumped the same border. Bruce's father and mother, David and Gerry Gordon, moved from Washington to the freshly bulldozed lanes of Hillcrest Heights in 1954, within months of the Stricklers. Unlike most of the other white families, the Gordons were Jewish-Americans, and they had to master a balancing act, learning when it was okay to exhibit their Jewishness and when it was not. On the baseball diamond at the Holy Family Catholic Church, green and splendidly landscaped, where Bruce went as a youngster to sign up to play ball, it was not okay. One of the coaches asked Bruce about his religion, and his answer, offered in all innocence, was met with a finality: "I'm sorry, no Jews can play. You have to be Catholic." It was okay, though, to be a Jewish-American doctor in a basement office. In the 1950s there were quotas for Jewish-Americans, the town doctor, the town lawyer, and the like, and Dr. Gordon fit the bill. He was a traditional family doctor, soon to be a suburban anachronism; he charged twenty dollars for an office visit and made house calls for thirty-five. But then there was a second balancing act. Doc had to learn how to handle relations with members of the other minority, the relatively few black citizens. "A doctor swears an oath never to discriminate," Doc used to say, a maxim no one would dispute, but most people do not live by maxims. Trying to sustain a general medical practice in the midst of Irish-Americans and Italian-Americans, he had to summon more than a little courage before welcoming African-Americans into his office. The ghosts of history were still on the loose in Prince George's County. Cross-burnings were still in vogue. White terrorists were a law unto themselves. White law officers routinely roughed up and, on occasion, killed the new immigrants under the color of the law. Yet Doc was conscientious; he laid on healing hands without respect to race. Virtually every black person in Hillcrest Heights received his medical help. Camilla knew him in the role of her doctor before she knew him as Bruce's father. In his doctor's office she had liked him—he seemed fair-minded, not greedy, a man with a civilized manner. It was only when she was perceived as a prospective daughter-in-law that he underwent a radical change. It was then she recognized him for a version of another traditional American character: the liberal hypocrite, quick to take your money downstairs but just as quick to shun you upstairs.

For his part Dr. Gordon believed that any serious association Bruce developed with Camilla would be detrimental to his son's career. "It's bad enough you're a Jew. You want to tie yourself down to a Negro woman? You're sick in the head, boy," Bruce would remember him saying. Yet Dr. Gordon believed he knew whereof he spoke. As a schoolboy in Washington he had experienced the brutal nature of prejudice. Boys would line up—"My turn, my turn!"—to punch him, the Jew boy. For Dr. Gordon, his Hillcrest Heights house on the double lot was the equivalent of the Statue of Liberty. Here he had escaped heredity. Here his Americanness was primary, his Jewishness secondary. The Gordon family had blended in. Why did Bruce want to stick out? For the sake of image, for the sake of career, Bruce must marry a woman deemed to be proper by the larger society, as his father had done. "I'm saying this for your own good," Bruce was told again and again.

Dr. Gordon could accept that people from differing backgrounds were capable of loving each other. He himself in a younger incarnation had behaved with a certain raffishness and fallen for a young blond nurse from the rural South, so different from the Jewish woman of the urban North he went on to marry. But he was from the old school where a line was drawn between private fantasies and public etiquette. Behind closed doors Bruce could do as he wanted; he could violate all the protocols. *Do as you damn well please. Screw her to your heart's delight.* And, indeed, Bruce had picked up on this, for in the letter he had sent to Camilla at Mount Holyoke, the letter that had preceded the breakup of the two young lovers, one particular sentence was like a neon sign: "Why can't you just be my mistress?" This was the balancing act Bruce had long ago put forth to Camilla.

Around the time Bruce arrived back in town, Merv and Dell Strickler attended a Democratic Party fund-raiser at the Officers Club ballroom at Bolling Air Force Base. The way to the ballroom is through a set of double doors and up a set of steps that takes one past a cathedral-sized, stained-glass mural of the flights of Icarus and the Wright plane. Merv and Dell found the party in full swing. The event had drawn a crowd almost exclusively of black people, which was of no bother to the Stricklers. They moved gregariously about and soon were mingling separately. Merv and Dell were not like some white people who, in such a crowd, cling together arm in arm, their social discomforts all stirred up. Anyway, for the purposes of tonight, everybody was a Democrat under the skin. The flow of the party took Merv to the high-ceilinged library. Gazing up at a succession of studio portraits of air force chiefs of staff mounted in frames on the upper walls, he wondered aloud who might be the next chief should Bill Clinton be voted in over George Bush. "I'd like to see what appointments a Democratic president might make for a change," Merv said. He has a habit of extolling things with wide motions of his big hands, and he was doing that now. He began to suggest various possibilities for the new chief of staff and then said, "I guess it doesn't matter, as long as it's somebody I don't have to call 'sir.' I've known every chief of staff since Eisenhower, and I haven't had to call anyone 'sir' yet."

This kind of evening was a familiar scene in a familiar place for Merv and Dell, lifetime members of the Bolling Officers Club. For nine years in the 1960s, while attached to the Civilian Air Patrol, Merv had occupied an office at the air base. It was a thinking man's military station, and Merv, who consulted the likes of Wernher von Braun for big-league advice, was in charge of devising prototype educational and training manuals that would be handed down to two generations of aviators. The whole Strickler family had gate passes to the base. Heather and her older brother, Todd, learned to swim in the Bolling pool, and Heather and Camilla had several opportunities to play out the role of prom princess on the hardwood dance floor. Any young international air cadet who was in Washington on a student visa, whose language of choice was French, and who was in need of an escort to a dance at the Bolling ballroom had a reasonable expectation of spending the evening with Merv Strickler's daughter or his daughter's best friend. Camilla liked "pushing the boundaries a bit." She would preach political heresy and when she got one of the military bigwigs clearly eavesdropping she would switch to speaking French. ("Of course, Mr. Strickler understood what I was doing, but he never minded.") Racially speaking, the exchange dances exhibited Camilla's solitary black face in among the white faces. ("Mr. Strickler would not blink an eye. Meanwhile, his superiors at the Civil Air Patrol were having strokes.") Whatever the shortcomings at Bolling, they were nothing like the official segregation in the public buildings of Prince George's County. Up through the 1960s the whites-only drinking fountains and rest rooms at the courthouse and in the public libraries gave Prince George's County bad press. By comparison, the air force base, just across the county line inside Washington, was ahead of the times, and whenever members of the Prince George's black establishment needed a place bigger than a church auditorium for a social event, they would rent the Bolling Officers Club.

The crowd tonight was an older one, well-heeled, more interested in schmoozing on the burgundy-and-gold carpet than in dancing on the wooden floor. The excuse for the party was to raise political money for the campaign of Albert Wynn, a Democrat expecting to be the first black politician from Prince George's County elected to the U.S. Congress. One month prior to the election, many on Al Wynn's side were already celebrating because he had just won the Democratic primary, which, in an area that had not elected a Republican congressman in decades, was usually all it took. The pitches for money therefore had the feel of going through the motions, and Gloria Lawlah, the state senator from Hillcrest Heights, hurried the pitchmeisters along. Gloria was euphoric. "Let the good times roll," she shouted at one point, swaying to the canned music.

Minutes later, spotting Merv, she rushed to kiss him. "Merv, Merv, I'm so tickled you're here." Hugging his shoulders, she pulled him over to be introduced to the congressman-to-be. Merv reached out a big white hand.

"This is my wonderful friend Merv. He's one of us!" Gloria exclaimed. She looked around for Dell. "His wife is around here somewhere. She's with us, too."

Gloria Lawlah, who with her husband lived in a house diagonally across the street from Merv and Dell, had been their neighbor for almost twenty-five years. Gloria was a black woman of above middling height, in her fifties, but with the soft skin and neck line of someone much younger. Slender and attractive, thick hair coiffed just so, she was resplendent in a black dress, Spanish doubloon earrings, a blue-green birthstone ring, and a simple gold bracelet. Squiggles of gold embroidery had been painted on her fingernails, like writing on Oriental scrolls. Luminous brown eyes danced behind designer glasses. To the cognoscenti of Hillcrest Heights she was the "first lady," the local politician who most closely resembled a mayor within the unincorporated community. To the rest of Prince George's County she was a political boss, a godmother of the county's emerging black political class. Within the pantheon of civil rights firsts, she had laid several claims. Most recently, in 1990, she had become the first black woman from Prince George's County elected to the Maryland Senate. It seemed very possible she could someday become the "first lady" of all of the county.

Later in the evening Gloria Lawlah would have a quiet moment, standing with a friend next to the big picture windows and brushing up against the velvet burgundy draperies, faintly musky. Out the windows was a view of the nation's capital, the city spilling almost featurelessly to the Potomac River amid a glitter of headlights from late-night tourists and revelers. Ruminating, Gloria remarked on the changes that had come to Prince George's County. "I remember my first job: September of 1960. I was such a young naive thing, and Prince George's was another world," she said. Just out of college, living in a Washington apartment, and starting out as a teacher, Gloria had found work at Fairmont Heights High. "If you'd have pointed to me back then and said, 'See that young black woman over there. She's twenty-one years old, and she's a nobody. Well, in thirty years she's going to be a somebody, an important figure.' Everybody would've told you, 'You're crazy, you're nuts. A black woman? It'll never happen in Prince George's County.' "

Earlier in the evening Merv, a lover of the classics, had made the same point. "We haven't achieved Utopia, like Sir Thomas More wanted, but we're working on it. We're working on it."

People who were introduced to Gloria Lawlah often got an impression of someone with old-fashioned glamour who hinted at a secret life. Although it was not exactly secret, Gloria did have an abundant other life. She was a teacher who had worked her way into the superintendent's office; she was a mother with three grown, financially independent children; she was a grandmother; and she was in the thirty-fifth year of a strong marriage to John Wesley (Jack) Lawlah III. The Lawlahs came from families that had been pulling up by the bootstraps for some time. Gloria's mother had also been a teacher, and her mother before her, and her mother before her. ("I was a little princess. I played the piano, I played the trumpet. I went out on the street and blew.") Gloria's father-in-law had been the medical chief of a Chicago hospital and a dean of the Howard University Medical School. Her husband was a civil engineer. By 1969, when Gloria and Jack Lawlah purchased their brick rambler in Hillcrest Heights, everyone on their block was assumed to be a professional. Their neighbors were a judge, an attorney, a historian, a physicist, and a National Symphony musician, as well as the aviator-educator Merv Strickler and the nurse-teacher Dell Strickler. Hillcrest Heights had the guild spirit of a medieval town. Only by virtue of their skin color did the Lawlahs stand out, which was, of course, the difference that mattered. Although they received a ritualistic welcoming dinner from the Stricklers and found in them astonishingly friendly soulmates, the Lawlahs got the icy treatment from other neighbors. Before being accepted they had to bide their time. In one case in particular, it took a while. ("He simply could not acknowledge our existence. It took him maybe five years. I invited him and his wife to a big party, and that helped. And then my packages were delivered to him by mistake, and he started to bring them over. He started to come in through the kitchen door, just like every neighbor. That broke down his reserve. Now we get along famously.") The Lawlahs also had a common interest with their neighbors in an Italian nightclub, Giovanni's, located in the Hillcrest Heights Shopping Center. Most everyone on the block was in agreement that Giovanni's had changed for the worse. Once upon a time the nightclub had been a hopping place for the Italian-American well-to-do. Revelries were carried on into the wee hours. The bosses of the Democratic machine held court in dimly lit corners while their shark-skinned crews assembled at the bar. By the early 1970s, however, drug deals were being conducted in unlit corners. It was a principal hang-out of the Grits, who hustled action at the pool tables and ambled out for other kinds of action at the alleyway forty paces away. They menaced not only young white teenagers like Bruce Gordon but adult black people. ("The Grits were notorious. They were the prime suspects in any cross-burning. They were known to be armed with chains and knives. Black people who had been victimized by them would be left on a sidewalk, bleeding, half beaten to death.") Giovanni's was a symbol of an era that in trendsetting Hillcrest Heights was being ushered out, the era of poor white trash. "Punks like that," Merv once said, referring to the Grits, "make you ashamed of being born white." It was an easy choice for the German-American Stricklers, the Jewish-American Gordons, and the rest of the up-standing white community when the African-American Lawlahs undertook an informal, unofficial boycott of Giovanni's. Within a few years the night-club was out of business, due to a lack of clientele and declining profits.

A few words mailed in 1976 between two college kids—that is, the "mistress" letter—had finished off a love affair, and it stood to reason this second time around that Bruce and Camilla must discuss those long-ago offending words. One word, actually—the illicit, old-fashioned concept of a *mistress,* of a "backstreet affair" as it seemed to Camilla. But when Camilla made reference to it on one of their disheveled, romantic week-ends Bruce claimed forgetfulness, "I can't remember one letter—there were so many." She let it pass, and did not return to it that weekend or in subsequent talks. It burned in Camilla's mind, though. One time she said on the phone to Heather, "I will tell you some juicy stuff. Bruce wrote me a letter back in college in which he said, quoting his father, 'Why do you have to marry her? Why can't she just be your mistress?' To this day Bruce has amnesia over that letter. He does not remember ever having written it. But, of course, that letter is the one thing I will never forget."

Of course, Bruce wanted only to avoid the subject. ("It was a stupid, stupid letter. I wish I could forget it.")

For Camilla, there had been times when the pain from the letter was so deep and intimate she felt like screaming. But why, exactly?

Camilla: "I have analyzed this for almost twenty years, and I'm not sure I know, except it pushed a button in me that maybe goes back to the days when the white plantation masters brought their slave mistresses into the big house for sex and did their thing and sent them back to the tarpaper shacks. Black women as white men's sexual property—I think that was the button it pushed. It's okay to be a mistress but not a wife. It's okay to be a prostitute but not a partner. That's a hard and grievous thing to endure."

Bruce: "It was crazy—I wanted to marry Camilla. I should never have mentioned the word 'mistress.' It was my father's word. I was hashing through things he was saying to me about the pros and cons of marrying outside your own race, and I made the mistake of repeating these things to her."

Camilla: "That was the saving grace. It was Bruce's father who raised this up, not Bruce. But was there some acceptance on Bruce's part? I was never sure."

Bruce: "I was young. I was the weakling agent of my dad."

Camilla: "Bruce's father was a bully and son of a bitch! But it's different now. We've grown up. Bruce is able to tell his father flat-out that the love of his life is a black woman."

Headlines in the *Prince George's Journal* predicted, correctly, that history would be made in the person of Albert Wynn. Having returned past the deadline for registering to vote, Bruce could not cast a ballot for Mr. Wynn, but he took pride in the news. ("This was George Wallace territory when I left. Okay, a few of us were throwing pebbles in the pond, making a few ripples, but who'd have believed the ripples could spread so fast and so far.") A number of observers, in trying to guess at the impact of Al Wynn's victorious run, were looking past this election to the next one, two years hence, because the stage now seemed set for a black politician to be elected county executive, the governmental overseer for all of Prince George's County. Black politicians had been elected at the top of the ticket in such large American jurisdictions as Detroit, Michigan, and Newark, New Jersey, but Prince George's County was not some old dead heap of a last-century city. It was a large modern suburb of spacious homes and clean air and peaceful streets and hundreds of thriving enterprises. "Mayors who won in Detroit and elsewhere represented a hollow victory. Just as blacks were taking over the city, whites were giving up and moving out," explained Professor Bart Landry, a University of Maryland sociologist who had studied the emergence of a new African-American middle class. "Prince George's can be the first jurisdiction where a black political establishment takes over a place that's on the way up. It would be an unprecedented event."

A generation ago such an event was a fantasy for Black America, and while success was now within reach in Prince George's County, it was far from guaranteed. The county executive had been time and again a white man who had either been born to or been claimed by the Prince George's political establishment. To have used "white" to describe the political establishment would have been, until recently, redundant. Now, finally, there was the likelihood of competition. In fact, a black political establishment had been officially incorporated under the name Prince George's County Alliance of Black Elected Officials, Inc., shortened for everyday use to the Black Alliance—a united front of the black Prince Georgians in elective office. Gloria Lawlah had been one of the incorporators, along with Al Wynn and state's attorney Alex Williams. They had selected a name measured and unprovocative, but the effect of their action was to pose a formal challenge.

"I get goose bumps thinking about it," said Gloria, who was herself the subject of avid discussion as a possible candidate for county executive. "In sports you have the Game of the Century. Well, this might be the Election of the Century, or maybe the Election of Three Centuries."

"It'll 'make,' " Merv said, speaking of the upcoming political season. "Do you know that term? It's a Pennsylvania Dutch expression that's worth a whole paragraph. It means it'll make a disturbance. It'll make people get excited. It'll make something!"

2 **Out among** the roadside merchants on Indian Head Highway, ribs were still cooked over hickory, and Maryland crabs and Carolina shrimp were hustled from the back of pickups, and flea markets were staged without a license, but the trafficking in lawn ornaments was not anymore than what it had been in the 1950s, when dozens of Saturday morning shoppers brought home to Hillcrest Heights a personal cast-iron jockey. Save for a red cap, the jockey would be done up in black: black face, black hands, black leggings, black boots. From an outstretched arm a lantern would hang. The original lawn jockey was thought to have been commissioned by George Washington as an honorific still-life of the slave Tom Graves, who froze to death while holding a lantern to light the way for Revolutionary War troops returning across the Delaware River. Right from the beginning the reports about Tom Graves had been mixed: Was he a hero, or had he carried obedience to an unnecessary extreme? Later, in the years leading up to the Civil War, replicas of the Tom Graves statue had been used for dire effect; plantation masters would light the jockey lanterns to signal the event of a runaway slave. In the twentieth century the lawn jockey with his familiar, simpering lean became a reminder of the Confederate South. So, as black homeowners moved into Hillcrest Heights, most of the jockeys had been quickly disposed of. But for certain of the new owners the funny-looking replicas held an attraction. These were the racing buffs who had moved to Hillcrest Heights because of its proximity to Rosecroft Raceway and who considered the jockeys to be a type of "gag" paraphernalia. Then there were those newcomers who thought the jockeys offered an opportunity for social commentary. Members of this latter group started a trend. They could be seen on weekends diligently, painstakingly working with artisan brushes. Eventually all the jockeys in Hillcrest Heights took on a new look.

On his walks with his dog Bruce noticed there was something different about them, but it took him a while before realization dawned: All the features now were painted white.

The old Prince George's County existed these days only in traces. But then there was Upper Marlboro, site of the courthouse and center of private grandeur and deep traditions. Founded in 1706 and dominated by a few old families, the population of Upper Marlboro had varied hardly at all in nearly three hundred years. The saying was that "nobody gets in and nobody gets out." In between the Censuses of 1980 and 1990, when the rest of the county was booming with new houses and new residents, the number of people residing in Upper Marlboro was affected only by the relocation of the jail outside the town limits, which lowered the population from 828 to 745. The town was four square miles. Limbs of big oaks overhung rooftops. Handpainted gold lettering was flaking off storefront windows on Main Street. Yodeling cries of auctioneers were still heard every fall at the tobacco auction houses. Change, when it occurred, proceeded slowly. The old post office, known for its WPA wall mural in celebration of tobacco, was about to be remade into a library, with the mural intact. The Southern States farm store continued in business despite diversification from plows and harrows into lawn chemicals. The *Enquirer-Gazette,* operating since 1851, had been purchased by an outsider, but the paper's smoke-choked newsrooms had not changed, nor its local page of bridesmaids. A pop-culture McDonald's with "No Smoking" signs was finally in the works to replace the Edelen Brothers tobacco house, although a couple of town commissioners swore it would be built over their dead bodies.

The courthouse, on Main Street, had an antique half and a modern half, joined in the middle. The new half was a $71.3 million addition finished in 1991, all spit and polish, with floors done in a black-and-white diamond pattern and skylights above and poured cement at the entrance. The old half was a stately building in an Italianate style, with a touch of the Gothic, and a front of squared-off lawn and boxwood hedges and walkways of old brick. The entranceway was studded with four massive columns. For a news conference on the morning of October 15, 1992, Gloria Lawlah set up next to the columns. They dated to the era of plantations, a not coinci-

dental backdrop. While television cameras rolled, Gloria, in a T-shirt decorated with American and Maryland flags, stepped to the microphone.
Shoulder to shoulder, faces scowling, stood eleven other members of the
Black Alliance, insiders who for this one morning were exhibiting an outsider's spirit—what used to be called a show of "black militancy," rarely
seen anymore, so rare it warranted front-page coverage in the local news
journals.

The militancy of the Black Alliance was directed at a thirteen-person
panel of Prince George's lawyers and laypeople, the Judicial Nominating
Commission, most of them white men, who held the power over the right
of ascendancy for any lawyer applying to become a judge. If the commission did not place your name on a judges-in-waiting list, your chances of
obtaining a judgeship were nil. If the commission placed your name on the
list but then removed it, your chances were reduced even more, and this is
what had happened to Elvira White, an attorney in the employ of the
Prince George's public defender's office.

Gloria, imposing and caustic, her good microphone voice revved up,
was the first to speak: "We are united unanimously to protest a terrible
travesty of justice which occurred Monday evening during deliberations of
the Judicial Nominating Commission. An outstanding attorney, Elvira
White, is being cheated out of a chance to be appointed a Prince George's
County judge based on an allegation that she is a closet racist. Ms. White
has denied this unfounded charge. However, the commission saw fit to remove her name anyway from the governor's recommended list, doing so
without one ounce of evidence or investigation into this incredible
charge."

Other members of the Black Alliance, among them Albert Wynn, did
their turns next, raising strident voices.

"How is it possible Elvira White passed the commission twice before
and now all of a sudden is unqualified?"

"Make no mistake about it, Elvira White is being made the victim of a
racist vendetta."

They blinked their eyes in the tawny autumn light. A late dry spell had
turned the flower boxes perversely bright and produced a bumper crop of
acorns. Off to one side, under a tree, stood the "victim," Elvira White.
Elvira looked crestfallen, as if she had, indeed, undergone the African-
American ordeal, had suffered the privations, was suffering them still. She
was a black woman, fortyish, with a heart-shaped face, her only adorn-
ment a choker of pearls, hair streaked with henna and cut in a bob and
brushed vigorously every morning. She was a short woman, not more than
five feet tall; her shortness and her emotional face added to the distinction

of her appearance. Born into a poor family in the poorest county of Maryland, she had come to Prince George's County in the mid-1970s, and until a few months ago her career had been characterized by nothing if not a rush to glory. Recipient of a "Woman of the Year" citation from the governor of Maryland, winner of the president's award for outstanding service from the Prince George's County Bar Association, the first black woman to be put in line for a Prince George's judgeship, Elvira had seemed incapable of doing any wrong. And then, almost without warning, God had stopped smiling on her.

In the shadow of a big tree Elvira fidgeted. Acting on Gloria's advice, Elvira was trying to make herself scarce, a change of tactics for someone blunt and ebullient, not the sort to go unnoticed, someone not from the school of subdued soliloquies and Ivy League window dressing. But Gloria had been quite specific: Above all, Elvira was not to say a word to reporters during the news conference. On today of all days, with her future perhaps hanging in the balance, Elvira could not do any free-speaking that might be turned against her. It was by expressing herself too openly that she had landed in trouble in the first place. She was well aware of this fault of hers and had tried, not always successfully, to bring it under control. "I have a tough mouth. I can really, really rub people the wrong way. So I want you to keep me in line," she would tell her assistants in the public defender's office when asking them to review her memos. Talking tough is not a felony, but a conversation one morning with her secretary, Ruth Jones, was currently being used to indict Elvira's fitness as an officer of the court and to disqualify her from the judgeship. The conversation in question had occurred in the spring of 1992 during the week of the Los Angeles riots, a time when racial tempers everywhere in America were once again on edge. A jury had acquitted the four white Los Angeles policemen who brutalized Rodney King, and vicious acts galore were being committed in the name of retaliation. A white truck driver, Reginald Denny, selected for the color of his skin, had been manhandled out of the cab of his truck by several black men and left for dead. Sitting on the other side of the country and arguing with Ruth Jones about the "rightness" and "righteousness" of the rioters, Elvira had said words to this effect: "I can really understand the frustration of the people in Los Angeles. Coming from where I come from, I can understand them." Elvira was herself wrought up over the acquittal of the cops, and possibly her actual words were not well chosen, as she herself later said, "I exercised my mouth too much." In any event, this set-to with her secretary had not been forgotten the way most office conversations are. Ruth Jones had committed a version to paper, and someone had gotten a copy and circulated it inside the public defender's office, where just recently Elvira had made enemies because of another "mouthing off" incident. In this second incident Elvira, taking tales outside the confines of the office, had reported on the "racist" behavior of an associate attorney, who then subsequently lost his job. So a kind of turnabout had been played on Elvira. Someone—acting with "malice aforethought," in Elvira's opinion—had forwarded a copy of the Ruth Jones letter to members of the Judicial Nominating Commission. Elvira's name had been high on the list of individuals to be appointed to judge-ships, but the letter, it was said, revealed Elvira to be too opinionated, too prone to fly off the handle. That Elvira was willing to "condone the vio-lence" of a race riot had caused several of the white lawyers on the com-mission to change their minds and remove her name from the judges' list.

Upon hearing of these troubles, Gloria Lawlah's first instinct had been to go to Elvira White's aid, and to go fighting mad. The constant in Gloria's life, beginning when she was a young child and continuing through her years as a teacher, a school administrator, an NAACP activist, and a politi-cian, had been her willingness to take on a fight. Subsequently she had en-listed her friends in the Black Alliance, and now, finishing the news conference, she held out a suggestion that she might carry the fight into the 1994 elections. Alongside a "Gloria Lawlah for County Executive" ban-ner there might also be one declaring "Elvira White for Judge." "Let me say to you that in 1994 there will not be business as usual," Gloria cried out. "We are going to put on a campaign that this county has never seen the likes of. Let me tell you that change is coming to Prince George's County."

Under the tree Elvira offered up a half-crooked smile. The smile did not part her lips; it was as if she had never quite mastered the knack of it. She said nothing. Of course, everyone knew of the fire concealed by the poker face.

At a luncheonette in Upper Marlboro, in the warm steam of counter food, two elderly black women smiled on Elvira White and pressed next to her ear with sweet urgings. *Hang in there, girl! You'll see, God is a good God!* And, at a Formica table, Elvira for the umpteenth time explained to an inquisitor what she had said, and what she had meant, in the comments she made to her secretary Ruth Jones concerning the Los Angeles rioters: "I never indicated I condoned violence. All I indicated was that I under-stood the feelings that drove these people to commit violence." Inquiring news reporters had heard Elvira's explanation, and so had inquiring court-house lawyers, inquiring police officers, even inquiring clients, tough dudes accused of malicious crimes who wondered how it came to pass that their attorney, this proper, extremely religious woman in her impeccably dry-cleaned business suits, her short-heeled pumps, and her deliberately unflashy cosmetics, should have to defend herself like someone at their level. How, indeed? Publicly, Elvira did not offer any theories, in keeping with the advice that she conduct herself with utmost judiciousness, but privately she had plenty to say. She had been duped, she had been set up; there was a plot against her. "Well, what else would you call it?" she said. "Don't you think it extremely odd that my secretary, a woman I've known for years, should sit down and write me a letter about a casual conversation we'd just had. Sure, it was a heated conversation, but it was just two people having a disagreement, and it was a private disagreement. Why would she make a record of it in a written document, something she's never done in eleven years? Unless . . . unless the document was meant to fall into the hands of my enemies." As for why Elvira might have enemies, there were many possible answers, but for her there was one passionate certitude: The world of the Prince George's courthouse had turned against her not because of "any remark I made about some black people out in Los Angeles," but because of "a remark a white male said— you know what I'm referring to, the Singman affair."

The Singman affair—yes, everyone in Upper Marlboro was well acquainted with the sorry details, and, circumstantially, at least, there did appear to be a connection between the controversy involving Elvira and the one involving Jeff Singman, formerly an attorney at the public defender's office. The Singman story went as follows: A few weeks prior to the Los Angeles riots, Jeff Singman had gone to the county police lockup in Hyattsville and had, not for the first time, encountered taunting. Mr. Singman had the misfortune of putting people in mind of PeeWee Herman, the squeaky-voiced children's television personality with cartoonlike features who, as worst luck would have it, had recently been arrested for misbehavior in a porno movie theater. The taunting of Mr. Singman was done by young black prisoners. "Yo, PeeWee! Over here, sweetie. We got a movie for you." After several minutes Mr. Singman stood, according to later accounts, and pointed a finger and screamed, "You're nothing but a bunch of black Sambos."

When informed of the incident, Elvira recommended a three-day suspension for Mr. Singman, who was subordinate to her in the office pecking order. "You've got to deal with this. It can't be brushed under the rug," she told Maureen Lamasney, the office director. "The word is out on Jeff's racial attitudes. I've talked to the sheriff. He can't guarantee Jeff's safety in the lockup anymore." Ms. Lamasney thought a letter of apology might suffice, but Elvira objected, "I am Jeff's supervisor. Why isn't my recommendation good enough?!" In her anger she forgot herself, "This annoys me. This pisses me off." Meanwhile, Mr. Singman wrote a letter of apology, which Elvira found wanting in its level of remorse. This put the situation at a stalemate. Several days went by without any decisive action while the rumor mill churned on. A local public defender said later, "Jeff Singman is just an interesting character and isn't a political threat to anybody, and several of us felt that for Elvira to be calling for his head was an overreaction on her part. It was an unfortunate choice of words on Jeff's part, but Elvira should have been willing to find a graceful way for everyone to save face." Among Elvira's friends on the circuit court bench was Judge Audrey Melbourne, a sort of mentor, who in her softly modulated voice gave Elvira some advice, "You're the one who's going to end up ruining your political future. I would just shut up and smile." But Elvira had lost patience and had already gone to a state senator, Decatur (Bucky) Trotter, who alerted Stephen Harris, director of the state office in Baltimore. A racial brouhaha was about to go public in Prince George's County?! Stephen Harris couldn't have it. Maureen Lamasney got a phone call from Baltimore. A friend of hers would later say, "Maureen had been hoping this whole business would fizzle out, but once it went up the chain of command, there was no way to avoid it. Things had to come to a head." Stephen Harris interviewed all the principals, including Elvira, who put forth her recommendation that Jeff Singman be suspended three days. "You're being too liberal," Stephen Harris countered, and thereupon had him fired. Elvira was on leave at the time, recovering from dental surgery, but when she reported back to her white-walled office on the second floor of the courthouse she was treated by many of her colleagues like a criminal returning to the scene of the crime.

Now, several months later, denizens of the courthouse were still expressing a widely held sentiment that Jeff Singman was "one poor unlucky bastard, guilty of a slip of the tongue, at most." At the luncheonette, even with Elvira sitting ten paces away, it took almost nothing to prompt this bitter talk. "The only reason Jeff got reamed is to keep Elvira happy," it was said by one white bailiff, waiting at the counter for stuffed pork chops. And waiting for liver and onions, a baleful-looking white litigator said with harshness, "Elvira might be a better lawyer than Jeff, but I, for one, am sick and tired of all her politically correct bullshit."

Dwight Jackson, a homicide prosecutor, came through the door and nodded to everyone. He was someone who had defended Elvira in the past and would do so again in the future, but he already sensed, as Elvira herself did not, the enormity of her miscalculation. "She has set off a chain of events over which she now has very little control," he said, responding to an outsider's question. "In her desire to be in the right, she forgot to take into account the personal consequences. The line she's crossed she probably did not know existed, but she's bringing unholy hell upon herself."

"Okay, it was a dumb cockamamie letter." This was said by Bruce during one of his late-night phone calls to Camilla. He felt sheepish and a little mournful. He was trying to patch up a quarrel. They had been arguing about something else, but he knew it was the deep-seated corruption of the "mistress" letter that had given rise to the quarrel.

"I'm glad to hear you've gotten over your amnesia," Camilla said.

For the time being, that ended the discussion, and the quarrel.

Camilla and Bruce were settling into a long-distance relationship, carried on mostly over the phone. Certain aspects of their whirlwind reunion had proved to have an afterlife—they enjoyed their rambling discourses, and on their infrequent dates they were wild for each other—but the idea of Bruce moving to Boston so they could become husband and wife had been put on temporary hold. For now they had agreed to remain unmarried lovers, and the historical sensitivity of this was something else left unsaid.

Bruce had seen to it that a three-tiered ramp was installed at the rear of the Gordon house, and his father, bundled up against the winter, spun his wheelchair down the planks and out to the garage and took some time looking at the elongated image of himself in the Cadillac chrome below the license plate. Dr. Gordon still had daydreams of himself cutting a Don Juan figure behind the wheel of his old Caddy. The previous night, shopping for groceries, Bruce had taken him along in the passenger seat, which wasn't the same. ("I felt like a damn basket case.") And Bruce had made such a big production of it. *Here we go, Pop! Here we go!* Who needed that kind of obvious cheering up? Why, in a month or two, he'd have enough life back in his right-side appendages to fend for himself. He was already in pretty fine fiddle, in his estimation. Anyway, Bruce was out of the house most of the time now and not hovering around. He had taken a job ten minutes from Hillcrest Heights, in the Prince George's branch of Banc One Leasing, the financial company that had employed him in Denver. Cooped up, he and his father were an irritation to each other's nerves. So a live-in "caregiver," Patsy, an emigrant from Guyana, had been hired to fill in for

Bruce during the day. Besides keeping company with Doc, she cooked his meals and assisted with his physical therapy. He was about to begin a session right now. He clapped his hands for her, "Let's go."

Bruce, jogging clothes on, went out the door into thin, sharp sunlight. Blimpie panted alongside him. It was almost noon on a Saturday after the holidays. The cool air was a blessing, and Bruce was getting reacquainted with the neighborhood.

He said hello to Rebecca, an elderly Jewish-American woman who often stayed overnight two or three times a week with a daughter in Virginia. "Every time I'm gone from my house my wonderful neighbor, Bob, a very thoughtful black man, will park his van in my driveway. To discourage burglars," Rebecca said. "You know, we're all sorry about your dad. We all think so highly of him. Bob said to let him know if there's anything he can do to help out."

Running through the strip mall, Bruce paused at the alleyway. A faint tang of urine hung in the air. The plywood, faded and bowed, had done the job. The hole in the wall was as without drama now as the litter of cigarette butts and candy wrappers and the outdated Christmas lights twinkling in the picture windows. At the Hillcrest Carryout, Bruce tied his dog to a lamppost. Mrs. Jones, an African-American woman past middle age but youthfully exuberant, served him a sandwich of barbecued beef. Her two daughters, working the counter, had hair rinsed with an orange-colored dye. "Next time you bring your dad around to say hello!" said Mrs. Jones in a brassy, nurturing voice. And she hollered as he left, "You tell Doc we miss him!"

Dr. Gordon did not lack for company. Many of his former patients made it a habit to stop by the house with home-cooked meals. At the time of his retirement, black people accounted for ninety percent of his practice, and ninety percent of the well-wishers with casseroles in their hands were black people. That Bruce's father should be such a well-liked figure among black residents of Hillcrest Heights was less an irony, Bruce decided, than a typical contradictory comment on the state of black-and-white relations in America.

Next to a bronze nameplate, Elvira White had placed on her desk a block of lacquered fruitwood engraved with a cheap-funny folkism: *You don't have to be crazy to work here, but it helps*. She would need her full reserve of humor to get through a day like today. On a bulletin board in the hallway, someone had tacked up a clipping from yesterday's edition of the *Prince George's Journal,* another news article about her turnaround in fortunes. To billboard unhappy news for all to see is a fairly normal office prank, but after Elvira had removed the clipping and balled it up in her tiny fists and dropped it with burning eyes into a wastebasket, and after its discomfitting effect on her was observed and spread about the office in a twitter of asides, the prankster had tacked up another copy. Except now it was more snidely positioned, up on the Sheetrock wall above the bulletin board. Try as she might on tiptoes, jumping, skirt hiking up, it was out of Elvira's reach. She felt demeaned by the silliness of her effort and yet had half a mind to drag a chair from her office and climb aboard. Instead she controlled herself—*Let those babies have their fun*—and walked stiffly back to her desk.

Ruminating, she said, "What you have to understand is that I've worked here eleven years, and for the first ten and a half years I did what I was told and didn't make trouble for anyone, and everything was fine. Then I asked for a simple, straightforward disciplinary action against a white man who got out of line, and it is as if I tempted damnation. I've spent eleven years proving myself, and now I'm back where I started from." She dropped her head.

It was possible the situation might yet be salvaged. Elvira White's name might yet be restored to the judges' list. But in a private moment one of her friends at the courthouse, a white woman, passed along a friendly warning: "You'll have to watch your back now and keep your opinions to yourself. Things can become extremely nasty if they think you are a threat to the system. I'm not saying you'll find a bomb in your car, but the people we're talking about can be very, very persuasive."

From the time they met at Potomac High School, and for several years afterward, Camilla and Heather's lives paralleled each other. On graduating from college they returned to the Washington area for their postgraduate work—Camilla in medicine at George Washington University, Heather in linguistics at Georgetown University—and then they were off in pursuit of careers—Camilla on a tour as a family doctor with VISTA, Heather as a translator for a variety of international networks. For both, dance was a second love. Whatever the locale, Camilla gravitated to hangouts where she could kick off her shoes any time of the night, whether classical or free-form dancing, folk or rock 'n' roll. For Heather, dancing was actually a second career. She studied dance seriously with a professional company and, as a stand-in with the Royal Ballet of England, had a brief time in the spotlights of the Kennedy Center. When Camilla and Heather were in their mid-twenties they both chose the married life, and within a year of each other they began having children. Prior to the birth of Heather's second daughter, in 1987, they had had a happy visit together. Heather, then in Charlestown, West Virginia, drove to Camilla's home in Cincinnati to borrow back some baby clothes. But since then they had not seen each other. Half the reason was Camilla's move to Massachusetts, and the other half was Heather's move to an isolated set of West Virginia hollows and then a second move to an even more isolated set of hollows. And the reason Heather kept moving farther away from people and toward civilization's edge had to do with her husband, Mike Holstine, and his ambitions for finding his nirvana.

Heather had met Mike in Annapolis, up Route 50 from Hillcrest Heights, when he was at the Naval Academy, a big, burly fellow who had tried out for the football team as a walk-on. Merv Strickler played matchmaker for his daughter by introducing her to the social swirl of navy football games, though the midshipman he intended for Heather was Mike's roommate. Instead, "Mike swept me off my feet," Heather recalled. As newlyweds, they considered settling in the old tobacco-farm section of Prince George's County but ended up outside Charlottesville, West Virginia, where five generations of Mike's family had lived. By 1987, suburban sprawl was crowding their first home, and Mike was itching to move on. For a few years they lived near Morgantown and ran a civil engineering company out of their house while Mike kept an eye out for ventures in more remote regions. Some years earlier an academic group affiliated with the National Science Foundation had searched the East Coast for a site, with a minimum of electrical lines and radio transmitters, to locate the world's most sensitive radio astronomy lab and had found no more remote a region than the wilds of Pocahontas County, in the eastern mountains of West Virginia. When the chief engineer's job for the lab became available in 1991, Mike could not believe his good fortune. He was hired for the job, and so Heather and their three daughters—Michelle, Danielle, and Christina— were now living in a place so bereft of the boutique spirit of the late twentieth century that the restaurants all closed down for the winter. In three hundred square miles there was but one stoplight. Deer roamed through the backyards, as did mountain lions.

Camilla felt Heather was disappearing into a cloistered existence. ("I

couldn't understand her willingness to shut herself away out in godfor-
saken Timbuktu! What was she going to do with herself? Who was she going to have a stimulating conversation with?") Merv and Dell Strickler,
whose concerns ran along the same lines, had recently hit upon a project
to bring about closer contact. Merv had an assignment to write a curriculum guide for the Federal Aviation Administration, and Heather, proficient
at research, copyediting, and punching the keys of a desktop computer,
was enlisted to perform those tasks. Every few weeks Merv and Dell com-
muted the five hours from Prince George's County to Pocahontas County.
To spend time in Heather's new world was to mingle among mountaineers
who wore CAT tractor caps, Harley-Davidson T-shirts, leather jackets, and
mud-splattered boots and who grew their hair long and kept rifles within
easy reach inside the cabs of their pickups—and who, to a man, woman,
and child, were of European origins. The color difference with Prince
George's County brought Merv and Dell up short. ("Maybe it's wrong for
us to be so aware of someone's race, but it's culture shock to see only
white people.")

Heather sat among her children's toys in her isolated house and tried to
think of what she had felt in that moment when it became home. She
thought instead of an excursion to New York City she had taken years earlier by car with Camilla, who, when they saw the skyline from the New
Jersey Turnpike, had gently informed Heather, "You better let me drive the
rest of the way. I'm not sure you're aggressive enough for the big city." A
part of Heather agreed; she was happy to steer clear of all the craziness of
closed-in spaces. As for the absence of black people in Pocahontas
County, it was something she took note of. "I want my children to be involved with people of every creed and color. That's important to me,"
Heather said. She had once thought of John Somersette as her "uncle" and
had listened to the casual dinnertime stories about his friends Nat King
Cole and Langston Hughes. "I suppose it is strange for me to end up here.
I would never have predicted it."

By noon Bruce had closed a deal for the underwriting of a dozen
portable classrooms at a local elementary school. But not every day at
Banc One was as satisfying or as down-to-earth. Fundamentally, his was a
wheeling and dealing job, and to wheel and deal you have to be keyed
up, always keyed up. Bruce's life was an alternation of high pressure at
Banc One and higher pressure at home. At home he was trying to do the
impossible—that is, he was trying to remake his life with his father before

moving on to be with a woman his father could not stand. This overload of stress gave Bruce a big appetite for barbecue at the Hillcrest Carryout. "I'm turning into a mound of unreknown," he confessed to Camilla, who had not seen him in person for several weeks.

Jogging with his dog and hefting the scattered-about free weights in the old X-ray room were like child's play against the barbecue. So, with his father dozing in front of the bedroom TV and Blimpie asleep on a throw rug, Bruce made a foray to the Marlow Heights Community Center and paid a $45 annual fee for access to a room of heavy-lifting equipment. The room had the Monday morning swelter of a Chinese laundry. A choke-hold smell of sweat and body oil rose stagnant from the floor. Bruce liked it immediately. About a dozen men were bench-pressing with an exertion that required gloved hands. They had rippling masses of muscles on the order of pinup models. Bruce's musculature probably placed him in the ninetieth percentile of men his age, but he was not in this league. "I'm interested in function, not form," he said to a man at the desk, who was gazing at him a little doubtfully. Bruce had once explained his bodybuilding philosophy thusly, "My buff is more like Reggie White than Arnold Schwarzenegger. I want to be powerful and quick like Reggie, not some clunky doughboy like Arnold." It was not exactly a rationalization. Tai kwon do had given Bruce a confidence he never had in his days of worry over the Grits, and it was his confidence rather than his physique that had caught Camilla's notice when they were reunited and when he had taken her hand and walked with her into the Telluride nightclubs and onto the beaches at the Cape. Gone were his skittish ways.

At the Marlow Heights center he filled in the membership form—height: 6 foot 3, weight: 248 pounds. In his first workout he pressed 200 pounds without trouble and worked up to 275 before quitting for the day. His goal was 350 pounds. On the bench next to him the gym champ was putting on a show, topping out at 500 pounds. The champ was a black man. Aside from Bruce, every one of the heavyweight lifters in the room was a black man. ("Their basic reaction to me was like: Are you lost? What are you doing here?") But after a couple more workouts, the gym mainstays began to buddy up, standing by to lift the power bars off his chest if Bruce miscalculated. One young man gave Bruce a standing invitation to go club-hopping. The mainstays were younger, unmarried men—a phys. ed. teacher, a landscaper, an accountant, a security guard, a guy in the music business—and were working off pressure from their own jobs. In time to come, Bruce would form a few friendships, slapping hands and bopping fists in the kind of sweat-soaked man-to-man brotherhood that is natural to a gym.

• • •

In these good new days for Prince George's County when a high percentage of the population had a task of value, there still remained men like the Hillcrest Heights neighbor who went by a single name, Delmar. Delmar was no shirker; yet he had no personal attainments to speak of and had been drifting on tough luck and scraping together a livelihood from odd jobs. One morning after a big snow, Delmar presented himself with snow shovel in hand at the Gordon house. Bruce had already departed for Banc One, and Dr. Gordon was happy to pay Delmar to clear off the front walk and the wheelchair ramp. Afterward, Doc asked the man in for coffee and a snack, as was his style of welcome. Back when Dr. Gordon had installed a small drug dispensary downstairs, he had paid a carpenter to cut a peephole into the front door, but with Doc's carefree attitude of accepting patients on a come-one, come-all basis, over time he had forgotten about the peephole. Anyway, he had no reservations about Delmar. A few years ago he had attended to Delmar's younger brother, dying of a fatal blood disease, and Delmar had kept a brotherly watch to the bitter end. Delmar was a black man in his early forties, a graduate of a neighboring high school from the class that came out several years before Bruce. Athletic, good-looking, he had played varsity football in high school and boxed locally. He came off as an earnest, gentlemanly fellow, not a street punk. No one in the neighborhood had ever observed him taking part in any hooliganism. It was simply that misfortunes seemed to befall him.

Before taking his leave Delmar inquired about the Cadillac. Despite many weeks of therapy, Dr. Gordon was no closer to regaining strength enough to drive the car, but why not go to the garage and induct Delmar into the admiration society? "She's a beauty, isn't she?" Dr. Gordon said. The winter assailed him. His breath smoked the air. It was quiet as night, the snow muffling the sounds of the streets.

Dr. Gordon mentioned that his need to be chauffeured about town was wearing on Bruce.

"I'd drive you around. You wouldn't have to pay me, excepting for gas money," Delmar said, and was quick with a clever invitation. "I accept tips, if you want to know."

So Delmar was not shy around an opportunity. Yet what harm is there in a man who wants a job?

Soon the onetime doctor and the onetime athlete were to become a common sight, tooling in the Cadillac through the sunny, spring-revived neighborhood. When the great, royal, heraldic vehicle was parked Delmar would examine it with such naked yearning that Dr. Gordon was moved to let the man borrow it for his own use. Delmar could then be seen alone like a Motor City monarch, taking advantage of Doc's generosity. But, figured Bruce, it was a small price to pay.

How did you come to be here? It was a collegial, clannish question on the tip of the tongue when one black person made the acquaintance of another black person in Prince George's County, and it was a question put many times to Elvira White.

Elvira's route to Prince George's County had begun in the rural town of Princess Anne on Maryland's Eastern Shore. Her family—eight children, a railroad-man father, and a housewife mother all named White (Elvira would keep her maiden name through two bad marriages)—made their home in a drafty dwelling previously used as a store. It was paid for in cash, hand-creased currency pulled from a fat glass jar. There was an outhouse out back, but the whole place was valiantly ornamented by Elvira's mother, rusty coffee cans golden with marigolds, the bottoms punched full of nail holes. With the coming of more babies Elvira's father built additional rooms, on a small scale, handyman style. Summertimes there were tomatoes to pick in the sandy-peat countryside, tomatoes by the hundreds of thousands. Ignoring red-horned worms that made other children jump, Elvira's fingers moved hungrily to heap up the red fruit. ("God, those baskets were heavy!") The Elvira of those years, a gaminelike, pigtailed girl at work in loose cotton outfits, was like a character out of Harriet Beecher Stowe, a yeoman character who might gain a foothold in lore. She would wolf down her lunch and then sit in a spot of shade and read books, not wretched juvenile books but serious books about history and politics. Elvira pushed so hard with her homework that her parents at times had to order her to bed. From age seven her favorite TV serial was "Perry Mason," and the lawyerly glamour formed her idea of a life away from the Shore. To be the first in her family to graduate not just from a high school but from a law school . . . it was indispensable she be a model student, academically superior, dignified, and so she was. ("All my life I've known what it takes, and I've gotten it done.") In 1970, Elvira went off to North Carolina Agricultural and Technical State University, paying her own way, a waitress on the night shift. She wore clothes sewn by her own hand. The partying she did was minimal. Weekends she tried to get home to the Eastern Shore, where her parents were caring for her young son, Andre, born to her when she was sixteen. Quiet tears flowed the day she finished college, one year ahead of schedule, magna cum laude. She hung the diploma in a frame. Law school brought Elvira to Prince George's County, to the campus of the University of Maryland. She completed her course work while holding down a full-time job and attending to Andre, who had come to live with her. Elvira also found time to be a founder of the Black Graduate Students Association. The University of Maryland subsequently hired her to direct a paralegal program, the first African-American in the position. By then Prince George's County was her adopted home. Elvira apprenticed herself to Arthur "Bud" Marshall, the white lord of the prosecutor's office, and to Alex Williams, the black attorney who would replace him, and to Judge James Taylor, perhaps the most revered black man in all of Prince George's. Writing to her parents, Elvira described how she had hitched her star to the courthouse and hoped to cash in on the quintessential American inheritance—the possibility of self-transformation. "I truly believe I have found the land of opportunity," she wrote.

In 1981 she landed a paying position with the public defender's office. In many jurisdictions a public defender's job would have been an automatic ticket for a cocksure young black attorney, but in Prince George's County the office had historically been the province of white men and women. Even after three years of volunteering her time, a licensed lawyer working for free, it required the intercession of state senator Tom Broadwater for her to be hired, the first black woman on staff. Immediately she entered into a Darwinian atmosphere ("I felt like I had to justify my existence.") She put up with snide remarks and petty harassments and with an explicit warning her failures would be held against the next black person to come looking for a job. A black person who is willful, one might presume, would never fit into an office where "go along to get along" was the first line of the first page of the rules of conduct and where "know your place" was the second line. Elvira knew it was unlikely she could achieve the level of easy camaraderie flaunted in the shiny-floored courthouse. Nonetheless she would try. Every day, in the teeth of tradition, she waved brightly to the cast of regulars, the lawyers and judges, the bailiffs, the clerks, the guards posted at the metal detector, the recidivist drunks. Over time many of them warmed up to this "affirmative-action baby," this "one-woman band." They seemed to appreciate her proper, posh accent (acquired, not inherited), her formal manners, and her emergence as a star lawyer. The courtroom did not awe her, and she held sway with a ferocity that was almost out of bounds. At the outset of each trial she would march up to the prosecution table and promise to raise Cain if anyone rustled papers or blocked her view or usurped her water glass. ("I wasn't going to suffer their little humiliations.") During jury selection, Elvira would look at each of the prospects with what one judge called "a gunfighter's squint."

Most of the judges thought of Elvira as someone with genuine and force-ful originality, but also someone very tightly wound. Yet her ride toward the top revealed a capacity for exuberant metamorphosis; she redesigned her courtroom face from trial to trial until she got it right. To go along with the harsh poses she was famous for, she developed the joshing side of her personality. Jeffrey Harding, a Prince George's prosecutor, said of her, "She defended her clients like it was a shootout to the death and she had to kill you to survive, but once you got to know her you realized you couldn't meet a nicer person." She found her place in the essential order of daily courtroom pressures and dramas. Violent crime was now part of the Prince George's scene, part of the definition of a place that was changing from sleepy to hardcharging, from rural to suburban (and, in places, to ur-ban), and Elvira took on more than twenty-five accused murderers, several facing death row charges. In the case of Antonio Gaskins, the killer of two bystanders who got in his way while he was collecting a debt at a pool hall a few blocks from the Gordon house, Elvira had to conduct the cross-ex-amination of a surprise witness while wearing her sneakers—she had for-gotten her dress shoes—but she handled herself with such aplomb she won a reduced sentence. Time and again prosecutors marveled at her. Elvira could strip away stereotypes from her young black clients. At other defense tables they slouched, put chin in hand, mouthed obscenities, pre-tended to snore. At her table they sat up straight. It did not seem to enter their minds to sass the legal system, let alone to sass her. "When these young men come to court, all they usually see is some white man who doesn't mean squat to them and who's telling them, 'You're probably go-ing down for twenty years.' They feel like they have no chance," Elvira once said. "With me, I treat them like their mama, like the lady who's raised them." She pressed their cases as if she would never dare think of representing anyone in whose innocence she did not believe. Her flow of adrenaline made for focused, straight-to-the-point performances. Her rate of acquittals was far above average. The *Prince George's Journal* featured her under the headline "Defender Stands Up for County's Hard Cases." Her admirers felt she made the adversarial system work. One prosecutor said, "As hard as she fights for her clients, not many innocent ones are likely to get convicted." Yet she had no patience with clients who gave up on them-selves just because they were born poor or made bad choices. ("With me, you get a lecture until you understand you do not accept the pit into which you are cast, but you crawl and dig your way out of it.") She gained the status of a senior felony trial attorney and then promotion to chief of the district court division, in which position she supervised fifteen white attorneys. She personified the transcendent ideal of the strong-minded, upwardly mobile African-American, and, by all outward appearances, she was accepted, even admired.

In 1984, eight years out of law school, Elvira formally put her name in for a Prince George's judgeship, the first black woman ever to apply. Were there any native-born inhabitants of the county who in their farthest-fetched imaginings thought they would see this day? Yet she was perceived as someone who knew her job, who was willing to put in long hours, and who also understood about collecting the right friends. Prior to her first appearance before the eminent members of the Judicial Nominating Commission, her courthouse friends schooled her to cut her Jheri curls, wear her blue dress with matching shoes, and scrape the polish off her famously long, highlighted faux nails. Still, her interview with the commissioners was not the smoothest of sailings. There was her teenage marriage. Why bring it up? Why not finesse the subject? The commissioners did not understand why Elvira had to be a stickler for correctness of every sort. Such "flapping of the mouth" bothered them, and the sharpness of her tongue, too. Asked about having enough time with her son if she had a judge's workload, she said that being a judge would be the easy life, comparatively: "Trust me, my workload will be cut in half." The commissioners would force on her two more oral exams over the next few years before stamping their approval. Elvira then had to pay a courtesy call on Maryland governor Donald Schaefer, an eccentric fellow who spent his entire session with her bantering about old-age afflictions. However, from all indications, the governor was on the verge of making Elvira's judgeship official when, almost without warning, she had become marked as a racialist and a troublemaker.

3 **The eleventh** of March was Elvira's forty-first birthday. On that same day at the Maryland prison facility in Patuxent, in a triple-locked high-security room with concave plastic chairs, there occurred an interview of one of the inmates, Amy Lynne Smith, a big-boned blond teenage girl with a gingery, coarse complexion (not improved by her confinement) who a year prior had been the most well known of Elvira's clients. Amy's inquisitors were the deputy state public defender Ron Kurasic and one of his staff investigators. Their line of inquiry was confidential, although Amy would write in a letter a few weeks later to G. R. Hovey Johnson, the Prince George's circuit judge, who had sentenced her to Patuxent, "They asked me questions concerning Ms. White." And Amy would add, somewhat cryptically, "To my knowledge no actions have been taken yet, but they are investigating the situation."

During the winter of 1992–93 a sense of missionary work had begun to emerge on Amy's behalf. Amy had been convicted of felonies related to a conspiracy in which the victims were meant to be her father, Dennis Smith, a local police officer, and her stepmother, Marialena (Marie) Smith. Derrick Jones, a black teenage boy who had dated Amy Smith for a brief time, was alleged to have been her co-conspirator. Derrick was deceased, the victim of a shooting by Amy's father. Early on, there had been an issue about whether Derrick's killing was cold-blooded—Amy was said to have faced constant harassment at home because of her romantic attachments to schoolmates of another race—but no charges were ever brought against the father, and the charges that went forward instead involved the two teenagers. The police theory was that Amy and Derrick had talked themselves into a murderous frenzy against her parents, and that the two shots of Mr. Smith's service revolver fired by him with deadly aim were an act of self-defense and the final proof of the conspiracy against him. The shots, striking Derrick in the chest and in the back of the head, were ruled justifiable. As the lone surviving conspirator Amy had been ordered to trial.

Since Amy's parents were to be star witnesses for the prosecution and could not be expected, or trusted, to hire counsel for her, and since she was without funds of her own, her representation became the job of the public defender's office. The case was assigned to Elvira, her last big case before racial controversy would overtake her. Of course, the Amy Smith case itself was racially charged and was bound to grab the attention of news reporters both legitimate and sensationalistic, but no one had challenged Elvira's ability to represent Amy in court. At the point Amy's case went to trial Elvira was still thought of as a trial attorney par excellence. Elvira was still on her way up, still the lady with the gift. Amy was lucky to have her, or so everyone said. Amy's maternal grandparents, with whom she went to live while the case was pending, wrote grateful letters to Elvira and sent her flowers, so pleased were they with Elvira's preparation for trial. Elvira approached Amy's defense with an "SOD" theory—"some other dude" did it. As she would later explain, "Either it was a cold, calculated murder committed by the father and therefore my client was innocent of all wrongdoing, or she was innocent by virtue of having been duped by the boyfriend. I would've been thrilled to find out Derrick Jones was a manipulator, a con man who had leverage on her, that he was the mastermind and had the strength to do evil. I'd have pinned it on him in a fast minute if I could have. It would've made life simple for me because he was dead and couldn't speak." Talks with Derrick's neighbors, teachers, and friends, and the findings of a private investigator, however, persuaded Elvira the dead youth could not be made into a scapegoat. "Everyone told me how Derrick was a wonderful young man, never been in trouble, never had so much as a citation for jaywalking. He was a talented young person, a singer and dancer. He had his whole future ahead of him. Why would he, out of a clear sky, come up with the idea of killing people he hardly knew?" Unable to fit Derrick Jones into an "SOD" theory, Elvira reverted to trying to make a culprit out of Dennis Smith. The trial was held without jurors, an option exercised by Elvira because of how she perceived the at-large mind-set of Prince George's County: "Common sense would tell you it'd be hard to find twelve people who did not harbor some prejudice against a white girl whose choice of a boyfriend was a young black man. I was concerned that even from my own African-American community there'd be anger at her because a young man with absolutely no blemishes on his record had been shot down." Circuit court judge Hovey Johnson, serving as judge and jury, appeared throughout the trial to be sympathetic to Amy's predicament and seemed intrigued by Elvira's arguments about Dennis Smith, but in the end the judge found Amy guilty. For five months now she had been at the Patuxent Institution, with many years ahead of her.

All along there had been staff attorneys at the public defender's office who felt Elvira made a mistake in not trying to shift more of the blame onto Derrick Jones, and now their feelings were out in the open. Elvira had done Amy a disservice by too glibly passing over Derrick's culpability and giving up on the most logical of the possible defenses—this was the basic criticism. The proposition that Elvira had wronged her client suggested a provocative possibility. Might the wrong rise to the level of reversible error? Was it possible for Amy Smith to win a chance for a new trial by now shifting the blame onto Elvira White?

The winter had moved on. Fallen dogwood petals lay in white masses under the trees.

Camilla was planning a return trip to Maryland. Perhaps she would visit with her father, William Brown, the Shakespearean director and drama professor who once had been one of the African-American success stories of Hillcrest Heights and who now, near the end of an illustrious career, was chairman of the drama department at the Baltimore campus of the University of Maryland. William Brown had previously taught for several years at Howard University, a "black" university, and though he counted these as happy years, he was proud to have been able to "break out" and win one of the classic struggles of well-educated black America. It had been the struggle of the generation born in the twenties and thirties, the struggle also of Camilla's mother, Alfie Brown, another success story, who had followed the proscribed course for black girls wishing to be actresses: studies at the all-black Dillard University and advanced studies at the Karamu Center in Cleveland, at the time one of three theatrical centers in the United States for people of color, where, as luck had it, she met William Brown, then a set designer and technical director. Camilla could remember being wowed by the pizzazz of her mother on the stages of "black theaters," the feathery plumes and the tiara of the Queen of Sheedy in *Defiant Island,* but on Broadway and in Hollywood there was next to nothing for her; older black actresses already had dibs on the maid and housekeeper roles. Camilla's mother did manage bit parts in *Car Wash* and *Hairspray,* but not until 1971, when Camilla was in high school, did Alfie Brown hit her jackpot with a part in the memorable *Being There,* which she then parlayed into a grandmotherly spot in a comedic soap opera that ran for seven years on PBS and became a model for the network show "Good Times."

Camilla's family had settled in Hillcrest Heights in 1968, one among tens of thousands of black families who, from the 1960s through the 1990s, would pack their belongings into rental trailers and exultingly leave Washington, D.C. ("We followed the Raisin-in-the-Sun model, moving to the suburbs, to a place Americans are supposed to aspire to.") Cancer had taken Alfie Brown a few years ago, and William Brown was now remarried and living in Baltimore. Homecomings for Camilla had become less and less frequent; relations with her stepmother were rather stepmotherly. Even though Camilla kept promising to make more room for her dad in her busy doctor's schedule, and even though William Brown was one of the considerations for her upcoming visit, it was not accurate to say he was the main consideration. The visit Camilla was planning had as its one true purpose a coming to terms with a more daunting man, the man who years ago might have been her father-in-law, the man who might yet be.

No definite date was set for Camilla's visit, but for a few weeks she and Bruce had been absorbed by the diciness of the idea—the idea of returning to the spot where years ago they had kissed under the stars and thrown convention to the winds and joined, near to the beginning, in a chain of causal connection.

"You don't have to do it for me," Bruce said when Camilla expressed second thoughts.

"I don't know why I'm doing it, but I'm doing it."

"I'll understand if you back out. I know my dad is the last person in the world you want to see."

"You got that right."

The humor writer Teresa Temple was one of the white people Bruce called the "Old Settlers" of Hillcrest Heights. In her heyday she had been much in demand nationally for her funny speeches. Now sixty-four years old, she resided by herself in the family home. Two months earlier a thief had slipped into Mrs. Temple's bedroom and helped himself to some of her jewelry. The one burglary had been followed in quick succession by four more, apparently committed by the same person. In vain, Mrs. Temple's three grown children, who lived in the area, argued with her to sell the house. She did agree to have an alarm system installed and to have the windows fortified by naked ironwork, although, because of a pile of leaves, the security crew overlooked a casement window at ground level. At 5:30 one morning, shortly after the security installation, an alarm sounded, but two Prince George's police officers failed to detect the casement window, its glass pane now shattered. The officers departed the premises but were persuaded to return three hours later by Mrs. Temple's daughter Sally. The house had been burglarized a sixth time. Mrs. Temple's body lay under a load of unwashed laundry. Her hands were tied with rag strips; one was lodged down her throat. She was dead of suffocation. The man subsequently convicted of the crime was thirty-one-year-old Michael Walker, an unemployed black man who, like Delmar, moved through the neighborhood doing handyman's work. Mrs. Temple had often hired him to rake the leaves from her yard and to mow her lawn and was said to have tipped him well. At his sentencing Mr. Walker apologized, saying, "Drugs were a big part of my life when this happened."

Among the riffraff of Hillcrest Heights there was a demented black man known for his ravings in front of churches, and he was heard proclaiming that the death of Teresa Temple was good for the neighborhood—it was like hanging out a "No Whites Wanted" sign. But Delmar was mortified by the violence. "I swear to Jesus," he said to Dr. Gordon, "I'd knock any sucker silly who messed with you."

What was the chance Merv and Dell Strickler would be struck down in a criminal act because they were residents of Hillcrest Heights? No matter how infinitesimal the odds, Heather believed it was her duty as their only living child to consider them. These were not pleasant thoughts, but, forced to articulate them, Heather said that while she thought of her childhood in Hillcrest Heights as "an ideal time in an ideal location," she now believed her parents would be safer somewhere else. ("I know they are connected emotionally to Hillcrest Heights, and maybe it is selfish of me to wish they would move, but, honestly, it would be a load off my mind. Of course, you can't predict when and where a handyman will turn into a murderer. That can happen anywhere. But if you are an older citizen living in Hillcrest Heights, I think you are more vulnerable. There are criminal types, not necessarily from Hillcrest Heights—usually they roam in from the other side of the line, from Washington—and they prey on the

old and the helpless. This has been going on for some time. It was a problem when I lived there.") Years ago, the "criminal types" from Washington—that is, rough-looking young black men—who ventured onto the
sidewalks of Hillcrest Heights were usually spotted from the kitchen windows of Neighborhood Watch sentries. Young black men then were oddi-
ties. If they dallied too long, a warning would go out over the telephone
lines. ("The difference now, since the complexion of the neighborhood
has changed, is they blend in more easily.") A question occurred to
Heather: Would Camilla see hidden racial motives in a daughter's wish for
her parents to live in a place that did not afford so much "protective coloration" for young black criminals? Heather would never think of herself
as "racist," not after growing up in such an open-minded family, but on
past occasions, Camilla had pointed out a racial dimension when Heather
was oblivious to it. One example: Back at Potomac High, the football
team's star running back, Obie Tucker, was involved in a car crash that
killed the team's quarterback, his best friend, sitting in the passenger's
seat. Obie Tucker, his legs maimed, his athletic career destroyed, had been
driving but was deemed not at fault; the other driver had been drunk.
Everyone at the school was grief-stricken, which is what Heather saw. ("It
was a toss of the coin who was behind the wheel and who was the passenger. It was a tragic accident, and I presumed everyone realized it
couldn't be Obie's fault.") Whereas Camilla saw white classmates holding
a black football player responsible for a white football player's death.
("More than blame was placed on Obie. It got to be a racial thing. It was
amazing how things had seemed to be fine, but all you had to do was
shake them up a bit and look what came out. There was a month or so of
really serious racial tension.") Another example: In 1974, on a trip to the
South with Heather's father, a white waitress at a restaurant took exception
to the two girls, then eighteen. The waitress threw silverware on the table.
Latecomers were served ahead of them. Afterward Camilla said to Merv,
"I'm glad you pretended like you didn't notice." Merv replied, "I didn't
want to give her the satisfaction." Recalling the incident, Heather said, "I
was baffled. I didn't know what they were talking about. Camilla said to
me, 'Didn't you see how the waitress acted?' I kind of shrugged. 'Yeah, but
I thought she was just grouchy, just being rude.' It never dawned on me
the waitress was giving us a hard time because of Camilla's skin color. I
think, fortunately or not, I did not grow up where anyone close to me
practiced racism and so I have to take particular pains to observe it. Otherwise it may happen in front of me, but I will be unaware."

The friendship between Camilla and Heather had lasted all this time because they did not hold back when they talked. They could say anything

to each other. The evening before Heather's wedding, Camilla had uttered a sharp warning, "Are you sure you want to commit to these vows? You want to promise to 'obey'? You want that kind of marriage?" To which Heather had answered, laughing and hugging her friend, "Yeah, it's cool. I'm not doing it for him. I'm doing it for me." And Camilla had squeezed her back, "Okay, as long as you're sure."

Heather said now, "Camilla's role has been to inform me of what I'm getting into. She is probably the shrewdest, most analytical person I know. Very aware of nuances. Of course, she can be analytical to the point of ad nauseum, which is something else I can tell her."

The subject of Merv and Dell Strickler's safety inside the confines of the old neighborhood was therefore something Heather planned to bring up to Camilla—at the right opportunity.

The term the kids in Prince George's County had for girls like Amy Smith was "whigger" or "wigger"—a white kid who tried to act "black," who talked the slang, who tried to look like a hard case, who dressed in the long, baggy look, who hung out, and who took someone black for a lover. No political statement was intended on Amy's part. To act black was to fit into Friendly High School, where white students numbered but one for every six black students. Yet behavior like hers was not without a degree of alienation and risk. There were night riders of the nineties, resentful white boys. A month ago a white girl at Bowie High School had been menaced at lunch and told to dump her black boyfriend. That night her car was covered with scrawlings in soap, lipstick, and shaving cream. *Wigger. Suck. Bitch die. Die Whigger.* How to deal with that cast of mind? Amy Smith could not go for advice to her father or to her stepmother. The narrative on which Amy was growing up did not go down well with Dennis and Marie Smith, or so Amy said in describing her home life to Dr. Ronald Schouten, a psychiatrist affiliated with Harvard Medical School who examined her prior to her incarceration at Patuxent Institution. The report Dr. Schouten filed with the courts pictured a girl deep in the throes of teenagehood, sixteen years old at the time, whose parents thought of her and her choice of friends as an effrontery. According to Amy, Mr. and Mrs. Smith's criterion was purely racial. All of Amy's white friends met with their approval, but she was forbidden to associate with anyone of color, boy or girl. Mrs. Smith talked of the white "tramps" who dated black boys. If Amy said "Nice day!" to a black friend at a softball game, her stepmother would "freak out." Once, while Mr. and Mrs. Smith were in the Bahamas,

Amy attended a church dance with a young black man; later the punishment, she said, was a hard slap across Amy's face. Amy also told of a time that Mrs. Smith had kicked a splintered hole into a wooden bedroom door trying to get at her stepdaughter. When Amy's friends expressed reluctance to come to her home they blamed her stepmother's bad temper. During the Christmas season of 1990, seven months before the incident inside the Smith house that would leave Derrick Jones dead, tensions between Amy and her parents "became particularly acute," according to Dr. Schouten's report. A Christmas card addressed to Amy was opened by Mrs. Smith; it was from a black youth Amy had dated clandestinely on and off for three years, and inside the card he had enclosed a photograph of himself. Up flew Mrs. Smith's hand. This time Amy slapped her back. Their fight was broken up by Mr. Smith, whose idea of peacemaking was to demand an apology of Amy. For church the next morning Amy had a shiner, and she refused to smear makeup over it. During the next few months, according to Amy, she was kept under strict surveillance. Letters that Amy tore up and threw away were taped back together by her stepmother. Amy was not allowed to leave the house after the dinner hour, neither weekdays nor weekends, under an indefinite sentence to be lifted only if she would abide by a rule prohibiting boyfriends of another race. "She finally agreed to do so because she could not tolerate being restricted from all activities," Dr. Schouten reported. Amy ignored the promise as soon as it was made. Sneaking out at night she began a period of trysting. Next she ran away, although her parents were able to find her in her hideaway and force her back home. By the spring she had lost thirty pounds from a kind of hunger strike and was sleeping in fits and starts. A defiant round of truancy followed, and then a suicide attempt with Tylenol, which her parents treated as a case of the flu. She would later be diagnosed by Dr. Schouten as suffering from a "depressive mood disorder," an "oppositional defiant disorder," and an "identity disorder."

This clinically depressed and unhappy girl, accused of trying to murder her parents had, after her arrest, come under the protective wing of Elvira White. In the detention center where they were introduced the attorney was perhaps a little too stern, too patently an adult, and the girl perhaps a little too sorry for herself, too ready to answer every hard question with a sob. But they seemed a good match. At this point in her life wouldn't Amy be more inclined to give her trust to a black person? And wouldn't Elvira be someone who could, without deprecation, accept a "whigger" for a client? In a letter to her grandparents Amy recorded her impressions of Elvira: "She seems nice and smart." The two of them, attorney and client, appeared to have a steady, well-adjusted rapport. After the verdict, when

Elvira visited with Amy in prison, there were no recriminations, no apparent hard feelings. ("Amy knew the job I'd done for her, a first-class defense. We lost, okay, but she was going to be paroled in five years. Amy had no intention of filing a claim that I was an ineffective counsel. Somebody from the public defender's office put that idea in her head.") The extent to which Amy may or may not have been manipulated by members in the public defender's office would remain unclear, and, legally speaking, it made no difference.

Soon enough two things did become clear, though. An appeal for a new trial was to be filed on Amy Smith's behalf, and the language of the appeal would put Amy's previous relationship with Elvira White into a wholly different light. Where Elvira had been the protector she now became the racially prejudiced miscreant who had ill used her underaged charge. The crux of the claim against Elvira was that she had blown the case because of her racial loyalties: she had not been willing to sacrifice the reputation of Derrick Jones to save Amy Smith.

On a wall in the Strickler dining room, Merv posted a blowup of a photograph he had taken last year during a campaign appearance by Bill Clinton in the Prince George's town of Clinton, named for one of the old county families. Merv had set up the shot with the president-to-be in the foreground and a Clinton town sign in the background, but at the critical second a Secret Service officer had thrust himself into the frame and Merv had to settle for a photo of the candidate without the sign. Still, it was an inspirational image—the overweight middle-aged Clinton looking somehow in fighting trim, looking somehow like a young Kennedy—and as soon as Gloria saw it up on the wall, she entreated Merv, "I have to have one of those. Can you get one blown up for me?"

It was the least Merv could do considering it was by Gloria's invitation that he had gone to see the presidential candidate in the first place. The host for the Clinton campaign stop had been the Prince George's white political boss, ruddy-faced Mike Miller, a lifelong inhabitant of Clinton, Maryland, and a descendant of one of the families that brought European civilization to Prince George's County. "Colleague" was now the operative term for the working relationship between Mike Miller and Gloria Lawlah they sidled together with arms on shoulders to pose for news photographers (with Democratic National Committee chairman David Wilhelm) at one of the Clinton victory parties at the swanky Martin's Crosswinds—but for some years the better term had been "antagonists," even

"bitter antagonists." The descriptions Mike Miller had applied to Gloria included "the lady without portfolio" and "the so-called reformer." In turn,
she had called him "a political throwback" and "the boss of bosses." Journalists pegged him as the leader of the "old guard" and her as a challenger
from a "new order." In the state capitol, where Mike Miller was the majority leader of the Maryland senate, his exercise of political power was second only to the governor's, and in Prince George's County, where he
directed the line of succession to the state legislature for the Democratic
Party and had given thumbs-up or thumbs-down to dozens of political careers, his power was, if anything, even greater. By comparison, when Gloria came onto the political scene, she was a nobody. In her first attempt for
the state legislature, in 1986, her brain trust consisted of three friends who,
like her, were strongwilled, professional black women with roots in the
civil rights movement and, like her, were novices in the nitty-gritty of electioneering. The conventional wisdom was against Gloria. History was
against her. The candidate Gloria would have to defeat had been hand-
picked by Mike Miller, and no black politician in Prince George's County
had ever prevailed over a machine politician. Of Gloria's candidacy, Mike
Miller had said, "It's either a hopeless cause, or a really hopeless cause."

But Gloria had a plan—later it would be referred to admiringly as "a
master plan"—that had begun to form by sheer inadvertence shortly after
nightfall one evening during the Christmas vacation of 1973. As number-
three vice-president, Gloria was hosting a meeting of the Prince George's
chapter of the NAACP. The number-one vice-president, a middle-aged
man, parked his car out front, on the side where the Stricklers lived. Dell
Strickler, at her dining room window, happened to see the vice-president
unlock his trunk lid and reach in for his briefcase. Out of the twilight two
young black men fell upon him; one, holding aloft a brick, bashed it
against his head. The man pitched face forward onto the edge of the open
trunk. The youths snatched up the briefcase and were gone. Dell wasted
not a minute in getting to the man, groggy, nose bloodied, two teeth broken, and helped him into Gloria's house. While Gloria drove him to the
hospital, Dell rode in a police cruiser and searched vainly for the muggers.
The police officers took the most direct route toward the county line because young black thieves in 1973 were seldom native to the settled society of Hillcrest Heights, but were more likely transients making quick
incursions from Washington. Gloria was beside herself. ("It infuriated me.
All the money we'd put into our house, now this criminal element was going to follow us into Hillcrest Heights and ruin it. I could just hear people
saying, 'Oh, there goes the neighborhood.' ") The next day, with Dell aiding and abetting, Gloria established a neighborhood crime watch. For

many weeks Gloria's phone was tied up; she was the lady who was going to run the bad guys out of town. Block after block of Hillcrest Heights joined in. Several dozen blue metallic Neighborhood Watch signs—$99 for the first one, $87 apiece for the rest—were planted in front yards. A top-drawer crowd of white people trooped to Gloria's house for meetings. Dell volunteered to be a block captain, in which capacity she was serving yet. The crime watch became a turning point for race relations in Hillcrest Heights. ("It brought everybody together. The reason was unfortunate, but it was a good mixer. A broad cross-section of friendships were formed. Race receded to the background. Everybody forgot about color and concentrated on the common interest.") Without quite realizing it Gloria had discovered her true calling. The solid-citizen network she strung together was the making of her political fortune. ("That was it, the neighborhood watch, all of us sitting around in living rooms, gabbing and taking the blinders off, because we were united against crime.") She gained the notice of reformers inside the Democratic Party, and at their invitation she ran in the 1982 elections for a spot on the Prince George's County Democratic Central Committee, winning by thirty-seven votes. White voters delivered the decisive margin. Her victory was a first; at the time no black person from her part of the county held any elective office.

By this time Gloria had gained an insight into larger political possibilities from excursions she took to the new Iverson Mall, a grand, glistening indoor emporium with covered pedestrian bridges that put to shame, and was trying to put out of business, the old Hillcrest Heights strip mall down the street. ("I told my husband, 'People think I'm nuts, but I walk through Iverson Mall with this big Cheshire cat grin.' I had never seen so many black faces, and I knew then that a great population shift was taking place.") Empirical proof of a large influx into Prince George's County of well-educated, well-off, civil rights–intoxicated Americans of African descent had first surfaced in the 1980 Census. Gloria and her three friends, the "Gang of Four," spent several evenings at her house with the Census tracts, double-checking those numbers against the voter rolls. Their findings portended exciting things. The subtraction of whites and the addition of blacks had changed the population of her local legislative district to one that was nearly fifty-fifty, black and white, and thus seemed ready for the overtures of an African-American politician. ("I felt giddy.") Yet a large number of the black newcomers, whose political allegiances lay in Washington, had not bothered to register to vote in Prince George's County. The local Democratic Central Committee, stacked with careerists loyal to Mike Miller, had no incentive to make the extra effort to recruit these newcomers onto the county rolls. But in 1984, the presidential campaign of

Jesse Jackson targeted Prince George's County for the Democratic primary held in March, as the campaign of George Wallace had done only twelve years earlier. A critical question was left unanswered, though: Would these same voters bother to return for the general election in November when Jesse Jackson would not be on the ballot? Because voting turnouts are not categorized according to race, there was no way to know for certain, short of stationing poll watchers outside each precinct house and marking notations in notebooks as to the race of each voter, which is precisely what Gloria and her three friends proceeded to do for State District Twenty-Six. Relying chiefly on their teenage children and friends of their children, they surveyed dozens of polling places. All day, as voters came and went, their crew scribbled in notebooks, checking off "white" or "black." Later, back at Gloria's house, the Gang of Four plugged the checkmarks into an adding machine. The reality in the notebooks was at considerable variance with conventional wisdom. Factoring in Board of Education projections, the women realized that black voters in District Twenty-Six would soon be in the majority. Excitement ran through the house. "Ladies," Gloria declared, holding up the adding machine tape, "I do believe we have the numbers." She placed the notebooks in a drawer for safekeeping. One day, she thought, they might be historical artifacts.

So when Gloria ran in 1986 for a seat in the state house of delegates she was not quite the novice Mike Miller imagined her to be. On election day the Miller major domos, who had once supped at Giovanni's, attempted to turn out their voters. These were voters identifiable from their outward appearances, white men in the garb of manual workers, wives with hair newly blued, people of recent European stock. Where had they gone? And from where had all the fancy-pants Negro men and their sharp-looking ladies come? That evening, while the votes were counted, Gloria's heart beat like a drum, a wonderful primal arrhythmia. Before she went to bed she knew she had won. No thrill from her later experiences in the government itself would be comparable.

Thereafter Mike Miller and his cronies talked of Gloria's success with the incredulity of primitives who are confronted with news of rocketships to the moon. "They thought we were these dreamy-eyed women," Gloria said. "But we had the plan. We had the numbers. They were the ones who were dreaming."

Did Dr. Gordon have any lingering feelings about the teenage love affair his white son had carried on with a black girl? You bet he did, and in the slurred, combative voice of a stroke victim he would register those feelings, even to strangers: "You think it's a picnic to have a son like him? You'd be disgusted, too, if you'd been through what I've been through." Dr. Gordon sat up stiff as a board, his soft, red doctor's fingers clenched in his lap. "I'm as open-minded as the next person, but it was too much, the way those two used to behave, all lovesick over each other. I'd come upstairs from my office, and they'd be sitting on the big couch, snuggled up real tight. I might as well have been a toadstool in the forest for all the respect they gave me. I might as well not have been alive. Their eyes were shut. They were listening to rock music. They most likely were stoned, for all I know. She had a goddamn big head of hair, what do you call it, an Afro? And he had his hair all puffed out, as big as hers. Weekends they'd take my car, my Cadillac, and go to Washington, go to Baltimore. I was upset to where I stopped giving Bruce the usual runaround money the way I had always done before. One time I told them, 'Get out of my house!' I didn't know what else to do. They looked at me like I was nuts."

On the afternoon Bruce and Camilla graduated from Potomac High, Dr. Gordon whiled away the time at the Rosecroft Raceway, placing fifty-dollar bets. "It was my regular day to go to the track, and why would I want to go see them graduate anyway?" His bad leg lay crooked on the footrest of a stuffed blue armchair. The leg would twitch every few minutes, and he would slap at it. His jut-jaw and pale eyes were not one bit less imperious than in the dresser-top photograph of him in white trousers standing next to a 1969 Cadillac, one hand caressing the rooftop. "You've got to understand where I stand. I made the money. I bought the cars. I bought the house. That's what I got for my life's work. I had an image to protect. I did not need to be wearing a big sign advertising to my neighbors that I'm a man who . . ." Here he paused, before struggling on in a strained voice, "who tolerates his son having relations with this black girl. And everybody knew it, too. Everybody knew what was going on. I'm sure they were doing it under my roof.

"So now they're starting up all over again. I've told Bruce not to bring her here, but what am I supposed to do? I don't know. You tell me: What is a man in my position supposed to do?"

Perhaps it was just wishful thinking to talk of the upcoming elections as "historic," to talk of 1994 as "the year of the breakthrough," but the people who made such advance claims believed the opportunity could not be more perfect. Since the early formative years of Prince George's County each political season had begun and ended with the incumbent office-holders or their heir apparents in control of most of the elected positions. The passing of the torch was usually up to the personal whim of the incumbents. But in 1992 the Prince George's electorate had voted to impose a limit on the length of any one person's stay in office. As a result, the current county executive and seven of the nine county council members were prevented from running for reelection. Term limits, a favorite idea of political outsiders, was supposed to open up county politics to all comers. "It really will be a golden opportunity, and I think it's time. It's time for some black folks to have our shot," Gloria said. Yet any reform will produce unintended consequences, and it was being whispered all over the county that Sue Mills, a longtime county council member whose career, according to the script, was supposed to be over and done, was instead going to declare herself a candidate in the wide-open race for county executive. Bruce, pumping iron, heard the rumor. ("When you hear something like that you don't know whether to laugh or cry.") At the gym Sue Mills's name was accompanied by exaggerated wolf whistles and epithets. Black people tended to speak of Sue Mills with exaggeration, and they invested the mention of her candidacy with even more drama, because the whole notion of Sue Mills as the person who late in the twentieth century would arise as the leader of America's "civil rights mecca" was stupefying.

The plantation era had endured longer in Prince George's County than in most of America, and Sue Mills was regarded by some as a living caricature from that era: a blond, syrup-voiced, overpainted, beehived, fifty-seven-year-old full-figured belle. She had come into prominence in the early 1970s through her opposition to the federal court order that tried to achieve racial mixing in the Prince George's schools by busing students out of their one-color neighborhoods. While she was not able to overturn the court order, she exhibited skills and charisma of a rare variety. For the Sunday afternoon of the Super Bowl game in 1972 she organized perhaps the most memorable political spectacle in Prince George's history. Despite the fact that most of her followers wanted to be at home in their game rooms locked tight to a TV set—it was an unprecedented day for local sports fans: the Washington Redskins were in the big game!—more than twenty thousand chose to show up in full cry at an antibusing rally in the stands of the Rosecroft Raceway, with Sue Mills front and center. "That's no small item. And the people were orderly, despite their very strong feelings," she remarked later. It was said at the time that, in a metropolitan area mad for the Redskins, no other politician could have called out such a crowd. The strength of her drawing power drove members of the civil rights movement to direct a countercampaign of harassment. Vigils were held outside her house. A coffin was marched up and down her street in a mock funeral procession, and she was hissed and booed by designated hecklers who followed her everywhere she went. She was spit on by people who saw in her a resemblance to George Wallace and Louise Day Hicks. Mrs. Mills was sent scores of hate letters, and her mailbox was blown up by a fistful of cherry bombs. Racial violence existed close to the surface. The Grits, who, naturally enough, volunteered themselves for Mrs. Mills's movement, spit on black students as they got off the buses and threw rocks at bus windows, and a few times they worked up a lather that led to attacks with chains at bus stops. At public meetings there was screaming, and the language was vile. The atmosphere of hate unnerved some parents, among them Gloria and John Lawlah, who chose to enroll their children in Catholic schools.

The prospect that Gloria Lawlah and Sue Mills might now face off against each other for the right to be the Prince George's chief executive recalled that time, just twenty years ago, when there was absolute clarity to race relations in the county. A 1994 campaign with Sue Mills and Gloria Lawlah at the center of it would, in a sense, have the same clarity. They would be foils of the highest order for each other. White Power versus Black Power. The Rural Hot Mama versus the Coolly Ambitious Suburban Newcomer. The Past versus the Future. By the summer of 1993, with more than a year to go before the election, the competition for county executive was causing a stir not just among academicians and journalists but among a few concerned citizens.

"The worst thing would be if this election destroyed all the progress that's been made," Merv Strickler said, sitting on his living room couch.

Dell Strickler, sitting with him, reflexively underscored his worry. "I just hope this election doesn't split Prince George's County down the middle."

In the final analysis there were three reasons Camilla decided to put herself to the test of returning to Dr. Gordon's home: her love for Bruce, her desire to be "big enough" to forgive, and, contradictory or not, an equal desire to express an attitude of "in your face, coming at you, whatever the expression."

Camilla arrived in Hillcrest Heights on a Friday evening in June. She forged straightforwardly into Dr. Gordon's massive bedroom. He was watching a show on his big TV and chose this moment to maneuver himself from his wheelchair into a blue armchair, a procedure that took more than a few seconds. He did not look at her but mumbled a greeting deep in his throat that Camilla could not make out. His big downturned slab of a face reminded Camilla of an Easter Island idol, your worst nightmare old coot. She searched for words to say. Bruce stood with her like he had on their first date, face extremely composed, heart pounding, anticipating the worst. Camilla could appear to be passive, even dreamy, but she could also charge up quickly, and right now her eyelids were in a flurry, which is not to say she was batting them. Nervous eyelids told Bruce she was about to say something like "Fuck you!" ("She was perfectly capable of it, too.")

Finally Dr. Gordon got out a clear greeting, "Good to see you again. You look like you've lost some weight."

At their last encounter Camilla had been in the prime of her youth, so the doctor's comment made no sense, except in the context of an older man trying to be flattering to a younger woman. "Thank you," Camilla said. "You're looking very chipper."

That night and the next night Camilla slept with Bruce on the king-sized bed in the old medical office downstairs and experienced a welter of conflicting emotions. ("Just to be back in Hillcrest Heights with Bruce after all those years was very intense, and to be sleeping with him in his father's house, which is something we'd never done when we were in high school, was melodramatic. And to make small talk with Bruce's father, it was very confusing. Could I really hate the father if I loved the son? I tried to face that question. Could I get beyond my own prejudices about Bruce's father. Okay, he is a narcissistic, racist bastard, but is that the entire picture?")

On the big-print living room sofa Camilla spoke to Dr. Gordon about his retirement. "What do you miss the most?"

"The people," he replied. "There were people in and out all the time. But, you know, some of the people still come by. They say hello. They bring me meals. And there's this young man, Delmar—his brother was a patient of mine—Delmar drives me wherever I want to go."

The talk moved on to Camilla's family practice in Cambridge. She said she had patients from both ends of the social spectrum, pregnant black teenagers popping gum and matronly white ladies with gastritis. Once a week she worked in an AIDS clinic at the Cambridge City Hospital; in the past year sixty of the clinic's patients had died.

"AIDS, boy, that's a horse of another color. We never had anything like that in my day," Doc said. "That takes real dedication."

"Thank you, but I think basically I'm doing the same work you did—treating sick people."

Bruce sat there wound up, but Camilla kept handling the awkward situation with spirit. "She was particularly gracious to Pop, and I have to say he was on his best behavior," Bruce said later, bursting with gladness. He would remember the weekend as "an important time, a kind of completion. We were all together in my father's house, almost like a family. My father was polite, and Camilla was polite. I think she mainly felt sorry for him, sitting in his wheelchair. They both probably choked on their words a little. You might think we were being hypocritical, and maybe we were. But hypocrisy is a very American theme, isn't it?"

In Cambridge no one had taken note of Bruce and Camilla when they had kissed in full public view. But a white man and a black woman strolling affectionately arm in arm through the Hillcrest Heights strip mall was still, in the 1990s, a sight to behold. On Saturday afternoon, before a big night on the town, Bruce and Camilla walked toward the People's Drugstore—she wanted eyeliner—and were followed by stares and snickers. In the parking lot, two young black men whistled at Camilla. One implied to the other that a black woman and a white man together must be a hooker and a john. Bruce was ready to do battle. "Forget it," Camilla said, elbowing him eloquently in the ribs. In the drugstore an elderly white man was unable to keep his eyes off them and bumped into the sunglasses rack. A middle-aged black woman wagged a finger. Bruce felt a rush of the old agitation. Even in a modern reconstituted place like Hillcrest Heights, it seemed, a black and white couple was not an easy fit. "It started me wondering, how provincial are these people? How lame are they? There'd been all this change in Hillcrest Heights, but how much had things really changed?" Bruce said later. "Most of the people in the drugstore were black, but they might as well have been white, the way they acted. I thought to myself, they're like that Pink Floyd song, kicking around on a piece of ground in their hometown. They haven't been anywhere, done anything. Not because they're poor. No way—they're driving fancy cars, wearing fancy clothes—but they like being stuck in their comfy little neighborhood with their comfy little uptight attitudes."

For Bruce it put a damper on the rest of the weekend. He could not relax. It made him think again that to have a loved one of a different color might mean being always on guard. To have Camilla for his wife might mean he was fated never to relax, else he would end up like the old man in a French painting who is walking in summer flowers, a little smug, oblivious, and behind him a sneak thief is cutting away his money bag.

• • •

For Sue Mills the spring of 1993 was spent making up her mind about a candidacy for county executive. "It's not an easy decision," she said. She was at her councilwoman's desk in county headquarters in a room she had decorated with an extraordinary devotion to a pinkish earth color and where, outside the door, as a kind of sentry, she had placed a pink-hued fountain statue of St. Francis of Assisi. On this morning she was dressed in a pink outfit, with purple and blue accents, and eyelids lined in blue.

"I feel like there's two voices inside my head having a debate," she said.

One voice told her to follow her destiny, a destiny she connected back to her father, the Reverend Robert Henry, who had moved from the Midwest to Prince George's County with her and her mother in 1938. The rector of two Episcopal churches, Reverend Henry operated as a politician might—in the settling of disputes, in the application of his influence on civic matters, in the use of his pulpit. Actually he was more important than a politician. People tipped their hat to him in the streets. "I wanted to be a minister like him," Mrs. Mills said, "but the church was not ordaining women, so I chose to run for political office, which, I felt, was akin to a priesthood." The PTA was her way into politics. She held every possible PTA position at the county level, and, having made herself known to the right people in the political establishment, she was invited in 1970 onto the Prince George's Board of Education. The offer came a few years early on the schedule Mrs. Mills had set for herself—her daughter, Cindy, was just a sophomore at Potomac High (Bruce Gordon, a year behind Cindy Mills, would remember Cindy as studiously apolitical), and Cindy's younger brother, Steve, the political child in the family, would not enter Potomac for another year—but there was no question about refusing the offer. PTA rank and filers, in an apocalyptic mood about the possibility of forced integration in the schools, were packing school board meetings. It legitimized their movement to have Sue Mills, their leader, seated up on the dais. For the next few years, while the fever over busing lasted, Mrs. Mills lived a fantasy; her name was a household word in Prince George's County; she was feted at dozens of town meetings. Her followers were as crazy about her as they were about Wayne Newton and Liberace. During a break at a school board meeting, out in a hallway, she experienced one of the ultimate sensations of celebrity: "There was a mob of people, and they had me pressed against the wall. These were the people who loved me, and I was scared stiff. I thought I was going to die of suffocation." A middle-aged man affixed his fingers to a button on her jacket and tore it off. Holding the button toward his wife, he cried, "I got it for you, baby! I got it!"

Yet for all the popularity Sue Mills had enjoyed and, to some extent, continued to enjoy, it was unlikely a sufficient number of her supporters still existed inside county borders for her to be elected county executive. "It would be a hard row to hoe" was what another voice was telling her. Each year there were more deaths and departures among the "Old Settlers" whose votes had kept Mrs. Mills in office as the councilwoman from District Eight. What could she say to attract a newcomer's vote in the modern and transformed Prince George's County? No matter how diverse her public life might have been, she would always be remembered as the woman who stood in the schoolhouse door. Her husband, James, an electrical contractor, had told her to be "realistic," which was possibly his way of saying he would be pleased to have his wife at home with him instead of out chasing her "destiny." Politics had taken its toll on the Mills family. At one point the boundary lines around District Eight, which Sue Mills began representing in 1978, were redrawn—deliberately, she believed, since the Mills house in Hillcrest Heights was left on the outside of her district by 150 feet on one side and 200 feet on a second side. (According to her, this was the handiwork of the boss, Mike Miller.) To preserve his wife's career, James Mills had agreed to sell the house, which had been in his family for years, and to relocate. "To this day I wonder why Jimmy has been willing to go along with all the upheaval in our lives, but he has. He's been a saint," Mrs. Mills said. As for daughter Cindy, now married and living by choice one county over from Prince George's, her mother had kidded her a few days ago about not being eligible, as a nonresident, to cast a vote for county executive, to which Cindy had replied, "What makes you think I'd vote for you, Mother?" This was not an unusual reaction for Cindy, who, Mrs. Mills said, "can't tolerate anything to do with politics. She is very desirous that I not run or, if I do, that I lose the campaign. She wants me out of politics."

Among the others who wanted Sue Mills not to run were the men who called the shots with Mike Miller in the white political establishment, with whom she had parted company long ago. Her favorite campaign line was, "I do not owe my soul to the company store." Although Mrs. Mills had served fifteen years, longer than anyone else on the county council, the honorary titles of council president and vice-president that are rotated annually had been denied her over and over. She was deemed "too loud and boisterous," "too demagogic," "too déclassé." Image was important. "You have everyone else in this county working hard to shed our redneck history and then you have Sue Mills and her little band of loyalists, who are of no help," said a man whose construction company was in the business of cutting in roads and contouring the underside of lawns and who had contributed handsome amounts toward the Miller machine.

What was central to the disparagements of Sue Mills, however, was her independence. "Mike Miller doesn't trust Sue because he can't control her," said Merv Strickler, representing the reform wing of Prince George's politics. "It is inevitable that a political hack will resent anyone who doesn't need him." As long as Mrs. Mills could latch onto celebrity, as long as her name was high in recognition and passion, her friends said, she would be able to survive without the power men.

In 1948, Merv and Dell Strickler, then teachers in Pennsylvania, quit their jobs and drove their black 1939 Ford coupe across the country so Merv could take a flyer at a Stanford doctorate. Due to a breakdown of the coupe in the California mountain town of Truckee, they found themselves at a whistlestop rally for Governor Earl Warren, who, according to the pollsters, was looking forward to being elected Thomas Dewey's vice-president on the Republican ticket. If not forty the car trouble, Merv would not have gone to the rally—he was a Democrat through and through—and he took it for a good Democratic omen that Governor Warren attracted a small crowd in Truckee. Omen or not, Dewey and Warren went on to lose the election, which proved a blessing for the civil rights movement because, in 1954, the former vice-presidential candidate was available for appointment to the U.S. Supreme Court, from which seat of power he more or less single-handedly fashioned the unanimous *Brown v. Board of Education* ruling. Years later, Merv saw the Supreme Court chief justice on 17th Street in downtown Washington, and, in his irrepressible way, Merv went up, shook the chief justice's hand and mentioned the Truckee campaign stop. "What if you and Dewey had won?" Merv said. "You'd never have gone to the Supreme Court. There might never have been a *Brown* decision!"

There was a round of appreciative chuckling when Merv and Dell collaboratively told this story at a party celebrating the fiftieth wedding anniversary of their neighbors, the Thompsons, held in a meeting hall at the Randall Memorial Methodist Church.

"I am always amazed at your stories. They're so, um, offbeat," Gloria Lawlah said. She was on hand not only for the fun of the party but to do a little politicking and to present the Thompsons with an ornamentally scrolled commemorative certificate from the state of Maryland.

Most of the partygoers were from Hillcrest Heights, who were getting up in years and for whom the *Brown* decision was a touchstone. The *Brown* decision had signaled the beginning of the end of legal segregation in America, even though in Prince George's County a generation came and went before real change was allowed to occur, and even then the change was not what Chief Justice Earl Warren had, in all likelihood, intended. For several years in Prince George's County the *Brown* decision was completely ignored. An official system of segregation continued to collect black students in one set of schools and white students in another set. When the school board did put forward a policy of integration it was done tentatively, and officials of the NAACP at last lost patience and hired lawyers, imported from Baltimore, to seek redress. In 1973, U.S. District Court Judge Thomas Kaufman ruled favorably for the NAACP and ordered the Prince George's schools to be integrated by means of cross-county busing. Judge Kaufman's order, compelling the school board to abide by the spirit and letter of the *Brown* decision, had changed the face of Prince George's County. More than anything else, it was the triggering event for the flight of white working-class families out of the county.

Might white people again pack up and leave if Gloria, or someone like her, was elected county executive?

"I don't think so," Merv said. "White or black doesn't matter to the people who live here now."

"It matters," said another of the guests, a black man. "Don't think it doesn't. If black folks start running the show, there goes our noble experiment in race relations."

"I don't think of Hillcrest Heights as a noble experiment. I think of it as a place with good neighbors," Dell said.

"So why did all those white people boogie out of here?"

Merv answered, "They left for the wrong reasons. But the people who've stayed are not going to jump up and leave if a black person gets elected county executive. That's a terrible thought. If that's how it's going to be construed, Dell and I will never leave. I don't care if we're the last white family living in Hillcrest Heights." He looked around. He and Dell were the only white people at the party.

Later, after the refreshments, the talk shifted to Sue Mills, whose name brought down bombardments of scornful laughter. On this score Merv and Dell were uncommonly quiet. They had extremely mixed feelings, which they had already expressed to Gloria. If Gloria was not going to run, they were tempted to vote for Mrs. Mills, who, although she had moved from the Hillcrest Heights area a while ago, was someone else they thought of as a neighbor.

• • •

The general sprucing up of the Gordon yard now was added to Delmar's jobs, and he became a regular visitor to the Gordon home. The more Bruce learned the more he grew concerned that beneath Delmar's genial nature was a guy with a precarious hold on the few good things in his life. Delmar lived with a woman, Jeanna, and her four children. He was as playful and loving with them as any father would be, and he gave the impression of being Jeanna's steady guy, not someone who was here today, gone tomorrow. Yet, away from the house, Delmar appeared to have had problems that caused him at times to show up for work in unkempt clothes and a growth of bristles. More than once Jeanna flounced into the Gordon house and at the top of her lungs accused Delmar of two-timing her with Patsy, the woman who served as Dr. Gordon's caregiver.

For all of that, Dr. Gordon had taken a keen liking to Delmar. "He's a good man," Dr. Gordon said. "He pays attention to me."

Here at the end, after Elvira White had exhausted all attempts to claim her judgeship from the Judicial Nominating Commission, it was said that if only she had uttered some magic words of humility, if only she had made a play for mercy, the prize might still have been hers. But had she not done all she could by saying nothing?

In every encounter with local news folks Elvira had bitten her tongue exactly as Gloria had counseled. "It's not in my nature to twist slowly in the wind," Elvira would tell reporters, voice shivering with the emotion of what she could not say. "I am trying to master the art of diplomacy, so help me." Her natural state was to strike back in anger, and she seethed even as she kept quiet. Indeed, contrary to Gloria's advice, other friends were telling Elvira she would gain nothing by her silence. One friend put it to her, "You got to get your head checked for sense, girl. You're living an illusion. No way they'll give you a second chance." However, Elvira clung to a hope that an exception would be made in her case because the chairman of the Judicial Nominating Commission was Judge James Taylor, someone to whom Elvira had once attached herself for mentoring.

For more than two months now Elvira had waited on help from Judge Taylor, who, strictly speaking, had but one vote on the commission, but who, in the black community of Prince George's County, functioned as a spiritual godfather to the politically ambitious. Judge Taylor had done the things with his career that Elvira craved to do. Born into a family of freed American slaves who came to Maryland in the 1850s, James Taylor never attended a high school (there was none for black children) but received a

GED and went on to the air force and to American University law school. In Upper Marlboro in the 1960s, he refused to go along with the standard procedures of segregation that still held at the courthouse—he drank at "white" water fountains, ate at "white" cafes—and yet managed to work within the system to such resounding acclaim that in 1969 he became the first black judge on the Prince George's Circuit Court. Judge Taylor had paid his dues in the prosecutor's office, as a deputy to the white reformer Arthur "Bud" Marshall, who said of him: "Jim Taylor gave no guff, and, by the same token, he took no guff. Jim never made a big issue out of the signs that said 'colored' and 'white.' He would walk into a restaurant with one of us and sit in the 'white' section and expect to be served, and, by Jesus, if he wasn't." At the time James Taylor was appointed judge there were but five black attorneys working in the county, all of them associates at his law firm. On the bench Judge Taylor had served for eighteen even-handed, scandal-free years, retiring in 1987 to a pension and to an elder statesmanship. If he had naysayers in Prince George's County they were hard to find. Gloria adored the man: "He is so, so dear. If the world could be full of Judge Taylors, there would be no stopping mankind." The positions he held now, chairman of the Judicial Nominating Commission and member of the statewide Democratic Central Committee, were honorary but not without power.

The situation of Elvira White was one he was dealing with privately. You had to seek Judge Taylor out if you were curious. He could be found in his spiffy, bricked-in office from where he represented a few select legal clients. "Here is a woman of great promise, but flawed," he said of Elvira. "Her flaws do not prevent her from being an excellent attorney, but . . ." He shook his head. A portly man with a half-moon mustache and curly hair flattened to his scalp, metal-rimmed glasses precarious on his nose, his face expressed bewilderment. "It would require an investigation beyond our means to examine all the allegations about Miss White, both the positive and the negative, and even then I'm not sure they can be reconciled. We did the best we could. Knowing what the judgeship means to her, I feel extremely sorry it did not work out for her." Years earlier, shortly after earning her law degree, Elvira had sought out Judge Taylor to clerk for him on a volunteer basis, and he had become a controlling influence in her life. "Oh, absolutely," she used to say. "I am his most loyal admirer. I just think there is no one like him. He is almost like my idol." When told of Elvira's gushing statements, though, he frowned. "She was never a protégée, no. Nothing like that," he said. "I can't say I even remember what kind of clerk she was."

Of course, as soon as Elvira picked up the news from the grapevine that

Judge Taylor would not exert himself on behalf of "her" judgeship, her attitude underwent a change, too. To act deferential was not going to return her to the good graces of the Judicial Nominating Commission; the decision against her was final. "Do I feel betrayed? I feel like what's happened is worse than a betrayal. I feel like I've been knifed in the heart," she said, breaking her vow of silence since there was no longer any point to it. Her tap-fidgety fingers stormed on her desk. She became sarcastic. "It's sad, it's sad. I thought Judge Taylor had the ability and the credentials to be the patriarch of our community. But no more. He has just demonstrated to me he has the backbone of a snail."

In her private store of hopes and dreams Sue Mills had always wanted it to be her son, Steve, to put the Mills name on the ballot for county executive—Steve, a 1977 graduate of Potomac High, the apple of her eye, "my political buddy," the one who could not get his fill of electioneering. "He knew strategy. He knew door-to-door. It was just a matter of time before he would've been able to step into my shoes," she said. Steve Mills did not carry around with him actions of twenty years ago that needed constant defending. He would have been a modern and acceptable candidate—although, perhaps, he may have been perceived as too modern. In any case, fate had destroyed Mrs. Mills's plans. Her son had died of AIDS two and a half years ago while she knelt at his bed. ("It was rough. Steve had been a strapping fellow of 180 pounds, but the AIDS cut him down to maybe half that. We brought him home to die in August. He'd been living in downtown Washington—he loved macadam, the sound of horns and screeching tires—but he wanted to be with us at the end. It was just a horrible death. At ten o'clock I'd pray for the Lord to perform a miracle. At ten-fifteen I'd pray for the Lord to take him. And all during that time I was running for reelection. I won the primary on a Tuesday. He died that Saturday.") When it came time to declare officially for the 1994 county executive's race Sue Mills filed the papers with the county clerk's office—"it was one of Steve's last wishes that I run"—and Gloria Lawlah did not.

For Gloria there was no all-or-nothing dilemma. Her spot in the state senate was not affected by term limits, and, for now, she decided, a state senator's role suited her fine. There was a long future beyond 1994. Besides, the opportunity of 1994, the opportunity for a singular African-American in this singular American place to reach the top, Gloria believed, would come in such an open and uncontaminated form just this once and must be handled with care. "We need to put our best candidate forward, someone who can unite the community," Gloria said. Her nominee was Beatrice (Bea) Tignor, the fifty-one-year-old overseer of the English department at Prince George's Community College. Bea Tignor was relatively new to politics—upon Al Wynn's election to Congress she had taken his place in the state senate through the grace of a special appointment—but she had lived all her life in Prince George's County. Her upbringing was on a fifteen-acre farm where chores began at five in the morning. Her school was seventeen miles away, a "black" school. She used to wear dresses cut from grain sacks. "Bea's a home-grown tomato, and I'm a transplant" was how Gloria saw the crucial difference between them. "Bea can talk to the Old Settlers better than I."

When Bea Tignor was asked to compare herself to Gloria Lawlah, she laughed out loud, "Well, I am a peacemaker, and Gloria is a hell-raiser."

The observation of Oliver Wendell Holmes that good judges reflect the felt necessities of their times is to say that judges are political creatures and should be answerable to the people. Yet there is another well-respected philosophy that judges should be able to ignore public caprice and be free of politics. In Prince George's County, the two philosophies existed side by side. A Prince George's judgeship was an elective office, but in practice it was unheard of for someone to gain the office through the grime of a competitive election. The men and women who became the judges of Prince George's County advanced through a system that rewarded them for steadfast fidelity to the courthouse code. Foremost they had to prove themselves to the Judicial Nominating Commission. Only then, after serving an appointed term, did they stand for election, as incumbents, unopposed, guaranteed a job until retirement or death. Of the six incumbent Prince George's circuit court judges whose terms expired in 1994, none had expressed a desire to retire. All were planning to register for reelection. Therefore, according to custom, those races were now closed.

On August 6, 1993, however, Elvira White announced herself as a candidate in a news conference at the old columned entrance to the courthouse. "Putting God first, I'm going for it," she said. She tried to be calm and pleasant, as if it was the most natural thing in Prince George's County to take on the established order, but before long an aggrieved tone crept into her voice. "They rejected me. They say I'm unqualified. Well, don't believe them. I'm extremely qualified. The bottom line is the good old boys don't want me taking what has been theirs."

The news that Elvira would seek to win through the electoral process the judgeship heretofore denied her came as no great shock. But what might it really mean? "Is she serious? I have no idea. Does she have a prayer in hell? I have no idea," said a court bailiff, who had been in his line of work for twenty-one years. "Why is she doing it? I have an idea or two on that. Basically she must be out of her tree."

A subsequent *Washington Post* article would say: "Both damned and deified by the county's legal community, [Elvira] White is the first lawyer in a decade to challenge a sitting judge in Prince George's County. Her portrayal of herself as the underdog, a black woman taking on a powerful white status quo, resonates with many blacks, who see the judiciary as one of the last bastions of inequality in the county."

Once, in 1979, while Camilla was in medical school at George Washington University, Bruce looked her up, and for an afternoon on a city park bench they had what Bruce called "an awkward who-are-you-to-me, who-am-I-to-you dialogue." All the closeness they had once felt was turned tenuous, and after they parted that time they ended all communication between them. The years went by, and then, as they sat in separate cities, pensive and out of sorts, something had come over them—an uncontrollable urge?—and they had resumed their love life in vintage storybook fashion, utterly without rancor and so fiercely passionate as to suggest that they had never stopped pining for each other. It seemed to them still like a pinch-yourself unreality, like a miracle, which was how they spoke of it.

Bruce: "I was in Denver when I started having these night visions, and I'd get up in the morning and all I could think of was 'Camilla, Camilla.' She was on my mind constantly."

Camilla: "A very specific event happened to me. I was at home, doing nothing, my mind wandering, and suddenly I felt this premonition running along my skin: Bruce is in trouble. So I acted on it. I picked up the phone and called his old number. That's the first I realized his parents had gotten divorced. I refused to tell Bruce's father why I was calling. But it was such a strong bizarre feeling I had. I thought Bruce had been in a car wreck or something. . . ."

Bruce: "I'd been in a life wreck."

Camilla: "I kept trying to track down Bruce's mom and finally got her number and called her. I started babbling, 'I don't know if you remember me, but is Bruce doing okay?' She was very sweet. 'Oh, yes, he's happily married. He married a princess from Mexico. I don't think he ever really got over you, Camilla, but he's fine. Why do you ask?' 'Oh, I was just checking.' I didn't tell her I was getting a divorce."

Bruce: "Camilla tuned in on the psychic airwaves and felt my longing for her."

Camilla: "It *was* kind of mystical."

Bruce: "And then I went through these spasms of agony trying to get her number. I was begging, 'Mom, give me Camilla's number. Please, please, I love Camilla.' For us to have this incredible desire to get in touch with each other when we were completely uninformed about each other's lives—I still can't believe it."

Christian solemnity is all well and good, but legal careers are often better served if you cut up once in a while. For several years it had been Elvira's habit to throw elaborate drinking parties for the Upper Marlboro crowd, one at the summer solstice, another over the Christmas holidays. ("I supplied everything. They only had to bring themselves.") The drinks engendered a collegiality and resulted in reciprocal invitations. To Mike Miller and the other well-settled citizens of the courthouse Elvira became something of a fascination. Describing that period of her career, a *Washington Post* reporter had written, "She is the darling of the county's legal community, a fixture at the parties thrown by the most established lawyers and judges in Prince George's."

However, since the firing of Jeff Singman, it seemed that Elvira's name had been crossed off all party lists. Likewise she had suspended her own biannual parties.

The feud that had enveloped her now had an air of being unstoppable, and it did not take an overactive imagination to envision the Amy Smith case getting caught up in it. Out in the courthouse corridors, Elvira was being freely blamed for Amy's imprisonment. Suzanne Clements, a young woman of Celtic background, slightly frumpish with a scramble of pretty blond hair, who, as Elvira's law clerk, had assisted on Amy's trial, was calling Amy "the real victim." Or the "three-time victim"—a girl victimized first by her parents, victimized second by her boyfriend, and victimized finally by her attorney. The elevation to victimhood is a normal process at any law office when it is decided to cannibalize one of the staff attorneys for the greater good of a client; breaking the lawyerly pact necessitates seeing the client as a sufferer of a gross injustice. But in this case, the talk seemed to make the women feel too holy. Their deeply moral purpose seemed overly conceived. The "ineffective counsel" claim registered against Elvira was so unusual, so pointed and personal, it seemed to have as much to do with settling a score as with rescuing someone from prison. Elvira was accused of being "ineffective"—not for goofing off the night before the trial, nor for a technical slipup, but for a mistake that supposedly grew out of her intrinsic loyalty to the "black rabble," her eagerness to go to bat for a kid like Derrick Jones, "probably a no-good kid," a kid who was not her client and whose interests were at odds with the interests of her actual client, the girl in Patuxent. Against these stinging accusations did a single one of Elvira's colleagues put in a considerate word for her? ("No, nobody, none of my so-called friends, these people who used to work with me all hours of the day or night, who used to come to my house and sit at my dinner table and eat and drink and tell stories and joke around with my son.") To the contrary, there was even a possibility Elvira's former friends might be willing to put their hand on the Bible and testify against her at a court hearing—the rite of legalistic cannibalism taken to a higher level.

Elvira had had intimations of this development, but she could not quite bring herself to believe that any of the attorneys and investigators who had worked alongside her on dozens of cases would go as far as to give evidence against her. Anyway, time seemed to be on her side. Everything to date had happened fast, but now there would be a period for reflection and sobering thought. Assuming an appeals court granted a hearing for Amy it would be several months before the hearing could be held.

In the meantime, Elvira was trying to find out whatever she could. Unfortunately, her few intelligence sources in the courthouse had dried up. There was no information to be had.

No one was more of a regular person than Sue Mills, a commoner without any of the old colonial blood in her veins, and the tragedy with her son had made her all the more regular. Who among us has been spared grief? In the Strickler family their only son, Todd, a jazz talent who toured with B. B. King, had also died a young man. Merv and Dell, to use the nouveau term, could "connect" with Mrs. Mills.

And in more ways than one. The Stricklers had always cheered Mrs. Mills's attentiveness to her constituents in her district, her attentiveness to white folks and black folks. Bang around the county with her in her big sedan and she would give you chapter and verse on libraries built, trees preserved, potholes fixed. *See those wooden benches. I need to put a memo through. They should be aluminum.* No politician could beat Mrs. Mills on making government work at the sidewalk level.

What then should Merv and Dell's judgment be on "the woman who stood in the schoolhouse door"? There was no forgiving her, of course, for her deliberate defiance of the federal judge's order—or was there? Even in the age of cynicism, it is wildly un-American not to believe that human improvement goes hand in hand with age, all our hearts growing bigger the older we get. Old sinners who do a few good turns are redeemed, or at least are afforded the cover of moral ambiguity. In the years since the Super Bowl rally, to Merv and Dell's knowledge, Mrs. Mills had not resorted to any public tactics giving aid and comfort to racists, the redneck kind anyway. Should her bygones be bygones?

Optimism was a motif for both Bruce and Camilla, and during the many months when they talked of living together and rang up thousands of dollars in long-distance bills, they had stopped their ears to common sense and refused to take heed of the difficulties that lay before them. Any outsider could have told them what, in real life, the likely outcome would be. In real life they would sooner or later have to face up to a dilemma that, in alternating forms, had haunted their romance from the beginning. How could Bruce make a family peace before his father died and at the same time marry the woman who was the source of the original enmity between son and father? How could Camilla give full devotion to a man who was unwilling to turn his back on the father who had so vehemently scorned her? How could a white man and a black woman, with so many challenges hitting hard against their string of luck, find happiness? What demons their dream invoked! In the weeks leading up to Camilla's return visit to Hillcrest Heights, which Bruce thought might be "a kind of exorcism," the bitchy words in their half-finished sentences were always about his father. But the two lovers kept postponing the "blow it out your ear" discussion that Bruce kept expecting.

Now, after eating at Dr. Gordon's table and exchanging even-up, doctor-to-doctor talk and after wheeling the old man to his room and watching him take off his unshined wingtips and sagging socks and seeing in his pouchy, heavy-lidded eyes a tacit surrender, it seemed less critical to

Camilla that she and Bruce had not yet resolved things between themselves. It was less critical because all plans for Camilla and Bruce to live together were off. They had come to a different resolution, a real-life resolution. No more of the heart-rent waiting game. Into the foreseeable future Camilla would continue to live in Cambridge, and Bruce would continue to live in Hillcrest Heights, and they would consider each other unbound and eligible for other interests.

Bruce: "Well, not exactly unbound. I love Camilla. Always have."

Camilla: "There is still this intensity between us. He doesn't want to get married, and I don't want to get married, but we can't pretend the intensity isn't there. So what do we do with it? With our history, he will always be my best friend who can talk over anything with me. There are pieces of me that he knows which nobody else will ever know because he's got twenty years with me."

Bruce: "A promise exists between us: We'll always be there for each other. We still talk on the phone once a week."

Camilla: "But after all the dizzying feelings, we've come down to earth."

Bruce: "We've agreed to give each other room to go on with our lives. We're not going to cramp each other's style."

To learn that two of your best friends might join even briefly with someone known for her racist reputation, join even for half a minute behind the cloth curtain of a voting booth—what should the normal reaction be? Should you get angry and give them what-for? *I can't believe you'd ever do business with Sue Mills! Don't you know a vote for her is a slap in my face?* But Gloria Lawlah's reaction was to invite Merv and Dell Strickler over to her house to break bread with the man most likely to be Maryland's next governor, Parris Glendening, the outgoing county executive who owed his career, in some part anyway, to Gloria's ability to turn out the vote for him in her district. Then, a few days later, Gloria paid a neighborly visit to the Stricklers and invited them, at their convenience, to sit for a private talk with Bea Tignor, her alternative to Sue Mills. "You'll like Bea," Gloria told them. "This lady raised two kids by herself after her husband died and then went back to school and got her doctorate."

Merv and Dell would, of course, oblige Gloria. Aside from friendship, the request came from one of the most important politicians in the county. Anybody who was anybody knew the way to Gloria's house.

Yet, in their own way, Merv and Dell were also voices to be reckoned with. Not to overstate their special status, but had Dell said "yes" instead of "no" to a phone call back in 1962, she might herself have become a First Lady. This was a call from Gladys Spellman, who pleaded with Dell to run for county council as a reform candidate. The two of them, two forceful ladies of the PTA, kicked the idea around. It was Gladys Spellman who ran instead and who became the original First Lady, so revered, at the time of her death, that the major thoroughfare of Prince George's County was quickly renamed Spellman Parkway. In the meantime Dell and Merv had been active all these years, furiously active, giving long and personally to the commonweal. That a library and not a gas station stood at 24th and Iverson was due considerably to the Stricklers. They also had helped rewrite the school curriculum. Public TV legislation was another of their pet projects, and the Bowie airport, and a Hillcrest Heights commuter train stop.

If nothing else, they were still trendsetters for the older white crowd. Were the Stricklers to declare publicly for Sue Mills it would make a difference.

A few minutes before quitting time on a Friday deep into autumn, Bruce joined the multitudes mixing with the loudly played rap music of Iverson Mall. He went straight to the Big & Tall shop for men. One look in the triple mirror at his mercury-lit pallor, and he groaned. "Ouch! I look like Wonder bread." By noon the next day he would be aboard a cruise ship on the Caribbean Sea, his first venture in years into the single life. "I need underwear. Silk bikini underwear," he said, slapping five with a clerk. Bruce was known at the store. The clerk pulled plastic bags of bikini briefs from a rack. "I got you covered, my man. What flavor you favor? Grape? Cherry? Lemon-lime?"

The cruise lasted two and a half days. The high moment for Bruce was his performance of the twist in the dance contest. Judged the most proficient, most exuberant twister, he was presented the first-place trophy. "For a white guy, you can really get down," a black woman in a sequined dress told him. She introduced herself, a married CPA. She was on the cruise with her husband and about fifty hard-drinking friends who called themselves "The Wrecking Crew," a civic club from Denver of the financially well-to-do. The Wrecking Crew members were the glamour personages on board, and Bruce became a special guest at their social hours. He was given kudos for his ability to keep up on the dance floor. They even brought him up to the front of the room and inducted him into the club, an honorary white member.

Back in Hillcrest Heights, he set on the nightstand next to his bed the trophy he had won, a gold plastic replica of the cruise ship bolted onto a wooden base. Some days later Bruce strolled into the Big & Tall. He was wearing his new green-and-purple sweatshirt stenciled with "Bahamas." The clerk winked broadly. "Man, oh man, sailing the Caribbean with a hundred and one foxes. How lucky can you be?!"

"I deserved it, I deserved it."

"Bet those silk underwear didn't stay on long."

"From my butt to the bedroom floor in, oh, maybe thirty seconds."

"You lying dog!"

"So what if I am?!"

Elvira approached her office door each morning with grim resignation. Yesterday, for the second time this week, she had found a note on her chair, informing her of a violation of procedure, this time for overstaying her lunch hour.

Now, hands politely clasped, Elvira said, "Everything is escalating. I cannot go through a week now without having some kind of complaint lodged against me. My whole career I compiled an exemplary record, and suddenly I can't do anything right?! Suddenly every time I turn around I've broken some rule?! Okay, I get the picture." She picked up a file folder and riffled briefly through, then tossed it down, the paperwork spilling out. "They will stop at nothing to prevent me from becoming a judge. I am the only one who has stepped to the plate and said 'Batter up!' They know that if I'm elected judge, whether it is in '94 or '96 or '98, all bets are off. Every black lawyer in Prince George's is going to step up to the plate then." She was up on her feet, pacing. She made a fist and slowly let her fingers unclench.

Commenting on Elvira's difficulties, a woman from the public defender's office said, "This is not easy for me to say, because I like Elvira, I admire her for having guts. But when you get right down to it, all this trouble, she brought it upon herself." The logic of this woman's argument was that Elvira could not catch a break now because she had been so loathe to give one when she had had the chance. For a decade everyone in the courthouse had watched as Elvira transmitted, with tight little grins, her high-and-mighty Caesar's wife judgments. "Elvira is possessed of a perfect assurance," the woman went on. "It never crosses her mind she

might be wrong. She thinks of herself as being always, always right."
When it was suggested that these sounded like qualities present in many
judges, the woman shrugged. "I don't agree. I think judges have to have a
little humility. But you're partly right. Elvira has an image of herself as
someone in black robes. I guess we'll have to wait and see if it comes to
pass."

The morning after his return from the Caribbean cruise Bruce slid into
a used Toyota Tercel, a gift from his mother. On some level of consciousness he had an expectation of problems and was not surprised to find the
odometer reading higher by 420 miles and the car's interior soiled and littered. The car had been ungratefully handled by Delmar, who had borrowed it in Bruce's absence. It was another mark against the man.

"You can only give the guy the benefit of the doubt for so long," Bruce
said to his father.

"Yeah, well, if you kick Delmar out, who's going to drive me around? I
don't see you showing much interest in doing it."

The following weekend Delmar came by the Gordon house to rake
leaves. Bruce expected some sort of apologetic gesture in regard to the
Toyota, and when none was forthcoming he decided then and there that
Delmar should be banned from the house.

The next time Bruce saw Delmar was several days later. Out walking his
dog, Bruce nodded hello, but Delmar, with angry eyes, slouched by. Bruce
knew better than to get a rise out of him. Half an hour later, as Bruce approached home, they met again. Delmar was across the street. Bruce
watched him dig rounded stones out of the dirt. Without warning the
stones were hurled in Bruce's direction. "I want my job back," Delmar
shouted. He spit in the air. "C'mon, man, I need the cash."

Bruce picked up his pace. He ran as hard as he could, burning himself
out.

"Okay, let's judge a person by the content of his character," Bruce said.
"Delmar has no character. I refuse to use the 'N' word, and I don't want to
hear the 'K' word, because they both rip the soul, but Delmar is a worthless motherfucker."

As Gloria went about her business, Elvira's name cropped up again
and again—in the hallways of the state capitol, on the phone with con-

stituents, on the sidewalks of Hillcrest Heights, at the dinner table. For the most part, people were just curious about Elvira, although a few were overwrought with concern. *She is being crucified. For being uppitty, that's why. That's the be-all and end-all. Every bone in my body knows it.* Perhaps the most interesting conversations were during family get-togethers when Dwight Jackson was in attendance. Tall, mustachioed, soft-handed, balding, the exhibitor of a fixed, smooth look, Dwight Jackson was a member of Gloria's extended family—his sister had married one of Gloria's sons. Dwight Jackson also was the deputy county prosecutor in charge of most homicide cases and thus the courtroom counterpoint to Elvira. In public situations he often struggled to find just the right cliché to describe Elvira—"a worthy rival," "an independent thinker"—but behind the scenes he was a friend and an admirer. He saw Elvira as someone who was defining the boundaries of permissible aspirations for black politicos at the courthouse. "For black people to get ahead at the courthouse someone has to push the envelope. She is that person," he would tell Gloria.

The seemingly unending controversies brought on by Elvira, however, placed Gloria in an unenviable position. In the beginning Gloria had taken up Elvira's cause with automatic fervor to the point that Elvira now assumed Gloria would be her principal sponsor in her run for judge. However, every time the newspapers made mention of Elvira's troubles it increased the potential for ugliness and divisiveness of the type to undermine all black office-seekers on the Prince George's ballot. Bea Tignor, at the top of Gloria's ticket, had the most to lose. "Bea can't win with strictly black support. She needs white support," Gloria told the people in her political crowd, getting straight to the point. Indeed, Gloria and the other Black Alliance leaders, including Congressman Al Wynn, had been engaged recently in deal-making sessions with Mike Miller, master of the hard-playing Irish school. The outlines of the deal called for Bea Tignor to be their unity candidate. She was to be the coalescing force, bringing into the middling span of the political spectrum the Black Alliance and the big white Miller machine. On the other hand, Elvira represented an extreme. She had no hope of ever obtaining support from Mike Miller, who was solidly for the six incumbent judges and who said of Elvira, much as he had once said of Gloria, "She could use a reality check."

When Gloria now walked into Mike Miller's office she had at her disposal tremendous political status and influence—"she's one of our success stories," Mike Miller now said—and because of that status and influence, Gloria herself stood to lose if Elvira's candidacy flew out of control. The decision confronting Gloria was whether Elvira was worth the risk

• • •

Several of the strategic thinkers around Gloria had tried to warn her off Elvira. *Stay away, she's poison, she's not like you.* Gloria had to admit, "She's not someone you can press easily to your bosom. She's prickly." Or as Elvira unflinchingly said of herself, "I have a rough-and-ready side." And yet wasn't Elvira's story also Gloria's story, the story of a girl from a shrunken, sorrily divided hamlet where railroad tracks twained the town into white and black sections, the story of a girl's hankering for a better life and the outstanding work ethic that brought each of them years of relentless good fortune? Weren't their longings the same, their resentments, their journeys of realization?

During their first encounters, when Elvira originally sought to win Gloria's sympathy, she had laid out her bittersweet history: the child who was everything John Calvin admired, up at dawn and in the tomato fields before breakfast, always hoeing one extra row, filling one extra basket, but all the time knowing it was a life for losers, for downtrodden Negro people. Freedom had come for Elvira with the Class of 1970, Washington High School, and she had said a fist-waving farewell. Until her senior year the schools as Elvira knew them had been segregated. The Eastern Shore had been a rebel territory during the Civil War and before then a haven for people outside the law. In the early nineteenth century the Chesapeake Bay oystermen lived in fear of brigands who fitted cannons onto the decks of fishing boats. Because of their isolation, and due also to a strangely powerful influence over the Maryland legislature, the counties of the Shore were often granted special exemptions from state laws—for instance, from the state's public accommodations act. It stood to reason then that the sudden throwing together of black students and white students at Washington High would produce tensions. The night before Elvira's baccalaureate ceremony, she met with her minister and a few friends who felt the honor of valedictorian had been stolen from her and given to a white boy. The next day, when it was time for the school song, Elvira and her friends sang "We Shall Overcome." Up on stage she raised a power salute. Fisticuffs broke out. Parents of white students hurried their children out of the auditorium. ("My mother wanted to hide under her chair.") A local newspaper reported: "Negro Students Disrupt Graduation." But Elvira already had received her acceptance letter to North Carolina A&T, a school she selected at least in part because of a day in 1960 when four A&T freshmen, having jacked up each other's nerve ("You really mean it?" "Sure, I mean it!"), slid themselves onto "whites only" stools at a Woolworth's counter and forever altered the world of segregation. At that audacious moment Elvira was eight years old and already aware. She then chose another school occupying a niche in African-American history, the University of Maryland. The once-segregated university had been successfully sued by the young NAACP lawyer Thurgood Marshall, who, after trying and failing in 1933 to become its first black law student, later returned for a legal skirmish that led directly to *Brown v. Board of Education.*

This was all familiar to Gloria, hailing, as she did, from Newberry, South Carolina, where, in the 1940s, teachers in the black public schools lost their jobs if they dared signal support for the local NAACP lawsuit that was later incorporated into the *Brown* case. The governor of South Carolina had empowered special deputies to identify these teachers, one of whom was Gloria's mother. She had heard in Thurgood Marshall's legal preachings the trumpet of deliverance, and she seized upon the governor's dare. An NAACP youth choir was organized—Gloria and friends in ribbons and white dresses. The upturned faces of the girls rose over a collection plate passed from church to church for Mr. Marshall.

Even so, Newberry had existed in a different time. There was more to fear than the governor's deputies; there was the Klan. The choir had to operate by word of mouth. It would have taken too great a liberty to post billings. You could not live through the era of the Klan without being tempered by it, and later on Gloria would wonder if this was what was missing from Elvira's education, the nights of cold fear. Then, too, on another level, Gloria had been a girl of the schoolhouse, not the fields. Gloria grew up in a family that had produced three generations of teachers. Gloria's grandmother ran a one-room school—"after hoeing and before picking, kids came out of the cotton fields, and she taught them reading and writing out of the Bible." Nor did Gloria's family know poverty. Their frame house was on a paved street not so far from the Georgian mansions on Main Street. Despite racial animus, Gloria had left Newberry on good terms and just recently had gone home to stand in an induction ceremony, a daughter of the South who had made good.

These were the sort of differences that could explain perhaps why Gloria did not like uncontrolled public outbursts, let alone any resort to violence. These were differences that might explain Gloria's reaction to the fires set in her neighborhood, and the stripping of store inventory, in the days after the 1968 murder of Martin Luther King, Jr. Gloria was living then with her husband and young children in Washington, D.C., in a section going to seed. She would remember the riots thusly: "My kids, when they saw the TV pictures of the burning and looting, said to me, 'What's going on, Mommy?' I said, 'The black people are looting.' And they said, 'Why?' And I said, 'Conditions are very bad, and Martin has been killed.' But my kids couldn't feel any connection to the rioters. The way we were brought up, you did not steal. You worked for everything. Black people did not act violently; they weren't bullies. Violence, bullying, that was part of the Klan culture."

It probably mattered that Gloria was older at the time, already a teacher on the job, already raising a family, whereas Elvira was a high school sophomore on the Eastern Shore. The fifteen years between the ages of the two women was the difference between the generation of the early 1950s and the generation of the late 1960s.

How had William Styron, in *The Confessions of Nat Turner,* put it? "An exquisitely sharpened hatred for the white man is of course an emotion not difficult for Negroes to harbor. Yet if truth be known this hatred does not abound in every Negro's soul; it relies upon too many mysterious and hidden patterns of life and chance to flourish luxuriantly everywhere."

In among trees and fields and a cattle pond, a last statement of colonial times, was the subdivision of Enterprise Estates, weedless and green under the streetlamps and scented by hybrid roses. Here Elbert and Daphne Jones owned a big modern house. Golden cherubs sat in sconces on the living room walls. The stereo shelves were of walnut burl. A statue of a cocker spaniel held open the front door. Mr. and Mrs. Jones were well-traveled and genteel people. He could turn a fine phrase and would sign off his phone calls with a cheery "ciao." She was a woman of culture and could declaim on many forms of music. They had arrived in Prince George's County in 1978, up from Miami, his hometown (she was originally from New York City) and had moved into the life of Enterprise Estates in 1989 by way of good-paying jobs with the local transit authority. Mr. Jones, a lithe, elegant-looking Korean War vet, was a rail supervisor, making the trains run on time, and Mrs. Jones, a beautiful woman of thin-boned features, worked with the transit police. No better a life could Mr. and Mrs. Jones imagine until the morning their hearts were ripped from their blooming roses and their two-car garage by a phone call. Their only child was dead—Derrick Jones, viewed by the adults on his street as a happy-faced, do-gooding youth welcome in everyone's home. ("A really, really lovable kid. He would carry in your groceries without you ever asking. And with the little kids he was a jokester like you wouldn't believe.

The best kind of big brother. There was never a moment's worry with him around.") At seventeen, Derrick had shot up into a tall lookalike of his father with one of those funny walks a little out of whack with the principles of mechanics. But get him singing and dancing, and he was a free flow of bodily movements. The delight he took in the art of entertainment led him to the D.C. Music Center, for which he sang bass in musical productions, and to the choreographer Marlene Davis, the first black cheerleader employed by the Washington Redskins. Under her tutelage he won auditions for music videos. The week before he died he traveled to New York for a rap video shoot in Central Park. The trip put him in a state of exaltation. Normally shy and stuttering around girls, he was inspired on his return to do some smooth-talking of the police officer's daughter, Amy Smith, and on the afternoon of July 31, 1991, he hitched a ride in a friend's car for a prearranged rendezvous with her. It was to be one of those whatever-strikes-the-mood dates, as far as his parents could tell. They gave him a midnight deadline, which he missed by a long shot. He was still absent, his bed not slept in, when they checked near dawn. So they were prepared for a measure of bad news. ("My wife was worried. She thought Derrick might be injured. I said, 'I hope not.' I thought he might walk in with some story. My wife stayed home while I went to work. Been doing the same job for over twenty years.") But this was a morning Mr. Jones would ceaselessly relive. The call from the police came about eight o'clock. *Your son's been in an accident.* When Mr. Jones got home, his wife was holding on to a next-door neighbor. ("That's when I found out my son had been killed.") Derrick was buried on an August afternoon, the headlights of the hearse dim in the hot sun. There was a boundlessness to the grief of his parents; it was unthinkable, "a raw ache." Derrick's room with the posters and school certificates could not stay as it was, could not be preserved in every detail as some parents do for a return that will never take place, because Mrs. Jones broke down and cried at the sight of it. Mr. Jones boxed up Derrick's belongings for storage or gave them to charities. But even a common event like a dinner party was too cruel for his wife if the exploits of other children came up for discussion. "I cannot be a hostess anymore," Mrs. Jones told her husband. One day on a commuter train the Joneses saw a young man, a dead ringer for their son. They made him uncomfortable with their stares. They could not help themselves and had to corner him and reveal their identities while he, wondering what to say, watched Mrs. Jones dab at streaked makeup. Everywhere the Joneses went there were playgrounds where Derrick used to romp, schools he attended, houses that looked like the one in which he had died. "I think we ought to get away," Mr. Jones suggested at last, and in the past two years they had

visited Spain and many parts of Africa and the Caribbean. They had become phantom residents of Enterprise Estates. Every day off from work
they went somewhere else.

Yesterday Camilla had phoned and asked Bruce to fly up for the
weekend, but because it was short notice and because it was foul weather
and because he did not feel like shelling out the dollars, he had said, "No,
forget it. I'm not at your beck and call."

This morning he was sorry for his churlish behavior, and moreover he
was racked by misgivings about ending their romance, if an ending is what
you could call it. Nothing was really settled in his mind about Camilla.
They had gotten back into the habit of constant communication on the
phone. They were trying to sort things out and were analyzing everything.

Bruce: "I was so desperate to set up house with Camilla, but I'm glad
we didn't do it right off the bat. That's where recently divorced people go
wrong. It's important to move beyond the ga-ga stage."

Camilla: "That initial stage was really a healing stage. We were wounded
from our divorces. I felt like maybe I'd go through the rest of my life making only superficial connections with men, but Bruce and I healed each
other."

Bruce: "It was a time of 'safe passage.' Camilla restored my manhood.
My ex-wife had emasculated me."

Camilla: "That was one transition, and this is another. I think it's a natural progression to reach a stage where we dwell on the differences between ourselves."

And what were those differences? Or, to ask the question as Bruce
framed it, "Is there something racial going on between the lines?"

Bruce's former wife, beautiful and brown and proud of Mexico and
things Mexican, used to shout in her best histrionics, "You can't understand!" It was a statement that still nagged at him. Even if he had no particular pride in being a white Jewish-American, could he appreciate the
stresses and tribulations of someone from another culture and heritage?
Could he understand? Could he break through to the soul? Could he
"grok"? There were married couples of his acquaintance, the husband of
one color, the wife of another, who appeared to be unstigmatized by
symptoms of racism and yet problems of race inveighed almost automatically in their relationship. All of their arguments came down, on some
level, to arguments about race. Bruce kept waiting for Camilla to say one
day, "You can't understand." What she had said was, "I don't know if we

can ever be right for each other. I've become sort of a witchy, spiritual, dance-and-drum woman. You've become very business-oriented. I'm a cat person, you're a dog person. We don't even have the same vocabulary anymore. We're always having to translate for each other. I don't know if there's a way to catch up to where we left off years ago." Bruce admitted to plenty of differences between them, other than race. There always had been differences. The life-slogan Bruce put for himself under his Potomac High yearbook picture was slapstick ("To achieve the perfect Barrrumsky") while Camilla's was earnest ("Be true to your own ideals, keep striving to achieve the goals you set for yourself"). They had different temperaments. Camilla addressed her highs and lows with Shakespearean moods; her face would proclaim vividly "Look out!" He preferred to sleep off his troubles, and in good times he liked to have a few beers. True, he was a workaholic moneyman, but with a few beers he could wax seductive; he could fashion appeals to her "sad poetic eyes." Wasn't there a creature in both of them that was entirely spontaneous and dreamy? What if, in trying to stifle their racial differences, in trying to put aside all prejudices, they were making too much ado over other differences? What if, by suppressing one thing, they were magnifying everything else? These were some of Bruce's thoughts.

The death of Derrick Jones in the home of the Smith family occurred around 3:00 A.M. on July 31, 1991, and occasioned rumor, racial innuendo, contradictions, and widespread suspicions. Two and a half years later the physical evidence and the testimony of witnesses gathered in the case continued to lend themselves to more than one interpretation, despite an "official" version of events put forth by the police and the prosecutor's office and despite the guilty verdict at Amy's trial.

For the most part the Prince George's authorities had adopted the version as relayed to them by Dennis and Marie Smith. It was a version that started the hairs and chilled the bones and went as follows:

About 1:50 A.M., having finished his night shift for the park police, Dennis Smith arrived at his home in Fort Washington, an area of expansion just south of Hillcrest Heights that had drawn, among others, the world heavyweight boxing champion Riddick Bowe in a customized $6 million Alhambra of gilt and chip technology. The Smith house was ranch style, with Florida colors. Upstairs Mr. Smith unfastened a gun-belt assembly for his nine-millimeter Beretta and hung it on a heavy-duty metal hanger in the closet of a guest bedroom. He crawled into bed next to his wife and fell into a light sleep. About fifty minutes later he bolted upright. Derrick Jones had burst through the bedroom door and switched on an overhead light, all in one move. The six-foot-three Derrick presented an otherworldly sight, smooth shirtless chest, ski-masked face, orange-gloved hands, handcuffs hung in the crook of a little finger. He wore a gold pierced earring in his left ear. Derrick also was clutching the loaded police-issue Beretta, which, the police would assume, he had located in the closet. Derrick stood spread-legged at the foot of the bed and aimed the gun. The half-awake Mr. Smith swung his feet to the floor. Derrick, moving forward, pressed the gun to Mr. Smith's forehead and, dropping the handcuffs in his lap, said, "Put them on." Mr. Smith shut his right hand in one cuff, and Derrick clamped the other cuff to the brass headboard rails. Again he aimed the gun. "I have no problem in killing a cop," he announced.

Mrs. Smith was awake by now. "I didn't move," she would say later. "I was scared of this man. I was so scared." Derrick ordered her to come out from under the covers and to lay by the footboard sideways across the king-sized mattress. On this hot July night Mrs. Smith had gone to bed nude, and she asked "Can I put my clothes on?" But Derrick would not let her. "I was scared he was going to rape me," she would say. He yanked the phone cord from the wall and went about the business of thievery. He rummaged through a jewelry box. He dumped the contents of a purse on the floor. There was about $300 in grocery money in a wallet and the ignition key to Mrs. Smith's Daytona in a red zippered pouch. "I got your car key," he said to her. "What are you going to do?"

"I don't care," she replied. Her panic had passed, and resignation was starting to set in. "I wasn't scared of him anymore," she would explain. "I wasn't scared that I was going to die. I knew I was. So why should I give in to him?"

Derrick inquired of the Smiths whether anyone else was at home, and they stalled him for a while, trying to protect Amy, whose bedroom was on the floor below theirs. But when Derrick turned angry, Mr. Smith answered, "Our daughter is asleep downstairs." Derrick left their bedroom but was gone just long enough for Mrs. Smith to secret her wedding ring under the mattress, and then, "within seconds," he was back. Along with the gun, he now held a serrated carving knife, taken from a ceramic container on the kitchen counter. He knelt on a padded hope chest at the foot of the bed and put the gun to Mrs. Smith's head. "You are going to take this knife and you're going to stab your husband to death," he ordered. Mrs. Smith said nothing. Derrick put pressure on the gun. "Did you hear what I said?" he asked. His voice was nasty, "full of hate." Mrs. Smith's reply was faint, "No, no." She pushed her face into the sheets and sobbed.

"And at this time I asked God to forgive me of my sins and to receive me now."

Mr. Smith saw murder in the youth's eyes and in that instant formed a plan. In school Mr. Smith had been a high jumper, and he still was able to lift his legs acrobatically. Planting his right foot on the floor, he thrust his left foot toward the gun, trying to knock it aside. Half crazed by his helpless state, he kicked with a force that broke his hand free of the cuff. Mrs. Smith gasped. "I thought he had torn his hand off." The movement threw Mr. Smith into a stumbling fall, but he caught himself and lunged again, now with both feet and both hands. He wrestled with Derrick, who was bigger by five inches and thirty pounds. He grabbed Derrick's wrists, jerking the gun and knife upward, and slammed his head against the closets, the walls, the bedroom door, trying to knock him out. Meanwhile, Mrs. Smith picked up her nightshirt from the floor and slipped it over her head. The two men, without letting go of each other, had jostled their way into the hallway. The nearest functioning phone was in the kitchen, and Mrs. Smith tried to get by them to reach it. At her feet she spied an ammunition clip for the Beretta, presumably taken from the gun belt earlier and dropped. "I thought to myself, 'That's the bullets that are going to kill us. I got to hide these.'" She ran back to the bedroom and slipped them under the mattress. Returning to where the men were struggling, now inside the upstairs bathroom, she heard her husband pleading, "Hit him, Marie. Hit him with something. Knock him out. Knock him out." Looking about frantically, Mrs. Smith saw the serrated kitchen knife on the floor, fallen from Derrick's grasp. She picked it up by the blade and began pounding Derrick on the head with the butt end. Her husband gave out a high-pitched yell, "Stab him." Turning the knife around to get hold of the handle, she stuck the blade into Derrick's left shoulder. Blood squirted out. "I fell back, and I dropped the knife. The man got like a surge of energy from the wound, and he knocked Smitty into the bathtub." A plastic butterfly broke off the bathroom wall. Derrick ran out and was lost from view on the steps to the downstairs. Mrs. Smith was relieved at this moment to see her stepdaughter in the upstairs kitchen. "Help us, please! Call the nine-one-one operator."

Mr. Smith was not nearly so alert to Amy's whereabouts: "I thought she was still downstairs." On hands and knees, huffing, gulping, out of breath, Mr. Smith made his way to the top of the stairwell. Halfway down the steps was the front door and a split foyer. To the right of the door a set of seven steps led back to the upper level of the house—to the kitchen, the dining room, living room, and master bedroom; to the left of the door were six steps down to Amy's bedroom and a family room. The steps were unlit, but Mr. Smith could make out Derrick on the landing of the foyer, between the floors. Something was pushed and fitted into Mr. Smith's right hand. He did not look at it but recognized it as his Beretta. "It has a certain feel." Mrs. Smith had retrieved it from the bathroom floor, where it had been lost during the hand-to-hand fighting. Mr. Smith was too exhausted to put a two-handed grip on the gun, but unsteady though the gun felt it was back in his possession. On the landing Derrick began to pivot. The Smiths believed he was about to turn and make a final, frontal assault on them. Then Mrs. Smith heard a shot and let out a scream. Mr. Smith was at the top of the steps, kneeling, half falling, his gun hand braced against the banister. "If you can't see a clear target, you fire at the center mass, and that is what I did," he testified later. "There was a blur that went down the lower set of steps. All I saw was this blur. I didn't know if he tripped, or fell, or what." Mr. Smith attempted a second shot, but it was a dud. The Beretta had jammed, he thought, until he saw that the ammunition clip had fallen out. He kept his focus down the stairs and felt a hand reach over his shoulder to give him a new clip. He inserted the magazine and cleared it. Summoning his nerve, Mr. Smith, who would be treated later for a broken toe and scrapes on his back and neck, bumped down the steps on his rear. "I said a prayer. I knew the intruder was down there, and I didn't know if he was going after Amy. I was out of breath so bad. I stopped just a second, and said another prayer, 'Give me three more breaths to get through this.' " Reaching the last step, Mr. Smith fired to his left. "I saw movement." The kick of the Beretta rolled him in his weakened condition off the step and against a wall, bringing down a candle-holding sconce. Upstairs, Mrs. Smith heard the second shot, followed by her husband's exclamation, "I'm okay. Everything's okay." Mrs. Smith peeked over the top banister in a furtive appraisal of the activity below. She saw Mr. Smith bending over a prone body. He was trying to find a pulse on an ankle. "Get an ambulance," he yelled up. There was no pulse. Derrick Jones had bullet holes in his chest and head.

For one of the paramedics who helped strap Derrick's body to a gurney, this was her second shooting of the night. She had worked the scene of the first shooting six hours earlier with Dennis Smith. By virtue of several on-duty and off-duty police functions both Mr. and Mrs. Smith were well acquainted with several of the official people who responded to Amy's 911 call. Jeffrey Gray, the officer who took charge of the scene, was known to Mr. Smith from the courthouse and was known to Mrs. Smith because, while younger, she had been a secretary to Officer Gray's father. When the Smiths began telling their story Officer Gray had no reason to doubt them and the evidence that lay out in the open—a sweaty, slightly injured fellow lawman (Mr. Smith's hair was "mustered," according to the report), a blood-soaked corpse, and the banged-up house—made the Smiths seem more than credible. The premises of two respected middle-class white adults had been entered in the middle of the night by a black teenager without the permission of the adults, and this had led, from all appearances, to a struggle to the death. To be honest about it, many people would have assumed Derrick Jones was the perpetrator and the Smiths were lucky to be alive.

Such a perfectly natural reaction would therefore help explain why the responding police officers seem to have acted with so little curiosity toward two inconsistencies in the evidence: the lack of any abrasion on Mr. Smith's finger where his ring should presumably have dug into the skin when he jerked his hand free of the locked handcuff, and the same lack of imprint on Mrs. Smith's whole and unmarked right palm where the serrated blade should have left some trace after trying to beat Derrick Jones into unconsciousness. In subsequent days the investigating detectives, without comment or explanation, would also apparently discount a report of David Chiasson, a forensic pathologist in the Prince George's medical examiner's office, whose scientific renderings were at considerable odds with the shooting sequence outlined by the Smiths. To start with, Derrick could not have been standing on the foyer landing when Mr. Smith fired the first shot. According to Dr. Chiasson, the shot must have struck Derrick while he was downstairs, in the vicinity of Amy's bedroom, and while he was off his feet, nearly prone, perhaps leaning or falling backwards, perhaps backpedaling on his hands, perhaps stretched out flat on his back. A nine millimeter bullet had gone through Derrick's body and was embedded in the downstairs flooring. Science indicated that this shot, into his chest, was the first one. Derrick's heart had disgorged four pints of blood into his chest cavity, an amount needing "several minutes" to accumulate. "This means the heart was pumping. I would never expect this amount of blood if the head shot was first," Dr. Chiasson would testify. The other shot to strike Derrick entered the base of his skull and stopped his heart within seconds; clearly, this was the second shot. The right-to-left trajectory of this second shot also meant, in Dr. Chiasson's opinion, it was highly unlikely Mr. Smith was correct in his statement about firing to his left while seated on the bottom of the stairs. Mrs. Smith's statement about keeping herself at a safe distance upstairs and peering down afterward as her husband examined Derrick's body for signs of life was not correct either, so a detective would concede on the witness stand; the body was not visible from the top edge of the stairs.

Dr. Chiasson's report, based on measurable factors like blood loss and bullet trajectories, had the value of being devoid of human bias and was the sort of evidence that in another case might have been determining. Elvira White, in her closing argument on behalf of Amy Smith, tried mightily to use the report to undermine the prosecution's case. "We don't have just inconsistencies here, we have lies," she argued.

Judge G. R. Hovey Johnson had other evidence to consider, however, evidence that in its preponderance persuaded him of Amy's guilt as to the charge of concocting with Derrick a plan to rob and murder the Smiths. Even so, the judge was troubled by the testimony of the Smiths, the heart of the prosecution's case, to the point he felt obliged afterward to comment from the bench. "I am not suggesting there has been any dissembling in the testimony," he said, but, at the same time, he was not willing to put their story into the record as gospel. In his opinion the prosecution's case contained "error." It was "impossible" for certain parts of the official version to be true. "I am stating on the record that the Court finds that the shooting did not occur exactly as it was related to have occurred," Judge Johnson declared.

It had to have happened some other way. That certainly was the conclusion that Elvira and her associates had reached in formulating a defense strategy for Amy.

Perhaps Mr. Smith had first knocked Derrick groggy or perhaps Derrick had slipped on the stairs and fallen on his back. From the evidence, Derrick must have been shot in the chest with Mr. Smith standing somewhere above. Then Derrick must have been left to lie on the carpet for some period, chest heaving, wound hemorrhaging. Derrick would have been badly frightened, with a premonition of his destiny. Perhaps Mr. Smith blacked out briefly or lost track of time, or possibly he debated with himself for a while and then delivered the follow-up shot to the head in a moment of cold decision. Because the bullet administering the coup de grâce entered toward the back of Derrick's head, there was also the gruesome possibility Mr. Smith had had an accomplice. According to the pathologist, after the first shot Derrick would have been prostrate on his back, face toward the ceiling. Perhaps he raised his head just before the second shot was fired, but it was also possible someone else pulled his head forward and held it for the killing act. The second shot was fired from a distance of eighteen inches or more, determined by the lack of gunpowder stippling, and it would have required unlikely contortions for Mr. Smith to have lifted Derrick's head while pulling the trigger. Might his wife have been his accomplice? One gruesome possibility led to another. Might it have been

Amy who cocked Derrick's head to the right angle? It was possible to speculate that Amy's father, offended and maddened beyond reason, had
forced his daughter to assist in the execution of her boyfriend. The more
one tried to figure out what had happened the more awful the sum of the
night's violence seemed. Was it possible a teenage romance between a
white girl and a black boy had created an event so devious all four participants were touched by evil?

The Stricklers got the use out of cars like nobody else in Hillcrest
Heights. Not until the seventies did they retire their 1939 Ford coupe from
active service, and these days they had on hand, either in their garage or
in their inclined driveway or out at the curb, a 1966 Mustang, the uphol-
stery still cherry, plus a 1971 Checker station wagon for which Dell scav-
enged spare parts in junkyards, a fully equipped 1973 Lincoln Continental
Mark IV they drove with style to the Bolling Officers Club, and a fourth vehicle, a 1990 Ford pickup with a covered bed, that Dell had wanted for
hauling her upright Troubador harps.

Before sunrise, the light a November gray, they loaded the smaller of
the harps into the back of the pickup, padding it with a thick blanket. After five hours of driving and an hour's stop at a roadside cafe, they came
to a mountainside clearing in Pocahontas County where radio astronomers
maneuvered tall, telescopic, perfectly machined devices toward deep
space to pick up spectral lines of atoms so sensitive their cumulative
power is barely enough to light a hundred-watt bulb. Just beyond the observatory was a cluster of frame houses. Merv honked the horn, and
Heather and Mike Holstine's three daughters sped outdoors and leaped
into their grandpa and grandma's arms and talked a mile a minute in their
West Virginian accents.

Later in the afternoon Dell plucked out Renaissance tunes on the harp
while the three girls squatted on the living room floor. Heather had ex-
cused herself and was at her desk giving copyediting advice to Merv for
his aviation guide. Mike was at a kitchen window. A mist from the mountains dripped off the poplar boughs. Two yearling deer stepped out of
scrub woods and stuck their noses into frozen tufts of grass in the meadow
across the road. "Come and watch," Mike said when there was a lull in the
lilting music. His merry Santa eyes were lit up above a thick black country
beard. A deer was an everyday occurrence, but he never tired of it. For
fifty weeks a year Mike was an admirer of deer, and the other two weeks
he went after venison. This year he had organized a controlled hunt with

bows and muzzle-loaders on the grounds of the observatory. Off limits to hunters for forty years, the observatory deer were meager, stunted creatures and had chewed a browse-line as high as they could reach on every tree on the property. Nonetheless a placard-waving band of animal rightists tried to stop the hunt. "If you were really animal lovers you would understand about checks and balances," Mike had reproached them in his mild voice. He thereupon had gone out and shot a buck.

It was as a hunter years ago that Mike first became acquainted with the roadside sights of Pocahontas County, the crumbled-down brick sawmills, the old turnblades and conveyors rusting in willow brush, vestiges of a former baronial economy. In the late twentieth century, Pocahontas County was a place of low technologies (if you did not count the observatory). Entrepreneurs lived here in double-body trailers set along steeply banked gravel roads and dealt in raw, hydraulic-split, heaved-together inventories of firewood they would truck out and sell for the fireplaces of suburban Washington. Merv and Dell had asked Mike in a roundabout way if he regretted moving Heather and the girls here two years ago, but what was there to regret? The girls had the best of two worlds. He was teaching them outdoor survival, and with his job came dance classes and baseball and soccer leagues; the firstborn, Christina, was quite the tomboy and was "Mrs. Babe Ruth" to the boys on her team. If anything, even with the closest fast-food eatery seventy-five miles away, life here was too suburban for Mike, at least according to Heather, who claimed, "I think the ideal home for Mike would be out with the bears somewhere in the middle of a forest."

After supper, up to her arms in dishwater, Heather said to her mother, "I'm thinking of bringing the girls to see the Christmas lights at the White House. We'd spend the weekend."

Dell beamed. "Oh, that'll be wonderful."

Whenever Heather could she tried to return home to Hillcrest Heights, but it had been four or five years since Mike had accompanied them. Heather's hometown was "too depressing" for him. "Hillcrest Heights used to have a pleasant All-American feel, a nice place to raise a family, but it's changed," he explained. "The course of history is right there in front of you. First the middle-class blacks moved in, which was a positive development because they upgraded the neighborhood, but, like night following the day, the violent criminal element was bound to follow and render it unsuitable for civilized living." For Mike the whole of Hillcrest Heights was ruined by an area at the border with Washington that was known locally as "Little Beirut." You could see along these blocks the start of a big-city slum by way of neglect and desecration—spray-can graffiti painted on the run, steel accordion gating across storefronts, plywood to cover broken windows, vacant lots with a filigree of barbed wire, sidewalks blown over with paper cups, ragweed in the cracks. Drug dealers did business with passing motorists. Mike said, "It's become close to frightening, people carrying on, talking trash on the corners. Even on the street where Heather's folks live it's gotten bad. The one time my father came along with us the police had the street barricaded for a drug raid. My father couldn't believe this is what decent upstanding people have to deal with. He kept saying, 'I should've brought my pistol.' "

Mike had said more than once to his in-laws, "I don't know how you can stand to live there. I couldn't do it. I couldn't sleep at night."

The Stricklers took such comments in stride. What was there to say? Mike was a man of the woods.

Another new mall had gone up, twelve minutes from Gloria's house, and she was renting space there. It was a drop-in center for the constituents of District Twenty-six. After supper one evening Gloria could not find the key to the office when she fished for it in her purse. Tires squealing, she drove to the home of Mary Larkin, who kept a spare key. Mrs. Larkin came to the door in a rainbow-colored floral dress. It highlighted the red tint in her hair. The daughter of an NAACP chapter president in St. Louis, Missouri, Mary Larkin had been used by her father at an early age to put the *Brown v. Board of Education* ruling to the test—all eyes were on her when she broke the color barrier at an elementary school. Her tour as a child star had turned her off to the civil rights movement ("I felt like I had to give up being a normal little girl"), and she did not lift a finger for it until she was middle aged and living in Hillcrest Heights and was persuaded by Gloria to join her so-called Gang of Four.

"Thanks for the key. I've got to hurry out of here," Gloria said, but then proceeded to stand in the doorway and talk away with delicious cheer.

"My, oh my, girl, what an election this is going to be," said Mrs. Larkin, who had run for the legislature herself once, unsuccessfully. Bright red fingertips smelling of nail varnish played with a necklace in the shape of icicles. "That Sue Mills—I know folks think she can't possibly win, but she is dangerous."

Gloria nodded. "She knows how to campaign."

"Elvira White? What is going on with her?"

"Elvira spoke out of turn, and now they are after her. She's a target."

"You supporting her?"

"I told her I would."

"You have to watch yourself."

"Look who's talking! You got your ticket for South Africa yet?"

"I got it!" The ticket would take Mary Larkin, a lawyer with the National Institute for Education in the Law, off for a two-month stay in the townships of Johannesburg, where, in preparation for South Africa's history-making democratic elections, she was to assist with the registration of black voters—a version of Freedom Summer for the 1990s. Students at Potomac High had raised $1,000 through bake sales and an art auction for the South African drive.

"First South Africa, then Prince George's!" Gloria sang out.

Mary Larkin was to be partnered in South Africa with a white man. "That could be very good, or very bad. Depending . . ." she said, obviously thinking about the rash of racially motivated street executions that had been in the news from her native continent. There was even a rumor that American tourists were to be singled out and killed, sacrificially, to send a message from white South Africans who wished to be left alone.

"You're not afraid, are you?" Gloria started to hoot, but she stopped, seeing her friend's doubtful face. Her voice dropped an octave. "Listen, honestly, I don't think anybody is going to kill an American."

"How are they going to tell? I'm as black as they are."

"They can tell who's an American, just by how we talk."

"I hope so, girl. It would've been okay to die in Mississippi, but I'm not willing to die in South Africa. I'm an American, not an African."

A few weeks later, while Mary Larkin nervously fulfilled the work she had signed up for in South Africa, one of the other American volunteers, twenty-six-year-old Fulbright scholar Amy Biehl, was killed. Amy Biehl was a white woman from California whose heart was with the black African freedom fighters. She spoke Xhosa, could do the jive dance phantsula, and had been registering voters. While she was stopped for gas at a filling station a marauding mob of young black men smashed a brick through the windshield of her old orange Mazda, on which she had placed the bumper sticker "Our Land Needs Peace." Yelling "Kill the settler," they dragged her from the car and stabbed her to death. Police would arrest teenagers associated with the Pan-Africanist Congress, a group operating under a slogan that could be translated as "one bullet for one white."

During the same period, with Mary Larkin still in Johannesburg, white extremists set off a car bomb outside the headquarters of the African National Congress, killing nine black people and injuring dozens more.

Yet the elections would be held. The wait in the lines would be four or five hours. It would be hot, there would be no water; babies on their mother's backs would wail. No one would leave the lines, though, and a flag-waving victory celebration would be bestowed on the ex-political prisoner Nelson Mandela. His inauguration would then draw dignitaries from 150 nations.

Back when Amy Smith's defense was first entrusted to the public defender's office, Elvira had not shown any signs of feeling proprietary about the case. She was more than happy to sit down for a serious but enjoyable "heart-to-heart talk" with some of the other staff attorneys over brown-bagged sandwiches in the homey comfort of the lunchroom. Most everyone seemed too busy for petty jealousies anyway, loaded up with assignments the way they were, and Elvira, for one, thought it helpful to take others into her confidence and to "share the burden" whenever she had a difficult who-did-what-when case. For the first several days of the Smith case Elvira solicited opinions, trying to arrive at an operating theory. "Lots of theories were going around the table, but we all believed the state's version was not correct," to quote Anne Gold-Rand, a white public defender who had taken up the law after several years in the public school system. Anne was as interested as Elvira in the possible pathologies of Dennis Smith, with whom the two attorneys were acquainted from other cases the veteran cop had worked. Suppose he had encountered a partially nude black youth sneaking out of his daughter's bedroom. Was he the type to have willy-nilly fired his Beretta in the urgency of the moment, not out of fear for anyone's safety but out of a pure sharp anger over the most outrageous violation yet of the racial taboos and sexual taboos that for months had incited harangues and episodes of petty violence in the Smith family? After the fact, after Derrick Jones had been wounded, might Mr. Smith have gathered a willingly complicit wife and a stricken daughter and made them partners in his crime? This was a scenario that fit with the astounding findings of the medical examiner's office and fit with an eye-witness account from Timothy County, a neighbor of the Smiths, who said he was outside his house when Mr. Smith's car barreled past and lurched into the driveway. Timothy County put the time at exactly 2:30 A.M.—he was positive because he was leaving for his job and had just checked the clock—and if Mr. County's clock was right, Mr. Smith could not have been asleep when the action inside the house began. The action must have begun within moments of Mr. Smith's opening the front door.

Dennis Smith was the guilty party—that's how the public defenders initially had the case pegged. And for a week or longer after Amy's arrest they were perfectly comfortable among themselves. "We figured Amy and Derrick had had a relationship, that this relationship developed into an intimate one, and the father caught them and went ballistic," Anne Gold-Rand would say in a statement made later. "We all thought this was really the underpinning of the whole fiasco."

In due time, however, the police apprised the defender's office of the things confiscated from Derrick's body, and it was then that Elvira and Anne's opinions began to diverge. The inventory included a front-door key to the Smith house found looped into the tie string of Derrick's shorts and several notebook pages stuffed in a shoe box, one page with directions to the house, another with a diagram of the house layout, and a third page of further incriminating notes—and while it was easy enough to explain away the key and the directions, routine exchanges between lovers, what about the mapping of the house? Why would Amy draw for Derrick a room-by-room exposition, "mstr bedroom," "lav," "gst room," if she wanted to direct Derrick to a love nest downstairs? With the photostats laid on a desk Anne rethought the defense theory. Perhaps the driving force of the case was not simple teenage lust after all. Perhaps Amy and Derrick had been bigger connivers than it initially appeared, with a plan to steal money and a car with which to run away together. Perhaps Derrick's death was the result of a bad plan gone more badly wrong. It was a possibility too obvious for the police to miss. Therefore Amy's attorney had to take it into consideration.

Elvira, however, was not persuaded to change her mind. Although a few years younger than Anne, she had senior status, and it was her case to manage. "Look, these were two smart kids," she argued. "If they wanted to commit a robbery, they wouldn't have done it when her parents were home. It wasn't money they were after, it was sex."

The one person who could have cleared up everything was not talking. Amy was plagued by crying jags whenever she was pushed to relate the true circumstances of that evening. "I think Amy's too closemouthed. I think she's holding something back. But every time I ask her to give me the truth once and for all, she bursts into tears and stonewalls," Elvira reported back.

All was therefore set for the defense attorneys to quarrel openly. Elvira and Anne were seen with hands on their hips, two women who bore a sisterly resemblance, conservative dressers, short in stature, hair dark and combed straight. "I think you have to plea bargain," Anne strongly advised. "Get Amy to plead to a b-and-e, but take the position she had no inkling anything violent would occur. Lay the violence on Derrick. It was his frolic. Harming the father and mother was at his own volition."

"A plea isn't necessary. We can win this." Elvira had remained confident, even jaunty, in the face of the mystery. Knowing the exact sequence of events was not necessary for her strategy. To her, Dennis Smith was ultimately responsible, his crime the only crime that mattered.

"I really, really disagree. Go for simple theft for Amy. Then you can say Derrick compounded it."

"I'm telling you, no, straight out. It's not fair to Derrick's mother. I'm not going to drag her son's name down."

"That's the holy principle you're standing on?! You don't want to hurt some woman's feelings?"

Two hours before sunup on a Sunday morning Mike phoned to signal Heather and the girls to leave Hillcrest Heights. A blizzard had blown into West Virginia overnight, and the roads were drifting shut.

"We'll get going right away," Heather said. "We'll skip church." At least she had had the foresight yesterday to canvass the shopping malls and show the girls the Christmas trees behind the White House.

"Promise me you'll drive I-64," Merv said. This was the long way home to Green Bank, skipping the mountains.

"I promise." Heather was trying to pack up the gift boxes out of view of the girls.

"Everyone's going to miss you at services," said Dell.

"I know. I'm disappointed, too." She had grown up with Sunday mornings at Ryland Epworth United Methodist.

Once Heather was on the road, Merv and Dell got dressed in holiday finery and made their way in their pickup to Ryland Epworth, a grand old institution. The walls were of gray and brown fieldstone, the windows of nineteenth-century stained glass in lagoon blue. It used to be that Christmas pageants, with Dell on the harp, would play to a packed house, but this morning half the pews were empty. The bad weather no doubt was a factor, and a boycott was keeping away some parishioners who derided today's service, "The Hanging of the Greens," as Druidlike paganism. But low attendance was the usual condition for Ryland Epworth, a congregation that had not adapted well to demographic changes. The irony that in the midst of a population boom a congregation with its 150th anniversary coming up should be down at the heels was an irony easily explained. A prejudice against black congregants had existed years ago at the church, and despite the best efforts of such leaders as the Stricklers and despite the presence of a black minister in the pulpit, the prejudice had not been entirely shamed out of some of the aging deacons. In their unspectacular fashion Merv and Dell had forced a public disavowal of segregation back in the 1960s, making it a condition of their membership at Ryland Epworth. ("When we were approached about joining the church we were told that the deacons did not feel black people would be comfortable attending services, and we said, 'Fine, okay, but we will not join until black people do feel comfortable.' ") In the 1970s and 1980s the Stricklers cooperated closely with Reverend Andrew Meeder, an engaging, expansionist white minister, who introduced a more open climate—free-form evangelism in the liturgy once a month and guest speakers hortative on the subject of integration—and now the Stricklers felt it fortuitous to have assigned to the parsonage Reverend Bruce Haskins, a tall, amiable black man under the age of forty. The congregation, however, was old. The natural line of succession—Heather's generation—had forsaken Ryland Epworth for other locales, and the church had attracted only a few walk-ins from the class of younger black professionals. Merv and Dell had tried without success to rally the deacons to launch a recruitment drive. "With your attitude you are condemning our church to death," Dell, who chaired the missions committee, had said. Reverend Haskins, who had come to Ryland Epworth a year ago after another black minister did not work out, seemed to represent a last chance. Now, while Dell in her choir robes stood among the fir trees in yuletide bunting, Merv led applause from the pews for a guest soloist, a black man introduced as "Dutch," loaned out by a Presbyterian church. Too soon the Ryland Epworth congregants became too quiet, and Reverend Haskins lit merrily into them. "Does anyone out there hear me?" He turned with a wink to the soloist. "You know, Dutch, you might think people would break with tradition just once, and when they hear 'We see the light,' they would pipe up with an Amen, just one tiny little Amen." Merv had been brought up in the mainline Protestant liturgy and was as self-conscious as the other white congregants about shrieking and clapping and stamping, that style of worship where you make the floors tremble and you come near to fainting. That was not his style, and yet he was determined to keep Reverend Haskins's spirits from flagging. During the sermon, amid a trickling of Amens, Merv lifted his voice with an animation that seemed to surprise everyone. There was a lick of fire to his Amens.

Afterward, on his way out, Merv gripped Reverend Haskins's hand and said heartily, "Keep at it. Sooner or later you're going to get us to be more vocal."

The minister threw back his head. "Or die trying!"

Dell was in the vestibule fussing with her overcoat and chatting with another woman. "It wouldn't seem so quiet if we could get better attendance," Dell said.

Merv gave Dell a helping hand with her coat. "What was the name of that sect? The Shakers? Yes, we might be like the Shakers," he said. "When we die the church is going to die with us."

The Stricklers, heads bowed in the blinding light, walked a friend to her car. Bare shafts of forsythia bent back and forth in the wind. The sun had come out. "I keep thinking my father wouldn't be letting this happen," Merv said. He was ever mindful of his father, the circuit-riding preacher who had made a life's work of saving souls and breathing life back into desolate congregations.

"But he didn't have to deal with racial problems," Dell said. "That was before his time."

At times Gloria would think back on a simple thing that came to her as a revelation on a day in 1968 when white people and black people appeared to be "at war"—when from the ghettoes there were regular reports of uprisings, America's cities ablaze with Molotov cocktails, cops acting as an occupying military force, Black Panthers killing and being killed, and when the Kerner Commission, embarking on months of scholarly research, would come to the solemn conclusion that America was a nation hopelessly divided, one race against the other. To Gloria the stakes had seemed very high. What if black Americans and white Americans continued on this way in varying degrees of unmitigated fury? What if this was to be the legacy of the sit-ins and marches Gloria had participated in at Morehouse and Howard universities? Her mother and father, born and raised in the old NAACP, would curse the modern civil rights movement. In the Lawlah home, Gloria's children, six-year-old John Jr. and five-year-old Gloria Jean, chased each other around a kitchen table where educated men and women sat and talked in long, ruminating sentences about the newly realized woes of racial consciousness. Or the children watched TV and saw the "war" for themselves. Black-gloved fists were raised on Olympic blocks; rocks and venomous insults flew through the air, and police nightsticks fell again and again on bloodied black flesh. There were lessons to be learned, and one day Gloria, shushing her children with a finger and arranging them on a couch with their knees crossed and hands in their laps, talked to them about being black in America. They did not ask any questions, and a wild thought entered Gloria's mind.

"What do you think you are? Do you think you're black?" she asked. Each of them, responding swiftly, said, "No, ma'am."

"Are you white?"

They shifted around, looking at each other. "Don't know. Don't know. You never told us."

The answers shocked Gloria, and thrilled her. Later, she would say, "I had always believed Martin's words, that color should not matter, that I should not notice your green-blue eyes, and you shouldn't notice my brown eyes. And here was proof it could happen that way. My heart was jumping, 'Oh, my God, yes, it's possible to hope, it's possible to dream.' Of course, my children learned they are indeed black. I taught them the African-American national anthems and told them of their heritage. But being black was never uppermost."

When the Lawlahs moved to Prince George's County after the riots, Gloria's mother told her, "You're a full-fledged American now." But on all sides there were white neighbors, and Gloria felt protective of her children. Later she would laugh with Merv and Dell about her nervousness, but in the beginning the Stricklers were strangers to her, and to get the skinny on Hillcrest Heights she sought out a black neighbor.

"Are the people around here the kind who use the word 'nigger'?" Gloria asked.

"No, the white folks on this street aren't like that."

"Thank the Lord. Because my children have never been called niggers, and I pray they can grow up without ever hearing the word."

Now that Prince George's County held an approximately equal number of black citizens and white citizens of voting age, per the 1990 Census, a strange quiet had fallen on the political front. Andrew Jackson's perturbed admonition of 1837, when he left the presidency, was that politicians of his day talked too candidly about race, that most "delicate and exciting of topics, upon which it is impossible for a large portion of the Union to ever speak without strong emotion." A century and a half later a majority of the Prince George's politicians euphemized when it came to race. It was not in official favor to speak of the racial side of politics. The politicians believed they had little to gain by calling things by name, especially such a loaded thing as political power based on the racial preference of voters. The Black Alliance leaders who went into meetings in Gloria Lawlah's living room did not come out with any talk to suggest a "black takeover" or a "black coup d'état." The insiders in Mike Miller's white crowd likewise did not talk in terms of holding on to the "white vote" or of gerrymandering boundary lines to maximize the number of "white districts." No politician traded openly on skin color. The strategies of "black power" and "white power" were carried out with almost no public comment, lest voters on the other side of the racial divide become spooked.

To understand that "blackness" and "whiteness" were not magically gone from local politics after all and that color of skin was still a local preoccupation you had to listen in on the ticklish jesting the politicians did with each other. If not about sex, their jokes were invariably about race. Or you had to read the impolitic newspaper columns of Frank Pesci, an Italian-American lover of plain talk and a disdainer of political niceties.

A few months ago Frank Pesci had handed in a column that his normally acquiescent editor at the *Prince George's Journal* criticized for its "us" and "them" tone.

Frank was adamant, "Somebody has to bring this out into the open."

After more give and take, the editor signed off on the column, muttering, "I guess if anyone can get away with writing this you're probably the guy."

In the days of the civil rights movement Frank Pesci had been an authentic local hero. He was introduced around. *Do you know who this is? This is the fellow from the college who* . . . In 1968, as dean of academic affairs at a local college, Frank had thrown his career to the wind by hiring the first black member of the faculty. He was summoned by the college president and directed to rescind the hiring. Instead Frank recruited a second black professor. In graffiti on campus Frank became the "nigger lover." He had been on course to be president of the college, but the chairman of the board of trustees hooted at him, "You'll never get it now. You've shown your true colors." A year later, when the presidency became vacant, Frank was indeed passed over. In turn, however, this would propel him into a political life, and he would serve sixteen years in the state legislature.

The newspaper column Frank Pesci intended as a "wake-up call" for a new generation of Prince Georgians minced no words. "Race matters in politics," he wrote, referring to the race for county executive. "Today, blacks vote for black candidates, and whites vote for white candidates pretty much exclusively. While the law has integrated the races, in one way or another we have become more segregated and polarized than we were thirty years ago. And that should be very disturbing to all of us, white and black alike. The polarization that has been festering in this country and this county is harmful to all of us. If it continues, it will succeed in dividing us irreparably. Does anybody care?"

A number of readers were insulted and vexed to the point of writing letters. They wrote with a vengeance, saying Frank Pesci was selling the people short. From a man named Fred Tutman of Upper Marlboro there was this comment: "I doubt that even an avowed bigot would agree with such a simplistic and cynical view." And from Kevin Trainor, also of Upper Marlboro, this: "Mr. Pesci is dead wrong in his assertion of how race will play in the campaign."

Gloria Lawlah did not write a letter to the editor only because she did not trust herself to keep to a diplomatic tone. In her reading of Frank Pesci's column she detected a separate agenda. She felt he was trying to hoodwink black voters into crossing over to vote for a white candidate out of a phony notion of interracial unity. "Between the lines Frank is running a guilt trip, which is okay as far as it goes. Yes, there should be more crossover voting, but in reality that usually translates into blacks voting for whites," she said. "That's the only kind of crossover voting most whites are interested in."

Elvira was in no hurry to risk romance again, in no hurry at all— "maybe sometime in the future, but not right now, not with everything I got going. I don't have the time for falling in love." Two failed marriages were said to be responsible for her "puritanism" and her wariness about having a man in the house. Elvira's first marriage, at age sixteen, lasted but a few weeks, although the son it produced, Andre, became Elvira's comfort through fifteen years of living single and was now with the U.S. Army, stationed at Fort Hood in Texas. Elvira's second husband had been the police officer Bertrand Lewis, with whom she had a second son, Bertrand Jr. (B.J.), but their marriage did not survive an incident in 1985 when Bertrand Sr., on a trip to California, took in a taping of "The Price Is Right" and was called impromptu to "come on down," a most unlucky fellow chosen by lot to be panned by a network TV camera as he sat next to a secret girlfriend, Charlotte Hamilton. A videotaped copy of the show was delivered by a friend to Elvira. ("They knew they'd been caught. They had a frozen look on their faces.") Elvira was willing to attempt a reconciliation, but Bertrand soon left for good on terms less than friendly. In a letter to the divorce judge, Elvira wrote about fearing for her safety: "As the victim in this matter I feel physically threatened because the defendant is (1) known to be armed, (2) is capable of traveling cross country, (3) has the . . . motive to flee if he causes great physical harm to me or our minor son." She lived alone now with B.J., a seventh grader at St. Philip the Apostle School, who dashed poems into a notebook and was six chapters into a novel and had hopes of a writer's life. During the worst days of her second divorce Elvira had begun to write her own book, a narrative explication of an African-American woman's predicaments at the end of the twentieth century, but she had abandoned her writing without trying to have it published. She had no way with words, she said: "I can't set a scene, and I can't write a flowery sentence. All I know are short, angry sentences."

5 **As we** know, the little things of life can get overblown. Over the span of a week Dr. Gordon, grouchy in the manner of castaway old men, worked himself into a lather about groceries Bruce had bought. ("Two hundred bucks at the supermarket! I'm paying half, and how much am I going to eat out of that? Thirty bucks' worth? My own son is taking advantage, screwing me over.") And about Bruce's weight-lifting equipment. ("I hear him working out, grunting like Tarzan of the Apes. The whole X-ray room is full of his fancy-schmancy barbells. What if I need storage? Where am I supposed to put my stuff?") And about the physical therapy Bruce was supposed to help him with. ("He told me, 'Just holler if you need me.' But he's downstairs with the music turned up, the big laggard. I can't holler loud enough. Does he give a hot damn if I ever walk again? You go ask him. He goes downstairs and stands on his head—Mister Levitation, all tuned in to outer space.") And Bruce, sniping back, would let nothing pass. ("It might've been a nice gesture if he'd let me use his Redskin tickets, but, no, he gives them to somebody else. I just want a little common courtesy.") The psychologists will tell you these are familiar tensions when middle-aged children move into the home of over-the-hill parents; everyone is prey to angry outbursts. A son who gives up his own home and his own life is not apt to gain gratitude; it is more likely he will be told he is trying to support himself less taxingly at the expense of his indisposed parent. Grin and bear it, the psychologists say; no good deed is without a selfish side. Besides, did not Bruce expect more than gratitude? Did he not want some grand apology for the past? Once, expounding on their relationship, he said, "My life might've turned out different, but I couldn't overcome the obstacles Grumpus put in the way. And Grumpus, he was the biggest obstacle of all." Grumpus—that was the nickname Bruce had tagged on his father.

The near entirety of Dr. Gordon's day took place in his massive bedroom, from bed to TV chair, with grudging intervals at the exercise station, the painful, useless motions with rubberized equipment. He was gimped up in his leg still and hating it. On his ten-step therapy program there was no progress beyond the fourth step. When friends visited, he could be as full of pretense as ever. "A year from now I'll be shaking a leg," he would say. But any realistic hope of recovering mobility on his right side had dwindled away, and with it more and more of Bruce's freedom.

And the cold, wet, soupy-gray weather added another layer of anxiousness and gloom. This was nothing like the clean winters of Colorado, where Bruce had caught the Wild West enthusiasm for the outdoors. Here, on the radio, there were warnings for the old and weak to stay indoors, and Bruce's morning jogs left his lungs feeling full of liquids. To venture outside was to inhale gusts of one of the Washington area's worst early winters of the century. "I should've never left Colorado," Bruce said one evening, feeling sorry for himself. "This is the pits, being cooped up here." He regretted immediately what he had said, for a fit of hard coughing seized his father.

But Bruce's stopover in Hillcrest Heights had passed the fourteen-month mark. The privations of the old doctor's office were not right for a man of his temperament. "I'm the bear in the woods who put his paw in a steel trap. Zang-snap! Gotcha!" he said, musing with an old school friend over beers. Bruce had stayed so long it seemed now next to impossible to leave. "Till death do us part," he said, laughing. His laugh had a chill on it.

A getaway weekend with Camilla in New York had been mutually agreed to, and for days Bruce was preoccupied by an itinerary—Rockefeller Center and its pirouetting skaters, Broadway lights, a hotel where the maids honored the "Do Not Disturb" sign till noon. But at the appointed time Camilla was held up by work and had to cancel. So Bruce went holiday shopping and bought a box of turtle-shaped "Pixies," candies made by Fannie Mae and not generally available in the Boston area. Camilla was cuckoo about them. As he packaged the box for mailing and signed a card, it occurred to him that like his father he was living inadequately off make-believe. Bruce drove to the post office through another overcast afternoon. The sky, the road, the leafless oaks and scrubby viburnum, all of life, everything was cast in shades of gray. He felt the paltriness of the past year. That evening Bruce phoned a friend. "I'm lonely," he said wretchedly. "I really, really need a girlfriend."

Busy as Frank Pesci was at the moment, two parts of his life would end with the close of the year. He would be taking early retirement from a lobbyist's job with a pharmaceutical trade association, and a month was all he had left in the care and tending of his dying mother. A bittersweet Thanksgiving this year at her house had been saved by his younger cousin, the actor Joe Pesci. It amused the children to hear the stories of Cousin Joe dating back to when he was a crawler, and after the turkey everyone had watched a video of *Home Alone*. The elderly Mrs. Pesci grinned in recognition at Joe the bad guy, and Frank was relieved the movie had none of Joe's trademark "f" words. One of Frank's many sidelights was his own arty endeavor, the Rose Company, a theater company named for his mother through which he produced Washington revues of Broadway and off-Broadway shows. This week he was casting for the musical *Starting Here, Starting Now,* scheduled for a cabaret at the Shoreham in downtown Washington. Would the feature role go to Jane Pesci-Townsend, his gifted daughter and a two-time nominee for a Helen Hayes Award, even though she was pregnant and suffering from a bad cold? "You better not leave me out. I'll go find some other company to star for," she tweaked him, and he knew he would give in to her; she had been a trouper since she was in kindergarten.

As a theatrical producer, Frank was not above inserting a little political commentary into the shows. For *Starting Here, Starting Now* he would be presenting a slide show of newspaper headlines culled from Prince George's County—homicides, muggings, urban life moving in on the suburbs. The issues in Prince George's politics today were different from when Frank started out, and so, it seemed to him, was the perspective of the politicians. "There was a brief shining moment when a lot of optimists got elected. We were going to make a better world," he said. "Now the pessimists have taken over. It's the influence of the street. Don't trust anybody. Your neighbor's son might rob you, he might shoot you. Watch your back. I myself am not the optimist I used to be. Who can afford to trust in people's goodwill anymore?"

Even so, Frank Pesci, for thirty years a college professor of political science, was and always would be a politician. "Ah, politics!" He breathed in. "Once a junkie, forever a junkie." Some of his old cronies were telling him he should run for his old seat in the legislature, and he toyed excitedly with the idea. "I think I'll do it," he said to his daughter Jane.

She placed a soft hand of restraint on his shoulder. "Please, Dad, tell me you're putting me on!"

Frank would soon enough decide he was not up to it. Running for office these days required the exertions of the damned, the endless grubbing for money and citizen gabfests and pig roasts and media manipulations. But to go through an election year without doing some sort of electioneering would be rare for Frank. There had been the good-hearted campaign of Stephen Sachs, "another optimist" and a Jewish-American who, having secured the Democratic nomination for governor in 1978, ran unprecedentedly and unsuccessfully with an African-American as his running mate, and there had been the insurgency of the icon Ted Kennedy in the 1980 Democratic primaries. ("God threw away the mold with the Kennedys and Martin Luther King.") And so on, election after election. Somehow or other, Frank figured, a niche would open up for him in 1994.

It was a Saturday morning, and B.J. was upstairs with a yellow pad composing a fantasy tale of young do-gooder warriors. From a pile of mail on a kitchen counter Elvira extracted a doll magazine and flipped through it. Fanciful collector's dolls were Elvira's "vice." A room off her front hall was reserved for her menagerie, nearly two dozen and counting, ceremonial African dolls, but also blondes in gingham, curlicue heads in velvet, and Amish-dressed dolls, some with hair like dry straw—bought through catalogs with thousands of dollars. For Elvira, the dolls were an "investment," no different in her mind from the grassy plot of property she had purchased in anticipation of future subdivisions. It would be a shame if she had to cash in anything prematurely, although that possibility could not now be ignored. Money was short. Every week the U.S. mails brought more computer-generated threats from collection agencies. Since her divorce Elvira had fallen slowly into debt—"not that it should be anybody else's business." However, according to a report in the *Prince George's Journal,* her personal finances had come under the official scrutiny of investigators of the public defender's office. No one had said anything directly to Elvira, but there it was on the front page. Elvira stood accused of making money on the side through the representation of off-duty clients, an insinuation of shady dealings. The salary of a public defender ($58,000 as of Elvira's last promotion) did not handily sustain the lifestyle she was accustomed to—a four-bedroom, two-and-a-half-bath Colonial-style house; a Mercedes in the driveway; private school for B.J.—and, as was common for Prince George's attorneys on the public payroll, she had some time ago developed a supplemental private practice. In 1989, one of her better years, her outside income had amounted to $19,500. Then new curtailing rules had gone into effect. Elvira was supposed to have given up her after-hours clients, and she had done so, she said, although, as was also common in Prince George's, she had allowed herself one exception, the divorce case of Jane Lloyd, daughter of Judge Audrey Melbourne. But the judge had known of Elvira's involvement. ("Not only was Audrey aware but she was the one who asked me to handle the case. It was a family matter. And it was no big secret. The divorce proceedings were in front of Judge Johnson, the same judge from Amy's trial.") At courthouses almost anywhere, it is business as usual when an attorney does a small and open favor for a judge. Besides, Elvira claimed to have permission to bend the rules from Maureen Lamasney, district director of the public defender's office. However, Ms. Lamasney was now denying ever countenancing this or any other infraction, and there was an additional sidelight—Jane Lloyd was the real estate agent who had handled Elvira's investment-property deal. In the absence of good feelings, even the most innocent and apparently straightforward of transactions might take on the reek of scandal.

At a memorial service for Howard McGuigan, dead of lung cancer, Frank Pesci made the rounds on the slick tile floors in the rotunda of the AFL-CIO building on Capitol Hill, shaking hands with backroom flourish, pulling himself up close and confidential. Frank was the picture of a pol who had not stinted on the people side of politics, the long nights out, the bad meals. His face was red with broken capillaries. His middle had grown stout. An open-at-the-throat type, he pulled loose the knot in his tie. It was yellow with blue polka dots, the kind once worn by arbitragers.

"Here we are, going to each other's funerals. I can't believe we've gotten to this point," Frank repeated with each handshake. "Where did thirty years go?"

The dead man—an AFL-CIO troubleshooter (the Newspaper Guild, United Food and Commerical Workers) and vice-chairman of the Democratic Central Committee in Prince George's County—used to dish out advice to the class of reform-minded, optimistic white men who came of age politically in the 1960s.

"I remember the first thing he told me, 'The walls have ears,' " someone said.

"Hey, to this day I don't take a leak in a public john without checking behind the doors to the stalls," Frank said, gleeful at the memory of conducting business over camphor balls in the urinals.

"Sometimes I felt we were dealing with the Cosa Nostra."

"Don't kid yourself. Some of those old boys would've made first-class mafiosi."

A generation had come and gone, and the neophytes of yesteryear were the movers and shakers of the 1990s. In the county executive race they were much in demand. Many of them were on Gloria Lawlah's list as she went about obtaining endorsements and money for Bea Tignor. One who was not was Earl Griffen, a retired liquor store owner with a renowned skill for tapping into the cash reserves of his fellow merchants at election time. He had surprised more than a few people by agreeing to be chief fund-raiser for the white hopeful Sue Mills.

Earl Griffen now approached Frank. "All the smart money is lining up behind Sue. She represents a new day in Prince George's County."

"That's a strange way to put it." Frank frowned.

"I know what you're thinking, but you've got to let go of those tired ideas about Sue," Earl Griffen said, going on about how Sue Mills would be flocked to by voters for her "independence" and "lack of bullshit." "The money's there, Frank. The only thing Sue's lacking is a good pro to take control of her campaign."

"Does she have anybody on the hook?"

"If I have my druthers, it'll be you, Frank."

"Me?" It was a flabbergasting thought. Frank would admit later to a queer sensation of "feeling a little bit flattered." He was "a warhorse looking for a final campaign."

"Are you interested?"

"I grant you, I might enjoy the action. But it's out of the question."

"Give me your business card, Frank, and I'll set up a meet with Sue. Then you can decide."

At that Frank looked severe. "No. No, thanks." Frank did not think himself a candidate for political sainthood, but he had always wished for an obituary that linked his name to the likes of Ted Kennedy and Stephen Sachs, not the likes of Sue Mills.

In Prince George's County the snows of winter usually hold off until late January, but on a morning in December, after Bruce had left for work and after an out-of-town visitor had arrived to kill time with Dr. Gordon, a cold north wind unleashed a white fury. A few hours of sleeting had preceded the snow, and a knobby glaze lay under the white drifts. Sparrows and purple finches deserted the bird feeder and the high-bowed wires for cover in evergreen shrubs. Overhead the sun would not get through for the foreseeable future. It was a good day for an old man to avoid the weather and be at peace indoors. Practically speaking, it was of no consequence to Dr. Gordon that his sidewalk was turned treacherous; none of his former patients came up the walk anymore bearing get-well dishes. And it was of no consequence that the wheelchair ramp out back was encrusted with ice and snow. Dr. Gordon had no reason to go down to the garage. Nonetheless, from his easy chair, he railed at the closed-off world. "You'd think that boy of mine could take a break and come home and shovel me out. What if the house caught on fire? I'd be in a fine fix."

Around noon the phone rang. Clomp-clomping on his walker, Dr. Gordon got to it. On the line was Delmar, shopping for jobs with his snow shovel.

"No, I can't use you," Dr. Gordon said. "I'd like to, but you've got to straighten out things with Bruce."

Clomp, clomp, Bruce's father sat down, his lower brow a prominence that shaded his eyes. He said to his visitor, "I have to laugh. My son thinks he's God's gift to the black cause, but he can't get along with black people any better than anybody else."

By December Elvira knew that naught would come of the official investigation into her alleged off-duty profiteering. The directors of the state public defender's office now said Elvira's activities were open "to more than one interpretation," indicating they had lost their stomach for formal charges. But any celebrating on Elvira's part had to be postponed. The Amy Smith case was going forward. The "favoritism" shown by Elvira to the family of Derrick Jones, according to a ruling from the appellate courts, was sufficient to bring into question a possible "conflict of interest." There would have to be a postconviction hearing in a Prince George's courtroom to sort things out.

Like an intricate novel, the Amy Smith case held many possible truths; it was a real-life plot overlaid with the twists and turns Elvira wished she could have constructed on paper. And at the center of the plot now was Elvira herself. She was in peril of having taken from her the reputation she had worked for and sacrificed for—or, anyway, what was left of that reputation.

• • •

Putting a gun to the head of a woman and ordering her to stab her husband has to be considered an archetypal example of what in cultural commentary is known as "the rage of the young black male." To many people, it is fair to say, Derrick Jones embodied the modern run of the dangerous black man in all his viciousness. To Elvira, these people had made an automatic but wrong assumption. The Derrick that Elvira saw was a victim, not of social misfortune but rather of puppy love. Derrick's life had become entwined with Amy's by the purest of accidents—a mistakenly dialed phone number. Neither Derrick nor Amy knew of each other until a day in the spring of 1991, four months before his death, when she misdialed and rang up the Jones family. Derrick, scrounging for a snack in the refrigerator, picked up the phone. His friend Gregory Drew was in the kitchen with him and said later that Amy must have begun spontaneously to flirt with Derrick because "his face kind of like started to dance." A few days later Amy, who had just obtained a driver's license, drove in a borrowed car to Enterprise Estates and rang the bell at the Jones residence and introduced herself to Derrick and his startled mother. Amy carried it off well; Mrs. Jones would later remember Amy as "polite and respectful, grown up for her age." In the next few weeks Derrick fell into a head-over-heels enchantment. Amy was not only the first white girl upon whom he had invested amorous intentions, she was his first serious fling of any kind. He was a novice in affairs of the heart. Except for a hayride back at Halloween when he had talked with a girl about stirred-up feelings and made overtures to her, there was not a great deal else to tell in the way of girlfriends. Of course, Derrick thought Amy was sexy. "He was like, hey, she can really shake that booty," Gregory Drew said. And very likely Derrick was drawn also to the thrill of Amy's rebellion, slipping out of her house through a downstairs window for covert assignations, living free in the malls with her parents unaware, a rebellion he probably figured was exceedingly safe. But if Amy was Derrick's Pied Piper to the semi-wild life of the suburbs, he apparently was to her a far more profound figure: he was to be her savior from the clutches of a father and stepmother bent on keeping track of her every move. Who knows whether it was just Derrick's fate she chose him or whether he volunteered, but any volunteerism had to have been preceded by a seduction, of this Elvira was sure. ("Derrick was in a better socioeconomic class than Amy was. There was nothing she could offer him, except her body.") Hanging out on the front lawns of Enterprise Estates in muggy, aromatic heat Derrick heard from Amy agitated, hissy reports of her home life. Gregory Drew, hanging out with them, wondered at Amy's obsession. ("She always used to talk about her parents, and I never had no idea why she wanted to talk about them.") Amy talked of her stepmother's quick temper. She called her father a "mother-fucker" and wished him dead. It took some talking for Derrick to give credence to the unrighteousness of the Smiths. With his own parents he got along well. He was little affected by the *Sturm und Drang* of teenage-hood. ("He would be trying to joke with Amy, to get her to chill, but she had this thing about her parents, and she wouldn't let go.") Amy was upset by the early curfews, the spying into her friendships, and the ban on black boyfriends. It may have been this last complaint that hit home with Derrick. Any black youth who thought he had prospects with Amy Smith would have soon realized he either had to elude her parents on a regular basis or somehow he had to get them out of the picture. For Derrick, involved in his first experience of sexual suffering, his reaction may have been an overreaction.

It was this motive, murder for the sake of teenage ardor, that Anne Gold-Rand had wanted to have articulated at Amy's trial, the motive Elvira could not bring herself to use against the dead young man. On a relative scale, Elvira believed that Derrick Jones had the least of the guilt, for which he had already paid most dear. Why should he be made posthumously to pay even more? "Elvira was adamant on this point. She would not relent," Anne Gold-Rand would say later. "She felt Derrick wasn't responsible. She felt Amy had seduced him. Anything he did was because of Amy. He was the victim."

By this stage of the case it was clear to Elvira that the police and the prosecutors had committed a basic mistake. Because the story of a black teenager's wanton attack in the middle of the night symbolized everything believed to be wrong with America, she believed the authorities had too hastily concluded Dennis and Marie Smith represented all that was right. But had Elvira turned this mistake on its head? Because Derrick represented the good kid, had she assumed Amy represented the bad?

The yearning of Americans to have their children instilled with explicit values, with rights and wrongs, is undeniable. Teachers hear this, Little League coaches hear this, and ministers, newspaper editors, professional celebrities, all the gospel-bearers of morality. But what should these values be? Is there a broad consensus for any particular values? Researchers for the Gallup Poll had interviewed a sampling of Americans and found that ninety percent of them placed a premium on four things: honesty, democracy, the Golden Rule, and, to Bruce's surprise, "racial tolerance."

The historian John Hope Franklin has said, speaking of strange findings like these in opinion surveys, "We've got a history of dishonesty and hypocrisy in this area. We pile one on top of the other, and have to lie and misrepresent in order to validate our original positions. It becomes a compounding of the hypocrisy that began in the seventeenth century."

"Yes, Americans are hypocritical," said Bruce, upon reading a news account of the poll. "On the other hand, we want our children to be better than we are."

The world was more understandable if you did not read the papers. Even so, Bruce had much time on his hands for reading and was not likely to miss a write-up in the *Washington Post* about the high-class Yacht Club and its singles scene featuring an over-thirty-five, business-suited, interracial crowd whose most requested song was Elton John's "Can You Feel the Love Tonight?" Bruce phoned for directions, and on a Friday night he appeared in the crowd. Looking everywhere at once, he felt silly and nervous and surely out of practice under the low, black ceilings. After a few drinks and a few dances, though, he was bumping his hip against the brass railings and swooning over a woman in a slinky, swinger's dress. Her name was Delphia—a lawyer, an African-American. Bruce had not come to the Yacht Club to exercise any social ideals, or remnants of social ideals. His intentions were entirely lascivious. ("As a veteran of interracial sex, I can tell you it's exciting. It's a different touch, a different feel, fuller lips, softer skin, a different scent. Interracial sex is hot. Socioeconomics are hogwash. It's the sex, and nothing wrong with that.") None of this meant he did not long for a steady companion and a human touch. "I'm tired of being single," he openly said to Delphia.

Magnificently tipsy, they went home to her town house. The perfect schematic globes of Bradford pear trees lined both sides of the street.

Delphia had two sons, a five-year-old and a fifteen-year-old, and they met Bruce the next morning in the kitchen. The fifteen-year-old yawned and ostentatiously banged the cupboard doors, provoked by the carelessly shaven white man who presumed to munch toast at the table. In the middle of pleasantries the teenager began to gloat about the moral superiority of black men. He baited Bruce, "I feel most white men have a curse on them from the way they've treated the African race. They deserve to die." It must not have been the first time he had spoken these lines because his younger brother was cued to chime in. "We like to fuck white girls, but if white boys come after our pussy we beat them up"—a five-year-old, a kindergartner, obviously parroting something he had heard. Bruce took it all in, hiding behind a blank, bleary-eyed expression. He knew enough to keep quiet and not put in his two cents, even though he was shocked to his toes. His thought was, "Where do these hatred vibes come from?"

Delphia phoned later that afternoon to say how sorry she was for the language of her sons. Point-blank she asked Bruce for a second date. But he knew he must stop this sooner rather than later. It could never work out.

He went upstairs and asked his father, "Got any candy to eat? My mouth tastes sour."

No one could pick Elbert and Daphne Jones out of a crowd, but for a while they felt strangely notorious. Their dead son was a household name—Derrick Jones, the would-be murderer. That had been the inferred judgment against him at Amy Smith's trial. The trial presentation of the bullet holes and the position of Derrick's body was ruled to have less probative value than the sworn testimony of Officer Dennis Smith. "Congratulations, you've just made me feel like dirt," Mr. Jones had said, walking out on the judge.

It is a fact of life in America that between a young black kid and an older white cop there is seldom a fair contest when it comes to getting the last word in a court of law—a fact of life little changed by one's station on a fancy street. "I am not naive, but I still feel the hurt," Mr. Jones said. He sat, hunched forward, on a rounded chair in his den. It was a coolish day, and he was dressed in a polo shirt, slacks, and sandals, a kind of Beat style. "Our son was killed, taken from us, by a cop who obviously went berserk because he hates black kids. And then, to make it worse, this cop isn't punished. He's never charged. Oh, no, sweet Jesus, they have the gall to say it's Derrick who went berserk, which in a million years I'll never believe. Derrick was as decent a kid as you'll ever meet. He had no reason to attack this man in his home. He had never seen Dennis Smith before that night. If you look at the evidence, the only logical conclusion is that Derrick went to the Smith home that night for hanky-panky with Amy. His only interest was in the girl, period, end of story." Mr. Jones stroked the side of his face with long fingers. "Yeah, well, except that wasn't the end of it. We still don't know what the end is going to be."

Mr. Jones was aware of the recent attempt within the public defender's office to gain a new trial for Amy. He had been trying to ignore the news in favor of reviewing travel brochures with his wife. Yet to have the case reopened was what they both had prayed for since the day of the verdict. "I know how the system works, how the deck is stacked," Mr. Jones said.

"Derrick is young and black—uh, was. I know in my head it'll be hard to get justice for him. But I feel we have to hold on to this little fragment of hope. The only chance the truth will ever come out is if there is a new trial."

At age twelve Amy Smith was shown for the first time a photograph of her mother apropos of questions Amy was asking her father. Aside from producing the photograph—in which an amiably grinning Judith Pickering Smith was seen as she once had been, full of life—Dennis Smith was not very forthcoming. The implacable answers he gave to Amy about her mother—how Judith Smith had consented to a legal separation soon after Amy was born on April 22, 1975; how a divorce was agreed to when Amy was nine months old; and how Judith left one morning thereafter to drive to a job interview and was killed by a hit-and-run motorist on the Baltimore-Washington Parkway—were attenuated, the details intact but the core missing. Whither the separation? Whither the divorce? What was the story behind the story?

Actually, as Amy told Dr. Schouten, she had already formed an idea of what the real story was from the family gossip whispered to her by her older stepsisters.

After Judith Smith's death Amy had been dispatched into the care of her maternal grandparents and then her paternal grandparents, and when she returned to live with her father, three years later, he was remarried. The new Mrs. Smith, Marie, had been one of Judith's best friends, and Marie's ex-husband had been one of Dennis Smith's best friends, a fellow officer. For several years the four had been steady companions, but then the relationships were reshuffled; the marriages ended; two couples became one. The fateful moment Dennis Smith first made eyes outside of his marriage was hard to know, but according to the version told to Amy, her parents began finalizing a divorce soon after her birth. Well in advance of Judith Smith's death it appears she was the odd woman out. As a youngster Amy ignored the family gossip about her father and stepmother, but upon reaching adolescence, Amy had the sensation of scales falling from her eyes. She saw with unwelcome clarity the backdrop to her mother's death. It was a disillusioning period, according to the psychological profile of her prepared by Dr. Schouten. Amy began to connect the deterioration of her parents' marriage to the hit-and-run scene on the highway, a scene, as she visualized it, of a woman's torn body inside a car with structural supports slammed into violent angles. "Amy became aware of the implications of the stories her stepsisters had told her, the suggestions that her father and stepmother were romantically involved and that this involvement led to the breakup of Amy's parents and to her mother's death," Dr. Schouten reported to the court. Although there was no proof of adultery nor any provable connection between Dennis Smith's relationship with Marie and Judith Smith's death, it seemed to Amy that her mother might well have been on the Baltimore-Washington Parkway looking not for a job but for a way out of things. Anyway, if not for the impending divorce, she probably would have been at home and out of harm's way. Not unreasonably, according to Dr. Schouten, Amy harbored "resentment toward her parents based on her belief that they are responsible to some extent for the death of her mother." Also, the tattletales of Amy's stepsisters about premarital goings-on by Dennis and Marie Smith added to Amy's adolescent discomfort. "She speaks with some resentment about her father's alleged sexual involvement with her stepmother before their marriage," Dr. Schouten reported. In sum, "Amy attributes the divorce, her mother's need to seek employment and subsequent death to her stepmother's relationship with her father. This belief, which she has held for many years, has clearly colored her relationship with her parents and has contributed significantly to the events in question"—those events being the alleged assault against Dennis and Marie Smith in their home and the killing of Derrick Jones in alleged retaliation.

In the halls of the state capitol in Annapolis one day in 1987, Frank Pesci extended a handshake and offered to fill in Gloria Lawlah on a few tricks of the trade. He was on his way out of the state legislature after a career of high-spirited, voluble, picturesque service on behalf of the goals of the civil rights movement; she was on her way in. Gloria would not years later remember the particulars of their meeting, but something in the handshake did not go over well, or perhaps it was something in Frank's attitude, or perhaps it was just a naturally occurring suspicion since none of the other white male legislators were rolling out the carpet for her. As Frank would remember it, "She stared down at the top of my head"—she was taller by several inches and had a thespian's flair—"then she waltzed away." Of course, plenty of rudeness had been shown her as well. But ever afterward there was no love lost between them.

During the 1990 elections their relations became worse. Gloria was trying to move from the lower to the upper body of the legislature, which placed her in a campaign against the incumbent 26th District state senator,

Frank Komenda, one of Frank Pesci's white pals. The two Franks had known each other since Frank Pesci happened into a hardware store on a Saturday in 1960—it was Frank Komenda's store, located in Suitland, a neighborhood then receiving an early onrush of African-American migration. The two men discovered they were both integrationists, and ten years later they ran for office together on a Democratic reform ticket. In time Frank Komenda had aligned himself with the Mike Miller machine and was in 1990 the chairman of the Prince George's senate delegation. Frank Pesci could have stayed neutral in the Komenda-Lawlah race—that would have been the politic thing to do—but he chose to place his loyalties aggressively behind his old friend. He could have kept black versus white out of the debate, but he chose to put it front and center. "Gloria Lawlah's message has been racist," he wrote in his *Prince George's Journal* column. "The 26th District is now predominantly black, and she thinks it should elect a black woman." Coming as it did late in the campaign, Frank Pesci's column was the sort of out-of-hand gambit that might have snatched victory from Gloria. "I felt like he might as well have slugged me in the face," she would say later. In an irritable panic she tried to get in touch with him, hoping he could be talked into writing an apology or retraction. No dice, and although Gloria had prevailed in the election ("It was those notebooks again! We knew which precincts had the numbers!"), she spoke to Frank now only through third parties.

Gloria (her voice revealing with every syllable her Carolina past): "Frank has labeled me a racist, but can a black person really be a racist? I question that. Because black people have no real power. We don't have an impact on people's lives. You have to possess power to be a racist."

Frank: "Racism is an attitude, that's number one. Number two, there certainly is a black power structure now in Prince George's."

Gloria: "We are about equal in voting power, but there are four times as many white officeholders as black officeholders, so there is no true parity. We do have Al Wynn in Congress now. It's beautiful. White people ask me, 'Why can't a white politician represent you?' I tell them, 'A white politician can, a white politician always has. We've always voted for your politicians.' "

Frank: "There have been good white politicians who worked for integration and deserved integrated support. And the same for good black politicians. But when black politicians send out the message, 'Vote black, vote black,' they're dancing with the devil.' "

Gloria: "I've always been opposed to any philosophy that advocates separatism. I'm a daughter of the NAACP."

Frank: "I've heard her in private be militant, very militant. Black power has suited her purpose, has suited the boldness of her ambition. To me, this 'vote black' strategy has no place within the principles of integration. And if we don't keep the flame burning for integration, it will go out."

Gloria: "To me, voting *against* someone for reasons of color is racism. But voting *for* a candidate can be done out of racial pride. That's the difference. Forty years ago we had to depend on the goodwill of nine white Supreme Court justices, but today the people of Prince George's can take it upon themselves to change the system. I don't call that black power, I call that people power."

One lunch hour, as Bruce pulled up in his car to a Hillcrest Heights sub shop, a man tapped on the passenger-side window. The man looked nineteen or twenty. "Hello, I need help out of a mess," he bleated in a thin voice, through the glass. "My car won't start."

Bruce rolled down the window. "Where's your car?"

The man pointed toward Pennsylvania Avenue. "Back there. I can show you. It's half a mile about. I left my parents with the car, and I been walking."

In this day and age such a response invites suspicion, and before unlocking his car door, Bruce had a debate with himself. Giving a stranger a lift may be of no great moment for the macho man, but anyone in touch with reality must think twice. In the past three months there had been two carjackings and three attempted carjackings within half a mile of the Gordon house. Another carjacking had been carried out in the parking lot of Potomac High. The dry cleaners where Bruce took his shirts and suits had been entered by pistoleros at noontime and robbed of the morning's proceeds. Four teenage girls walking outside Iverson Mall had been picked up by two men, who took them to an apartment and raped them after failing to win their favor with malt liquor and bootleg porn videos. In each instance the perpetrators were described as "young" and "black," just like the man asking to get into Bruce's car, just like the sort of person called to mind by the abject admission ("When I see a stranger walking toward me on the street, I'm relieved if he's a white man") of the Reverend Jesse Jackson, who lived over the county line not far away on a middle-class Washington street and whose comment, which had caused much ado, may have been said in a tired moment but also came from a high stage of frustration.

As for this young black stranger, he had gotten himself up in a sport coat and tie for his day's activities. But what did that mean? For being well-attired and polite was he deserving of an extra benefit of doubt? Why should Bruce be the gullible stooge?

While Bruce hesitated, the young man kept talking. "We was driving back from Upper Marlboro, and the car stalled. The battery is run low. She goes ur-rr, ur-rr, but she won't start."

"You got cables?"

"No, man. I was hoping you had some."

"Now that you mention it, I do." Bruce remembered having to get his own car jump-started a week ago and leaving jumper cables in his trunk. "Okay." Bruce flipped up the door lock on the passenger side. "Hop in." Well, what's a person supposed to do? Stop helping people?

But on closer inspection he sized up the young man as someone probably not accustomed to job-going clothes; the sport coat was new, just off the rack—not a good sign.

"I appreciate you helping me out. I been walking and walking but wouldn't nobody give me a ride."

"No problem," Bruce said, but without conviction. How frequently foolish is the man of high ideals!

Half a mile away on Pennsylvania Avenue the truth was revealed: a late-model sedan pulled to the side and inside two middle-aged black people dressed as for a church service. "This here's my mother and dad," the young man said.

Bruce got the motor up and firing, and the young man and his parents were profuse with their thanks. Bruce felt good about himself. He had fulfilled the duties of the good white man. He was not after all one of those paranoids who misinterpret so much, who see in the aggressive thievery of a few the good-for-nothingness of all black men. "I was on my high horse," he would say later. "How many white guys are willing to let a black kid into their car? How many are willing to take the chance? But then, when I was putting the cables away, it came back to me that the guy who'd stopped and jumped my car the week before was a black guy. He never made a big deal of it. So how rare an occurrence is it to find goodness in people? How big a deal is it? Here I was making myself into a moral crusade for doing something that should be routine in a civilized society."

Bruce lingered on the avenue, striking up more of a conversation. The young man lived with his parents in Washington, a few blocks from Jesse Jackson's house. Their car had stalled out while they were traveling home from the Prince George's courthouse where the young man (one of Elvira White's charges) had been arraigned in a criminal court, accused of breaking into a Hillcrest Heights home—"a false arrest," his mother said. He had been remanded into the custody of his family. The young man, introducing himself by name now, changed the subject. "I'm looking for a job, man. You got any work I can do?" Minutes before, Bruce had been complimenting him, telling him how as a hitchhiker he had presented himself in upstanding fashion, and Bruce had been halfway convinced the young man would be an excellent choice to handle Delmar's old chores at the Gordon house. But what was Bruce to make of the information about the pending burglary case? Had the young man gotten fouled up by one of those mistaken identities the authorities can make, or had he gone wrong on his own?

In the end Bruce took the young man's phone number but never called him. Bruce had no instinct he could trust. Some people are not what they seem, but then again some people are exactly what they seem. It was unknowable.

The court proceedings in the Amy Smith case almost always took place under the personal appraisal of Daphne Jones, mother of Derrick. She would sit on a bench and listen and watch, waiting for any new revelations. During the days when Elvira was the attorney of record the two women had instigated gossip by walking together from the courtroom to Elvira's office. Anne Gold-Rand said they acted like "soul sisters." Elvira took this as an insult. ("Mrs. Jones and I had never laid eyes on each other before all this happened, but that doesn't matter. Black is black. We must be soul sisters.") What the two women had between them might better be called a courthouse friendship—each had a stake in the Smith case. The friendship took hold less because of a common ancestry than because of an act of intimate kindness shown by Elvira, who, soon after Derrick's death, had called on the Jones home in Enterprise Estates and listened solemnly as Mrs. Jones, weeping into a hanky, poured out her heart. Some things are simply not done, and conveying condolences to the families of victims when you are an attorney for the other side is one of those things. But it had always been Elvira's highly individualistic, go-it-alone practice to be a comforter to mothers whose children lay dead or wounded at the hands of her clients. ("I can zealously represent a client, and I can also be a compassionate human being. Every mother's nightmare is to wake up and learn her child has been shot. But for the grace of God there go any of us.") In all previous cases nothing untoward had come of Elvira's Good Samaritanism. In the courtroom her allegiance to her clients had never been questioned. But in the Smith case Elvira was accused of having assumed that Amy's best interests were also the best interests of the Jones family. A misguided assumption, it was now said, although at the time there had been a logic to it. If Amy wanted a clear not-guilty verdict then it was necessary for Elvira to present Derrick in court as likewise without guilt. On this basis Elvira felt justified in making the acquaintance of the Joneses. Their information might be of value, and she was within ethical bounds. From the talks with Mrs. Jones, however, Elvira came away mainly with a powerful sense that she and her husband were people deserving of fair play, people of integrity, salts of the earth. Elvira had not tried to hide these sympathies. But had she crossed the line? Had she become a legal advocate for the Jones family? Had the friendship jaundiced an objective defense of Amy Smith? This was the claim being made in legal papers. Should the claim be proved Amy would get her wish for a new trial.

And Daphne and Elbert Jones would get their wish, too. The Joneses would get a reexamination of the facts surrounding Derrick's death.

Of course, Elvira's career would be diminished. That was the hitch.

"So they're trying to use Elbert and me to ruin you?" Mrs. Jones said, shaking Elvira's hand at a White-for-Judge function.

"They're trying to ruin me any way they can."

"It is so distressing."

For Elvira to be the "scapegoat," as Mrs. Jones said, was "intolerable because a person who lets truth be their guide should not have to suffer as a result." What good was the uncompromising majesty of the law in a case like this? Still and all, Mr. and Mrs. Jones were reluctant to give up on the one recourse left to them to clear their son's name. The quintessence of their dilemma was expressed one day by Mr. Jones: "We want to be loyal to Elvira White because she was the one who defended Derrick's honor, and we also want to be loyal to Derrick's memory and pursue all avenues to set the record straight. But we can't do both. Because of the way the appeal process is structured we have to choose one or the other."

6 **For almost** a generation prior to the Amy Smith case the name in Prince George's County most associated with deadly racial violence was the name Terrence Johnson, a young black man, just fifteen, when he came to prominence on the night of June 26, 1978, for ending the lives of two white police officers. Incarceration had been Terrence Johnson's fate, and it was his periodic right now to seek parole. Thus far he had not come close to obtaining one, but each time he sat down with the parole commissioners there was, up and down the hallways of the Prince George's courthouse, a revived state of high anxiety. It would be a travesty for Terrence Johnson to be set loose, so said most of the white people of the courthouse. As for the black people, they said with equal predictability that if Terrence Johnson had been a white teenager who killed two black men under similar circumstances he probably would not have had charges laid on him in the first place. All that could be agreed on inside the courthouse was that "Free Terrence Johnson" were fighting words. Once, when Elvira brought up Terrence Johnson's name to a white bulge-chinned bailiff, he bellowed out, "I hope to God that little shithead, excuse my French, never walks. He's a killer through and through. I've seen his eyes. I was here when the Claggett case went to trial."

The "Claggett case" was how white old-timers referred to the killings. The best known of Terrence Johnson's victims had been Albert M. Claggett IV, whose surname evoked the lost heroic heritage of the Prince George's gentry and in whose features were centuries of British stock. Albert Claggett had descended from one of the original Maryland colonists, Captain Thomas Clagett, who in 1671 was granted land in America for his previous support of Charles II when the monarch was in exile from the commoner Oliver Cromwell. Lore had it that the spelling of Clagett was changed during the Revolutionary War by a Tory ancestor, a second "g" being added to honor George III. In 1792 the patriot Thomas John Claggett was consecrated as the first Episcopal bishop in the Americas; he would be remembered for gaining the independence of the Episcopal Church from the Church of England and his remains would be interred at the National Cathedral. By the early 1800s the Claggett family owned a tobacco plantation outside Upper Marlboro. As elsewhere in southern Maryland, the land was worked by slaves from Africa. At least two of the Claggetts joined the renegade Second Maryland Regiment that fought for the Confederacy in the Civil War and were among those who laid down their arms at Appomattox. The police officer Claggett, who went by the nickname Rusty, had entered into America's modern history of the war between the races well before his death at age twenty-six. In 1975 a Prince George's prosecutor had cited Rusty Claggett for "a prima facie case of excessive force" in the beating of a black motorist, Thomas Peet, who had given offense by refusing to append his signature to a ten-dollar traffic ticket. A request for a grand jury indictment of Rusty Claggett was made, but, as with all previous county grand juries impaneled to hear evidence of police brutality, tradition held—that is, the Prince George's tradition of never bringing into the dock a white lawman accused of violent behavior against a black man. Subsequently another grand jury declined to indict Rusty Claggett's brother officer, Peter Morgan, for shooting in the back of the head a black thief, William Sonny Ray, on Christmas Eve 1977 during a tussle that began with the shoplifting of two supermarket hams for a holiday dinner. This time, though, public furor toward the Prince George's justice system was such that, on June 21, 1978, to quiet things down, Officer Morgan was fired for his action. Rusty Claggett and dozens of other officers, not all of them hotheads, reacted with great consternation to the firing, complaining that it constituted "the breakdown of law and order."

Five days later Rusty Claggett was on patrol along Route 450 when, past nightfall, he pulled over the driver of a Plymouth for operating without headlights. The driver was Terrence Johnson's older brother, Melvin, who earlier in the evening had busted open a Laundromat coinbox and helped himself to thirty dollars in quarters. With the shine of a flashlight Rusty Claggett spotted a chisel, a tire iron, and a sock containing the quarters and put two and two together. He arrested Melvin Johnson for theft and took along Terrence Johnson, a passenger, for questioning. The younger Johnson had not been involved in the crime and had no criminal record, but evidence would be proffered later that he possessed a violent streak. He had broken the glasses of a varsity wrestler at his school and swung a cafeteria tray at an assistant principal. The treatment accorded the Johnson brothers inside the processing room was not out of the ordinary, which is to say it was brusque and prejudicial. While the brothers were manacled and while their father, a postal worker, and their mother, a nursing home orderly, were given no notice of their sons' whereabouts, the policemen exhibited a far different attitude toward two white teenage boys picked up that same evening for trespassing at a private pool; one of the white kids asked playfully if he could try on a pair of handcuffs, and an officer went along with the joke; then the fathers of the white boys were welcomed in, and the boys were released with jovial warnings about next time. This was the prelude for Terrence Johnson's smart-alecky antics. Trying to show up the police, he slid his chair into a forbidden zone, and when a white officer knocked him to the floor, the black kid with his cuffed hands picked the chair up over his head. It was behavior that went against the wisdom of the Prince George's NAACP, which for years sponsored forums at which black youths were shown the protocols of an encounter with white policemen. (Hardi Jones, the current NAACP chapter president, explained, "Our aim was to instruct you how to handle yourself so you lived to talk about it afterwards.") Terrence Johnson's attitude played terribly on Rusty Claggett's cop pride. Mostly silent all this time, but clearly full of bile, he took over and escorted Terrence Johnson into the Breathalyzer room, a separate cagelike cubicle, and closed the door. Simultaneously, and far too conveniently to the minds of jurors who later sat in judgment, every other officer in the processing room chose that moment to run errands or go to the men's room, creating the impression that they knew full well Officer Claggett, a strapping man who stood six-four, planned to administer a version of police justice. Passions inside the Breathalyzer room boiled up quickly, like a tornado, but of the two who went into the room, only the fifteen-year-old boy, diminutive, doe-eyed, able to pass for a much younger kid, lived to report the events that took place, which were over in less than a minute. According to the survivor's tale, Rusty Claggett proceeded to throw his prisoner against a table and choke him with a headlock. Flailing about, Terrence Johnson got his hands on the .38 Special at the policeman's belt. The shock for both of them must have been incredible. Rusty Claggett called out, stupidly, "Why you black motherfucker!" Terrence Johnson would testify that "the gun went off. I saw red spots on his shirt, and he just looked at me with his eyes wide open." Running out, Terrence Johnson was like a madman, shooting wildly. Bullets zinged. His brother had to duck for cover. Officer James B. Swart came into the line of fire and was struck fatally. Over the next several minutes, as Terrence Johnson was captured and taken to a holding cell, he suffered the blows of hysterical white officers. Finally he met for the first time that evening a black officer, Ray Evans, who had responded to a distress signal on his cruiser radio. "Brother," Terrence Johnson implored, "don't let them do this to me! They're beating me." Saying not a word, the black officer punched the young man twice in the face.

By the time Terrence Johnson went on trial, however, the black community of Prince George's County had come together with a surpassing unity on behalf of the accused murderer. A frenzied crowd of demonstrators gathered each day at daybreak outside the courthouse, bearing hand-lettered posters: "Cops and Klan Work Hand in Hand." Fearing the worst, a phalanx of blue coats stood watch, and sharpshooters were posted to Upper Marlboro rooftops. Members of the white crowd, separated from the black crowd by a sidewalk, stood and hollered in support of the dead officers and held aloft their own banners: "Insanity: A License to Murder in P.G. County." Inside, Terrence Johnson's lawyers argued to a jury that he was a kid of decent values driven temporarily mad by an officially tolerated state of racist terror. The jurors deliberated for seventeen hours and then asked Judge Jacob Levin to relieve them of their duties. He told them to sleep on it, and in the morning, a Saturday, they delivered a compromise verdict: innocent by virtue of insanity in the death of Officer Swart and guilty only of voluntary manslaughter and illegal use of a handgun in the death of Officer Claggett. One white police officer, Paul Low, overcome by anger, yelled "No, no!" and slammed his fists against a courtroom wall. The following Monday all of the 138 white police officers and 4 of the 12 black officers stayed off the job in a sickout. Three days later Peter Morgan, the white cop who had killed a black man over two Christmas hams, was given back his badge, revealing, as far as many members of the black community were concerned, the true heart of the police brass.

There were five declared candidates for county executive, a white woman (Sue Mills), a black woman (Bea Tignor), two black men (Wayne Curry and Artie Polk), and a white man (Richard Castaldi), and at a candidates forum in Temple Hills the five were collected together at a plastic-covered table. A foreigner with knowledge of American race relations gleaned mainly from television sitcoms would have found a comfortable wonderment in the scene. The five candidates acted happy-go-lucky. The wonder was they could act so well with the campaign at a win-or-else stage. But they were professionals. It was only out of the public eye that blowups were occurring—blowups particularly between Bea Tignor and Wayne Curry, the two best-credentialed black candidates. The problem boiled down to a lack of room in the campaign for two major black candidates. A week ago, over dinner, two of Bea Tignor's allies in the Prince George's delegation, Gary Alexander and Tim Maloney, had been leaned on by John Davey, a courthouse lawyer and a political financier in league with Mr. Curry. The gist of their advice was that Mrs. Tignor should withdraw and clear the way for Mr. Curry. Even Bucky Trotter, dean of black politics in Prince George's, who had earlier said of Mrs. Tignor's entry into the race, "This is the year we can elect a black County Executive," was saying now, "I'm disappointed we can't get one of the black candidates to disappear. Unless Bea or Wayne drop out, Sue Mills will win." Neither Mrs. Tignor nor Mr. Curry was willing to take the hint. Mrs. Tignor, a very perturbed spirit, had put out dozens of calls in the past several days, telling friends and foes, "I'm not dropping out. I'm in this to the bitter end."

Sue Mills was keeping away from the fray; it was a black-against-black thing. But the point of it was the same racial dynamic as always. The point of it was to reduce the campaign to black against white.

One after another, Bruce's protestations had dropped away, and he now sat cologne-splashed in the driver's seat of his mother's Toyota, all nervous qualms, headed toward a synagogue in Silver Spring. Bruce's mother figured it was the perfect solution. *There are so many nice marriageable girls there. You can have your pick.* The night was white and wicked; snow whipped slantwise past the car. At the synagogue door Bruce was met by discouraging canned music, and on top of that he had to contend with the doubts of a gray-haired chaperone. "I'm afraid you're too young. You won't have any fun," she said. He was wearing his "black" outfit—leather jacket, black slacks, black boots, a Torpedo Factory T-shirt. He said, "Ma'am, the doctor fills out my medical form as middle-aged."

But when Bruce got inside there was a woman with a charming, lilting voice, another brave soul putting her best foot forward. The woman— Betsy—had on a black cocktail dress, and Bruce's getup, the mysterious dark stranger, put him on provocative terms with her. On the dance floor Betsy had pizzazz, while off the floor, fumbling with her purse, she seemed as much a greenhorn as him, another plus. She had grown up in Calverton, near Hillcrest Heights, and among her vital statistics were a CPA degree, a nine-year-old son, and a one-year-old divorce. She had been raised in the Saturday faith but no longer observed it. "I'm glad to be talking a common language," Bruce said to her.

New Year's Eve was a few days away, and they made a date—Lulu's in downtown Washington, a loud, hopping place of Golden Oldies. They lushed it up and engaged in too many dance contortions, and Bruce began the year 1994 with a pounding head and pains in his joints, but, as he said, "Who cares?" Two weeks later he brought Betsy home to be introduced to his father, only the second woman to cross the Gordon threshold on his arm.

"Finding her might be the smartest thing you've ever done," his father said that evening.

For a change, might the old man be on the money? ("Is that the answer? Stick with your own kind? I don't know. I don't know.") Anybody could see Betsy was a find: a dynamite looker and a vivid, systematic, characteristic Jewish-American woman doing the right things by her boy, Hebrew school and the Boy Scouts, a woman who believed in the strong bonds of family which Bruce with willy-nilly shabbiness had ignored for so long. He could do a lot worse than her. Why not get hitched and father a child and carry on the Gordon patriarchy, as a childless, middle-aged son ought to?

During closing arguments at Amy's trial the prosecuting attorney, Beverly Woodard, had come up with a rhetorical question meant to put to rest the idea that Dennis Smith's shot to the back of Derrick Jones's head was a brutal, criminal act. "Would Amy out of the goodness of her heart sit here and keep quiet and go along with her father's murder of Derrick, if that is what it really was?" Ms. Woodard had asked. "Would Amy sit here and keep quiet when she'd been telling her friends she hated her father and wanted him dead?"

News reporters covering the trial found it hard to reconcile any answer in Amy's favor. Moreover, the lack of a good answer is likely to have played a part in Judge Johnson's verdict against Amy. Elvira herself was troubled by it, especially since she knew of information, kept out of the trial, that seemed to reinforce the prosecutor's point. In talking to Thomas and Elizabeth Pickering of Cape Cod, Massachusetts—Amy's grandparents on her mother's side—Elvira had been informed they were dead-set certain the phantom driver of the van that ran Judith Smith's car off the road was either a killer hired by Dennis Smith or Dennis Smith himself. (Elvira, with customary alacrity, fitted this allegation neatly into the shooting of Derrick Jones: "If Mr. Smith was capable of planning his wife's death, the hand of God surely wouldn't have stayed him from executing Derrick Jones.") There was no proof Judith Smith had not died an accidental death, and even if there had been foul play, the "evidence" against Dennis Smith was very circumstantial; all that could be said was that he had owned a van at the time of the accident and, shortly beforehand, he had purchased extra life-insurance coverage on his wife. Nonetheless, Mr. and Mrs. Pickering had continued to hold an intense dislike for their former son-in-law, in part because his new wife for years kept them isolated from Amy, intercepting and destroying their letters to her (as they would later learn). Thus, when they were finally able to make contact with Amy, they had let her know of their suspicions regarding her mother's death. Given Amy's predispositions, this must have sounded like a further and logically consistent damnation of Dennis Smith. It must have been the easiest thing in the world for her to believe her father was the unseen instrument on the Baltimore-Washington Parkway the day her mother died.

Thus, the question posed by the prosecutor: How could Amy sit quietly in the courtroom and protect someone she so despised? How could she not rat out a man she thought responsible for so much villainy?

Elvira had pondered the question and believed there were ways to understand Amy's stubborn silence. Even before Derrick's death Amy seemed to have held twin secrets: She was hiding from her father the romance with Derrick, and she was hiding from Derrick the fact that her interest in him was based mostly on the color of his skin. At the same time Amy had set no stock in keeping the first secret, just the opposite. Why else did she drive down her street with Derrick seated next to her? Why did she invite him to her house? Why did she flout the chance of discovery? And sooner or later wouldn't her father with his strength of suspicion have been sure to unmask her juvenile game? From the start, in Elvira's opinion, Amy had hoped with all the willfulness and vulgarity of youth for a climactic moment in which her black boyfriend would be revealed, knowing it would drive her father crazy. *Look who I brought home, daddy-o!* Perhaps the night in question was to have been the night. In any event, it requires no special psychological insight to understand that Amy's love-hate state of confusion toward her father was the primary thought streaming through her mind, and that her off-chance fling with Derrick was an afterthought. Whatever her intentions at three o'clock the afternoon of Derrick's death, or at six o'clock, or at nine o'clock, whatever the fluctuations in her plan as the evening wore dazedly on, Elvira was convinced that everything revolved around her father. When the night was over, in jungle terms, in the ceremony of death and survival, Dennis Smith was the victor, and Derrick Jones was not. The fatal shooting, even if committed solely by a predatory Mr. Smith, was an experience Amy had shared with her father. Victims sometimes become attached in an empathic way to the criminals who victimize them; psychiatrists use the Stockholm syndrome to explain the inverse compassion that develops during kidnappings. Might not a strange closeness have developed between Amy Smith and Dennis Smith? Regardless of everything, they were blood. And together they had survived. Elvira believed that to listen to the tape of Amy's phone call to the 911 dispatcher was to realize that partway through the evening Amy had hardened her heart against Derrick. Amy can be heard beseeching the dispatcher in an initially berserk, unendurable wail, but then the tone of her voice steadies, and she speaks as if Derrick was a total stranger, saying a "prowler" has broken into the house. A shot is heard, followed by dead space. Amy has lain the phone receiver on the kitchen counter and is exploring on bare feet the half-lit house. The fifteen-bullet clip for the Beretta has fallen to the floor, and perhaps she steps on the clip or stubs her toe against it. At any rate she picks it up and finds her father, crouched on the staircase, deciding on his options. It must be that Amy then hands the clip to him because this is the most reasonable interpretation of the faint, eerie comment of hers that breaks the silence: "Dad, here, do you need this?" Was Derrick downstairs, waiting, incapable of flight, limbs twitching on a carpet splashed with his blood? Did Amy intend to give her father the ammunition for a finishing shot? *Dad, here, do you need this?* Elvira had been thunderstruck! ("I felt like I'd gotten to know Amy, but after listening to the nine-one-one call I realized I didn't know her at all.") The tape also put a different perspective on the testimony of Jeffrey Gray, the supervising officer who sat with Amy at the kitchen table while the paramedics attended to Derrick's body downstairs. "I took Amy's hand and tried to console her. She was crying and saying it was all her fault," Officer Gray had said at her trial. "I explained she might have to look at the body and identify him, and she became very emotional, hysterical, crying even harder." Whatever the extent of Amy's complicity in Derrick's death, it was possible to believe, in this family of secrets, that she was in possession of a secret so unbearable she had been traumatized into silence.

Traumas can fade away, but afterward there might have been legal practicalities for Amy to consider. She may have concluded her most prudent course was to say nothing and take her chances in court. "I honestly believe Amy decided to take the fall because her father told her she would serve only a year or two in a juvenile home," Elvira said. "Remember, she was just sixteen." If such was the daughter's reasoning, it did not take into account that she would be tried and convicted in adult court and sentenced to an adult prison.

In January the most freewheeling of the five circuit court judges up for election, Vincent Femia, took a crack at Elvira while soliciting campaign funds at a cocktail party. "I wish we didn't have to spend your money on politics and could give it all to charity," he told the people handing him checks. He also used the word "illegitimate" in connection with Elvira's candidacy.

Elvira seized on this chance to get ink for herself, saying without irony to local reporters, "It's sad to see a member of the bench resort to innuendo and name-calling." This was how quickly she could outdo her opposition. Those rumors about a woebegone Elvira sunk in dejection were false, it seemed. She had not lost her flair.

Now the incumbent judges were declining to make any comment whatsoever about her. The garrulous Judge Femia, the judge who had appeared on "60 Minutes," for sentencing the rogue parolee Willie Horton to a life term plus eighty years in the rape of a white Oxon Hill woman, wagged his head and cocked an eye and said when approached, "You are witnessing a great moment in history: Femia tongue-tied." To present a united front, and perhaps to keep each other from talking out of turn, the incumbents were attending all parades and forums in a group. Despite their disparagement of Elvira's campaign, they took her seriously. In Judge Femia's last campaign he had been so confident he had returned all contributions unspent, but this time he and the others were putting the arm on strangers at unfamiliar events, not just the lawyers from the courthouse who were dutybound to ante up. Thus far, the judges had raised $130,000, more than any of the county executive candidates.

A couple of blocks from Dr. Gordon's house lived Duane Void, another Potomac High graduate and ex-jock. Bruce had gotten to know him in a casual way from the basketball courts at the Marlow Heights gym. Duane Void was twenty-one years old and living at home, but he had plans. He was enrolled in classes at Prince George's Community College. One Sunday at twilight Duane Void was drawn outside by the panicked yelping of his German shepherd. On the front lawn he found his dog in a throat-biting struggle with a pit bull. There was a .22 pistol in the house, which Duane Void ran for. This wild scene of a gunman and two pain-crazed dogs turned even wilder with the arrival of Kenneth Milling, the owner of the pit bull. According to the account Bruce heard, Duane Void fired three shots toward the ground to scare the dogs but accidentally struck the pit bull, angering Officer Milling—he was a District of Columbia cop—who would claim later that he thought the shots were intended for him. Officer Milling shouted and cursed and aimed a Glock nine-millimeter handgun. Duane Void, twisting around and backing off several paces, may have been trying to move out of firing range, or he may have been trying to position himself for a shootout, but it is certain the twenty-six-year-old policeman blazed away with the Glock. None of the social constraints that might have welled up inside him—the fact that minutes before he had been enjoying dinner with his mother, the fact that he had been a teammate of Duane Void in three-on-three pickup games in the neighborhood, the fact that he had police-academy training—held back his trigger finger.

Word on the street reached Bruce the next day, and the word was that a gun-happy cop (who would later be tried twice and then acquitted on the grounds of self-defense) had shot to death a young black man. In the total sum of Bruce's knowledge, cops who killed black men in Prince George's County were white cops. He said to his father, "How come we have a redneck cop living in Hillcrest Heights? I thought all the rednecks had been run out of here." But the killer of Duane Void was a black police officer, as Bruce was to learn, and strange as the details of the killing were, this was the strangest detail of all. How to explain a black cop who, surrounded by the sweetness of a good middle-class life, would be so quick to fire on one of his own?

Now that Elvira was a candidate for judge, now that she needed a sensation-provoking case or two to attract media coverage, her job had turned into a succession of misdemeanor cases unworthy of her skills. For months all of her major cases had been kept in limbo because the circuit court judges were recusing themselves. The recusals lent the judges a certain high-mindedness—they claimed to be preserving the neutrality of the courtroom—but they had to know they were also depriving Elvira of her usual means of getting her name out to the public. ("I was generating too much publicity for myself, too many high-profile cases. It's okay for the sitting judges to preside over big cases. They have the advantage, and they are pressing it. They want to squash me flat.") It was as if a secret agreement had been reached to declare her a nonentity.

Then, several weeks ago, Elvira had been driven even farther out of the arena. She was taken to lunch on a Friday by one of the administrators from state headquarters, Phyllis Hildreth, a black woman. It was her role to smooth the way for Elvira to be transferred. "I think it'd do you good to get away from Prince George's," Mrs. Hildreth suggested, not unkindly.

Elvira was almost amused. "What choice do I have?" She had a mortgage to pay, a son to think of.

The following Monday she was assigned to the public defender's office in Charles County, one county to the south. The effect of the transfer was to strip Elvira summarily of her position and to banish her during the workday from Prince George's County.

Today, at Sacred Heart Church in Bowie, final respects were to be paid to Charles (Buzz) Ryan, dead of a heart attack at age fifty-seven. Buzz Ryan had been one of the good-spirited pals of Frank Pesci in the state legislature and on the Kennedy campaign, one of the Prince George's politicians of Boston-Irish sensibility who kept a bottle in a bottom drawer for late Friday afternoons.

"Is this when it starts? Is this when we start going to funerals in order to see the survivors?" Frank said hoarsely at the wind-blown men in gray and black woolen overcoats taking the steps with him, one at a time, up to the cavernous Catholic cathedral. The men had all been together with Buzz Ryan a little more than a month ago at the wake for Howard McGuigan. Red-cheeked from the wind, Frank shook his head. "We're too young for this."

In the vestibule, in a dirge of down-tempo music and steamy breaths and tolling bells, Frank spied a robust Mike Miller, with his peacock-blue eyes and a touch of gray in his ginger-tufted brows and curlicue locks. Mike Miller was holding court at the rear of the church. Members of what Frank referred to as "the brotherhood"—Steny Hoyer, Bud Marshall, Tim Maloney—were coming through the massive wood doors and saying their hellos. (For much of the twentieth century it seemed everyone involved in politics in Prince George's County was of Irish or Italian heritage, the English plantation men having retreated from political life to their patrician farms where they paid emancipated Negroes pennies a day to strip tobacco leaves or, in some cases, having fallen themselves onto proletarian times, their offspring forced into such as police work.) If Mike Miller made an appearance at an event, it was routine for the rest of the brotherhood to show up, too. But, Frank wondered, would Paul Pinsky show? A white man of Bruce Gordon's generation, Paul Pinsky had come to Prince George's County in 1978 in search of Martin Luther King's "beloved community." He had purchased a house on a well-integrated street, and periodically he would get himself arrested outside the South African embassy to remind his two children that integration was a lifestyle still being contested by whole governments. As coach of a state champion Prince George's basketball team, he was given the affectionate name "White Shadow," and in 1986 he was elected to the legislature. The old-timers had muttered in their scornful way, "Communist!" When the 1990 Census caused district lines to be redrawn, the new boundaries placed the Pinsky house in a district where black voters constituted a large majority. Paul Pinsky could take his chances with these black voters, or he could sell his house and change his address, or, as Frank later suggested in his column, he could reach an arrangement with the Miller machine.

As Frank moved to his seat he heard a stage whisper, "There he is. Boy, does he look like he's been through the wringer." It was Paul Pinsky, tall and lanky and morose. Mike Miller rocked on his heels in a mock gangster pose and gave him a thumbs-up.

A few minutes later Frank glanced about and saw Sue Mills enter. In her sheer hose, high heels, foundation, blusher, mascara, eyeliner, lipstick, and frozen-whip platinum beehive, Mrs. Mills still maintained an eye-catching style, but no one waved or stuck out a hand. "The brotherhood treats her like she's diseased," Frank had said of her. Mrs. Mills knelt at a pew in the rear and crossed herself, awkwardly, being Episcopalian. She sat by herself on the curved wood. For the duration of the funeral no one would sit with her or pay her any acknowledgment, although Frank, thinking to play once again the contrarian, was tempted to join her. The politics of the idea warmed him, on a day so raw. ("That'll goose the brotherhood. They'll go nuts. They'll figure that SOB Pesci is up to some kind of trick.") But he waited until the last dirge was sung and the organ music had stopped, and by then Mrs. Mills had left, skipping the Irish wake and the stews and scalloped potatoes. Frank ate and drank his fill and reminisced with the guys about Buzz Ryan. It was twelve degrees outside, too cold for the gravediggers, and the priest canceled the saying of words in the cemetery on the hill behind the church.

• • •

In the middle of winter the Stricklers made a pilgrimage to a Pennsylvania farm high in the Alleghenies, near the hamlet of Penfield and within a few miles of the Continental Divide. It was the place of Dell's upbringing. As with many farm children, Dell had in her youth wanted to get away from the fields and see the world, but that her homestead had stayed in the family was now a source of great joy. ("Whenever I come to the farm I feel my real roots.") Each year Dell and Merv met with a freelance farmer to approve a regimen for the eighty-seven acres. ("Dell's the boss. She's the one who knows farming.") The era in which Dell was raised, the era of plow horses, had emphasized stewardship, and she would not give permission for any of the modern farm men to plow up her fields until she had investigated their conservation practices. This year corn and oats would be planted, and hay would be taken off one of the old meadows. A valley lying fallow had sprung up in feral apple and pine trees and was to be clear-cut, and the useless wood chipped into mulch. The rest of the farm was a hillside of older hardwoods abutting publicly owned forests and was to be left alone.

The summer after their first year of college Bruce, Camilla, and Heather spent a weekend with the Stricklers here. The farmhouse was ancient, without refrigeration or a shower. Sleeping was done on bare-wood floors or in sagged beds. Yet the three college kids were loathe to leave. They woke up to Dell's breakfasts of fresh eggs and sausage and melon. Sweet corn was in season. The air was sweet, stars were in the sky. "It was heaven," Bruce recalled.

In Heather's mind, no more perfect a retirement place existed anywhere for her folks. ("In the early morning you go outside—there's no traffic, no human noises. You feel like time has stood still.") Indeed, the Stricklers had always planned to retire to the farm, but each year they kept putting off the date of their retirement.

Heather: "Every Christmas I have the same discussion with my folks, 'Is this going to be the year, or not?' This has been going on now for eight years, since Dad turned sixty-five."

Merv (putting on a scatterbrained face): "I may look like a guy ready for a rocking chair, but I've still got a few projects to finish. Maybe this year we can talk about moving. Last year was my year to write."

Heather: "That's weak. I can't think of a weaker excuse. He knows he could've set up his word processor at the farm."

Dell: "The house has to be winter-proofed, and we want to put up an addition. A lot has to be done."

Heather: "They could at least spend summers on the farm. Maybe if they hung out in Penfield a little more, they'd find a local contractor who could fix up the place for them."

Heather had tried to find the right moment to remind her folks they might regret these years lost dallying. Her quandary was in whether to continue to feign bemusement or to sit them down and talk turkey? "If it was me and I had a house located in beautiful country and money to fix it up as cozy as can be, I'd have been gone from Hillcrest Heights zippity-do-dah! If Mom and Dad told me today they were ready to move, I'd jump in the car and be there tomorrow to load up a U-Haul. But for some reason they won't say the word. So I keep hesitating. How far should I push them? What's my proper role as their only child? Am I supposed to shove them out of their beloved nest, or am I supposed to respect their wishes and let them wait as long as they want?"

All over America ribbons were being cut for new brick-and-cement public schools named in honor of Thurgood Marshall, the great man from Maryland, perhaps the greatest African-American success story of the late twentieth century, who had died in 1993. The Prince George's version of this ceremony drew state senator Gloria Lawlah, the columnist Carl Rowan, and the Miss Black Maryland beauty pageant winner, who sweetly belted out "Lift Up Every Voice and Sing" to an audience of black parents shouting hallelujahs. No ribbon was cut, though. No new school was being built. The Thurgood Marshall inscription was being placed on the already existing Roger B. Taney junior high school with its dinged-up walls and foot-worn floors, and Gloria would not have had it any other way.

"Yes, we're celebrating," Gloria declared with the fervor of someone who had waited quite a while for this day. "In with the good and out with the bad"—that is, in with the man who made *Brown* the law of the land and out with the man who made *Dred Scott* the law. Roger B. Taney was the nineteenth-century Supreme Court chief justice, also from Maryland, who had gone down in history for his authorship of the *Dred Scott v. Sanford* decision of 1857, and his acceptance of the southern view that black Americans from slave states remained chattel even when they crossed into so-called free states. "Most of us have been cringing for years whenever we'd go by the school and see Taney's name up there. It was an insult," Gloria harrumphed. "This change was long overdue."

Leave it to Frank Pesci to be the one person in all of Prince George's County to take exception, publicly, to an evolutionary action that for everyone else was the way of the world. Writing in his *Journal* column Frank went straight to Justice Taney's defense, claiming he had been overly judged—he was not all bad; he had freed the slaves passed on to him as inheritance from his plantation-master father. "It should be noted that Taney was a product of his time, not an evil man," Frank wrote. Not stopping there, Frank went on to compare Gloria and the other name-changers with the mobs that swarm through village centers seeking vengeance against the statuary of past leaders. He noted that "for more than a century an imposing statue of Taney has stood before the entrance to the Maryland State House in Annapolis, looking down Francis Street to-ward the Annapolis dock and the Chesapeake Bay beyond. What should we do with it now that Taney is out of favor? Topple it?"

How to understand a rebuke of black Prince Georgians for whom the change of a school name was historical fair play? Being lectured by Gloria (her statements were published in the *Prince George's Post*) made Frank feel contrary. "Once more they're dividing up the world according to race, which I'm tired of," he said, explaining himself. "Thurgood Marshall should be a hero to all Americans, not just black Americans, and Justice Taney should not be anybody's antihero. He was more complex than that. I've had a lifetime of seeing people placed into black-and-white pigeon-holes. Did you know I was blackballed not once but twice from a college presidency? You may know about the first time in 1969, when the white board of trustees did me in, but then there was a second time, a few years later, at a historically black college. The presidency became vacant, and I applied for it. A lot of people were pushing me for the job, friends of mine in the legislature, friends from the civil rights movement, but the search committee was an all-black committee, and all the finalists recommended by the committee were black."

It is impossible to be an above-average citizen every day, but when a deep frozen glaze of winter lays over the pokey crocus stems what else is there to do? For five days the ice storm of the century had locked Dell in the house. Wasting not a minute, she worked her way down a list of chores. She made phone calls for Ryland Epworth Methodist and for the PBS station WETA, where the Stricklers belonged to the Pledge Week team. When Dell's ear hurt from the phone, she wrote letters. One went to the editors of the *Washington Post* informing them of her opinion that a large fee for a flattering speech to a Fortune 500 group should not be part of a politician's entitlement.

Meanwhile, Merv was in the Egyptian capital of Cairo. On his birthday, officers of the Federation Aeronautique Internationale surprised him with the Nile Gold Medal, the highest international award in the field of aviation and space education. He was proclaimed "America's foremost aerospace educator." The timing of Merv's trip had been worked out so that he would get back to the States for the spring thaw in the Alleghenies where, if all went well, he and Dell would be tromping in rubber boots.

For some years the most effective way to win political office in Prince George's County had been to get yourself onto a slate of candidates pre-ordained by Mike Miller or, failing that, to get on the slate of one of the other political bosses. The least effective way was to run on a slate of your own making. In Gloria Lawlah's first campaign, when she was still the up-start and the renegade, her slate was lacking in names with proven pull, especially white names. Then someone had a brainstorm. Why not make common cause with the one white politician perpetually on the outs with the bosses but who had a way with crowds, who excited people? Thus it was that in 1986 none other than Gloria Lawlah and Sue Mills appeared on the same slate.

This was one of those oddball, contrived partnerships that come about sometimes in politics. Gloria, when she explained it, would say with a little defensive hitch in her voice, "With Sue, what you see is what you get. Everybody knows where she stands. There's no guile to her." And Gloria would then tell the story of a dentist who befriended her father back in South Carolina in the 1950s. Gloria's father was working at the time as the super in a building where this bespectacled white man with his big break-fast smile had his dental office, and such were the overtures of the dentist that he was regarded as an honorary member of the Negro community. At the supper table Gloria was regaled by examples of the dentist's outstanding qualities, a man who, assuredly, would have no truck with the night-time KKKers running cars up and down the unlit, rutted dirt streets of "Niggertown." Gloria's father, in his NAACP capacity, one day declared himself on the trail of the night riders, and his plan, undertaken with other self-conceived sleuths, was to find and identify those cars caked with mud the morning after any raiding party that took place in the rain. The NAACPers inspected parked cars the length of Main Street, and they queried the black wash-boys who were employed to rub down the vehi-cles of the town's high-toned gents and ladies. License plate numbers were jotted on lined sheets of paper. A frequently muddy car could be construed to belong to a night rider since white folks had little legitimate reason to drive through "Niggertown." Gloria's father did not take the dentist into his confidence, perhaps out of old tribal instincts, which became a critical decision when it came to pass that the dentist's car was among the repeat offenders. ("One thing led to another, and my father discovered the dentist was the local Grand Dragon. My father was shocked to his core. He never got over it.") The point was it's better to know your devils.

Sue Mills was not just any devil, of course. She had star quality, and the alliance Gloria made with her in 1986 proved to be mutually advantageous. Both of them, the two outsiders, won election, and there was reason to believe that, urged along by their say-so, a number of voters crossed racial lines, white voters for Gloria, black voters for Mrs. Mills. As such, it was an exercise in a type of integration, although neither candidate made any high claims about something so expedient. On the other hand, an opportunity for a more authentic integration, the person-to-person type, had presented itself to the two candidates. Prejudices are supposed to tone down when the enemy gains a human face—this is a guiding principle of integrationists—and seeing each other up close, all the times they were thrown together by the campaign schedule, the two women learned things, unexpected things, humanizing things. Such as: Sue Mills had once been an elementary school teacher, same as Gloria. When not out on their free-spirited campaigns, both women were neat and prim homebodies. Both women had saintly, self-effacing, long-suffering husbands. Gloria's children were disengaged from politics in much the same fashion as Mrs. Mills's daughter. And such as, the person Sue Mills chose for a political heroine was not anyone of a conservative bent but was instead the late Gladys Spellman, a liberal, reform Democrat (and close friend of the Stricklers) who was the first modern-day woman elected to the county council. Mrs. Mills, not normally a collector of political souvenirs, had laminated an uncashed $200 check Gladys Spellman donated in 1978. ("I greatly admired her. She talked common sense, and I would go to her for advice, even though we never voted the same way.") Between Gloria Lawlah and Sue Mills there also were separate political agendas, but they had developed a human-faced truce. In the eight years since they ran on the same slate they had held their tongues in public comments about each other. It was seen as a sign of enlightenment in Prince George's County that the two women could politely shake hands and trade pecks on the cheek.

There were those who, having assumed the candidacy of Sue Mills would bring shame to Prince George's County, took gladsome pride in the absence of racial innuendo and in the large doses of dispassion and civility on display thus far in the county executive's race. At the same time, people talked unhappily about the "black eye" being inflicted on the county because of Elvira White's uncivil race for the circuit court.

Had Elvira been in a traditional campaign she might have enjoyed very different reviews. After all, her political biography contained the kind of All-American eccentricities and specifics that make for good exhilarating copy—a woman so postmodern she favored the right to bear arms, so devoted to her son B.J. she was the best-known mother at his elementary school, such a thrill-seeker she leapt from airplanes at high altitudes (although her palms trembled with sweat on arching bridges), and so clean-living she hewed to biblical injunctions (she did not swear and thought bare midriffs "sleazy" and would not listen to off-color stories). In addition, she had the kind of pugnacious, acutely rural charm that wins over skeptics. However, Elvira was not in a traditional campaign, nor was she a traditional campaigner. Forced to commute every day to Charles County she felt at loose ends, removed from the place she thought of as home ground. "I'm losing control over my campaign," she said to friends. Her schedule was fitful. Luncheons had to be canceled. And she was out of the headlines. ("I've been kicked out of Prince George's and no one has read a word about me since. The word on the street is I've dropped out of the race. That's why every chance I get, I speak out.") Speaking out had become Elvira's strongest suit. She was the militant again, speaking out in a disconcerting language, the language of heat and aggressiveness learned in the schoolyards of the Eastern Shore. Describing the Prince George's courthouse scene she reveled in terms like "good old boys" and "house niggers" and "plantation mentality," terms of such incorrectness to keep away from her news conferences all other courthouse lawyers. ("They are what they are—slave lawyers instead of free lawyers!") It made many white people fit to be tied to hear such free-associating from Elvira. To sermonize about racism when you yourself are brimming with racial animus is akin to a marital bounder holding forth for fidelity.

Then again, all people who preach about sin need only to look at themselves to find the original suggestion of it. It happens all the time.

Recently, circuit court judge James Magruder Rea, a lifelong Prince Georgian, of the old white school, informal to the point of interrupting witnesses to chat them up, had retired. Sylvania Woods, a lower-court judge passed over seven times by the Judicial Nominating Commission, had been promoted into the slot. Judge Woods was a black man who had grown up in the rural South. At age fourteen he had enlisted in the navy to go off to World War II. He was now sixty-six years old, four years shy of mandatory retirement. Elvira was quick to swell with indignation, calling his appointment an "obvious political ploy." She gave a blistering, cantankerous account of how he had gotten the judgeship she coveted: "Judge Woods is a very nice man who's wanted to be a circuit judge all these years. The Judicial Commission . . . wouldn't send his nomination to the governor. But one morning they wake up, and he's a valuable commodity. He's got a black face. They need a black face in with all the white faces. Just like that the Judicial Commission gets his name on the list, and he's appointed by the governor, and he's sworn in, boom, boom, boom. My only question is: Are they going to pose him in the middle with the white judges when they take the class photo, like an inside-out Oreo?"

Elvira was regarded now as someone who loved to hear her own voice raised in public disputation to the point that her supervisors felt it important to try to curtail her. She had been reprimanded and officially told to cease and desist with the terms "plantation mentality" and "house nigger."

Of course, what did people at the courthouse call her? *The crazy bitch!*

That "crazy bitch" should be understood by so many to signify Elvira underscored the extent to which she was no longer a mere figure of controversy but a full-fledged outcast.

• • •

There were places Bruce wanted nothing to do with—the Rosecroft Raceway, for one, with its foul universe of horse manure and smoky air pressing down on the memory of his long-ago graduation day. Conversely, Dr. Gordon loved Rosecroft for its raucous energy. The racetrack regulars knew him as "Mister Racetrack" for all the money he had dropped over the years. Last week, without consulting Bruce, he had rehired Delmar to drive him there to play the ponies.

Why should it matter to Bruce, who was dating Betsy every weekend and was less and less a presence in the house? But Bruce considered it another dictatorlike surprise. An argument erupted.

"Delmar is a parasite, Pop," Bruce said. He was at the stove mixing ingredients for hamburger goulash. "All Delmar wants is somebody to latch on to, and you can't let him. You can't be the dog that doesn't scratch."

"What do you want me to do?" Dr. Gordon was immediately sarcastic. "Take out an ad in the *Washington Post* for a chauffeur?"

"Why not?"

"What do I look like? A millionaire? I'll be a pauper if I follow your style of doing things." Dr. Gordon, in his wheelchair, pulled knives and forks from a drawer. "He's not bothering you."

"Yes, he is. I feel totally violated because he goes everywhere in the house when I'm not here. He pokes into anything. He probably brushes his teeth with my toothbrush."

"Boy, you're something. I can't figure out why you got such a bug up your ass about Delmar. He's your kind of person."

So went the huffy rhythm, Bruce all the while mystified. Didn't the case state itself?

Later in the evening Bruce talked it over with a friend. Might he have a hang-up? In household matters he was inclined these days to be conciliatory—except when it came to Delmar. There was a sense of the carefree desperado about the man Bruce did not like. Delmar's chief claim on the household was predicated on his many hours of free time. But why did a hale and hearty and well-spoken grown-up man not have a steady job?

The Grits used to keep switchblades and chunks of metal pipe in their jackets the way you might keep pocket change. Bored, they would beat up on each other (a form of self-hate, the psychotherapists might say). Other times, the Devil provided a substitute.

One day in the spring of 1972, in the middle of the afternoon, the Grits pulled off an ambush from the alleyway of the Hillcrest Heights strip mall.

They chose for target practice a heavyset, isolated-looking black woman with a shopping bag in either hand. Exulting in their advantage, they laughed and yelled, "Run, nigger, run!" When she did, they attacked from behind with pellet guns popped with CO_2 cartridges. The woman ran in a certain, headlong charge through the parking lot and across 23rd Place toward the office of Dr. Gordon. In Doc's diary he could have entered the incident as "Grits Send Me Another Patient." The wounded woman collapsed short of the front door, on the fat hill of the Gordon lawn. Bruce, then a fourteen-year-old on his way home from school, arrived at the same spot. The woman was breathing unevenly. In the back of her flowery yellow dress were splotches of blood, emitted by slow hemorrhages. She seemed ready to bolt again. Bruce had a sharp and immediate apprehension of what it might feel like to be a black person in America. The woman implored him, "Hurry, oh, Lordy, hurry!" A few adult bystanders looked on ineffectually. Although Bruce was able to calm her down and help her inside, he would later remember most of all his fear. He would remember frantically turning his head, scanning in all directions for the Grits. And years afterward he would reflect back with tough-guy, poolroom contempt on his younger self.

Gambling had no stigma in the Prince George's culture. On a recent evening Sue Mills's minister, paying a visit to Gloria Lawlah's office to consult about a new church, was hurried along because Gloria was on her way to Atlantic City for a night of to-your-heart's-content gambling. Everyone knew Gloria had a yen for the slots, for chanciness. "I'd love to build a big Vegas-type casino right here in Prince George's," she said to the nonplussed minister. Lots of people had the yen. The firefighters in many Prince George's towns did elbow-to-elbow trade on casino nights in firehouses and gyms. The legal skim went to buy fire trucks. The financing regimen for a few of these deals was currently in Bruce Gordon's hands. In fact, casino proceeds were a crucial part of the financial packaging Bruce handled in his job.

Across 23rd Place from the Gordon house there were also bingo nights in a brick building on the treeless backlot of the strip mall. The bingo profits were spent next door in a whitewashed Quonset hut, home of the Hillcrest Heights Boys & Girls Club and for thirty years the second home of Bob Magruder. A couple times a year, when the spirit moved him, Bob Magruder would walk over to the Gordon house and holler, "They're off and running," and he and the doctor would head to Rosecroft. There was an old-time dash in Bob Magruder's slicked, unparted hair and his backlit blue eyes and his striped Pinehurst National golf shirts. When Bob Magruder was growing up as a street-savvy, fatherless kid—seven years ahead of Bruce—Doc Gordon had been one of the influences in his life. Not only had Doc stitched up those local residents who had the misfortune to encounter the Grits, he had also taken several of the tough boys under his wing, in particular boys like Bob Magruder, willing to come in from the pavement and let themselves be trained in Golden Gloves pugilism at the Quonset hut. Doc had been the gym physician. The young boxers went to him for checkups and shots of penicillin and a spray of ethyl chloride on their hurting, swollen knuckles. He was with them in the locker room and in their corner at ringside. Bobby Magruder used to wonder, "Who is this guy?! What kind of upstanding citizen is willing to volunteer his time for a bunch of wild kids like we were."

Extraordinary attributes of nerve and recklessness were what were esteemed at the Quonset hut, and, above all, the ability to fight. Bobby Magruder was all fighter and then some. For many years his champion fists could not be bested in the Washington area. When Bobby Magruder was fifteen a crucial event had occurred, prompting him to make a bargain with the Almighty and to forsake the life of a Grit. "Everybody knew me, a punk, a hardcase, always in trouble, headed toward prison" was how he described his early reputation. His father had deserted the family, and his mother was out of patience with him. Summer nights he slept at the Hillcrest Heights strip mall, up on the roof of the drugstore. At three or four in the morning delivery trucks would roll in behind the Safeway, and he and the rest of the pack would run off with Sealtest milk cartons and factory-baked pies and have food fights on Doc Gordon's lawn. The police would sneak up on them in pitch-black squad cars, and there would be scuffling and swinging nightsticks. Food fights built up to fiercer, more desperate action. One night Bob Magruder pressed the small of his back against the bulky front-end of a parked Pontiac Firebird and watched in horror as a kid at the wheel of another car accelerated two thousand pounds of motorized mayhem toward his stomach. At the last second Bob jumped straight up, saved from sure death by instinct or divine device. Even so, the doctors talked of sewing surgical rods into his fractured legs. In the hospital room he lay on his back and gazed heavenward and negotiated. ("My deal was if God would let me walk again, I'd go straight.") It was a year before he could return to classes at Potomac High, but just two years later, with Doc shouting encouragements from below the red and white ropes in the Quonset hut, Bob wowed the Golden Gloves audience. He could take any punch thrown. What was momentary pain to him?

Bob Magruder had gone straight, and more than anything else it was boxing that had saved him. His goal now was to return the favor. Evenings, weekends, spare afternoons, he was a trainer and manager of young talent at the Quonset hut.

In the same vein, he took the time to escort Dr. Gordon to the racetrack.

Steam rose in whitish wisps from a vent on the roof of the Hillcrest Heights Community Center. Television crews set up their strobe lights in the gym, near a hand-lettered sign: "No Personal Basketballs Allowed." Someone had spiffed up the room with freestanding flags—the Maryland crest, the Stars & Stripes. A sheet had been lain artfully over a trestle table, and gray folding chairs arranged in rows. The chairs were filling up. A white, earring-studded youth sat holding hands with a black girl, her head a bevy of tiny braids. These youngsters were the exceptions in an audience of men in suits and women in dresses. More than a hundred people had come out on a blustery night as cold as crystal to hear and to see the candidates for county executive, the largest gathering ever of the Hillcrest Heights Civic Association. Merv and Dell, present at the creation of the association, had emeritus status and took front-row seats.

After making sure that Bea Tignor posters were well positioned, Gloria's operatives distributed buttons, pens, bumper stickers, brochures. "It looks like a Bea Tignor rally," Dell observed.

Dell nudged her husband as Bea Tignor herself glided into view, a short, smooth-faced woman in an appropriately dashing outfit of black nylons, pink jacket, white skirt. She was passing out pens. Merv heaved up from his chair and put out a hand for a Tignor pen. "We need to talk," he boomed at her, a big, eye-crinkling, cheek-puffing grin on his face. "My wife and I live across the street from Gloria, and she insists we sit down with you."

Mrs. Tignor was game. "Fire away."

"Well, I thought we could meet somewhere . . ." Merv paused; he had picked up on her playfulness. "Okay, I have a question. Why would an educated woman in her right mind—in your case, a good-looking educated woman—want to run for county executive?"

Some of the people swirling around had stopped to listen. Mrs. Tignor's expression changed. A sincerity came into her voice. "I'm running because I grew up here," she said, expressively but by rote. "I grew up just down the road in Brandywine. I care about these people. I care!" She had a grip on Merv's thick arms and was pulling herself up on tiptoes. Her chin was inches from his. This was her beseeching in-your-face campaign style, an automatic reflex.

Sue Mills, masses of golden hair piled up as always, had come into the room. Seeing the commotion, she made a beeline for Merv and insinuated herself between him and her rival. "Okay," Merv said, neutrally, "Sue, I'll ask you the same question I asked Mrs. Tignor." He repeated it word for word, including the part about being "good-looking" and "being in her right mind."

"Because some of us aren't in our right mind. That's why we're running," Sue Mills cackled, letting her Adam's apple play, the better for all the world to notice her self-ridicule.

For Bea Tignor the conversation was now queered. She was not going to stoop to this level of satire. She went off to give away the rest of her souvenirs.

Mrs. Mills jabbed Merv in the ribs. She was wearing a red-orange jacket and skirt. A big gold brooch on the jacket matched big round earrings. The outrageous outfits and hairdo were so striking that the configuration of Mrs. Mills's face was an afterthought to most people. It was a hard, slashing face, a brittle face like a painted Easter egg, with thin pinched eyebrows and eyelids and lips that tonight were colored a purplish red.

When everyone was seated, Mrs. Caster Lett, president of the civic association, introduced the candidates and led an opening prayer. "Please, Lord," she said, "please stop the killings."

Mrs. Mills was the first to rise for a short speech. "I was born in a podunk Illinois town, but Prince George's is my home. My children attended public schools here, from kindergarten through Potomac High, and I was PTA president at every level." Then, defiantly, she herself brought up the one issue synonymous with her name, restating her infamous opposition to court-ordered busing: "I think we need to stop busing and spend that money instead on textbooks and teachers." As Mrs. Mills sat down on a folding chair, her skirt rode up over her knees. It was a distracting sight, shiny knees, shiny as doorknobs, and cheerleader's legs in sheer nylons.

Mrs. Tignor, whose skirt was a crucial three inches longer and stretched demurely downward, was next. She utilized the question Merv had posed to her: "Why am I running? I'm a leader. I'm results-oriented. These young men who are heading down a life of crime? I've introduced a bill for a shock boot camp. These dilapidated, vacant buildings in Hillcrest Heights? I can assure you, they'll be torn down." Her speech ran long and she had to be belled twice by the timekeeper before she sat down.

Wayne Curry, making his first run at political office, sported eyeglasses, a barbered mustache, and a natty double-breasted suit and was a more polished speaker. "I like to dwell on the positive," he said. "I like to dwell on the fact Prince George's County is the only jurisdiction in America that has changed from a majority of whites to a majority of blacks where income per capita has gone up, not down." Mr. Curry had an additional word for the Stricklers and the other white people in the audience. "I'm not trying to put you down nor am I trying to praise black people per se. I'm pointing out the progress we've made as a county. And the issue before us in this election is will we remain a county of the new or will we go back to being a county of the old?"

When the candidates were seated again, Merv went to the microphone at the back of the room, the honorary inquisitor. He glanced at his notebook, into which he had been diligently jotting. He was grading the candidates by the tall standards of an idealist. "I don't wish to be insulting," he said, gruffly irreverent, letting everyone know he was serious now, "but I have to say our politicians have a habit of lying to us. So give us the facts, please. No baloney." A give-and-take followed. Mrs. Mills made a reference to "an influential politician" who had rerouted the commuter train line away from Hillcrest Heights in order to have a terminus at Rosecroft Raceway. Merv, who had served with Mrs. Mills on a study group dealing with mass transit, piped up, "That was Mike Miller." It was a line to bring down the house—the boss was not a favorite here—but the applause faltered. Mrs. Tignor's supporters began to remember that in this campaign she was on the Miller slate. In her seat Mrs. Tignor took off her glasses. "I had nothing to do with the Rosecroft decision," she said finally. "I wasn't part of the government when that came up." One of the marginal candidates, Artie Polk, gave his selling point: "I'm the only candidate who isn't connected to political bosses or have political baggage." He looked piercingly at Mrs. Mills. "I don't have to spell out what that baggage is. I think we all know what it is." His remark was calculated to get her goat, and her mouth tightened, and she began to fidget. She leafed through her notes and lifted purple-tinted, gold-rimmed reading glasses off her bosom and set them on her nose. Caricature was attached to Mrs. Mills's every movement. And yet, for this evening at least, she saved herself with a reply to one of the final questions. Could she envision herself living in Hillcrest Heights? While the other candidates ducked the question, Mrs. Mills said, "I did live here for most of my life, just off Wheeler Road. I'd be living here still, but Mike Miller gerrymandered me out of my district. I've always been loyal to Hillcrest Heights." The audience clapped in appreciation.

Afterward, out in the parking lot, Merv commented, "On a scale of one to ten, I'd rate them all fives."

Dell nodded. "I was disappointed, too."

The Stricklers had come here looking for someone who would speak confidently of a black-and-white future, but no one had. The days of messianic optimism were past.

Merv reminded Dell of the political opportunity she had turned down years ago. "I do wonder sometimes what would have happened if I'd run that time instead of Gladys Spellman," she said.

"If I was twenty years younger I'd be running right now. I really would," Merv said.

Sticking his hand into a pocket for his truck keys he lost his balance on a patch of black ice and landed in a pratfall. When Dell saw he was okay, she helped him up. "But you're not twenty years younger, and never will be."

Violence begets violence, and the origin is lost. The shooting of a twenty-four-year-old black construction worker, Archie Elliott III (whose father was a district court judge in Portsmouth, Virginia), had been submitted to a Prince George's grand jury. The killers were two white Prince George's police officers, Wayne Cheney and Jason Leavitt. In setting a course to defend themselves the officers had persevered by firing fourteen chattering rounds into Mr. Elliott, who was described as "acutely intoxicated" and was handcuffed in the front seat of a patrol car. The officers were standing three or four feet from the car when Mr. Elliott extricated a .22-caliber handgun he had hidden in his undershorts. Only later did they learn the gun was unloaded. Now, after due consideration, the grand jury was declining to return a true bill, keeping intact the long streak of absolution for white Prince George's law enforcers involved in violence against black citizens. On the other hand, Officers Cheney and Leavitt seemed entitled to fear for their lives. This was the cycle that kept repeating, the white policemen in fear, the black civilians in fear.

It was lunchtime at a Ramada Inn. A Ray Charles song, low and jazzy, was in the air. The melancholy mood suited Elvira just fine. She sat, weary-eyed, at a cloth-covered table and sipped a glass of iced tea. The postconviction hearing for Amy Smith had been posted on the circuit court calendar, and Elvira felt strangely endangered by it. Soon the intentions of her old friends would be a matter of public record. The smart guess was

that Anne Gold-Rand, with her strongly held opinions, would willingly testify to Elvira's detriment. But what about the three other women with
whom Elvira had worked so closely prior to the trial? Might better feelings
prevail? Or not?

There was Bonnie Aldridge, the investigator, fifteen years a friend, who
had been the first to pick up on the significance of the medical examiner's
report and who had found the next-door witness; there was Gale Saccarelli, the associate counsel, seven years a working partner, who from the
front row of Courtroom 201 had passed notes on slips of yellow Post-it paper to Elvira at the defense table; and there was Suzanne Clements, the
law clerk, who had been a protégée of Elvira's and was sponsored by
Elvira for admission to the bar. Over the course of several cases the
women had developed a sort of compact. Elvira would make the big
strategic decisions and be the one to sway the jurors; the others would
take care of details. The compact had served them well. "We were a team.
I'd like to think that counts for something," Elvira said. Momentarily overcome by nostalgia, she averted her eyes. "There's so much emotion in this
case. I've never been involved in anything like this."

Thinking about it, Elvira had decided the turning point for her at the
courthouse had come not with Jeff Singman's firing ("Jeff's already been
forgotten!") but with her assignment to the Amy Smith case. Feelings in the
office had run high. The scene of an "adamant" Elvira keeping at bay an
increasingly "belligerent" Anne Gold-Rand had reoccurred as well with
Bonnie Aldridge and Gale Saccarelli. Days before Amy's trial they were
still at odds. In the heat of the argument rash things were said. *This is my
case. Just because you're white you can't order me around.* Elvira had been
in a tizzy, wanting to go before Judge Johnson and portray Dennis Smith
as a berserk, throwback father who had killed on behalf of his daughter's
white virtue, but she had needed more factual information. "There must be
something else we can use against him," Elvira had egged on Bonnie
Aldridge, who was trying to turn up evidence of father-daughter incest (a
rumor had gone around) but was not meeting with success.

The attorney and investigator were an odd team, the short, fiery Elvira
and Bonnie, a tall, nervous-looking former policewoman with a blond coif
of hair, but they worked well together. Bonnie, having grown disconsolate
at the clanking of so many prison doors and at the deaths of two friends,
had quit the Prince George's police force a few years ago and returned to
the defender's office to work with Elvira. Their disagreement in this case
was a fairly subtle one and hinged on the emotional scope of Elvira's trial
strategy. Rather than putting on a drama about race and sex, Bonnie argued for prudence—take the emotions out, and also take the theater out.

There was a mundane but plausible way of explaining what transpired the night in question. Amy might have enlisted Derrick to help only with the removal of an expensive set of silverware from the Smith house—an act not even constituting robbery perhaps since the silverware had belonged to Amy's dead mother and was marked for Amy's dowry. And Mr. Smith, awakened by a noise, might have assumed Derrick was an unknown intruder and might have fired with no other provocation, and then, discovering Derrick to be his daughter's unarmed boyfriend, Mr. Smith might have forced his family into a cover-up. But this simple explanation, undramatic, with not much of a racial tinge or a sexual tinge or a Hollywood tinge, was totally unacceptable to Elvira, who was carried away by stronger feelings. ("Elvira couldn't be budged. None of the discussing did any good. She was a majority of one.")

On trial day, lacking no confidence, Elvira stuck to her strategy of Mr. Smith as "pure villain" and Derrick Jones as "pure victim," and lost the case for Amy. Could it be Elvira deliberately lost, out of a dislike for her client? Not very likely, everyone agreed. Elvira's desire to come out ahead in all contests was such that little stock was set in any theory she had tried to throw the case, even on a subconscious level. There was a popular theory, however, that Elvira, vainglorious and arrogant and presuming herself unbeatable, had set aside common sense and gambled to win twice over—trying to get Amy off and also trying to protect Derrick's good name. The theory was that Elvira had relied on her ability to give a movielike performance, a performance meant not incidentally to add to her star image, and had blown it. Attendant on this theory was the much-discussed idea that this case was the sort to which professional scriptwriters and directors might bring their intelligence to bear. Right from the start producers for such as Diane Sawyer, Sally Jesse Raphael, "Hard Copy," "Current Affair," and Oprah Winfrey had made known their interest. To Elvira's credit the hounding of the TV people had not moved her; she had refused to be their stage guest. (If the situation called for it Elvira could be quite adept at dodging cameras. A few years back, in 1989, an excruciatingly personal "media circus" had been forced on her—the bigamy trial of her husband Bertrand, charged with (and later acquitted of) forging papers and jumping the gun in marrying his girlfriend—but, according to Judge Melbourne, "despite all that going on, all that enormous personal stress, Elvira went right into the courtroom and did her business, cool as you please.") Toward the end of the Smith case, however, Elvira had given in to the enticement of fame, or so the accusation went. Gale Saccarelli—who, without saying so directly, gave every indication she planned to be a hostile witness at the postconviction hearing—claimed Elvira had tried to line up a tour of the talk shows to commence right after the trial was over: "She asked me to contact the shows. I told her, 'You can't do this.' " In addition, there had been a running skit in which Elvira, primping and standing on tiptoes behind her desk, would rehearse lines from her closing argument as if an actress might someday repeat them in a movie version. Gale Saccarelli remembered it as "a big office joke: Who was going to play Elvira in the movie?" However, Ms. Saccarelli added, "Speaking privately to Elvira, I believed she was serious." Elvira's awe at herself had grown to fantastical proportions, it was said. Her desire for publicity had influenced her thinking to the point she undertook only a halfhearted effort to keep Amy's trial in a juvenile courtroom, from which news reporters are barred, and instead was glad of the move to an open, adult jurisdiction where she could grandstand for journalists she imagined to be her helpful talent scouts—this was the office theory. Their consensus was that Elvira really expected Hollywood to come calling.

As these remarks were repeated to Elvira, she listened, elbows on the table, a half-eaten salad pushed aside, iced tea melting away, and did a riveting slow burn. What really got her attention was this last mortifying insinuation. She rolled her eyes. "That's incredible. Talk about bending things to their view of reality," she said in a tight voice. "Yes, that business about a movie was a joke, a real joke. You know, I can't believe this. Everything I've ever said or done is being twisted or shaded to alter the connotation. I swear to you, the whole courthouse was in on the joke. The prosecutor on the case, another black woman, was talking about actresses who might play her part. Everybody laughed about it. But, see, the problem was these white women were the ones who actually took it seriously. They couldn't stand it. A black woman was going to be put up on the big screen?! A black woman was going to be the hero?! In their heart of hearts they couldn't stand it!"

The nature of their motives was clear now to Elvira. The case had released hidden jealousies—that was her theory.

Tent worms massed in a kwanza cherry, a screen door dangling on one hinge—chores for a man Friday, but where was Delmar?

The return of Delmar to the Gordon home was destined not to last. What chance did Delmar have, even on his best behavior? As it was, he hastened along his second banishment by doing a poor job on the late-winter shoveling and by leaving unfinished the spring raking and by forgetting to shut the gate when Bruce's dog was off his leash. There were also the sloppy shakedowns for money ("I need twenty dollars real bad to buy a birthday present") and the frequent trips to a Burger King where Doc got wired on coffee and watched, out of earshot, while Delmar table-hopped and talked to his pals in recessed booths. There were more unexplained solo jaunts in the Cadillac and items missing from dresser-tops. The disappearance of Bruce's expensive watch was the final straw. He couldn't help but wonder if Delmar had snatched it.

"Come on, Pop, Delmar's used up his chances," Bruce said. "If I catch him in my room one more time, I'll have his ass in jail."

So Dr. Gordon gave his doleful blessing, and Bruce delivered the news: "You're trash! Stay away from my father, and stay away from me. We're through with your shit."

Looking at it with full objectivity, Dr. Gordon was of two minds about Delmar. "Yeah, yeah, he has only himself to thank for getting kicked out again. But what wrong did he really do? He was happy to put up with me, an old eccentric. Which is more than I can say about Bruce. Yeah, Bruce puts up with me, but he's not happy about it." And Bruce? He had to admit it was a piddling victory, as if a poor schmuck trying to make a half-honest buck was responsible for wrecking the Gordon family! But this thought came later on, after Delmar had been put off the premises and Bruce's anger was spent.

The trip to the Deep South in the summer of 1974 was Merv's idea—a gift to Heather and Camilla on their graduation from Potomac High and a means of continuing their education. They went by car, with Merv the driver and chaperon. In Virginia and the Carolinas the sunburnt, skinny-armed attendants at the pump-and-go's filled Camilla with dread, and she refused to get out of the car. ("We were this little integrated group from the North sticking our nose where we didn't belong. The only precedent for people like us were the Freedom Riders. I kept thinking we were going to get jumped or ambushed, but Mr. Strickler acted like we shouldn't have a worry in the world. He was so weird.") This was his debonair Gandhian style, to give no outward sign anything could be out of the ordinary. It proclaimed Merv Strickler wherever he went. Hitting Georgia, Camilla was prodded by his subtle encouragements to place a tentative foot inside the moccasin joints and pecan stands. Merv treated her to a box of candies. They reached Florida and its reptile emporiums. In Daytona Beach a young white university professor who wanted to pick Merv's brain about aviation insisted on standing them to a restaurant dinner. The place had a dance floor, and with nervous gallantry the professor did a few spins, one girl at a time. After Camilla's turn a carrot-topped white youth, glaring with furious repudiation, yelled out, "What you doing dancing with her, boy?" The young professor blurted out, "She's my sister," and Merv haw-hawed. It tickled Merv no end to see the professor flushing with pride. ("Mr. Strickler was always impressed when people rose to the occasion, never thinking it might create a backlash. Whereas I was thinking 'Let's get out of here before this redneck goes and gets his cousins, and we have to deal with Round Two.' ") Merv tried to explain to Camilla how much worse things once were, how during the war he and a couple of black GI friends were met in their swim trunks by Miami beach signs saying "Dogs, Jews, Niggers Not Allowed," how he was ordered off a bus for sitting on a "colored" seat with his friends, how even after the war he and Dell had waited an hour for service at a Hickory Pit in liberal California because they were in the company of the black man John Somersette—but thanks to people of good intentions the beach signs were now uprooted and the bus drivers and waitresses reoriented and even poorly intentioned people were coming around. As far as Camilla could see, however, there was no resounding success, and if their little threesome had so far been lucky enough to escape a beating then luck was all they could credit. ("Maybe he could afford to be blasé because he had some kind of white cloud that follows him around, but I just couldn't buy his philosophy that good always triumphs over evil.") In Alabama, they were treated boorishly in a diner. Again Merv put on his unflappable face, and the waitress grew progressively nicer. It may not have been a life lesson, but Camilla was beginning to get the point. ("It was one of the best put-downs I've ever witnessed because he got the waitress to give us the proper respect without getting down to her level. I remember thinking, 'Okay, so that's where Mr. Strickler exists. Up on this plane where he expects everybody to join him.' He and I talked a lot on the drive back to Maryland, and he listened to what I had to say. I felt very grown-up. It got me over a little bit of snobbery because in my house I had the impression the only insightful, thinking people in the world were poets and actors.")

"Racism" was no longer an automatic vote-getter among black Prince Georgians. "Racism" was part of Old America. In fact, "racism" was becoming so rapidly obsolete that Elvira, expecting to find bad in white people nearly everywhere she went, seemed like she was from the wrong generation. Two times in the past year Elvira had gone into Denny's restaurants, once in her churchgoing duds after Sunday services, another time after taking B.J. to an amusement park, and both times she had felt a lack of respect from the white staff—white patrons were seated and served while she was left impatiently in line, and a waitress then brought her cold food on a plate stained with somebody else's breakfast eggs. After the second incident Elvira was overcome by indignation. She borrowed a notebook from another customer and loudly asked for names, writing them down while B.J. hid his face. *Oh, Jesus, why is it my mom who's always popping off?!*

Then again there is cause sometimes to believe no black American can ever be too paranoid. In the process of going to the Washington Lawyers Committee on Civil Rights to file a declaration about her mistreatment, Elvira learned there were dozens of complaints on record against the Denny's chain. A certifiably racist idea seemed to have become imbedded in at least a few Denny's managers. It went something like this: What with the deadbeats and obnoxious bombasts in the African-American population ("A-A's" according to corporate lingo), the restaurant chain was considered better off if a "closed" sign was put up whenever a black person came to the door, a policy carried out at a couple of Denny's restaurants in California. Not long after Elvira's declaration the clincher came in the form of six young black brushed-down, pedigreed Secret Service agents who at a Denny's in Annapolis had an experience not unlike Elvira's. When the complaint of the president's protectors was registered, the owners of Denny's felt obliged to buy some goodwill, and a settlement of $54 million was now in the offing. Apparently thousands of black Americans had been given a hard time by Denny's hands around the country—for several days now a lineup of people in Los Angeles had milled through a car showroom, emptied of cars, where the dealer was helping them fill out claim forms—but these thousands had suffered in silence until the headlines about the Secret Servicemen made it permissible to come forward. How to account for such silence? A tiredness at being a victim? A red-faced shame? A "what's-the-point feeling," as one man said? Or perhaps, for some, a pride in finding their own solution—as in Prince George's County where more and more restaurants were owned by black entrepreneurs?

Bruce: "**Here's** a good one. Which person has come closest to achieving the Zen center of racial harmony: the person who can identify racism from a million miles away or the person who can't see it at all? Which person most improves society?"

• • •

Amy Smith, for whom temporary freedom was now in the offing, had written a short hopeful letter in her prison cell to be sent to the Massachusetts home of her grandparents. Might she, by her twentieth birthday, one year hence, be able to celebrate full freedom in the precious mad intimacy of a shopping mall somewhere? What did they think?

A more formal letter concerning her postconviction hearing went from Amy to her new attorney, Larry Polen, a slightly built white man who practiced law in an office of thin paneling in suburban Baltimore. Bubbly and optimistic though Amy might have felt, the task at hand was a mighty one. Everything was contingent on Mr. Polen's ability to assemble a set of courtroom witnesses willing to swallow their pride on her behalf—witnesses drawn from a group of people with no particular liking for the task or for each other. To start with, out of a family disunited by dark deeds and rumors of dark deeds, Mr. Polen had to find a way to give the appearance of unity. Gentle white-haired souls Thomas and Elizabeth Pickering had to be convinced to cooperate with the despised Dennis Smith. (When Amy was sentenced to prison, Mr. Pickering had said, "I feel like we're losing another child," to which Mrs. Pickering had added bitterly, "And we're losing her at the hands of the same man.") As for Amy, she would have to sit in court and smile sumptuously upon her parents whose high-pitched tones and devastating glares had been memorable up on the witness stand at her first trial. (Amy believed that her worst suspicions about her father and the woman who replaced her mother were confirmed one evening prior to the trial. Sorting through old snapshots at the home of the Pickerings, Amy had stared with dumb recognition for some minutes at a photograph of her father standing happily with a woman, dated 1975, prior to the death of Judith Pickering Smith. But the woman in the photo was not her mother; it was the woman who would later marry Amy's briefly widowed father.) Given all that had passed between Amy and her parents, and between the Pickerings and the Smiths, how might Larry Polen compel them to breathe the air of the same courtroom?

Not to mention Anne Gold-Rand, Bonnie Aldridge, Gale Saccarelli, and Suzanne Clements, who would have to put on a face at considerable variance from the face they had presented when they were assisting Elvira. For a staff attorney to testify voluntarily against another staff attorney was a rarity of the first order for the Prince George's public defender's office. Probably the biggest asset Larry Polen brought to the case was his far remove from the intrigue, although even he could tell what Elvira's standing at the courthouse was. "Boy, I wouldn't want to be in her shoes," he had said soon after his first briefing. This dislike of Elvira, he had thought, would stand him in good stead. But now that the date for the hearing was approaching he was not at all sure he could get any of the staff members to disown the job they had helped Elvira do. The four women were still agonizing over their decision. Was it really necessary to go beyond routine cooperation? Bonnie Aldridge, who had earlier written a letter to the governor recommending Elvira for a judgeship and who had stood by Elvira in regard to allegations about her off-duty clients, said, "I don't want people to say we're testifying because Amy is white and Elvira is black. Let Larry Polen subpoena me. I'd rather do this by the book. Maybe then everybody will feel better."

The Mervin Strickler Leadership Award?! Merv was not yet aware of it, but officers of the National Congress on Space and Aviation had it up their sleeve to establish an annual award in his honor. After a long run of service in promoting the academic study of mechanical objects that fly, Merv had become an aviation celebrity. Accolades were coming his way, thank-yous for a job well done. At several technically minded colleges, his name had been thrown into the hopper for vacant presidencies, and he might have cashed in had he not preferred his independence, a world-traveler's independence. It had been his life's ambition to sell educators of all varieties on the value of aviation as an interdisciplinary vehicle, and this ambition had taken him—with Dell at his side when they could swing it—to the far corners of the globe, to Siberia and Puerto Rico, to Outer Mongolia and Hawaii. He had finagled his way into Moscow in 1970, ahead of detente, and later he was one of President Nixon's designated peacemakers. A favored guest, he was invited back to Moscow time and again. Must be CIA or a secret Red, the talk was. But Merv was enjoyed by the Soviets because he knew chapter and verse on Igor Sikorsky and the other great Russian aviators. The strange part of these travels is that they had kept Merv and Dell rooted in Hillcrest Heights—"You have to have a place to return to, a place to call home." Constant comings and goings, by the same token, did not leave them much time to undertake a serious business, like moving their possessions to an old farm in the Alleghenies. A decision was at hand, though, and Merv and Dell had decided they would take all the steps necessary to change their address.

"If we don't do it soon, we never will. My roots have always stretched back to the old sod, but, after a while, the elasticity starts to wear," Dell was saying to a woman named Cheerful, a friend from Ryland Epworth Methodist. Worship services were over for another Sunday, and the parishioners were jostling at the coatracks.

Merv joined in. "What hung us up this past year was my FAA book, but, thank God, I'm done. The manuscript is off at the printers. Now, if we can get a break in the weather, we can do a survey and see if there's a suitable place to build."

"The old house isn't really habitable anymore. We'll have to build a new one," Dell explained.

"I'll be ready as soon as I'm back from Egypt," Merv said, adding in a low, excited murmur. "The government of Egypt has asked me to prepare a curriculum based on space and aviation."

A here-we-go-again expression came into Dell's face. She tugged at his coat sleeve. "Just a minute, I didn't know Egypt was definitely on the agenda."

Merv's cheeks reddened. "It's not definite, but they're waiting for my answer."

"Just remember, last year was your writing year, this year is supposed to be our building year. We don't have time for another traveling year."

Merv gave Cheerful an imploring look. "Didn't I five minutes ago tell you I couldn't give you a guided tour of Russia this year? You're my witness."

Dell laughed and patted him affectionately on the back. He grew ever more florid. "I swear, I've been turning down travel invitations right and left."

"Except for Egypt, and God knows where else." Dell's expression contained a merriment at Merv being Merv.

In the matter of the county executive's race the Stricklers had liked the original scenario of Gloria Lawlah versus Sue Mills because it would have shown the outside world how a black politician and a white politician could be opponents without a hate-thy-neighbor undertone. And it would, they believed, have resulted in a victory for the black politician. Ninety percent of the white liberal vote and ninety percent of the overall black vote—this was to be Gloria's winning coalition. But it was not unfolding like that. With Gloria out of the race, there were—believe it or not—credible projections of a Sue Mills landslide. Several months into the campaign Mrs. Mills held a three-to-one lead in the public opinion polls. The magnitude of her lead seemed to surpass any margin of error attributable to her high-flown name recognition. The rest of the field had been served notice. "She is the person to beat," a *Washington Post* article reported. If black Prince Georgians split their votes between Bea Tignor and Wayne Curry, then Mrs. Mills would carry the election. Simple math in America of the late twentieth century: One strong white candidate is mightier than two strong black candidates—assuming people will vote along racial lines, which is what many political observers, not just Frank Pesci, assumed. According to the *Washington Post* article, Mrs. Mills was "well positioned to win a fractured Democratic primary, especially one in which some analysts say racial identification may be a strong predictor of voting patterns."

Having said that, there was more to Sue Mills's good fortune than racial indicators. She was a charismatic leader who believed in the efficacy of the thirty-second sound bite, and she was also the lady-next-door who would phone a dispatcher to get your cat out of the tree. The *Washington Post* credited her with redefining herself over the years as a politician in the style of a big mama, personable and responsive. "You call her, the sun doesn't go down before she calls you back" was her approach with her constituents. Hence her popularity with neighborhood activists, even the likes of the Stricklers. Moreover, Mrs. Mills appeared to be making a good-faith effort, correctly, astutely, toward voters of every color. On a Saturday, hammer in hand, she had pounded nails for the refurbishing of a broken-down house where lived a ninety-two-year-old black woman, part of Operation Tom Sawyer and part of Mrs. Mills's people-helping-people politics. And recently she had campaigned at the Hillcrest Heights strip mall. It was a scene the integrationists might have scripted, the lady in the beehive grabbing feverishly for black hands. At the carryout rib joint, meat slabs sizzling on blackened grills, the cooks in their sauce-smeared aprons watched with near astonishment as Mrs. Mills, all smiles, breezed in and out the door with her chatty calling card: "Remember me on Election Day. You know who I am."

Elbert and Daphne Jones once held dear the social contract. They hoped to influence their son, Derrick, by their enviable position in the grand pattern of American endeavor. They thought something good would rub off on him if they moved into Enterprise Estates with its nitrogen-green, parklike yards and neighbors such as Wayne Curry. And they thought Derrick would learn law and order if he sometimes tagged along with Mrs. Jones to the precincts of the transit police, where she was as-

signed, in a desk job, to the internal affairs division. By Derrick's deport-
ment, by his excellent standing with the neighbors, they believed he had
proven them right. "Derrick never had one hassle with the police, nada.
He was a good-behaving child, not mischievous, not acting up or cutting
up," said Mr. Jones. "Most of the transit officers knew him because he
would come in with his mom and interact with them. He had a lot of respect for police and authority and for adults, period. He knew how to
carry himself around adults. He wasn't the type of kid who did the way a
lot of kids do, tell adults where to kiss it. That wasn't our son. Our son followed the letter of the law." Stories always come to mind after a death,
and the one Mr. Jones lingered on involved a run-in Derrick had had with
another teenager on a sidewalk in Enterprise Estates. The other boy had
produced a gun and stuck it shakily in Derrick's face—it belonged to the
boy's father, a police officer. More than one teenager has pushed such a
moment to a do-or-die conclusion, and Derrick said afterward he was confident his training in karate would have enabled him to overcome his tor-
mentor. But Derrick's training in the life arts enabled him to walk away,
with a flip of the hand. He came home and asked his father to call the police. Mr. Jones was proudest of this moment, a boy fancying so adult a solution, and it was this image of Derrick Jones his parents wanted to have
officially recognized at the courthouse—the wholesome, bright-eyed boy
who went by the commandments.

But for months, since realizing what the cost of a second trial might be
to Elvira, the Joneses had felt self-conscious about it. Painful though it was
to give up on Derrick's last chance, they had decided they must throw in
their lot with Elvira. Mrs. Jones had agreed to witness on Elvira's behalf at
the hearing.

"It's become a race issue," Mr. Jones explained. "All the witnesses testifying against Miss White are white people." A strongly protective look
swept over him. "Miss White doesn't bite her tongue or hold back. She
doesn't dress it up, doesn't sweeten it up. I'm somewhat the same way. I
like how she is. But the bosses don't. She doesn't know her place. That's
been the thing black people have had to deal with as long as I've been
alive, the Yessir Boss thing."

All through the first stages of the Amy Smith case Elvira had maintained
high-powered connections. Her law intern was Catholic University student
Melissa Miller, daughter of Mike Miller. Placing his young impressionable
daughter under the mentoring of the steely tough-mouthed litigator had
been Mike Miller's idea of "a can't-miss valuable experience," an experi-

ence to get his daughter ready for "the real world." When the internship was over, Elvira duly lent her name to Melissa's application to the bar, and, according to Elvira, Mike Miller had knocked on her office door one day to declare with a wink of a blue eye, "I owe you one"—a promise now worthless. "Although I wish I had it on tape, just so I could play it at a press conference," Elvira said bitterly on a spring morning.

She was passing, quick and manic, through the waiting room of the brown-bricked, orange-trimmed Charles County public defender's building with its editions of *Country America* and *Country Sampler* in the magazine rack. Slamming shut her office door, she began rattling off the things irking her. This was Elvira's style now, no perfunctory courtesies, no small talk about children or holidays. Elvira was willing now to tell everything, to name names and burn bridges, since she was thoroughly finished and disgusted with her earlier time at the Prince George's courthouse, the time of accommodations and role-playing. "That courthouse is one of the most controlled, incestuous, inbred, to-the-manor-born places you will find anywhere in America," she said. She talked with the conviction of someone who has discovered afresh truths that have always been known. "It's seventeenth-century political incest. The lawyers and judges all have a sister in the domestic relations bureau or a mother in land records. Sons and daughters start off here as part-time help when they're sixteen. If you're not born into a job, you've got to worm your way in, and to do that you've got to be connected. Everybody's connected to everybody. Maureen Lamasney is a protégée and friend of the first public defender, Edward Canans, whose law partner, Tim Maloney, sits on the Senate Appropriations Committee that controls state funding for the public defender's office. Another former partner in the firm was Darlene Perry, who's a circuit court judge and whose good friend Ned Camus sits on the Judicial Nominating Commission that rejected me. Tim Maloney's brother was a law clerk for Judge Perry and now works in the state's attorney's office. The son of the chairman of the Prince George's County House delegation, Joe Vallario, also works in the state's attorney's office. I remember going to the courthouse fifteen years ago and asking someone why all the officers of the court were white, and he said, 'That's the way it's always been.' A few black folks have been allowed in since then, but not many. There was a young black woman volunteering in the state's attorney's office who wanted a summer job but was told there were no openings. The next thing you know Melissa Miller gets the summer job, and she gets an internship with me. That's how it works. Some of the people who control the purse strings threatened to reduce funding for the public defender's office if they didn't get rid of me. The way I heard it"—Elvira had come by private information from a friend who, she said, was too scared to go public—"three of them got together, one from the legislature, one from the state's attorney's office, and one from the Judicial Nominating Commission, and they went to Martha's Vineyard to interview Amy's grandparents. The real purpose was to turn Mr. and Mrs. Pickering against me because during Amy's trial the Pickerings had lavished affection on me. They sent me flowers; they sent me cards; Mrs. Pickering was going to do this or that for me. I'm sure a successful hatchet job was done on me. I'm sure my name is mud with them. That's been the strategy all along. I am accused of reducing everything to black and white, but, when you are black and all the people against you are white, that's black and white, isn't it?"

Yes, Elvira had plenty to say, and most of it validated what black Prince Georgians on the outside had always figured went on at the courthouse. To them the courthouse was the id like center of the county. Progress lay in the green grass and black asphalt of the subdivisions, but the courthouse was still a primitive place, overrun by racial spectres and haunted by tribal ways. Little doubt existed that a campaign was under way to declare Elvira unfit for the courthouse, and each day the campaign was getting more obvious. All the hobnobbing she had done, all her efforts to fit in, it seemed, could not save her now. A celebrity of the courthouse, someone the system had helped create, was being destroyed by the system. But did Elvira's turn of fortune add up to a conspiracy? She had compiled a list of wrongs done her, the violations of protocol filed against her, the official investigations imperiling her law license, plus other random events that perhaps could be construed as organized activities meant to destabilize her. There had been a break-in at her house on June 23, 1993. "Forced entry" was noted in the police report; the "valuables" taken were papers from her personal files. She believed strangers had entered her house to inspect her files on two or three additional occasions; her bank records were mixed up, the pages out of order. She thought a man in a car had her under surveillance. She believed her phone was tapped, and she paid a security firm for debugging services. "I say certain things on the phone, and I hear them later on the grapevine," she explained. "I don't know exactly who would order a wiretap on me, but only judges have that power, and the people with power over the judges are the political bosses."

Where institutions are capricious and heavy-handed, people resort to conspiracy theories. So it was with Elvira and the courthouse, a place like most courthouses, without Caesars, no Darrows, no grand dukes of the law, just petty pols, a place where everyone's job is based on acts of hurt and fraud and lust, and motives are constantly colored by impurities. But the Prince Georgians who assumed a conspiracy had been hatched—and for a while they included not only Elvira but some of the people Gloria Lawlah associated with in the Black Alliance—did not credit the old courtesies of the courthouse. In such a milieu conspiracies are not necessary. When you are on the inside you know without being told what is expected of you. You know, and everyone knows. Elvira herself had to know; she had been on the inside not so long ago.

8   ***The thoroughbreds*** were in the paddocks at Rosecroft, and on a day that ranneth over with light Bobby Magruder came by the Gordon house and hollered.

All that afternoon Doc's horses finished out of luck, and he complained about jockeys who cheat and track stewards who do not dry out muddy patches around the turns. But these were happy complaints. Mister Racetrack was full of piss and vinegar again. Who cared about a few lousy fifty-dollar bets?!

Back at home, still in a gay mood, Dr. Gordon embraced the rejuvenating exercises for his leg. Dust from months of disuse flew off the rubber contraption. He was still at it when Bruce walked in. "I had me some fun at the track today. Went with Bobby Magruder," Dr. Gordon informed his son.

"Great!" Bruce said unctuously. He had had a surly day at Banc One. "If you're not hanging out with Delmar, you're hanging out with smelly horses."

"You don't know." Dr. Gordon's chest heaved. "You don't know the friends I've got at the track."

"More lowlifes! I'm sure they love you. They love anybody who burns money."

"You have no call to talk to me like that. This is still my house."

"You're the one who's always going on about money."

"You watch yourself. I may be an old cripple, but I bet Bobby Magruder can still whip your ass, Mister Kung Fu!"

• • •

To be a black person who judged by color among white people who judged by color: in the paranoid atmosphere of the courthouse you were sure to end up badly.

A *Washington Post* reporter, Jon Jeter, had been assigned to write an article about Elvira, and he began by asking people at the courthouse for their opinions. Few of them wanted to be quoted, and fewer still wanted to be quoted saying anything of a complimentary nature. Dwight Jackson, the homicide prosecutor who in another interview had been willing to talk of the courthouse as "a very informal place, where you can go in, put your feet up on a judge's desk and talk deals" and had called the courthouse "the last line of defense for the white establishment," was about the only one.

Dwight Jackson's father, a police officer, had been among the first modern-day black immigrants to Prince George's County, settling his family in Landover in 1964. Dwight Jackson was then a long-legged kid playing roughhouse games in the tunnels and on the slopes of the not-yet-opened Beltway. Later, but before he became a respectable burgher, Dwight Jackson was a gypsy newspaperman, a lawyer in a firm with Wayne Curry, and an aide in the breakthrough campaign of Alex Williams in 1986 for the chief prosecutor's job. (The white courthouse establishment had been partially dispossessed by the election of Alex Williams, friend and political ally of Gloria Lawlah and a founder with her of the Black Alliance—and also a senior partner of a law office where Elvira had worked on her way up. "If white folks can have their political networks, why can't black folks?" Gloria once said.) During this past winter Alex Williams had been nominated by President Clinton for a federal judgeship, and just recently Dwight Jackson had decided to file candidate's papers to try to succeed Mr. Williams as chief prosecutor.

A politician now, Dwight Jackson was advised by his campaign aides to say nothing about Elvira to the *Washington Post* reporter, or, if he felt an obligation to talk, then he should use words that said nothing. But how do you justify being an equivocal friend when someone is beset. Even in her crankiest moments Elvira had been able to hang on to some nobility. He went ahead with the interview. "Elvira elicits some very strong feelings in a lot of people" was how he explained her. "Some people's perception is that she is this loudmouthed black woman always stirring up trouble, and some people think she gets in trouble simply because she talks too much."

Dwight Jackson might have cut himself off right there, but, pulling himself up to full stature, he gave the *Washington Post* man the kind of quote he knew would get printed. He compared Elvira to the baseball player Curt Flood, whose career a generation ago was lost when he challenged a system that made players beholden to team owners but who today gets credit for creating the new system of free agency. "From an institutional dynamic, what Elvira's doing is challenging the way things are and have been done," Dwight Jackson said to the reporter, for attribution. "The more they beat up on her, the stronger she gets."

On the morning the *Washington Post* article was published, under the headline "On the Road Less Traveled," Dwight Jackson, related by marriage to Gloria and by social kinship to Elvira, was stopped several times as he made the rounds of the courthouse. "The reaction I got was very, very intense," he said later. "It was the first time I realized what it feels like to be on the receiving end. These people were on my case. 'You said that about Elvira White?!' "

Bruce was not cut out for a choir, but he could belt out a song with verve, and belt out he did for the Passover ritual at his sister's home in Boston. It was a family sing-along—his sister, an aunt and uncle, although not Bruce's father, who, defeated by skinny airplane aisles, had stayed behind in his wheelchair. The lead singer was a best friend of Bruce's sister, a black woman, who hit the high notes and complimented Bruce on his good try. Honorary family member Camilla, with her two preadolescent children, came for breakfast the next morning, and she and the kids took Bruce out and about the wind-rustled spring foliage. The children preened a bit, reciting titles of books they were reading, and showed a tender, protective sense, pressing their heads warmly against their mother, but later they consented to take Bruce's hands.

"You have the most wonderful kids in the world," he said, when he and Camilla were alone. "Interracial kids must get the dominant genes, not the recessive ones. It must be the opposite of inbreeding."

Pleased as Camilla was with her offspring, and she was quite pleased, it was a tricky business figuring out what was best for them. To wit: which school to enroll them in? Camilla had tried the public system, but, despite classmates from Haiti and Cape Verde and Japan, there was a distinctly white-honed cast to their learning. They were now in a private Waldorf school, entrusted to a setting that lacked diversity, but Camilla judged the results to be strangely more satisfactory.

"I can't make up my mind," she said to Bruce. "I kind of think I should transfer them back to public schools. The older they get, the more I think of us at Potomac. Yes, it was turbulent, but I feel we learned a lot about life, and Hillcrest Heights learned a little from us: We were the positive example."

"I'd say transfer your kids. We lived through it, they'll live through it. Public school is the real deal."

"You probably don't know how real it is. The level of racial harassment can be horrifying. I have a friend whose daughter was tormented to the point she had to secure a restraining order from a judge. I don't know how far I should go to throw my kids into a situation where they basically are sacrificial lambs."

Who could fail to swell with admiration at such a woman, trying her utmost to balance the betterment of society with the betterment of flesh and blood? Going head over heels for Camilla was a highly irresistible proposition, but on this weekend, for the first time since high school, Camilla was being chaste with Bruce—out of "solidarity" with Betsy. "Camilla wants to keep me right," Bruce would say later. "She doesn't want to sabotage anything or leave her mark. Camilla has tremendous integrity. She believes sex is wonderful and great, but you can get beyond it." As for Camilla, she would explain this latest phase in their long crazy sojourn thusly, "Our relationship is evolving, but it feels to me every bit as solid, if not more so, than the commitment I made to my husband when I said those wedding vows. I have a very non-monogamous, pan-fidelidous, bizarre code. It's fluid and flexible; it's not limited. Unfortunately, sex between Bruce and me is out for now. I feel a need to be respectful of any woman in his life."

Things between Bruce and Betsy, however, had become more tentative, and in a matter of a few weeks she would be a moot part of his life. Whatever the reason, incompatibility, jealousy, the impossibility of meeting standards set by Camilla, it was quits for Betsy.

Promptly at ten o'clock the morning of June 1, 1994, in Courtroom 201 of the Prince George's County courthouse, the same courtroom where two years earlier Amy Smith had been adjudicated guilty, her new postconviction hearing was called to order by the clerk for Judge William D. Missouri. With two deputies at her side, Amy then entered the room, walking slowly, impeded by leg chains attached to her ankles. Later, at a break, Judge Missouri would tell the deputies to remove the chains, but for a while Amy sat pigeon-toed at a table up front, feet fidgeting, her convict status well-advertised. Amy's long, equine face assumed an attitude uncommonly jaundiced and mature for an eighteen-year-old—a prison face. She was dressed in a throat-high purple blouse and a tweedy, flowing skirt. Her long dusky blond hair, looking combed and cared for, was slipped into a ponytail. At the table some murmuring passed between her and Larry Polen before he called her to the stand. Speaking in fractured English, she made but one statement relevant to the claim of Elvira's racial bias. She said Elvira had informed her early on that it would be more strategic to have a single veteran judge sit in judgment of her rather than twelve jurors, some of whom were sure to be offended by her choice in boyfriends. "Being as how I'd been involved with black men, Ms. White told me there'd be a racial tinge to my case," Amy testified. "Whites would be prejudiced against me. And blacks would be prejudiced because of how it happened, Derrick Jones getting killed in my house." From the hard-felon's face issued a little girl's voice, eager to please. Her hands were crossed in her lap.

There soon followed Dennis Smith's turn. His footsteps sounded loud in the quiet of the place, quiet as a funeral home. Ashy-faced and unsmiling, looking himself somewhat funereal, Mr. Smith swore the oath. Scarcely any resemblance between him and his daughter could be discerned. Where she was on the big side, he was not, standing shorter and weighing less than she. Everything about him was diminished and receding, his eyes, his chin, the flat, untidy streaks of hair. Larry Polen had brought Mr. Smith to court with the assurance that he would not be asked about his relationship with his daughter, only about the legal performance of Elvira White. Mr. Smith's criticism of Elvira was that she had not succeeded in having Amy tried as a juvenile. "Amy should not have been treated as an adult because she wasn't an adult, either agewise or emotionally," said Mr. Smith, in a hollow voice. He blamed Elvira for not giving him a freer hand in trying to work out a plea bargain that might have sent Amy to juvenile detention. Elvira's formula for dealing with Mr. Smith instead had been to limit his contact with Amy to one jailhouse visit. "You have to consider your father an adversarial figure, and you cannot discuss the case with him," Elvira had told Amy, and Elvira herself had refused to return several of his phone calls. In their few personal encounters, Mr. Smith said, Elvira had been a tough customer, keeping her arms folded, and communicating with shrugs or curt half-sentences. The thrust of Mr. Smith's testimony, while unflattering to Elvira perhaps, was not a particularly instructive critique of her job performance, however. The real point to Mr. Smith's appearance in court this morning was symbolic, suggesting a father's forgiveness and the chance for reconciliation with Amy. Larry Polen was hopeful that if Amy should have her conviction thrown out Mr. Smith might find it in his heart to decline a prosecutorial role in the second trial. For now, whatever lay in Mr. Smith's heart was his to know, and Amy seemed not to care. She watched with a vacant stare, locked in thoughts of her own. Mr. Smith's eyes were downcast, his hands worrying the wooden arms of the witness chair. He wiped some dust or moisture from his eyeglasses and took a few seconds to study them. Then he lifted his head, flinching at the sight of his prisoner daughter and the deputies seated behind her. His visage was that of Dante contemplating hell. Stepping down Mr. Smith walked gingerly past Amy's table. He gave her a searching look, but no acknowledgment was asked for or given. In fact, she turned away, and he veered slightly off path and touched the back of her chair. Quickly, as if burned, he pulled his hand off. He stood, feet akimbo in that familiar lawman's stance, looking baleful, and then he took a seat toward the back of the room, slumping into his red-brown sport coat. A brooding, uneasy, almost disembodied presence, he listened but a minute to the next witness and then quietly left, hastening away from news reporters who tried to detain him.

The next witness was Mr. Smith's former father-in-law, Thomas Pickering. He spoke of how he and his wife had gotten a call out of the blue after Amy's arrest but had gamely posted her bail with their house as collateral, had taken Amy in, had seen to it she lived a normal school-going life prior to trial, had traveled from Massachusetts for all of Amy's courthouse appearances, never wavering. (Elbert Jones had said of Amy's grandparents, "Wonderful people—my heart breaks for them.") Once again Mr. and Mrs. Pickering had made the trip to Upper Marlboro, and during the two days the hearing would go on they would be faithful court watchers, mouthing endearments to Amy, confirming their loyalty. But as a witness Mr. Pickering was not any more germane than Mr. Smith. Mr. Pickering had little to say that put Elvira in a bad light. He and his wife had once thought of Elvira as a member of the family, inviting her with gracious enthusiasm to the Vineyard. *Come any time. Do you like seafood? Oh, but of course, you grew up on the Eastern Shore!* To save his granddaughter Mr. Pickering was willing to go to many lengths, but he was also pledged to the truth, and he said straightforwardly that he had not witnessed any racially prejudicial behavior on Elvira's part.

It was left to the four women from the public defender's office to deliver such evidence. The first was Bonnie Aldridge, looking haggard, who outside in the hallway told reporters, "I'm here because I was subpoe-naed." On the stand she had difficulty keeping her composure. She had known Elvira a long time. "I would say we were friends, very good friends," she testified.

"What was it that Elvira said to you when Dennis Smith called for her on the phone?" Larry Polen asked.

"You want the exact quote?" Bonnie replied. "Elvira told me, 'Fuck Den-nis Smith!' "

Bonnie Aldridge had no basic disagreement with Elvira's attitude to-ward Mr. Smith, saying of him, "He bent over backwards to say he wasn't a racist, but my gut feeling was that he is a racist." But Bonnie did not agree with how Elvira had imputed to Mr. Smith's racism an entire se-quence of behavior: Amy sneaking away from the house through a down-stairs window in pursuit of black boyfriends in order to "taunt" her father and then, tiring of that game, turning her seductive wiles on Derrick and inviting him into the house to "provoke" a face-to-face confrontation, knowing it might fly out of control.

"What, if anything, did Elvira White say about Derrick Jones?" Bonnie Aldridge was asked.

"She referred to him more or less as 'the victim.' "

"And Amy Smith?"

"Elvira referred to Miss Smith as 'the white bitch!' "

"Did she say this on more than one occasion?"

"Constantly."

The white bitch!—a universal put-down, streety and vulgar, and racist to boot. No doubt of it now, this case would belong to the folklore of Prince George's County. And no doubt, for some people, that "white bitch" would be the sum of the case, just as for others the words used through-out the courthouse against Elvira, "crazy bitch" and the whispered "black bitch," would say it all.

Dismissed from the stand Bonnie Aldridge lingered for a while in the hallway, as if she had something else to get off her chest. "I had no choice but to testify," she said to the news reporters. "I felt like I was between a rock and a hard place."

The courthouse reporter for the *Prince George's Journal,* Tim Maier, queried her, "I assume you're no longer friends with Elvira?"

"Well, I don't know how Elvira feels, but I feel I still am."

Soon the other women from the public defender's office were sworn in, and one by one they contributed to a general impression of Elvira as a vitri-olic, race-conscious attorney who also, not incidentally, lusted after fame. Anne Gold-Rand, looking composed but uptight, said she had had occasion outside the courthouse cafeteria one day to talk to Dennis Smith—"I knew Mr. Smith from other cases"—during which he offered to testify on Amy's behalf to keep the case in juvenile court but that Elvira had vehemently rejected the offer. *I don't care what he's willing to do, I will not speak to the man.* The thrust of the Gold-Rand testimony was that Elvira's judgment had been clouded by a racial hatred of Amy's parents and a racial empathy for Derrick's family. "Elvira had gotten close to Derrick's mother, and she wouldn't go after Derrick even if it meant saving Amy," Anne Gold-Rand said. Concurring, Gale Saccarelli, whose expressive Italian features and big brown eyes made her one of the most recognizable attorneys working the courthouse, testified that Elvira had been in repeated contact with Mrs. Jones and that when anyone in the public defender's office raised an idea like portraying Derrick as the deranged suitor and Amy as his relatively innocent sex object Elvira would say, "I can't do that to Derrick's mother." From start to finish Elvira had not wavered in her assessment of where the guilt lay, all on Dennis Smith, none on Derrick Jones. For her the case boiled down to a trigger-happy white cop–father's avenging of a black boy's sexual congress with the white temptress daughter. Although that sort of reasoning may not have been in Amy's best legal interests, Elvira, according to the testimony, liked her clichéd, elemental black-and-white calculus to the extent that she tried peddling it to the entertainment industry. Gale Saccarelli testified about Elvira trying to solicit the TV talk shows, and Suzanne Clements, who sat forward in the witness chair, testified that, at Elvira's request, she had queried the author Jerry Bledsoe, who had done well selling movie rights to his books, to see if he had any interest in writing about the Smith case. A lesser known author had expressed an interest, Suzanne Clements said, but Elvira was holding out for "a writer with a bigger name."

The four women witnesses were able to speak their piece outside the presence of Elvira who, as a prospective witness herself, had been cloistered since early morning in an upstairs room. When the women finished Judge Missouri ordered a recess, and three of them—Anne Gold-Rand, Gale Saccarelli, and Suzanne Clements—dallied briefly with him in a cordoned-off area reserved for officers of the court. Breaking a mood that had been intense and fraught, Judge Missouri asked Anne Gold-Rand if she had changed the color of her hair. "No, Your Honor, but thanks for asking," she answered. "Do you think I should?" There was light skittering laughter all around. A clerk dialed a number, spoke a question into a phone, and, hanging up, said to the women, "She's coming down," referring to Elvira. The announcement induced a giggle from one of the women, which set off a paroxysm of giggling. Embarrassed now, the women exited. Their passage out the door was stealthy, a quick look up and down the hallways, as if they expected Elvira to come screaming at them. But she was nowhere to be seen, and Anne Gold-Rand paused to issue a prediction to a group of news reporters, "I bet you Elvira won't testify. She's not going to add perjury to her troubles." Pressed to elaborate, Anne Gold-Rand said protestingly, "I better not say another word," and flung her suit jacket up over her face like a schoolgirl.

"Elvira should have conceded and spared us all this grief," Gale Saccarelli added in a peevish tone.

"It's not too late," Anne Gold-Rand said with what might have been taken for earnestness. "Elvira should go in there right now and admit her mistakes, cut her losses, and get on with her life. It would not harm Elvira's career anymore than it has already been harmed for her to admit she was wrong. Elvira is not going to become a judge of the circuit court, not through appointment, not through election. She knows that. So the right thing for her to do ethically is not to contest this hearing. She should let Amy have a new trial. Amy has her whole life ahead of her."

The two women went off breezily. "You know what? I could use a stiff one," Anne Gold-Rand said, and they made a date to go drinking after work.

Not until the coast was clear did Elvira appear, walking alone down the wide, dark wood-paneled hallway, arms swinging in short strokes. ("Maybe it looked like I was walking to my execution, to my doom, but I felt like I was walking out of darkness toward the light.") She had often wondered how her clients dealt with adversity, how they relaxed their minds before entering court, and had been informed that sleep was a good preparation. ("So, while these women were busy downstairs doing the devil's work, I was upstairs taking a nap. When I woke up I didn't feel alone anymore. I felt like I was surrounded by a force much greater than myself and much greater than the people in that courtroom. Walking down the hallway I felt incredibly at ease, lighter than air, like I was being carried, carried by the Lord and all the spirits of those who had died for the cause.") The proceedings were at last upon her. Elvira took the stand at 3:55 P.M. Judge Missouri noted the late hour and said he planned to call it a day soon but asked her to begin. She did, admitting that because of Amy's interracial romantic history Elvira had forgone a jury trial: "In this county, which I know quite well, I didn't think Amy's sexual encounters with black males would play well with jurors," she said. "In a jury trial, I would have had to put it all out there, the white-black thing"—but without a jury, Elvira thought she would be able to downplay the subject. Elvira also admitted instructing Amy not to have anything to do with Mr. Smith, a decision arrived at, she said, only after interviewing both him and his wife and hearing their "false, one-sided" version. The most "delicate" part of the case, according to Elvira, came when she had to tell Amy what her parents were saying: "Amy sat there and sobbed."

Then, soon enough, the question on everyone's mind was launched. Had Elvira ever described her teenage client as "the white bitch"?

"No, never." Elvira jutted out her chin and spoke in a raspy voice. Against her Irish green blouse a pendant shone, a crucifix hanging on a thin gold chain and set with a small diamond. "I do not use that kind of language."

Asked to rate her overall level of commitment to the case, Elvira called it "zealous, hardworking." She recalled she had put off major dental surgery for Amy's sake and had gone to the hospital immediately following the trial—the Pickerings, though saddened by the verdict, had the good grace to send flowers—and when it came time for Elvira to return to the courthouse to plead with Judge Johnson for a lenient sentence for her client, she had done so. "I came in with my mouth swollen up, crawled out of bed. I was in terrible pain, but I did not shirk my duty," she said.

Did she consider the outcome of the case to be a "tragedy"?

Elvira drew in a long, careful breath. "Yes, I did. Here were two good kids, Derrick from a loving family, Amy from a dysfunctional family. One ends up dead, the other in prison. Of course, it's a tragedy."

At 5:30 P.M. a sober-minded Judge Missouri, with billowing robe, took his leave. There was almost no chatter as Elvira walked slowly to the door, only the din of traffic through the walls.

The weather stayed hot and gray.

The next morning the deputies unlocked Amy's leg chains right off, although, if appearances were any guide, she had overnight become more of a security risk. Her makeover was startling, her attire now tarted up with tight pants, heels, brassy blouse, and hair loosely fluffed. Since adolescence, by Amy's own admission, she had been trying to be two different teenagers, regularly composing and recomposing herself to fit the circumstance. The one Amy was a "ponytail person" who played sports, maintained good grades, laid out plans to be an air force pilot or a computer jockey, and socialized with a small circle of white classmates. The other Amy was a prodigal who made the scene after hours with the black friends of whom her parents were so disapproving. "Amy described this pattern of living a double life as very difficult but something she had to do to keep her friendships and meet her parents' demands," Dr. Schouten had reported, noting further that, upon reflection, Amy had come to the wisdom that "neither of these two extremes are 'her.' " Yet, it seemed, even locked away from the world, the two Amy's continued to co-exist.

Any inquiry into Amy's state of mind, though, would have to wait for another day. She was not the one to be cross-examined this morning. She was not the one the distinguished oglers in the courtroom, including a member of the Judicial Nominating Commission, had come to see. Elvira was the one caught in the glare of attention, Elvira in a plain red-and-white dress, her wiry frame thinned down not from the gym but from long hours and hardships—her one beauty statement her fingernails, this morning in a paisley of purple and pink. The look on Elvira's face was her classic look, registering wariness and moxie. She had no lawyer to represent her; she was comfortable being her own champion. As Larry Polen, yellow legal pad in hand, went through a long, time-consuming, far-ranging, possibly irrelevant list of particulars—Elvira's bankruptcy, her list of off-duty clients, her dealings with writers—Elvira grew more and more agitated; her eyes were dark and charged and angry. On a polished bench in the back row a young, brown-haired woman, an investigator with the public defender's office, was scribbling copiously, and every once in a while the courtroom door was cracked open and Anne Gold-Rand's head poked in. At a recess Elvira, making a beeline to the hallway, tried to plead her case to news reporters. "Can you see the pattern here? Can you see the agenda?" she said with barely suffocated anger. "These questions don't relate to Amy Smith. They relate to an attempt to discredit me, to sabotage my election. And now there's an investigator at the back of the room taking notes to report to my superiors so they can develop more smears, more character assassination. Please, please believe me! Don't you realize what a ruse this hearing is?"

The break ended, and inside Courtroom 201 the court clerk asked Elvira, "Are you all right?"

"I'm fine." Elvira winced, and a fit of shivering shook her. "It's the air-conditioning," she said weakly and accepted a white sweater from the clerk.

Her responses to the ongoing interrogation—it was to last altogether six hours, a long time for a lawyer to endure—were not up to her characteristic sharpness. Wrapping the sweater tighter and tighter around her, she begged off more than once, saying she had been denied a chance to undertake a proper review of her files because of a burglar who had ransacked her home office. Partway into the fifth hour, when Larry Polen seemed to imply Elvira was using the missing files as a dodge, she completely lost control. "Why do you keep persecuting me?! You have the files! You have my phone records," she shouted at him. He tried to get her to stop, but she went on, positively prattling. Judge Missouri put up a hand. Outside a car alarm was sounding off. "Don't try to compete with that," the judge said. The noise lasted a couple of minutes, and then Elvira picked up where she had left off, her voice as apoplectic as before. "Don't ask me. Ask the people who started this!"

"Your Honor, the witness is not being responsive to my question," Larry Polen said.

Judge Missouri nodded. "Miss White, please refrain from these outbursts."

In the spectators' section there was stirring. Here was a sign of the craziness attributed to her! The chastened Elvira worked to recover her composure. "I'm sorry. All I'm trying to do is to get Your Honor to see the whole truth. These people have a political agenda."

At the next break Elvira sat on a bench in the hallway and read from a well-worn Bible. Red ribbons marked her favorite passages. One of the reporters asked with an element of mockery if she thought her tribulations were worthy of Job. "No," she said. "But Job is a good example. Like him, I will endure and see this through to the end."

Anne Gold-Rand also saw the hunched, soulful-looking figure of Elvira and remarked, "Is it penance?" But Elvira did not hear, or chose not to.

On the stand for a final go-round, a question came up about the public defender's office. "Before the office got cliquish, we always helped each other out," Elvira said with poorly affected equanimity. The ordeal of testifying had altered her face; it was gray, drained.

"You were friends?"

"Yes," she croaked out.

Shortly before noon, Elvira left the courthouse. Tropical heat steamed up off the macadam. She put a hand to her forehead, panting for air. She squinted from the sun. A fizzing sprinkler threw out bright, soaking, iridescent spots over thousands of green, machine-cut blades of grass. To the west, the sky was clouding up. Lightning flashed. A five-minute rain-greased storm was on the way.

At the appearance of Daphne Jones in the afternoon there was new murmuring in the courtroom. *That's the dead boy's mother, a sharp dresser—I didn't think she'd look so young. Yeah, but look at her eyes, she's got old eyes.* Adding to her burdens, Mrs. Jones had been diagnosed with breast cancer. She had elected surgery, which she now thought might have been hasty and mistaken. But after the loss of a son, how shrewd is anyone's judgment in matters of death?

Mrs. Jones took the stand to counter the white women who had preceded her. Whatever complimentary tribute Elvira might have wished for, Mrs. Jones was pleased to testify to it.

Something else preyed on her mind, though, and she wanted Judge Missouri to know it: "My husband and I hired a private investigator to look into this case. We wanted to get at the truth. We don't believe the truth has come out yet."

All the time Bruce lived in Denver there was just one visit between him and his father. Dr. Gordon took the initiative, flying out, but the climax of the visit was a yelling match, full of recriminations over the loss of Camilla from Bruce's life and also over the loss of Mrs. Gordon from Dr. Gordon's life. Bruce's mother and father were divorced soon after he finished college. Bruce was back living in Prince George's County then and bore witness to the final days. No one could blame him for the divorce, but he had taken his mother's side, a kind of aiding and abetting role, and he was the one who had delivered the news to his father. Dr. Gordon later gave this account: "Bruce came by one Sunday afternoon—he had his own apartment then—and he started telling me, 'Do you realize how much trouble it is for me to come visit you?' I said, 'Don't take a lot of trouble just for me. I can do without it.' So then he invited me to dinner and put the screws to me. Told me his mother wanted a divorce and I better give it to her. He said, 'It's the best thing that could happen to you.' I said, 'You're making that decision for me?!' " After the divorce Bruce had moved to Denver. He felt little or no ache of homesickness for his father, and even now the long estrangement from his father was far from over. The two of them had settled into bad routines that had become normal, Dr. Gordon cantankerous and resentful, Bruce acerbic and resentful, both of them acting out their old feuds, every wrong word more raw gasoline on the wounds. It had been a year and a half now since Bruce's return home, and only recently had he begun to understand the extent of his father's bitterness. Yes, Dr. Gordon's stroke was the cruelest blow, denying him the King Cadillac retirement he felt he was owed, but even before the stroke his life had been coming unglued. Living by himself, Dr. Gordon was working six days and six evenings a week in his downstairs clinic. ("One day I said to myself, 'What the hell am I working for?' After that I took Thursday evening off, then Wednesday off, then Friday off.") Freed up, he frequented the track and ate voluminously. After gaining seventy pounds he binged on diet drugs. Then came an allegation of sexual harassment. Dr. Gordon's ver-

sion was that one of his female patients flirted with him, and he accidentally touched her high on her chest, but he had to hire the big boss himself, Mike Miller, to avert the courtroom. Doc's blood pressure shot up. ("I
was in bad shape. I was lucky I wasn't dead already.") He gave up his
medical practice and closed off the downstairs, but three months later he
was struck down by the stroke. All this time, to most everyone in the family, Dr. Gordon remained the hard man who imposed on everyone his
sense of white-coated superiority carried over from his clinic. ("Even after
the stroke, the basic reaction in the family was 'Screw him!' ") Only now
was Bruce getting a fuller, more sympathetic picture. This information
came not from any heart-to-heart discussions but from partially realized
conversations with Old Settlers or from Doc's non sequiturs dropped into
dinner talk. At least Bruce was beginning to grasp what many sons fail
ever to grasp: A father does not go through life unscathed, no one is free
of personal failure. ("I'm a smart guy, but I haven't been smart enough to
see my dad is human. Fucking up is part of being human. Everybody has
done it. If you aspire to be human, it may be necessary to fuck up. That's
my new philosophy: Where there are no fuckups, there is no life.") Finally
Bruce and Doc were striking terms. The son saw his father now as an old
man, needy for help but unable to ask for it. The enemy was pride, from
whence all sins flow. So Bruce had initiated a new routine on Friday
nights—restaurants, movie theaters, the malls.

And how was that proceeding? On one of their first Fridays out Bruce,
having reserved a table at the Fireside restaurant in Beltsville, brought the
Cadillac around back to the wheelchair ramp. In his hurry, the roof of the
car caught the garage door, scoring the vinyl and bending the radio aerial.
Rather than dampen his father's spirits Bruce concealed the damage
through the evening, then owned up to it the next morning, handing over
a signed blank check for repairs. But all Saturday long Dr. Gordon made
life miserable in the house.

On the June 26 anniversary of the night Officer Rusty Claggett took into
an interrogation cell a black juvenile and lost his life to the said juvenile, a
slow-moving column of men and women with lit candles in their hands
filed past the police station where the crime took place. In suits and ties
and in dresses and heels, they were a sober, sweaty, somewhat dispirited
tracing of a hallelujah train. Against all odds, though, they continued to believe they could free the killer Terrence Johnson, who, at age thirty-one,
had lived in penitentiaries for sixteen years. Their tired march was in-

tended for local TV coverage. A young black woman, Cynthia Green, with a day job of assistant supermarket manager, was the organizer. A small item in a weekly newspaper had inspired her. When, in 1978, Terrence Johnson became a celebrity for his moment of gunplay—perhaps an act of self-defense—black political leaders in Prince George's County had given speech after speech invoking his name in full cry. "We are tired of seeing our sons brutalized, we are tired of seeing our sons railroaded" was the galvanizing theme of the Johnson case, and the message for black voters was to vote "black" in order to put a check on the Prince George's police system. In subsequent years, reforms had been arrived at. A reformist police chief, David Mitchell, had increased black representation on the police force. Instances of brutality were no longer commonplace, and Terrence Johnson nowadays was no longer a holy cause. Although Black Alliance leaders Al Wynn and Bea Tignor were present to address the candle-carrying marchers, they were careful to be respectful of the slain officers, saying, "We have sympathy for the loss of all life." The righteousness of securing Terrence Johnson's release had been left now to an eclectic group of true missionaries who called themselves the Concerned Citizens for Terrence Johnson and to a few mainly anonymous benefactors who sent along small checks (Elvira White was one). There was also a singularly dedicated attorney, Charles Ware, who had taken a fatherly interest in Terrence Johnson and was ready to have him join the Ware law firm at the earliest possible date. This was the future for the prisoner painted brightly, a law degree and a fine house: prosperity. It was not so far-fetched. The file of Johnson's various stops at Maryland prisons told of a model life behind bars. There were letters of praise from one prison warden after another as well as a college diploma earned through the inmate program of Morgan State University, and, without an application ever being filled out, an offering letter of a five-figure scholarship from the dean of Howard University Law School. Members of the Concerned Citizens for Terrence Johnson had knocked on more doors than any politician ever would and collected seventy thousand signatures on a petition for clemency. Yet Terrence Johnson remained in prison, having served twice the normal time for his sentence. And if he wanted to keep a grip on reality, it seemed like he ought to circle a date nine years hence when his maximum would be served. All his chances with the parole board had been exhausted. His last option for freedom depended now on the lawyerly machinations of Mr. Ware, who was candid with his client: "Do not expect a miracle."

In other circumstances Terrence Johnson might have been prosecuted as a juvenile and been freed automatically at age twenty-one, or he might at least have been accorded run-of-the-mill leniency. Instead, Judge Jacob

Levin, a man considered a soft touch for Prince George's County, had imposed the stiffest possible sentence for the killing of Rusty Claggett, ten years for manslaughter and fifteen years for deadly assault. Instead of the usual practice of running the two terms together, Terrence Johnson was ordered to do his terms back-to-back. "The punishment must fit the crime," Judge Levin had intoned from the bench, with the teenager standing defiantly before him. "You have absolutely no respect for authority of any kind, and, secondly, you have some kind of psychological problem. In my judgment, you are a walking time bomb, and you exploded on the night of June the 26th, 1978, and caused this senseless tragedy." It was not the mercy of God but the limits of Maryland law, the judge added, that kept him from locking the prison door and throwing away the key.

Of course, it was not solely one judge's pronouncement that hung over Terrence Johnson. The historic philosophy of Prince George's County held that the violence of the black man must be controlled through the severest of sanctions. In the 1950s the reigning county executive had said, "No one will be safe if the Negro is allowed to take the law into his own hands"— a viewpoint commonly embraced then and hardly abolished now.

Lansdale Sasscer, the county executive who made the remark, was descended from the extended family that produced Rusty Claggett and also produced, across the American centuries, a line of imported aristocratic bourgeoisie: an English lord, a Revolutionary War officer, a Maryland governor, the first Episcopal bishop in the Americas, and the first white person to lay claim to the land where the White House is located. The life of Mr. Sasscer, born in 1893, was one of housebound gentility, when creature comforts were still demanded of black servants. He inherited a large tract of plantation land outside Upper Marlboro on which grew tobacco and corn tilled by black tenants. He also owned the *Enquirer-Gazette,* the local weekly that was an extension of the Sasscer social and political callings. At an early age he told his family, "I know God will make me whatever I want to be." He wanted to be "Mr. Prince George's." The political reign of Lansdale Sasscer lasted from the 1940s into the 1960s and coincided with the final heyday of absolute political-bossism, when Mr. Sasscer could handpick for sheriff a man publicly compared to the slow-witted, second-banana TV deputy Goober. But Mr. Sasscer had no direct political heir, and with his death in 1964 his power went up for grabs and was subsequently assumed in large part by Mike Miller, with family roots in one of the rival English clans. The Sasscer name slipped from the headlines. Then, a few hours after the last of his children, Lucy Claggett Sasscer

Sanders, had presented a racing cup named for her father to the winner of the Marlborough Hunt steeplechase races, the body of the seventy-one-year-old Miss Lucy, who in her youth had been the Miss Tobacco Festival Princess, was found murdered in the dark, wood-paneled dining room of the family manse outside Upper Marlboro. An electrical cord was wrapped around her neck. The crime had the markings of prosaic money-grubbing: a break-in, the intruder caught in the act, a vicious silencing of the eyewitness. But no young thief was to blame. The murderer was Miss Lucy's psychotic, vagabond son Walter. His criminal development had taken years. Even as Miss Lucy kept up the Sasscer family obligations, her duties with the Marlborough Hunt, the Forest Garden Club, the Vansville Farmers Club, the Maryland Club, the Metropolitan Club, the Sulgrave Club, and the Chevy Chase Country Club, her son was allowed a life on the loose. Off and on he'd hole up in monasteries and translate Shakespearean sonnets into French. Mainly he hung out on the Left Bank in Paris. Sometimes his spoiled, amoral nature got the best of him. A year earlier, he had strangled to death a French lover with another electrical cord. He was returned to America, escorted by a French psychiatrist, who recommended he be institutionalized, but the family could not bear the shame and kept him at home and told no one. Walter's berserk assault on his mother came after she threatened to cut him out of her will. Now Lansdale Sasscer's grandson received visits in his prison cell from attorneys of the Prince George's public defender's office. They would be handling the trial defense for him, a legally defined indigent.

At one time, when Elvira was in good standing, the case of Walter Claggett Sasscer Sanders might well have been assigned to her—a daughter of a slave family appointed the legal stand-in for a son of the colonial line. But this was not to be.

The two-day hearing in the Amy Smith case was likened by some at the courthouse to a formal and public breaking point in a love affair. For more than a year Elvira had spoken to her old friends only when spoken to, and since they were communicating with her primarily by memo she had occasion to say very little. Nonetheless a certain code of conduct had kept things civilized, and it was the hearing in Courtroom 201 that ended the pretense and pulled the hard feelings into the open.

A humorless Anne Gold-Rand tried to smile professionally as she walked from one courtroom to another. It was a busy morning, and she saw no point in trying to discuss the ramblings of an overwrought woman.

This was what she said at first, pleading "No comment, no comment." But, halting outside one of the big swinging fortress doors, she decided to let fly with a few choice words, speaking not in the spirit of lawyers who lift a glass to each other after an adversarial day in court but in a disturbed, disquieting voice, all the time curling and uncurling her fingers around the handle of a valise: "Elvira is not the same person I used to know. Elvira used to be a regular person, and I'm not sure what it was that changed her. Maybe it was things going wrong in her personal life. Anyway, she let herself get in deeper and deeper to the point where things went wrong in her professional life and she developed this enormous martyr complex."

In Elvira's office in Charles County country music was playing on the audio box overhead. "I'd like to take an ax to it," Elvira said.

Elvira was at all times a champion talker, of the type adored by writers. She delivered enlivened diatribes on the Disraeli model, the trenchant, illusionless monologue that cuts to the quick. And her face was so dramatic, the tone of her voice so mobile, and her way of dealing with the world so instinctive, everything yes or no, right or wrong, black or white; there were no neutral parties in her life, only true believers or traitors. A friend once remarked about Elvira: "She's brilliant, top of the charts, so it's surprising how simplistic her outlook on life is. She believes in good and evil." Now that friendships had been betrayed, Elvira was bursting with the utmost revulsion. She went into high gear, sparing no one in her temper. "You want to know why Anne and the others were afraid to stay in the courtroom and listen to my testimony? You know why they went skittering away like scared rabbits? They couldn't dare look me in the eye. They were afraid to look truth in the face!" A laugh. "They might've done the smart thing, though. If they'd stayed, if I'd had to look at their hypocritical faces, my testimony might've been a whole lot different. My memory might've become suddenly very clear. They're lucky I'm not a vengeful or bitter person because I could have paid them back in spades. I could've been as nasty as they were. There are things I could have done to wound them the way they wounded me. For instance, I could've let slip some information to challenge Bonnie Aldridge's credibility, the fact Bonnie had to retire from the Prince George's police force because of a psychological disability. (What a thing to say! The two of them, Elvira and Bonnie, both country girls, had started out together at the public defender's office in the late 1970s and were reunited in 1990. In between Bonnie had been a policewoman, assigned to hostage negotiations, and her departure from the force had indeed come at a time of emotional distress. But the distress was caused by the immolation-suicide of a brother officer—his body was still smoldering when Bonnie got there—and the accidental killing of another officer by his best friend, all within the space of three weeks.) I could've brought up her psychological problem, but it would've served no purpose except to give me momentary pleasure. That is all they are getting from this, momentary pleasure. All I can think is how incredibly empty their lives must be. Anne Gold-Rand? She is consumed by jealousy. Suzanne Clements? I sponsored her for the bar. . . . That was fine. She didn't have a problem with my ability then. But now she does?! Okay, you figure it out. Did you know Anne and Suzanne phoned one of the other staff attorneys here in Charles County. I guess they wanted to gauge how sorry they should feel for me. I guess if they'd found out I was miserable and unhappy they would've sent me a cheer-up card. Linda McCaulley? Do you know who she is? She was the young woman in the back of the courtroom writing down my words to be used against me at some future date. Now if someone was to ask Linda the question: Who immediately came to the hospital for you when your mother and father suffered simultaneous strokes? Who gave you free legal advice about your divorce and child-support situation, advice for which you didn't have to pay a dime? I mean, I guess she truly has forgotten what I did. (But why explain yourself when the other person is past the point of caring?) Considering what I've done for some of these people and the way they've reacted, considering how they went out of their way to impeach me, I could be a very bitter person, but I'm not. I don't have time for it. Let them sit awake at night scheming and planning. The Lord is cognizant. He will strike down all wrongdoers on the Day of Reckoning."

Elvira was interrupted by a Garth Brooks song. You had to admire her candor. In pursuit of what she called "God's work" she was not afraid to delve in and make judgments about people. She was no computerized personality; no one could say that. During the course of this diatribe she had put on a vibrant, radiant smile, which before long was established not to be a smile. Her mouth writhed with mock pity. Her throat cords stood out below a face swollen from lack of sleep. Her eyebrows rode up and down with her emotions. Her mood was bitter, punk, fairly spitting, and yet at any moment tears could have flowed. It was as if the talk, caustic and unabating, was holding her together.

Another nonstop string entered her head, and she laid it out. She talked louder, over the music and the thrumming of the air conditioner. "I invited these women into my life, but they never really reciprocated. There was always a consciously erected barrier between us. They palmed themselves off as friends. They ate my food, drank my liquor, but I don't think I was ever invited to their homes. They kept me out. They never let down their guard with me."

The hard edge in Elvira's voice did not prevent a heart-stung face and did not prevent wet eyes. Her words trailed off. She swallowed. The past year had jaded her. Who in her position would not want to squeeze from memory all the sweetness? And yet, according to those who used to work with her, the good feelings had once seemed genuine. The women from her office invariably noted their previous regard for Elvira as a "friend" and a "running buddy," "someone I thought highly of," "someone like a sister, yes, a sister, close to my heart." Elvira's one-room office with the African artwork on the walls had been a drop-in spot. Anyone might show up, unannounced, like a visitor in Chekhov. Kibitzing went on, and gossiping, and crying on the shoulder—a lot of "girl stuff," in Elvira's words. She, too, in better days had expressed her pleasure at how companionable and easy everyone in the office had been, helping each other through divorces and bailing each other out of financial jams, how they exchanged notes and nudges during trials and would compare what-ifs afterward, how they gossiped in breathless, wait-till-you-hear-this voices and how they would in more somber moods tell things only good friends share, confidences entrusted and now regretted all around.

Elvira wiped her eyes at the corners and turned to look out a window onto a parking lot and, in a startling gesture, struck an open palm on her desk. Her eyes lidded over. Her expression was numb, poignant. She asked, almost inaudibly, "Do you think the judge saw how personal this whole thing is?"

Midway through the 1994 elections Frank Pesci had this to say, over lunch at a Marriott: "I like Bea Tignor, and she may win, what with Mike Miller and Gloria Lawlah behind her. Gloria is just as important now as Mike. Gloria's a boss in her own right. However, since I never belonged to Mike's gang and I'm persona non grata with Gloria, I have to have my doubts about Bea. Inexperienced as Bea is, if she gets into office, how's she going to keep it from becoming the Mike and Gloria show? Frankly, if Mike and Gloria are against Sue Mills, that's the best recommendation anyone could give me in favor of Sue. That's why a lot of independent-minded people are looking at Sue with a fresh eye. It's a fluke, but Sue might be the person in the right place at the right time. She's the only real independent. I don't know, but it's possible she can put together a coalition of people who hate machine politics."

• • •

Looking into the lights on the backstreet where once again the new neighbors had parked their car inconsiderately at the foot of Dr. Gordon's wheelchair ramp, Bruce had to fight feelings of annoyance. And they had again placed their trash cans in a dead space where he liked to park, these neighbors with direct ties to the professional, BMW-owning sector of black America. Six months after they had moved in they were still cold-shouldering his hellos and brushing off his attempts at friendly cooperation. Black people who did not respond to his overtures Bruce found profoundly troubling. On his night out with his father, he was indignant enough to say, "Clearly they have no interest in getting to know us. They act like they hate all white people."

Nor were these neighbors the only ones who seemed clannish. A week ago the basement of the Gordon house had sprung a leak, and Bruce had gone for advice to a black neighbor who did construction jobs. The man, unsmiling and wordless as he went to get his tools, left Bruce standing outside on the doorstep and gave Bruce the impression he was embarrassed to have his teenage son see him do a favor for a white man.

Had Delmar been poisoning the neighborhood against the Gordon family? Or was it personal prejudice?

White flight was one of the subjects Frank Pesci wanted to write about in his commentary for the *Journal,* and he set out to conduct his own random surveys. An intractable phenomenon of asking white people about white flight is that they go mum. He found communication hard to come by even among his neighbors in the pleasant, professorial town of New Carrollton.

In the 1960s, New Carrollton had been known for real estate agents who would tell black couples wishing to buy in white neighborhoods, "Nothing's available at present." If a black couple should happen to see a "For Sale" sign, the couple would be told, "That house has been sold, and we forgot to take the sign down." Back then Frank had had words with some of the realty agents, who told him they were trying to protect his property values. "Don't do me any favors" was his line. He threatened to blow the whistle on them to federal authorities, and he threatened civil litigation. This led to the arrival in 1968 of the first black family in Frank's neighborhood. He practically bounded over with a welcoming plate of cookies baked by his wife, Dorothy. Later the same day Frank got a visit from a white neighbor who had witnessed the cookies. "Bad enough we have to let them move in here. Don't you go making them feel at home," the man said. Frank told the man, "Get the hell off my property." This man, old and decrepit now with emphysema but still a resident of the street, had vowed to go to his death before he would speak to any of the several black families who had moved in and, as far as Frank knew, had kept to his vow. Frank thought it would be an interesting moment of decision if someday the man suffered an attack of chest pains and had no one to ask for a ride to the hospital but a person of color. ("Talk about the agonies of the damned: I'd like to know if he's ever had nightmares about what he'd do in that moment.") Still, for this man, things in Prince George's County had yet to reach his "tipping point"—what real estate agents like to call the state of racial affairs that turns white homeowners into runaways. The central question of Frank's survey was whether a large number of white people might consider it a "tipping point" if a black politician were to occupy the office of county executive.

Most of the people he asked shrugged blankly—they knew he wrote for the *Journal*—or they said, "Well, Frank, you know . . ." Only one neighbor looked him in the eye and admitted, "I'm white, and I don't want to be in a minority. Is that a sin?"

Frank's conclusion, listening between the lines: "There will be a lot of slow, quiet flight."

Alvin Thornton, a Howard University constitutional law professor and a Prince George's school board member who had recently traveled to Johannesburg as an "international observer" of Nelson Mandela's election, had this comment on the county executive's race: "You have decent, good people who are accustomed to living in a county where power has been white-controlled. Now there is a chance of a black person taking over, and good white people are concerned about that. There is a fear of the unknown."

On an outing to see *Schindler's List,* the double doors of thick glass and shiny alloys at the Beltway Plaza presented a struggle for Doc's wheelchair. Bruce needed an extra hand, and, two feet away, there were extra hands belonging to a black teenage boy who stood and looked on and did not move a muscle. Bruce believed he saw on the young man's face an intelligent assessment in favor of passive hostility.

In prison the test of manhood begins with small courtesies. Hold a door open for the next man or walk through a door held open, offer a cigarette or accept a cigarette—make a move like this and you have revealed yourself to be weak. No experienced criminal bandies civilities or exhibits kindness, knowing such will lead to rumors of sissiness and rape in the shower. But did the rules of prison pertain now in suburban malls?

The first neighborhood in Prince George's County to experience blockbusting on a wholesale level was Hillcrest Heights. In the 1960s, scare flyers were deposited in mailboxes. *Don't be the last one left on your block!* Sue Mills, then a young PTA mother, made a show of ripping up the flyers. She went up and down her street telling her white neighbors, "Nobody is going to run me out of my home." And the Mills family did stay on, through the graduation of Cindy and Steve from Potomac High, and even now, after being compelled to sell their house, Sue Mills and her husband lived less than five miles away. Among those who knew Mrs. Mills there had long been a disagreement about how much of her loyalty to Hillcrest Heights was sentimental hoax, how much was canny politics, and how much could be taken as evidence of warmth in her heart for a black neighbor. But now the disagreement was taking a different twist. Could it be that the election of Sue Mills as county executive was the most effective way of preventing a new wave of white flight from Prince George's County?

It was a point Frank Pesci thought worth considering. It also seemed to help explain, in part, the big lead Sue Mills had in the polls and to explain her value as a candidate to such voters as John Kirwin, an electronics scientist retired from civilian naval research, and his wife, Jenette, a retired nurse. The Kirwins—he of the rational, reserved Alan Laddism, the square Irish face, white hair combed straight back; she of the same handsome Irish features, the flinty eyes, a touch of poetry in her upright mannerisms—were two of Merv and Dell's best white friends. The Kirwins were in Sue Mills's corner because they believed they knew her well enough to know she was not evil incarnate. Sue and Jimmy Mills had been neighbors. Jimmy had rewired the Kirwin house. But for the Kirwins, who in their prime had done battle with the old realities of Prince George's County, it was nonetheless a strange turn to think Sue Mills might be the candidate most likely to have a positive effect on race relations.

A number of period pieces with respect to the Kirwins can be related, such as the one involving the private swimming pool where they paid dues and where in the summer of 1965 a banner was hoisted, "AFS Students Welcome, Swim for Free." This was to ballyhoo the exchange students arriving on U.S. soil through the American Field Service. The Kirwins happened past the swimming pool while an AFS student was in their car, a young black man freshly off a flight from his native Panama to the terminals of Dulles Airport. As of 1965 no black person had set foot behind the gates of a Prince George's private pool except to perform minimum-wage labors, so the Kirwins had more than an inkling that the bannered welcome did not extend to their particular AFS student. Nonetheless it was too good an invitation not to be put to the test. Their oldest son, John Jr., then eighteen and full of pep and idealism, escorted the Panamanian youth in for a dip but did not make it to the water's edge. ("They were stopped by whoever was in charge. The terminology used was 'No niggers allowed.' ") The Kirwins registered a complaint with the governing body of the pool and called the *Washington Post,* resulting in a crisis meeting at a school auditorium. Their son wrote a four-page letter, which Mrs. Kirwin read out loud. ("As someone who grew up in the church, he did not understand why people did not believe in their hearts what they professed to believe in their prayers.") While only ten pool members took the side of the Kirwins, about six hundred raised hands against them. ("Some of these were people we had better expectations of, and it was very hurtful.") Two years later, as lay leaders of the Oxon Hill Methodist Church, the Kirwins attempted to merge their all-white congregation with an all-black congregation from St. Paul United Methodist. At the time the two congregations were in opposite straits, Oxon Hill accustomed to prosperity, St. Paul struggling. A meeting of the white congregants was held. ("All kinds of reasons were expressed against the merger. It would cause mixed marriages and so forth, just about every conceivable excuse you can think of.") There was a vote, and the Kirwins lost once more. This was the segregation era. To change things the Kirwins were willing to hear the "nigger-lover" talk. They had moved from the Eastern Shore to Prince George's County in 1948, purchasing a house in the Barnaby Manor Oaks subdivision, across the road from black squatters. Only after the sale did the Kirwins find out black people were precluded, by virtue of a covenant in the deeds, from buying in the subdivision. It would take consultations with lawyers and days in court and pressure on reluctant real estate agents, and it would take a changing of the times, but Barnaby Manor Oaks, where the Kirwins continued to live, now counted nine black homeowners for every white homeowner. To understand the Kirwins you had to know how they gloried in the integration of their subdivision and, once the worst bigots had taken petulant flight, in the eventual integration of their pool and church. You would then also get a glimmer of their unhappiness and bafflement at those expressing an "all-black" philosophy. These days the Methodist congregation at Oxon Hill was badly diminished, down from seventeen hundred to nine hundred, a punishment from on high perhaps. However, the white congregants who had stayed with the church were actively recruiting black families into the fold. At St. Paul, meanwhile, there was now twice the membership of Oxon Hill, but no white congregants, and there was little interest anymore in a merger. An all-black faction appeared to have the same hold on St. Paul that an all-white faction once had on Oxon Hill. "Black prejudice has gotten to be as bad as white prejudice used to be," Mr. Kirwin said. "You encounter it everywhere, on the highway, in grocery stores. The youngsters are the worst—too much black consciousness, as if that's their sole thought."

In this context it seemed to the Kirwins that Sue Mills had matured and now accepted the proposition of brotherhood and sisterhood under the same sun. An appropriate time would come for a black person to be the county executive, but at this point in history the Kirwins believed that Sue Mills, with all her shortcomings, was preferable to any black politician who, regardless of personal intentions, would serve to make "black consciousness" more of a fait accompli.

The Prince George's County police were investigating as a hate crime the defacing of a sign at St. Paul United Methodist Church. Someone, perhaps from the rear gate of a pickup truck, had hand-stroked red paint across a wooden sign, set in concrete on the front lawn of the 201-year-old whitewashed frame church and bearing the popular message "Free South Africa." The Reverend Leonard Felton gazed upon the sign—it had a weirdly religious look from the blood-red drippings—and said, "I think we'll leave it the way it is. We'll let the community drive by and maybe take a lesson from it."

9 **Bruce, with** a good reputation in his chosen trade of financier, had switched to a better-paying company in Reston, Virginia. But now he had to negotiate a commute lousy with morning glare, fumes, horns. He had tried a couple of different routes across the Potomac, but there was no fast route. To idle the time he would talk on his car phone or check his hair in the mirror or gaze upon women in other cars, any distraction. One summer morning, a couple of blocks from the U.S. Capitol, Bruce turned up the ramp from South Capitol Street to the Southwest Expressway. The traffic roared but did not move. His way was blocked as far as he could see. The Howard Stern show was tuned in on his radio, and it was during a commercial break, as he was reaching down to switch to DC 101, that his Toyota banged into a Dodge Dynasty.

The driver was a black woman, about twenty-one.

Bruce got out. "Gosh, that was stupid." There was a slight bow in the rear bumper of the Dodge.

"Don't worry. We're okay," the woman replied. She introduced herself and an elderly man with her, her grandfather.

Bruce offered her the use of his car phone while he wrote out his name, address, and insurance policy number on a piece of paper. The woman dialed her mother. "I had an accident, but it's nothing, just a dent."

An officer from the U.S. Park Police stopped and made sure no one was injured, then drove off since he was out of his jurisdiction. A District of Columbia officer happened by and likewise checked for injuries. "We're not hurt, not a scratch," the woman said. Her grandfather nodded and went back to sit in the Dodge. The officer sped off to another call, and while the wait continued on the dewy green embankment, the woman took a second look at the piece of paper Bruce had handed her and made note of his address on Iverson Street in Hillcrest Heights. "I've been to Iverson Street, been to the mall," she said. "It's great you live there."

Bruce gave her a puzzled look, and the woman smiled, "I mean, it's great you don't live in Chevy Chase or a place like that," which was to say a place inhabited extensively by conventional white Americans who believe their lives safe because their neighbors are also white and conventional.

"I'm definitely not the Chevy Chase type." Bruce made a face to indicate he looked down his nose at the type, and she laughed. His irritation at having to start his day in the company of a young woman who must think him a dolt was being lessened by her stately manners. While they talked, a civilian car pulled over. The amplified pop voice of Whitney Houston poured from the car radio. A door opened for a man decked out in a tailored suit. He motioned the young woman over to him. "You okay, sister?! This looks like it could be pretty bad. Try moving your neck and your shoulders." She did as he indicated, twisting her head and arching her shoulders and, in the Dodge, her grandfather followed suit. "Nothing hurts, not really," the woman said. "I got like a little twinge is all."

The man offered the sage opinion that she could not be too careful. "Whiplash doesn't always manifest itself right away. You hear what I'm saying? You might be better off going to a hospital to get yourself X-rayed. Your pappy, too."

Bruce had the man pegged now. He was a Good Samaritan who would be friendly to a stranger in trouble in order to make action off the stranger. That a man so well turned out should be a hustler disappointed Bruce. He felt his adrenaline pump, like in tai kwon do. He stepped over. "This is ridiculous," Bruce said. "Look, she says she's not hurt. You can see yourself there's hardly any damage to her car. How can she be hurt?"

Bruce would say later, "I looked at the guy and it was one of those knowing looks where you look deep into his eyes and see the truth. There was a twitching in his face for a minute like he was embarrassed because he knew that I knew he was running an insurance scam. A guy like that goes through life thinking he's an entrepreneur—let's get the system, let's get some free money, ten grand, fifty grand, this white boy's got liability insurance. It wasn't so much a racial thing as a money thing, but I had the distinct feeling he figured I was a chump because I was white. I was an easy score. The young lady looked very confused, and I was trying to read her mind. I thought, well, she's confused because of the screwy lesson she's learning from this man who's old enough to be her father. The lesson was how to get one over on the system, how to get rewarded for doing nothing. Which pissed me off, but I didn't want things to escalate, so I tried to reason with the young lady."

The incident did escalate, though. Bruce spoke severely to the woman. "Why don't you get in your car and go to your job? You can get your bumper straightened out anytime. You're covered. My insurance company will pay for it. Get in your car and go to your job. That's the thing to do."

"Don't you be telling me what's right to do."

"It sure as hell isn't right to try to rip me off for some insurance money!"

"I want an ambulance." The woman turned to the man in the tailored suit, her voice rising. "You got a car phone? Call us an ambulance!" She put up her right hand, warning Bruce, "Don't you be coming near me." The reversal in her attitude sent a chill through Bruce. "Minutes ago I had been the nice guy and now I was the racist capitalist pig"—his characterization of her characterization.

The woman and her grandfather spent the rest of the day at Washington General Hospital. They were examined for whiplash, and, although Bruce said the tests were inconclusive, the woman in due course filed a lawsuit asking for $25,000 in compensation.

Everywhere Elvira went she wore a crucifix as a symbol of her devout Christianity and her affiliation with Gibbons United Methodist Church, where she served on the usher board. Gibbons United Methodist had been a small country church until the handsome, energetically political Reverend C. Anthony Muse came along in 1984. The congregation now had more than 1,500 members, and building tradesmen on scaffolding were doing wondrous work on a brand-new sanctuary. The groundbreaking at Gibbons United had attracted Sue Mills, Bea Tignor, and Wayne Curry, who stood at prayerful attention while the enthusiastic congregants swayed and sang. Several new or newly invigorated black Christian congregations were relocating from Washington to the Route 202 corridor running through the communities of Hillcrest Heights, Oxon Hill, and Temple Hills. The Full Gospel AME Zion Church now had a membership of 15,000 in Hillcrest Heights, with a 10,400-seat sanctuary. The bill for construction, $24 million, had been paid off without a bank loan. As the churches were raised up so, too, was the political power of their ministers. Gloria Lawlah had accepted the Reverend Muse onto her slate as a candidate for the house of delegates. The Reverend Muse, religious sanctifier and political adviser to Elvira, had run for the same office in 1990, and lost. Now he was favored to win.

With unremarked-upon efficiency Dell set out a meal of baked chicken and mashed potatoes. The Strickler home squealed with three granddaughters. Heather was home for a visit, and over dinner she parceled out newsworthy updates. For instance, Camilla was living now with a boyfriend named David in Cambridge—"or partner, I should say. She hates the word 'boyfriend.' "

"Too bad things didn't work out with Bruce," said Merv, who was someone who still expressed disappointment whenever reality had its way in the world.

"Think about how rare it is for people to have a simple, honest friendship when they're not the same color," Dell reminded him. She marveled that Heather and Camilla's friendship was intact and ongoing, considering all the circumstances.

By circumstances Dell was referring to the years and the miles and also to the normal frictions that can be aggravated by the issue of race. Dell mentioned as an example Heather and Mike's wedding. This was news to Heather, who had no memory of anything spoiling the picture-perfect Catholic ceremony with tuxedos and white lace in a big West Virginia stone church, on May 17, 1980, the day the volcano blew off the top of Mount St. Helens. ("We woke up the next morning, and the earth had moved.") However, it had not been the straightforward event Heather remembered. Without her being aware, another drama had unfolded, and the casual mention of it these several years later stirred Heather to find out more. Of course, the literal history would be hard to come by now. Anything said now would be freighted with situational meaning.

Heather: "My mother had never said boo about it—I guess she didn't want to cause hard feelings."

Dell: "It was a beautiful wedding, and it went off without a hitch. And afterward there was no reason to bring up this other thing."

Heather: "Everyone in my family always knew Camilla would be my maid of honor, but it seems she was made to feel unwelcome by some of the relatives on Mike's side, and she almost bowed out, without me knowing it."

Dell: "At a party before the wedding some of the in-laws were taken aback to find out Heather's best friend was a black woman. This was a foreign concept to them. They tried to discourage Camilla. They said things like 'I don't expect the photographer will want any pictures with you'|and 'You're not going to stand in the reception line, are you?' "

Heather: "Mike does not have a prejudiced bone in his body—he was close to a lot of black kids who were on the football team with him in high school—but he comes from a line of coal miners who used to live in a hollow called Campbell's Creek. There's a mountaineering legend that goes with Campbell's Creek. It's said that no black man who ever went into the hollow came out alive. I sort of pooh-poohed it, but one day I asked a friend of mine who's black if he'd ever been to Campbell's Creek, and without batting an eyelash he said, 'Never have and never will. No black man's ever come out alive from Campbell's Creek.' So, you know, I suppose it's possible some of Mike's relatives could have been less than friendly to Camilla."

Dell: "Camilla came to me before the wedding and asked me, 'What should I do?' She didn't want to have Heather's wedding ruined. I asked Camilla, 'You do want to be the maid of honor, don't you?' And she said she could not imagine not being up there with Heather. That was the only answer I needed to hear. I told her, 'Well, I can't imagine it either!' "

Heather: "It's probably better to let sleeping dogs lie, but I had to bring it up to Camilla. I wanted to know: Did this really happen? She hedged at first when I asked her, which is not like her."

Camilla: "When Heather asked me about it I realized she had forgotten the incident. Which is understandable—it was one of many things she had to contend with as the bride. But she did know about it at the time. The in-laws had gone to her, in fact. A few days before the ceremony Heather called me and said, 'I'm having a problem because Michael's family suggested maybe you'd be uncomfortable at the wedding.' And she told me how the conversation had gone with the in-laws. She'd asked them, 'Why would Camilla feel uncomfortable?' And they'd said, 'Well, maybe she wouldn't feel welcome.' And Heather had said, 'Wait, I don't get it.' And they'd said, 'Well, you know, there won't be another black person for fifty miles around.' And then Heather said to me, 'You don't mind, do you, Camilla?' I said, 'Of course not.' "

Heather: "After talking to Camilla I racked my brain. I did remember Mike's grandmother saying, 'You're not all going to stand together for pictures?' Maybe there were some other comments that didn't register."

Camilla (who at her own wedding, the same day Prince Charles wed Lady Diana, wore a plum-colored Mexican folk sundress and played Frisbee barefoot, with Heather as her maid of honor): "I didn't want to cause a scene at Heather's wedding. But I do have a little bit of the troublemaker in me. So for the wedding reception, this big soiree, I brought along my husband-to-be, an Irish Catholic from Kentucky, and I made sure he danced with me in very public ways. Some of the in-laws were bug-eyed to see a black woman and a white man. I was having a great sexy time, smiling but making it obvious."

Heather: "If Camilla says it happened, then it happened. Her antennae are always up where mine are not."

Camilla: "Heather was such a good friend she didn't get it that they were trying to insult our friendship. They were trying to pound it into her head, but it went right through her. She may be the only person I know who actually fits the description of 'colorblind.' "

Heather: "The way I was raised, I didn't learn to factor color into every equation. Does that mean I'm not tuned in to all the racial undercurrents in society? I think I see people for who they are, but maybe I don't see all of life for what it is."

It was while Bruce was driving around metropolitan Washington, staring at the world through a sunstruck windshield, that he contemplated the meaning of racial conflict in America. Could black Americans and white Americans be disagreeable, or even venomous to each other, without it devolving into racial conflict? That was Bruce's question, and he applied it to a lifetime of personal experiences.

The odd thing was, if he did not count the recent run of incidents with the insurance scammer and with the mall kid and with Delmar, there was not much to go on. His school days Bruce skipped over. The conflicts with his father from that time so overshadowed everything else he could not think of other memorable incidents. There were none either from his first two years after college. As a photocopier salesman ("that's what you do with a sociology degree from the University of Florida") he dealt every day with black people in rundown sections of Prince George's County and Washington, D.C. The old alkies slouched in the parking lots at his regular ports of call were like street comrades. He called them by the names they called each other, "Zeke" and "New York" and "Guts," and they would show their affection by refusing to say his name, playing the game of "You white folks all look alike." The younger guys in their Afros gave him the fist salute or a desultory passing nod. His own hair still had frizz, and maybe they took him for a hippie in shirt and tie. Anyway it was the 1970s, before crack. Denver, when Bruce lived there with his wife, was a city of many colors, and he could say with satisfaction that one of his best friends was a black man named Trevor, who had played football for Morehouse

University and had come west to practice law. Bruce and Trevor went together to all the parties, to weddings and birthdays and job promotions, all
the milestones reached within their circle. They went together to karate
classes, and one bleary Saturday morning, bleary in Bruce's mind because
on Friday night he had binged on tequila trying to get out of his system an
inane tongue-lashing given him by a corporate vice-president, he was
matched with Trevor in an exhibition bout. Each feint, each slashing blow,
was stuck in Bruce's mind. Trevor had committed a minor violation of etiquette with a stiff jab to Bruce's nose, but Bruce's counterattack had been
inappropriate according to the rules, according to the regulated physical
passion of karate, and according to any standard of friendship. (Here was
a personal experience to which he could address his question!) What was
the reason Bruce "saw blood and went apeshit and tried to take Trevor's
head off" with a reverse turn and kick? Why the follow-up heel that broke
his friend's ribs, and why, with Trevor sliding toward the mat, did Bruce
finish him with a blindsided, cheap shot left hook that knocked him un-
conscious? Why had "a switch flipped on inside me, triggering all this
rage"? Did he imagine his friend to represent all the petty-minded corporate vice-presidents of the world? Bruce thought that must have been it
and explained it so to Trevor, saying he was sorry for "being such a shit,"
and Trevor, bandaged up, was "a mensch about it, which was a relief to
me because I dearly loved the guy." Bruce paid his meted-out punishment
of thirty extra push-ups, and their friendship resumed its course. They par-
tied as usual, and Trevor would bring along his mother, who had earlier
adopted Bruce into her family. But now she would not look at him. The
beating of her son had to be an expression of submerged racial anger; it
had to be her son's blackness that had set Bruce off—she could not
fathom it otherwise, and she went to her death without forgiving Bruce.
Her attitude did not come between Bruce and Trevor, not so far as Bruce
could tell, but whenever they were on the karate mat afterward there was
a certain wariness between them, a hint of stifled aggression, of a private
tension struggling to stay beneath the surface. Bruce did not know if
Trevor was wondering, as perhaps any sane person would wonder: Could
a real friend have inspired such deep-down viciousness?

The NAACP and such groups, transmitters of racial togetherness, the
Nobel laureates of all-is-one, are out of fashion. Martin Luther King is idol-
ized but who follows his ideals? Perhaps the problem lies in the current
definition of racial togetherness. When people refer to it these days, what

do they mean? Does a political marriage of convenience between the likes of Mike Miller and Gloria Lawlah qualify as "integration"? How about a mutual understanding between the incumbent circuit court judges and Congressman Albert Wynn?

Along with almost everyone else in the Black Alliance, Congressman Wynn was being standoffish about Elvira White's candidacy. If Elvira was, in the eyes of the white establishment, an overbearing woman getting her comeuppance, then to the black establishment she was a representation of the "uppity Negro" who, despite elocution lessons and the acquiring of excellent table manners, was too angry to fit in. She was a representation of a character supposedly purged from the Prince George's scene, a character many of Prince George's black politicians found embarrassing.

At an earlier time Congressman Wynn had met with Governor Donald Schaefer to lobby for Elvira's judgeship. But that was before all the controversy. Doubts had now developed in the congressman, and he was quietly exerting himself to get her to withdraw her candidacy. All her outlandish talk, he felt, reflected poorly on her fitness for office. "I did everything I could to get Elvira appointed, but this recent series of problems has raised a question of whether she's temperamentally suited," Congressman Wynn said now. He was a heavyset man in a three-piece suit behind a mahogany desk on Capitol Hill. "You have to say, wait a minute, if this person wants to be a judge should she be having all these problems, finding herself in all these situations? I've talked to a lot of black people who are politically active, and they have all expressed a degree of reservation about her." To be a judge, sitting in judgment on the variegated masses, was not a dream vouchsafed to any black American with a law degree. You had to earn it, the congressman said.

Elvira was not someone who took rejection lightly. Nor would she stand for lectures from someone like Congressman Wynn, who would not be where he was, she felt, if not for the outspokenness of earlier black Americans and who, when Elvira's name was sparkling and marketable, had come to her for support.

At a Waldorf restaurant, her suit a somber black, fingernails unpainted, Elvira was fuming and feeling tough. "It was good ol' Al Wynn who called my house when he didn't have ten cents in his pocket to run for Congress, when he didn't have a staff, when he didn't have anything except his big belly. He managed to ring my phone at ten o'clock one night right after the state of Maryland, of which he was a senator at the time, had furloughed us at the public defender's office, costing me a week's pay. He managed to disturb me in my home and ask for money, and I managed to cough it up. And it was good ol' Al Wynn, before he was elected to Congress, who was happy to get the publicity when the Black Alliance held a press conference for me at the courthouse. I have a videotape of him standing with the others on the courthouse steps, saying rah, rah, rah, we're gonna run Elvira for judge. We're gonna run her. Al Wynn's body is quite visible on that TV screen, and his voice is quite loud, and he can't deny what he said because you can see his lips moving. So now two years later I am being hung out to dry, and he's running for cover." Elvira was all anger. Her professional friendships had turned to ashes; all she had left was contempt, not just for her white friends, but for all people who once had marveled at her brashness and her potential for greatness and who had patronized her even as they served as her patrons. "I want Al Wynn to know he owes me. I'm going to make certain I call his name regularly. He can't afford to stiff me. He can't afford not to give me money. He hasn't given me one dime, but I'm going to call him and specifically say I'd like to have a check. I've supported him all these years. I'm going to ask him to look at his campaign records to see whose name has appeared each and every time. Time to pay up!"

The personal could not be separated from the political in Elvira's campaign. But, fancy Elvira or not, feud with her or not, there was no disputing that her candidacy had placed members of the Black Alliance in a predicament. Elvira had introduced her gambit in an election cycle tricky to predict. Mike Miller was in a wheeling-and-dealing mood. He had a long-held animosity for Sue Mills and a long-held animosity for Wayne Curry's white patron, Parris Glendening. Therefore Mike Miller was willing to come out whole hog for Bea Tignor, the candidate supported by Congressman Wynn and by most other members of the Black Alliance. To obtain Mike Miller's blessing for a black woman in the county executive's race was more than a pragmatic move; it was a lucky break, heaven-sent. By the same token, to deal with Mike Miller, a defense lawyer and well-known figure at the courthouse, was to accept the incumbent judges. Members of the Black Alliance ordinarily had little brief with courthouse politics—they were teachers, ministers, entrepreneurs, not lawyers—but this easy deal with Mike Miller on behalf of Mrs. Tignor had turned complex and nasty because of Elvira. She would call out anyone. The bitterness flowed freely from her. That you were Congressman Wynn, of the highest local rank, did not faze her. That you were Judge Taylor, revered by everyone, did not faze her. When she heard that Judge Taylor, the man who might have been her mentor, had endorsed the incumbent judges, she said loudly, "It must be that he likes the social life too much, the fine pleasures with the good old boys. They're still paying him, and he's still flying that plane."

The love of money—that, to Elvira, was a root of the evil: "Prince George's is supposed to be quote, unquote 'the mecca of the highly educated, higher-income black people in the world'—the mecca of the entire world! But they're still slaves, living behind their ritzy gates. Slaves in suits and high heels, still with their shackles on. One man volunteered to take a position in my campaign but then backed off. He stumbled and stuttered when he came to tell me. He couldn't look me in the face. As long as you're a slave in the trappings of success, you'll never be anybody. Before I'll be a slave I'll be buried in my grave. Kill me, because that's what they'll have to do to stop me. I feel the black people in South Africa today are enjoying more independence than we in Prince George's County. The white minority will continue to rule here until these educated middle-income African-Americans get some spine to their step and quit being afraid of losing their little four-by-fours. I get very incensed when they talk about all the things they could lose. They were able to earn their college degrees because people in the civil rights movement sacrificed their lives. Material things are easy come, easy go. I've seen both sides. Those forlorn black men on the street corners . . . I know them, I can talk to them. Where I started out, we just had an outhouse till I was ten years old. After I got here, I was in middle-class heaven. I wined and dined with the best of them behind the big Woodmoor gates. I danced the dance, and it was fun, but I had to be stripped of the good life before I got my freedom papers, which arrived in the form of Chapter Thirteen bankruptcy papers. Yes, I'm in Chapter Thirteen, but I still get up every morning and look myself in the mirror. I don't give a kitty about losing x, y, or z because x, y, or z does not define me as a human being."

Elvira had put her finger on it: Some black people in Prince George's County had too much money for the likes of her. The uptick of black wealth was decipherable from the 1990 Census—a doubling in the previous ten years of the average household income, now up to $50,393; a raise in the median price of houses from $55,000 to $120,000; a lowering of the poverty rate to 6.5 percent (compared to an average of 23.6 percent elsewhere in Maryland). The spread of luxury could be seen on a Sunday afternoon drive. Elvira would say, "The only thing I need money for is to run my campaign. To all those who are carrying around the heavy burden of the middle-class blues here is the chance to lighten your load. Contribute to my campaign. You don't want to put it in your name, put it in the name of a cousin or an aunt. I don't care if it's in the name of your dog." A coffee klatch in Enterprise Estates might be worth a thousand dollars if you knew what to say. But in Elvira's usual speech she might call up the name of Terrence Johnson and would certainly talk about her courthouse tribulations. She assumed there would be total and abiding interest, but her listeners were put off. She had raised less than five percent of the funds raised by the incumbent judges. Whenever affluent black Prince Georgians had to choose where to contribute political money—on the one hand, to the county executive's campaign and its influence over the whole kit-and-kaboodle of bond sales, development deals, and government prerogatives; on the other hand, a judge's race and the power of a single circuit court courtroom—the choice seldom went in Elvira's favor. With the courthouse, the good property-owning black Prince Georgian took an approach much like the maharajah in the Indian story who, when solicited about Christianity by a missionary lady, is noncommittal: "But of what use is that to me?" What could Elvira offer them? Her money-poor campaign went begging, unable to afford the slick brochures and massive mailings of the incumbent judges. She had difficulty reaching voters, except when she made news, and for quite a while now all the publicity attending Elvira in the media had been bad publicity.

There was always a handful of sociable people as Dr. Gordon toiled on his walker up and down the sidewalk. This morning there was Mrs. Jones, apron off, bustling to make a bank deposit in the middle of the day. "How grand to see you out and about, Doc. That's so good," she gushed. And there was Mr. Crittenden, a shopkeeper from the era when the Grits were the troublemakers. His Cadillac Eldorado had been stolen last week and recovered yesterday. "A couple of black kids took it," Mr. Crittenden announced, as if this was a revelation. And there was Bob Magruder, who never failed to wave. Dr. Gordon yelled out, "Hey, Bobby, slow down," and the old boxing champion pulled over to the curb in his waxed sedan with its cracked windshield, damage done by a wayward golf ball. They made another date for Rosecroft—"soon as I get the windshield replaced."

Later in the day a few of the Old Settlers, a retired police chief and a half-retired lawyer, along with Mr. Crittenden, gathered in the Gordon living room to drink lemonades and fool with Doc's old blood-pressure devices. Not for the first time, they got around to boasting about Bob Magruder. "The best pugilist ever to put on gloves and grace Hillcrest Heights," said Dr. Gordon.

At age ten Bobby Magruder had been a seventy-pound, dirty-finger-nailed, lit-up firecracker fighting all comers in the hayseed roadhouses of southern Maryland. He was paid five bucks for a win and any dimes or nickels tossed his way on the wood floors. Milky-white farm girls in bikinis dangled circuslike on go-go swings and wolf-whistled at him. For years the gift of a hard chin and his brawling style made him all but unbeatable. Finally, in 1971, word came of a worthy opponent, and a club match was arranged. Twenty-one years old, Bobby Magruder was then the main card, at the top of the amateur game, voted the outstanding fighter of the previous year's Golden Gloves tournament. His opponent was to be a seventeen-year-old kid from over by the Landover Mall, name of Sugar Ray Leonard, said to be lightning fast but whose fame still lay ahead. The kid had never fought in front of a big crowd. A quarter-century later the Magruder-Leonard fight would be remembered as a classic. Just a few days ago Bob Magruder had been interviewed about it again on Channel Eight.

"Oh, boy, they really duked it out, and Bobby kicked Sugar Ray's fancy butt!" crowed Dr. Gordon.

To a man, this was the consensus of the Old Settlers. Bruce, in his downstairs room, could hear the whoops. He came up the stairs into the living room and said, "No, no, that's not what happened. You guys are wrong. Sugar Ray won. Magruder lost."

"Bullshit!" his father said.

"I'm not going to argue with you." Somewhere in the house there were old newspaper clippings of the fight, but what was the point of hunting them up? The Old Settlers were blissful in their revised history.

There was a fair amount more to the story of Bob Magruder and Sugar Ray Leonard, however, beyond what the newspapers had ever reported— or, for that matter, what Bruce, on his account, knew. The 1971 fight, it was true, had been credited to the underdog. Bob Magruder had been overconfident, and Sugar Ray won on points with a bup, bup, bup and gone. Their second Golden Gloves fight, a year later at Suitland High School, was actually more of a classic. In those days everyone knew Bob Magruder, and hundreds of his idolators shoved their way into the gym— teenage girls who adored him, over-the-hill pugs to whom he was a second coming, the cops who used to roust him. Right from the bell, Bobby moved in for a quick finish, throwing roundhouses, showing no mercy. Sugar Ray hung on but figured he had lost. "You got me, Bobby," he said. But the ring judges decided against the Hillcrest Heights boy on a split decision. The crowd went berserk. It was a police scene. Then, a few months later, the two boxers fought again, open-class, AAU tournament. Sugar Ray caught Bob flush on an eyebrow cut and put him on the canvas for the first time ever. It ended up another decision for Sugar Ray Leonard, and this time the once indomitable Bob Magruder, looking at the youngster's arms raised in celebration, felt himself sag on the ropes and knew his future would not hold any big TV bouts in Las Vegas or license plates that said "CHAMP." And yet the story went on from there. The two boxers became friends. The rough-edged white guy became a member of the high-mannered black kid's entourage. They traveled the Americas for Sugar Ray's title fights, and, when not on the road, their hangout was the Quonset hut across the street from the Gordons. Sugar Ray brought the entire 1972 Olympic team to the hut for training, and even after Sugar Ray hit it big the hut was his favorite place to spar. These days he lived in Los Angeles, a young, rich retiree, and, except for the occasional banquet or black-tie exhibition, the two men had drifted apart, but when they did get together they were like brothers, squeezing the bejesus out of each other. Meanwhile, the Quonset hut remained an active landmark, and the grown-up Bob Magruder, the hometown hero who had stayed behind long after most of his hero-worshipers had moved away, still had the run of the place and kept it alive and well. His workday job was to collar bail jumpers, a job once called bounty hunting, but, off hours, inside the hut, he was somebody the kids looked on like a godfather. For all the young mean-eyed roughhousers he had hauled back in handcuffs to the Prince George's courthouse he had probably saved dozens more from going wrong. He had proved the old culture could be resilient.

The grief of Elbert and Daphne Jones for their son and for his lost life, a life he might possibly have lived with Amy Smith in a world the Joneses once idealized, had become a search for a truth other than the official one. Mr. and Mrs. Jones had hired a private investigator and had consulted with lawyers about filing a "wrongful death" suit against Amy's parents. But nothing new had come out of the private eye's search, and the lawyers were of the opinion a lawsuit could become an interminable enterprise and would probably result in little more than a rehash of the testimony already sworn to by Dennis and Marie Smith. "I can assure you the Smiths will simply restate everything they've already said. They can't change a word without getting hung up on perjury," one lawyer told the Joneses. "But you might be able to win a settlement. It might be worth it to the Smiths to pay you to go away."

"No thanks, we're not interested in money," Mr. Jones replied. "We want to know what happened in that house that night—the real story."

Beyond the central question of how the Jones family line had come to such a violent end there was other information Mr. and Mrs. Jones wished to know. What had been on Derrick's mind before he arrived at the Smith house? Was he in a cunning mood? ("Inconceivable. Derrick was naive about most things in life. Amy is a hundred times more cunning than Derrick could ever have been.") Might he have been in a reckless mood, though? Was it conceivable he got talked into an act of criminal derring-do for a lady love? Amy was the one with these answers, and, from the day of the crime through the day of Amy's sentencing, Mrs. Jones had entreated Elvira for five minutes alone with the girl—"As one mother to another, do me this one favor!" But Elvira had to refuse Mrs. Jones. Anything Amy said outside the attorney-client privilege might have compromised her at trial. Afterward, however, after Amy was debriefed by Dr. Schouten and after she was processed into Patuxent Institution and issued a jumpsuit, Elvira arranged to give Mrs. Jones her five minutes in the prison visiting room, face-to-face.

It was an awkward meeting. Mrs. Jones tried to remember the gushy, well-mannered young lady who introduced herself one afternoon at the front door of the Jones home and who had laughingly, teasingly pulled Derrick by the hand into her borrowed car. Mrs. Jones tried to remember how likable Amy had seemed. She tried to think of Amy as a girl who might have married into the family. She tried not to ask questions that were too direct or too demanding, leaving it for Amy to settle accounts.

There was not much to report when Mrs. Jones returned to her husband. Amy had talked blandly of the inconveniences behind bars and of her desire to take classes toward her GED. She had begged off saying anything about the circumstances surrounding Derrick's death.

"Did she even say she was sorry?" Mr. Jones asked.

"No."

But why would she?—this was the thought that had occurred to Mr. Jones. Why should someone who believed that the bad had always been done to her ever think ill of herself? Mr. Jones no longer expected anyone from the Smith family to make a confession. It was up to a higher power now. "I don't do lots of things that so-called true Christians do, but I do serve God," Mr. Jones said, mouth grim. "And I have to believe that somewhere sometime these people will be punished." At night Mr. Jones had a recurring dream in which he would run to where his son lay calling out his name on a shag carpet. In front of him a staircase led to a heavenly light. He tried to reach Derrick, to lift him up, but a man walked out of the light with deliberate footsteps and pointed a snub-nosed gun. Mr. Jones would awake thinking he had been a witness to his son's death. But he was as uninformed as before. He had no idea whether his son had died silent and forlorn or howling into musty basement air.

At one time Elvira's success in the courtroom had a logic behind it. "As the mother of two young African-American males, I can identify with both sides," she would say. "I identify with the defendant because of what's happening with my people, and I identify with the victim for the same reason. My people are getting killed, and my people are getting jailed." But Elvira's equipping of young black men with a surrogate mother's love that earlier had won her praise in the local newspapers was now turned against her. What had then seemed like savvy was said now to be a blind spot. What had seemed like a sensitivity in her handling of black clients was said now to be an insensitivity toward white clients. And where Elvira's ambition to be the first black female public defender, the first black female judge, the first black everything, was once held up as laudatory, her ambition now confronted her like an indictment.

Other members of the Black Alliance had begun to distance themselves from the defeat everyone assumed was in store for Elvira. Bea Tignor had endorsed the incumbent judges, as had Wayne Curry. Only Gloria Lawlah, alone among the officially powerful, was willing to be enthusiastic about Elvira in public. Gloria's word had been her bond. She had put Elvira on her slate, and Elvira's name was included on Gloria's brochures and in her mailings. It was a risk for Gloria—not a risk to her own election but a risk that Frank Pesci might write once again in his column about Gloria playing to the black vote. "Yet what is Elvira's crime?" Gloria had said. "Her only crime is being a black woman."

Probably, without Gloria's support, Elvira would indeed have given up. Depression had finally descended on her. She was experiencing bad, sleepless nights. She would prowl the house, trying not to wake up B.J. under his covers. She had taken her troubles to a psychotherapist, Dr. Frances Rankin, who had prescribed Prozac for her. While she was in Dr. Rankin's therapy room, B.J. would wait outside and afterward would say, "It's going to be okay, Mom." Yet what kept Elvira going most of all was the single shining light of Gloria Lawlah—not just the solidarity Gloria was extending now but also the example she had set four years earlier when she ran against Frank Pesci's friend, the incumbent Frank Komenda.

In her office, sipping water, Elvira harked back on Gloria's run. There had been one Saturday night when limos and town cars stacked up along the curb in Elvira's subdivision and big-timers piled onto a nearby lawn for a steaks-and-ribs fund-raiser. Governor Schaefer and Mike Miller and a dozen prominent black politicians were in attendance. Curiosity got the better of Elvira, and she moseyed over. "I saw all these major politicians, black and white, rubbing shoulders and writing checks for Frank Komenda," Elvira remembered. "But a few weeks later, when the votes were counted, Komenda had lost. Gloria beat him. So whenever I think of how difficult it is for me, I think of that barbecue, and how Gloria came out a winner anyway."

On their way to a South Carolina beach vacation Heather and Mike and the three girls detoured to Hillcrest Heights to leave their dogs with Heather's folks. The girls had another agenda: Could their grandpa pull strings to get them tickets to the sold-out World Cup soccer games at RFK Stadium? Merv laughed at their awesome faith in him. "I'll give it my best shot," he promised. The troupe then clambered back toward their van. Kisses and finger-tight hugs were traded.

The melancholy premonition of death in saying good-bye to old people did not lay so heavily on Heather because her folks were healthy as mules. They could go to bed at eleven, get up at six-thirty and put in a full-tilt day without naps.

Like newlyweds, Merv and Dell had been at work the past few months at the farm in Penfield, reversing years of neglect. They had thrown themselves into the task—a prayer answered for Heather. (She would periodically check on them, and in the course of these trips she had discovered something about herself: "It hit me one day how much Penfield resembles my little remote hole in West Virginia. I think I've chosen to live where I live because it's my way of going back home, back to the original family home—that's what I finally figured out.") Finding their own way, Merv and Dell had freed the old, two-story frame house from loops of briar and honeysuckle vines and thickish saplings, undergrowth brought forth in the bellies of birds and on the tips of winter winds. The cold cellar had been returned to its historic utility. Next in store was the remodeling of the pitched-roof, gray-planked garage, two wings and an attic to be added. Dell was deciding between unadorned linear windows or curved tops; Merv wanted stairs and a trapdoor to the attic where the grandchildren could play on rainy days. Merv's aviation records, those not already sent to archivists at Stanford University's Hoover Institute, would go into safekeeping in one of the new wings. In the other wing would go either the

Continental or the Mustang or the Checker. Their 1939 Ford coupe was already in the garage, tires sunk down, dusty and cobwebbed, but preserved for a time of restoration among piles of firewood and museum-quality tools hung on nails. The house itself was too antiquated, past hope, but the Stricklers were hatching a scheme for a new house in a woods across fields of hay, a quarter mile from the nearest road. A house in that spot, on a hillside, would command a stupendous view. With sharpened axes and a crosscut they made a clearing, just the two of them. They breathed in the smell of sap. One weekend turned into ten.

And yet, returning each time to Hillcrest Heights, there was a sense of relief at being again in a comfortable place. The house on Foster Place had less of a transient feel than did, for all its history, the homestead in Pennsylvania.

10

The politicians appreciated having Bob Magruder at their rallies because he was a walking advertisement of a white guy unfazed by the racial divide. He might show up with his friend Robert "Pappy" Gault, the first black Olympic boxing coach, who had been handed the flag by George Foreman and who lived in neighboring Capitol Heights, or he might bring young guys like the black boxer Greg Truman and the white boxer Joe Fitzpatrick III, another pair of advertisements.

At this very moment, had Bruce Gordon gone across the street and into the Quonset hut, he would have found Bob Magruder in a white shirt and blue tie, towel on a shoulder, pacing the linoleum floor and directing the workouts of the thickly muscled Truman, about to turn pro, and the rabbity-legged Fitzpatrick, a jolter, undefeated after four pro fights. They were doing rapid turns on the heavy canvas bag and the light leather bag. "Don't stop moving," Bob Magruder said. Joe Fitzpatrick and Greg Truman were from the Magruder stable; he was their manager. They put on headgear and vaulted into the ring, four sections of white painted wood on two-by-four stilts with a red apron and blue stools in the corners. Bob Magruder, an old tiger who could keep guys in line with just his soft tenor voice, encouraged them. "Relax in there, relax, push off, relax, set it up. Short stuff. No uppercuts. Slip that hook, Joe, slip it. One, two. Quick, one, two."

Joseph Fitzpatrick II, the boy's father, walked in and asked, "How's he look today?"

"Tough as a hammer," Bob Magruder said.

"Just like they used to say about you." Joe the Second was one of his old sparring partners. "Toughest, roughest kid on the street."

"Yeah, well . . ."

Joe the Second turned to another man at ringside, a stranger to the Hut who had come to interview Bob Magruder about his recent nomination to the Maryland Boxing Hall of Fame. "Every cop in Prince George's knew Bobby by name, that's how tough he was," Joe the Second said.

"Don't bring that up. I was a kid."

"Oh, everybody knows you're a model citizen now."

All of this might have been evident to Bruce had he popped over, but it had been years since he was inside the Hut, not since he was twenty-two and put in a month of workouts and called attention to himself as the biggest guy in the gym with the heaviest hit on the punching bags. Bob Magruder, into his scout-and-trainer phase by then, had given Bruce a few pointers. The Magruder ring strategy is the lost art of the body attack: pound the midsection, make the guy's knees quiver, and slam home the uppercut. Bruce seemed to have exceptional skills, but he would not go toe-to-toe with his trainer. "I was scared of Magruder—even with gear on, even for so-called fun, you can get hit a lot in three rounds" was Bruce's memory of it. His personal dignity had been hurt. It was a needling thought even now. But was it not reasonable for Bruce to avoid a fight with the former street punk who had been doted on by Bruce's father and who in conspiracy with his father might have been planning to teach a lesson to a callow college youth known locally for loving a black woman? How was Bruce to have known he could have shucked off his terrified awe and embraced the ex-Grit with real pride?

When Is it not valuable to have a benefactor in a high place?

Television crews, a hearing room in the state capitol, an inquiry into the types of racism Maryland state employees were contending with in the 1990s—it was a sterling opportunity for Elvira to secure an appearance on the six o'clock news. Gloria instructed her staff to send Elvira an invitation to the state hearing, along with a day parking pass. Just when Elvira was thinking a good break might catch up with her, though, a minor courtroom case in Charles County was compounded into an all-day ordeal, and she missed out on the TV cameras. She was at home feeling sorry for herself when Gloria phoned. "How about tomorrow? Can you come testify tomorrow?" Gloria asked. The following day, with a second invitation and a second parking pass, Elvira drove to Annapolis and said her piece. Late in the afternoon, back home, she turned on the news. Her face leaped up on the Channel Thirteen lead-in. Elvira punched the remote, and there she was on Channel Eleven also.

Thus the TV audience heard of Elvira's view of herself as a "plantation hand." No use in being so judicious as to overlook how she had been sinned against!

Yet would her statements rouse anger against the Prince George's incumbents, or would she come across merely as a paranoid?

Many of those who sat through the full hearing at the state capitol decided it was, all in all, a good portent for Elvira's campaign. A host of state employees, it turned out, had personal stories not unlike hers. Maryland lawmakers heard how jobs were denied to black people, promotions were denied, offensive names were tossed offhandedly into office talk, even Klan literature was passed around. The three days of testimony recalled an American era when a seat at the lunch counter was a thrillingly real-life goal, before the full range of racial integration became a social idea.

A few weeks later, different testimony but with the same undertone was reported at a hearing chaired by Congressman Al Wynn, who, in his position on the U.S. House Committee on Banking, Finance and Urban Affairs, was investigating banking practices in Prince George's County. The owner of a construction company, a black man, told of having to conduct business at a Largo bank where the doors were locked through the middle of the day and customers had to pass a visual inspection before the key was turned. A bank regulator said he empathized with the bank tellers, since they were not protected by bullet-proof glass. At the largest savings and loan association in the metropolitan area, Chevy Chase Federal Savings Bank, the attitude of the loan officers was being investigated by the U.S. Justice Department because only three percent of the Chevy Chase loans between 1976 and 1992 had gone to people living in "black" areas of housing.

Gloria took it hard, hearing all this testimony. "I'm so distressed. I'd thought we'd gotten past this kind of discrimination," she said during constituent-hour at her office in the mall. "When I was young, it was 'Just get your diploma, girl,' and now to have a place like Prince George's County chock full of black people with education, with careers, with beautiful homes, cars, immaculate clothes, people who speak standard English, who do all the things every American does, and then to be slapped in the face again. This banking thing really messes up my mind. It's incredible.

Why wouldn't a bank lend money to college-educated black people? A bank is in the business to make loans. Why shut us out? I don't want to make it into such a racial issue. It would be wonderful to completely move away from race, but every time I try to forget about race something like this comes up. Look what Elvira's been through. You keep hoping racism is dead, but it's not. How many times do we have to go back and fight this battle? I'm tired of it. Oh Jesus, I'm so tired of it."

A ruling on whether Elvira had, or had not, played racial favorites in the Amy Smith case was at hand, but Judge William Missouri was holding it up. Because of the delay, there was grousing at the courthouse that the judge must be "staying up nights to figure how to let Elvira off the hook." People who would not have been the least bit troubled if a white judge had been sitting in judgment of Elvira were troubled because Judge Missouri, who had made his way to Prince George's County from the cotton fields of South Carolina, was a black man. Had they been privy to the judge's past relationship with Elvira—he had been her study partner in law school, he had written to Governor Schaefer on her behalf, and he had been a guest in her house—they might well have chorused, "The fix is in!"

Yet it was Elvira who had sought to have Judge Missouri recused from the case. It was she who was positive he could not be a dispassionate arbiter. It was she who believed "sad to say, he's sold his soul to the devil." Her thinking was that since Judge Missouri cared about his career at the courthouse, he could not afford to rule in her favor. When speaking of him she used the familiar bludgeons of "Uncle Tom" and "handkerchief head." She said, "Black people are allowed into the courthouse club because they ingratiate themselves, and that's how you stay in the club." So it was that the issue of race continued to dominate the Amy Smith case.

In the town of Clinton, in the privacy of a dingily lit, virtually deserted Italian cafe, Frank Pesci was getting down to blunt, unvarnished talk with Sue Mills. Since her surrogates had failed to lure Frank into her campaign, she had picked up the phone one evening and personally asked for his help. But Frank would commit only to meet at the cafe. "I have a few questions," he said. The questions would perhaps be impertinent, and he apologized in advance.

"I don't mind. I'm pretty impertinent myself."

Twenty years earlier, as a state legislator, Frank had sponsored the legislation that changed the Prince George's school board from an appointed into an elected body, and, into this opening, Mrs. Mills's barnstorming political career had taken off. An unintentional favor, but Mrs. Mills always had had a soft spot for Frank, even when he was setting the world on fire with his liberal ideas. But could Frank be comfortable with Sue Mills as the county executive? Was the "new" Sue Mills a credible creation—that is, the matured, statesmanlike Sue Mills who spoke now for integration?

At the restaurant Frank commenced with his battery of questions. Rantings and ravings were part of the Mills's legend, and he wanted to provoke her, to animate a true self. He asked about the slights she had suffered from the political establishment. Sue Mills laughed her brassy laugh. "So what?" she said. She was casual, as if chatting in a supermarket line with a PTA mom.

Frank pressed. "You're the senior member on the council, and they won't let you serve as president?!"

"It's their loss." She had control of herself. She held a cigarette over her shoulder. Smoke swirled. This was her sort of stylishness, the style of a nightclub singer—heavy makeup; provocative dresses—the affectation of glamour lent to her generation by Lauren Bacall and Elizabeth Taylor. It was something else that made some people uncomfortable, and Frank decided to bring it up.

"It's who I am."

"The impression it creates, though . . ."

Mrs. Mills had heard the talk. "Hey, come on, I've got a husband who loves me. I've raised two kids. I'm a grandmother. I dress the way I do because it presents a positive outlook. I've had my share of dark times—I've had a son die of a rare disease; I've had to sell my house because of Mike Miller. But I've tried to stay positive. Put it this way: I'm an ordinary woman who likes to look dressy. That's who I am. People who talk about my looks don't like me because of my politics. They use my hair and my dresses as an excuse."

Frank thought she was only partly right. The look of Sue Mills was discomfiting because it was the look of the past. Still, a cosmetic makeover at this stage would have made her unrecognizable to the voters. Let the professional pols dismiss her as the crass, dolled-up PTA mother. That was her appeal to the public!

"Enough about that," Frank said. He asked her if there was a "main motivating force" behind her candidacy. He knew she had put together a slate to take over the Democratic Central Committee from Mike Miller. "Are you after revenge? They didn't let you into the club so you're going to show them? You're going to be the top boss. Is that it?"

"I'm too independent to be a political tycoon," she said. "I wouldn't even be running for county executive if the term-limits law hadn't forced my hand." In the act of running, however, she said, her view of politics, her view of people, her view of herself, everything had grown more expansive. She was discovering what it might mean to be in charge of a place that was "damn near unique in the annals of American history."

This introduced the subject of race. "Where are your black supporters?" Frank wanted to know. "You talk about them, but where are they? Why aren't more of them out there posing with you?"

He seemed finally to have hit a nerve. She fiddled agitatedly with the silverware. There were many black people who had pledged their votes to her, she said—James Hammonds was one, an army man and a longtime resident of Hillcrest Heights who had been alienated from her during the busing era but was now converted ("Even if you disagree with Sue Mills on some of her past concepts there are good things about her that balance the equation"). But the past was her millstone. To be really and truly reincarnated, to be a force for unity, Sue Mills would have to be more than just the candidate most likely to prevent white flight. She needed, at the end of the day, to show with flesh and blood that she was the candidate of all the people.

Frank had some free advice. "Get your black supporters out front, and go on TV and promise that all your appointments will be independent and interracial if you get into office."

"That's been my plan all along."

Sue Mills was more complex than her reputation, Frank thought, and more simple. Afterward, in his summation of the restaurant meeting, he would say, "She seems to have come a long way, but I know her past too well."

Two decades had come and gone since Heather and Camilla and Bruce engaged in plots to make themselves the talk of the Class of 1974. But how could they not take up their old roles? How could they not delight in proving to their old classmates they were still true-blue spitfires?

This new plot had been prompted by a discussion between Heather and Camilla about the ten-year class reunion in 1984, a reunion memorable for not having a single black member of the class present. And where were they? Were they boycotting out of a collective pique? A school reunion might be an ideal Rorschach of the passing decades, but apparently no statement was being made by the missing black classmates. Apparently they had not been invited. At least Camilla and other black leaders of the class had not received an invitation in the mail. At the reunion Heather went up to a woman who had helped organize it and asked the obvious, "Why is it that nobody who is black is here?"

"I don't remember ever having any blacks in our class," the woman replied.

A horror came over Heather. What powerful longings had shielded this woman from the actualities of life? Perhaps, after all, there was such a thing as being too colorblind.

Neither Camilla nor Bruce had attended the ten-year reunion, and they had little interest in attending the twenty-year reunion until presented with Heather's radiant outrage. "I was mad ten years ago, and I am madder now because . . . well, because it was as if somebody had come up to me and told me my friends didn't exist or, even worse, didn't have a right to exist," Heather said. "Literally, that's the way I felt."

So the plot was for Camilla, cheerleader and salutatorian, to attend this year's reunion hand in hand with Heather, her oldest friend, and with Bruce, her old lover.

Three days short of the third anniversary of Derrick Jones's death Judge Missouri, who admitted to having spent a few late nights with the case, finally issued his ruling. The length of his ruling was twenty-seven double-spaced pages.

Elvira White, at her office, flipped through the pages like a speedreader and was trembling with rage when she finished.

Amy Smith was notified by her new attorney late that afternoon. "Good news!" Larry Polen said. Amy went into the exercise room at Patuxent and high-fived everyone in sight.

Daphne and Elbert Jones heard about it at their home from a news reporter. They confessed to having exceedingly mixed emotions, but they talked bravely. *The truth will out!*

Judge Missouri, the former law school partner of Elvira, had ordered a new trial for Amy. His ruling overturned Amy's 1992 conviction by reasons of "prejudice." He had reviewed the relationship between Amy (referred to as "Petitioner") and Elvira (referred to by her surname) and had come to this hard conclusion: "White's view of the Petitioner was negative. That negative view of the Petitioner by White prejudiced the Petitioner to the extent that she was deprived of the counsel guaranteed by the Sixth Amendment to the United States Constitution. Therefore, this court concludes that the Petitioner has established that White was ineffective due to her concern for the deceased co-defendant [Derrick Jones] and his family, and that this concern was equal to or greater than the concern White had for the Petitioner. This amounts to a conflict of interest because White's loyalty to her client was breached. . . . Because of White's split loyalties it is obvious she did not give her full attention to a defense for the Petitioner."

Elvira was adjudged to have done right by the Jones family but to have wronged Amy. "Tragic though Derrick Jones's death was, Amy Lynne Smith was the person who was entitled to Ms. White's entire devotion," Judge Missouri wrote. Elvira's transgression was not simply an altruistic breaking of the rules. Morally she may have walked a narrow ledge, but legally she had fallen off. With or without prior intent, according to the judge, Elvira had played false with her client. Judge Missouri could not say whether Elvira had uttered the infamous "bitch" comment, but, in his reading of the trial record, such an uttering was consistent with Elvira's attitude. "Ms. White's view of Petitioner was negative," he wrote. The way it seemed to him, Elvira had been too keen on presenting trial witnesses of overenthusiastic and indiscriminate report, leaving an impression of Amy as a "loose" young woman. Cross-examining one of Amy's former boyfriends, a young black man named Anthony Harding, Elvira had asked, "Did you have a sexual relationship with her?" The trial judge had ruled the question out of order. "This is totally irrelevant," he had admonished Elvira, "and, quite frankly, I don't understand why you want to bring it in. The fact that she may have had a sexual relationship with someone, as far as the public is concerned, isn't going to do her any good, and I don't see how it's helping her at all in this trial." At the same time, Elvira had tried to put on witness after witness to give good accounts of Derrick, the solid young citizen of Enterprise Estates. Elvira had tried to call Ralph Daniels, friend and neighbor of the Jones family, to testify that Derrick had no propensity for violence. Judge Missouri, in his ruling, was querulous. Why concentrate on Derrick's good character instead of Amy's? It appeared Elvira was bent on "protecting the memory of Derrick Jones and the Jones family to Petitioner's detriment." Building up Derrick was the legal equivalent of tearing down Amy and was the pivotal point for Judge Missouri. "If taken to its logical conclusion, such testimony would have the effect of suggesting that the Petitioner, by whatever means, corrupted Derrick Jones to the extent that he, contrary to his character, committed a crime."

But "corruption," or rather seduction, was exactly what Elvira believed had happened. Elvira was comfortable creating Amy in a sexual image. This was Elvira's moral high ground, her conception of her client as a junior harridan. Any disloyalty Amy had experienced was less disloyalty than she had dished out to the boy, seducing him to his death. In Elvira's mind her handling of the case had an upright and sound basis in the law. In a bench conversation at the trial she had pleaded to have the sexual evidence allowed in. "There is a method to my madness." To Elvira, the revelations about Amy's sex life were not just spellbinding. To Elvira, the sex explained everything. Once the father realized the daughter was sleeping with young black men, the father was capable of the most heinous of acts. This had been Elvira's theory from the beginning, and she had not let go of it.

At the courthouse there were overdrawn expressions of regret to see Elvira so publicly rebuked by Judge Missouri.

Dwight Jackson joked grimly, "It's like the beneficiaries pretending to mourn the millionaire on his deathbed: 'Is he dead yet?' "

Mr. Jackson was probably the only good friend left to her at the courthouse. "It's sad," he said, "because I have this memory of all of us with our arms around each other, drinking Elvira's liquor, having a good old time."

It used to please Bruce and Camilla when, as a man in the company of a black woman, he would be mistaken for a wild-haired, bearded, light-skinned *black* guy. They liked to think Bruce was a forerunning American, someone with no fixed racial identity, and that their children would be forerunners, too. "Everybody should be able to pass as either black or white," Bruce would say. "That's the way it should be." To speak of a "mixed" marriage may be out of style, but the phrase has a certain aptness. Only by mixing and melding the racial genes will true integration be achieved, so it seemed to Bruce and Camilla. How absurd to have the measure of American idealism be at the mercy of so quack a contrivance as separate races! To bring into the world children through sanctioned, popularly blessed interracial couplings would be the obvious solution— that is, if such couplings did not involve sex.

Where were you when you first got clued in to the taboo regarding black and white sex? Camilla was at an audition for the female lead in a junior high performance of *Romeo and Juliet*. The precocious Camilla brought considerable qualifications to bear, with training from her Hollywood-actress mother and her drama-professor father, but the selection of a white boy for Romeo preordained that no black girl could be Juliet. The casting director gave Camilla a sorry excuse: "You're too qualified to play Juliet! Why not try out for the nurse?" Camilla, full of hurt, said, "I don't think so."

The end of the century was now upon us, but had we adjusted our American minds any better to the idea of men and women having sex without regard to race, color, or creed?

At least in the 1990s the statistics had become unstuck from America's historical norm. For three centuries not enough interracial couples took wedding vows to make a statistical import, but now, in the part of America that lays outside the Dixie South, marriages between black men and white women numbered ten percent of all couples and marriages between black women and white men numbered five percent. (In Prince George's County, the percentage of interracial marriages was slightly higher than the national average.) Statistics are facts about people, not their attitudes and certainly not the people themselves. And yet—and this was one of Camilla and Bruce's beefs with the rest of us—why is it that we, in a society riven by race, are such an ignorant lot when it comes to the facts about common blood and racial genetics? Why is this a subject about which intelligent Americans are wont to make sincerely believed assertions that are dead wrong? The few people like Bruce and Camilla who have a handle on the scholarly research might amaze the rest of us with scientific and historical facts routinely ignored in the great head-kicking debates about race. Among behaviorists, for instance, the conservative deconstructionists have made a prodigious intellectual exercise out of finding differences between white Americans and black Americans. Black Americans are alleged to have a propensity toward violence, a tendency for out-of-wedlock childbearing, and, on average, a lower level of intelligence—"the doctrine of immutable difference and inferiority, the eternal strategic positioning of white over black" in John Edgar Wideman's phrase. This debate is a bugaboo for liberal behaviorists who wish to downplay any differences but who wonder in private whether race might be, just maybe, an unfortunate determining factor in human conduct. The geneticists, however, have established that the debate is moot. Big differences among sentient beings may exist out in the universe, but humankind is united by a common and recent ancestry that began in Africa. We are all members of the family *homo sapiens*. Believe in the image of God or not, we are all created the same. Consider the comment of the anthropologist John Moore: "The question to ask is not, 'Do we have any African ancestors?' but 'How many?' " From Africa the original humans migrated first to Europe and then

to Asia, where weather conditions influenced changes in skin color and fa-
cial features and tricked early anthropologists into thinking the world is divided by the three racial groupings of Negroid, Caucasoid, and Mongoloid.
But when a team of Stanford University geneticists, led by the pioneer
Luigi Cavalli-Sforza, investigated Australian aborigines, who fit the physical characteristics of the Negroid group, they discovered instead far greater
genetic similarities between the aborigines and Mongoloids. A logical explanation can be extrapolated: Dark-skinned African migrants who over a
long expanse of time and under a milder Eastern sun became paler-
skinned Asians subsequently found their way to Australia and adopted
again a darker epidermis because of the heat and aridity. Skin color therefore is irrelevant to everything except climate.

Indeed, there is no gene that predetermines "race," and there can be no
intrinsic worth in being a "Negroid" or "Caucasoid" or "Mongoloid" because there are as many genetic differences within the three groupings as
there are between the groupings. Strictly speaking, there are more than
four hundred "races," but the DNA distinctions making up these "races"
are so incidental, hardly a dime's worth, it is more reasonable to accept
that there is only one race, the human race. "Black is a shade of brown. So
is white, if you look," John Updike wrote in the opening line to one of his
books. The wisdom of the geneticists is that American social life has been
operated under a defunct version of science. If you are unconvinced—*I
ain't no ace of spades, I ain't no white coon-ass*—forget science and consider history. Consider the mixing of the bloodlines just in America, just in
the past three hundred years. The exotica of sex between men and women
of differing skin tones is not a titillating invention of pulp writers. Sex
without regard to color has been an American condition since the arrival
of the first slaves. In the Ralph Ellison essay "What Would America Be Like
Without Blacks," he contends that African-Americans are at the center of
America's complex immigrant culture, having come to these shores not
long after white settlers. "Africanism is inextricable from the definition of
Americanism," he writes. "Whatever else the true American is, he is also
somehow black." This is a cultural observation that is also a biological observation, as substantiated faithfully by government census-takers. In the
era of slavery, pure-blooded African slaves were counted as "black" while
those of mixed African and European blood were "mulatto." By the late
nineteenth century, mulattoes were subdivided in the U.S. Census into
"quadroons" (one-quarter African) and "octoroons" (one-eighth African).
By 1930, the attempt to quantify by percentage of ancestry was given up as
a lost cause since three-quarters of the "colored" population was of mixed

blood. A breaking down of racial distinctions had occurred, driven by sexual impulses that disregarded legal and social impulses. So why not acknowledge it? Because, unhappy to say, this is a history of racial integration by sexual union but not very often by marriage. By and large, black women were impregnated by white men, and then deserted. Among the forebears of longtime African-American families are white plantation masters, but who among us would want to claim rape and concubinage in our family background? Who would care to be reminded of the caste period of America, the power drive carried onto silk sheets and into haylofts, part of an intricate shame, part of many heartsick rages? Read the poems of Langston Hughes to understand the degrees of denial and exorcising that have gone on in the black community. And, in the white community, was there not a great subconscious fear that revenge for all those sins would be visited on their daughters?

On a spring break from college, Camilla sat in the Potomac High auditorium and watched a black boy and a white girl play a hillbilly man and his betrothed in *Dark of the Moon*. In a pivotal scene the hillbilly becomes demented over a dark, fantasyland love affair that has beguiled the girl, and he takes her by force on a church pew. The scene by itself would have been enough to bring a blush to the parents of most high school students, but to stage it so that a black boy rapes a white girl in a place of worship?! To stage a downright freak-show Caligula manifestation of White America's burden?! The play was received by Camilla's liberal parents with incredulity. ("They were absolutely mortified. In our seats we were saying, 'What the hell are they doing? Why did they choose this play? If they want people to accept biracial sex why not choose something middle-of-the-road?' ") The other parents were almost eerily subdued. They may have been in shock, or they may have been putting on a chic air of knowingness. ("Everybody in the audience was so polite. They were saying to each other, okay, okay. I guess everybody wanted to pretend that this tension between the races was totally under control.") But it was not under control then and was not under control now. Everybody knows the score.

On the other hand, the statistics about interracial marriages were a sign of hope, if you were inclined to be hopeful. Only sex through marriage can do the job in intermingling the races. Or rather sex through love. Love—a supreme force that rises above fickleness and abandonments and double-crosses. Love—more of a taboo than sex ever could be. Love—glorious, magical love.

Might it be possible in America to eliminate race, color, and creed from our idea of love?

• • •

Sometimes when you are about to leave a place you feel a surge of appreciation. You might be living in a metropolitan area known as Murder Capital, USA, but a place like that can also produce an interesting whir of people and events. You can put on formal duds one evening for a dinner in honor of an old friend, the first black man accepted into the air-racing business. You can, if you are a volunteer tour guide for WETA-TV, take in tow one afternoon twelve Japanese businessmen full of questions about the racial headlines always in the news about America. After they tell you from the perspective of their one-track culture that separate and distinct races cannot thrive together and that no country can hold up under the differences, you can say to them, "Yes, it's a challenge for a country to have diverse cultures, but come visit Prince George's County and see how it works." Not that you have complete faith in America, but these Japanese tourists are themselves a symbol of the power of common ground that can come with the passage of time. (You remember well the night your bright-eyed, bushy-tailed lieutenant husband, a bombardier instructor then at a New Mexico military base, flew a night run in a DC-3 and saw a clandestine, headlight-covered truck convoy near Los Alamos and was told by his commanding officer, "Lieutenant Strickler, you never saw a goddamn thing, you got that?" and how a few days later there came on the radio the news of Fat Boy and Little Man). And you can spend a week, if you can free it up, with another symbol of hate overcome, a Russian schoolteacher from czarist-communist St. Petersburg, someone you got to know in the bad days, who is coming at your invitation to view America's big stone citadels and painted rotundas and world-famous obelisks and other holy relics.

These are the sort of things you would miss if you sold your house on Foster Place and moved to the top of the Alleghenies.

There was a new and sudden twist in the Terrence Johnson case. The attorney Charles Ware had managed a rare type of judicial hearing, to be held in a courtroom outside the bounds of Prince George's County. The court date was granted on the grounds that Terrence Johnson's imprisonment had reached a point where it might be deemed excessive and discriminatory.

Anne Arundel County judge Warren Duckett gaveled the hearing to order. Terrence Johnson executed his entrance well, head up, brisk movements despite the cuffs and leg irons. There had never been any doubt of Terrence Johnson's dignity. Even as a sixteen-year-old in an adult prison at Hagerstown, Maryland, he had handled himself with such aplomb he suffered none of the familiar initiations at the hands of experienced cons. Of course, he had a reputation. During his first decade in prison Terrence Johnson refused to see the taking of the two white policemen's lives as anything other than a necessary, valiant act. "It was just unfortunate that people died as a result of trying to save my own life," he would say. He would not acknowledge any feelings of repentance. "He felt society was to blame for his situation," said Devon Brown, an exacting, highly moralistic black man who oversaw psychotherapy sessions at Patuxent, where Terrence Johnson spent the years 1980 to 1987. "He had a long way to go before he rolled up his sleeves and got into the difficult process of introspection." But why should Terrence Johnson look into his heart when in the popular consciousness of the black community his imprisonment was the work of white devils? An expression of remorse on his part would have made nonsense of the headlines—"Miscarriage of Justice"—that had appeared in many African-American journals. The tightly amoral Terrence Johnson, to whom parole could be routinely denied, had a role to play out. Not until a few years ago had he stopped quoting Malcolm X and George Jackson to the parole board. Not until 1991 had he offered what might reasonably be termed an apology. "I feel bad that anyone had to die," he had said finally at his parole hearing, "and I accept my share of the responsibility." A few deliberate words, but they had the power of redemption, or the beginning of it.

Today, for the Anne Arundel courtroom, he was devoid of militant imagery. His face was shaved, his hair trimmed in the style of police academies, and he was dressed in a white shirt and a brown suit, pants sharply creased, a Victorian gentleman. It was Charles Ware's plan to turn the tables on the parole commissioners. The prisoner's keepers, not the prisoner, were to be compelled to put forth articulate, plausibly heartfelt answers. No first-time offender in the history of the Maryland penal system had ever suffered the doom of serving out a full, long-term sentence. Why should Terrence Johnson be the first and only? What justification did the parole commissioners have other than that they were faithfully carrying out the wishes of the Prince George's courthouse gang? Dan Zacagnini, a white, stolid civil servant, was the parole commissioner designated to testify. Gazing at a courtroom of spectators in which partisans of the old white order were badly outnumbered, Commissioner Zacagnini took the oath and said to Mr. Ware, "Parole is not a given thing in Maryland. It is not a guarantee." Then he fell quiet. What a blasé, uninspired sort of reasoning! Terrence Johnson, watching in his seat with keen-eyed composure, felt a quiet surge. Did he imagine it, or were the judge's eyes rolling? Yet Commissioner Zacagnini was speaking out of a legal and political reality. If the system demanded full punishment, who was this judge to say the system was wrong? Who was he to usurp the authority of the parole board and of the Prince George's courthouse for the sake of a black cop-killer?

Indeed, who was Judge Duckett? He was an older white man and a former Anne Arundel County prosecutor, an admirer of the blue uniform all his life. This was Commissioner Zacagnini's main comfort.

After a single day of testimony, however, Judge Duckett had heard enough. He ordered a recess of eight days and made a point-blank suggestion that the eight days be used by the parole commissioners to reconsider Terrence Johnson's future. "I think Mr. Johnson has strength—strength of purpose, strength of character, strength of dignity. I admire him very much," Judge Duckett said in an extraordinary statement from the bench. "I'm telling you, folks, this man is going to make it. And boy, do I wish him luck." Afterward, in the hallway, Judge Duckett's enthusiasm became breathtaking. He maneuvered about to shake Terrence Johnson's back-cuffed hands and kissed on the cheek the killer's mother and aunt.

The mother of Brian Swart, the second police officer slain in Terrence Johnson's shooting blitz, rushed from the Anne Arundel courthouse, and, as soon as possible, phoned Arthur Marshall, the white prosecutor who years earlier had delivered the emotional demand for Terrence Johnson's maximum sentence. Mr. Marshall, beaten out of his prosecutor's job in 1986, was currently campaigning (against Dwight Jackson) to try to succeed Alex Williams, the black man who had succeeded him. Mr. Marshall had missed Judge Duckett's pronouncement, and he had trouble believing Mrs. Swart's report. She was beside herself. "What can we do? How can we stop this crazy judge?" she kept asking. Perhaps she did not mean crazy in a medical sense, but ever since Judge Duckett had agreed to let Terrence Johnson into his courtroom there were rumors the judge had lost full use of his faculties. Mr. Marshall, to say the least, did not discount the rumors. "I never heard of a judge kissing a prisoner's mother. It's a very nonjudicial thing to do. I have absolutely no idea if he's gone over the deep end," he would later tell a reporter, and he suggested to Mrs. Swart that she press a complaint against Judge Duckett with the Judicial Disability Commission: "Maybe you can get him disqualified for reasons of incompetence."

• • •

Staying home with an invalided father on a Friday night may make you think you live in a mausoleum, or a madhouse, but Bruce belonged to a school of deal-makers who believe an arrangement with fate is possible. The steady and fair will inherit peace of mind. Therefore he had become the dutiful bachelor son who took his father out. Tonight their main stop was the Woodard & Lothrop department store in the Iverson Mall for the purchase of a higher-comfort mattress. Doc kept up a puckish banter, and Bruce was a good sport, wheeling his father through the bedroom section and thumping on the springs. By the time they were through Dr. Gordon had splurged on a selection from Stearns & Foster, plus pillows and sheets. Outside, on the cement apron by the front doors, Dr. Gordon pulled himself out of his wheelchair and leaned on a thick-handled cane to hop the curb. Bruce slung the chair over one shoulder. They stepped into the driving lane, some two hundred yards from a late-model car moving at parking-lot speed. Instantly the driver of the car stepped on the accelerator. As the car bore down, Bruce could see the occupants, four young black men, heads hanging out the windows. They were not happy with two white people claiming the right-of-way—this according to words they hollered out the windows. At the last second, a proper fear having been put into Bruce and his father, the car swerved away. Then, apparently so they would not be seen committing an act of mercy, the young men turned in their seats and yanked their bodies half out the windows to launch viler and more creative epithets and to make the sign of a gun with their fingers.

At another time in his life, after a bad scare like that, Bruce would have had a good laugh, but not these days. "All the way back home my heart was going thump-thump-thump. Man, oh man, I could feel that heavy cloud of shittiness in the air. I really expected a shower of bullets to go flying. I guess I have Grumpus to thank. Evidently it was against their code to kill a crippled old man," Bruce said.

He was talking to Ray Norris, his best friend since junior high—a pal in that sacred league of pals, a soul brother who was lost and then found. Bruce had been matchmaker to Ray and his wife, Nancy, and had been best man at their wedding—it was the only trip Bruce made back to Prince George's County during his time in Colorado—and now, after years of

separation, Bruce and Ray were again beer-and-poker buddies. An executive in a small engineering firm (his most recent gig was the parking lot at
the new major league baseball stadium in Baltimore), Ray was a sandy-
haired, mustachioed father of three. Though he had taken his family out of
Hillcrest Heights for a finer house and a bigger yard, Ray still made trips
back to the neighborhood to throw down iced beers with Bruce and talk
in the spirit of old college bull sessions about race and prejudice and issues they once upon a time identified as paramount.

Bruce: "I am sick and tired of these carpools of black kids at the beautiful age of nineteen or twenty acting so charming. Is it my imagination or
are things getting worse? When I moved back here I had the impression
Hillcrest Heights was yuppiedom, or buppiedom—American meritocracy
at its finest."

Ray: "That stuff was in your head. This stuff is real. It's on the street."

Bruce: "The people I see when I'm out jogging look like people who've
worked hard to get here, to leave the ghetto behind. So where does this
ghetto attitude come from?"

Ray: "You're saying 'Why don't they just assimilate?' But you don't leave
your color behind. When you're poor and white, at least you're still white.
You can blend in and move up the ladder. Look at my family: My grandpa
was a dirt farmer; my dad sold eggs to restaurants. They were working
stiffs . . ."

Bruce: "I remember your dad used to bring my dad his extra cartons of
double-yolk eggs."

Ray: "Your family—same thing, right?"

Bruce: "Right. My mother's mother didn't speak English. She emigrated
from Poland. Her sister died on the boat. My father's parents came from
Lithuania and worked seven days a week when they arrived. They put all
three of their sons through medical school. But, okay, I'm not so arrogant
as to believe their accomplishments were solely the result of their efforts.
There's an advantage to being white."

Ray: "Anyway, these black kids are young. You're always full of yourself
when you're young."

Bruce: "I don't have a problem with a black kid in an 'X' shirt. Black
power? Great! Black pride? Great! But these black kids wearing shirts that
say 'White Men Can't Jump' or 'White Men Can't Pump' are over the limit.
I'd be crucified if I wore a shirt that says black men can't do this or can't
do that. Those are hate slogans. These kids are the new purveyors of racial
hate."

Ray: "The new Grits?"

Bruce: "Except they don't even know who the Grits were."

Ray: "You know, when we were at Potomac, black kids actually had less attitude."

Bruce: "Sometimes I think the good old days were really the good old turned-on days. Marijuana took the edge off everyone. Otherwise Camilla and I would've been hassled a lot more than we were."

Ray: "The black kids who had an attitude back then were the kids from D.C., remember? They invaded Potomac and took over the cafeteria and pelted us with gobs of ice cream. And they used to come marauding across the border and take over our basketball courts. They stalked Ray Kelley, a nice, intelligent white boy, and hospitalized him."

Bruce: "They were genuine ghetto hoodlums. But, in a way, I never blamed them. We had a basketball court, and they didn't, so they took ours. These kids at the malls today are middle class. They've got it made. They don't have the same excuse as a ghetto kid. The ghetto kids I could identify with. They wanted to wage their little campaigns to settle the score, and so did I. When I was deemed an unworthy Jew by the baseball coaches at Holy Family, you know what I did? I snuck onto the baseball field and rigged up an M-80 under the pitching rubber. That M-80 packed a wallop. It obliterated the rubber. Then I picked up stones and ran around and broke every window in the rectory."

Ray (with a skeptical smile): "Okay."

Bruce: "Maybe being Jewish doesn't measure up to being black, but my people, the Gordons, experienced pogroms in Russia where homes were burned. My sister and her classmates went into the South to march for civil rights in the sixties. She knew some of the white kids who died for the movement."

Ray: "You're still white."

Bruce (raspingly): "I'm white, but the Gordons have no history of owning slaves. There is none of that in our lineage. There is nothing in my own personal history to justify a black person terrorizing me. That's what makes good white people goofy. It makes me goofy. I feel like I'm being told, 'Whitey, hit the road'—to get picked on for no reason other than you're white. What I see, frankly, is black people turning Hillcrest Heights into their own enclave, driving everyone else out. I watched *Schindler's List,* and this kind of Maccabean instinct came over me. Don't take any shit! I refuse to go marching off to the ovens. The old Jews in their beards and skullcaps abhorred violence. Only goys were brought up to kick ass. But where's the honor in letting yourself be the victim? I can be shoved only so far before I see red. Kill me if you must, but let me go down fighting. I'm ready to take a stand. That's how I feel: Put your dukes up, let's get on with it. They have an attitude? Okay, I'm developing an attitude."

Ray: "You're taking it personally."

Bruce (with a long sigh, and an absentminded draining of another beer): "Life is personal. You know, I used to be able to empathize. I'd see a black dude, and I'd think 'Yo, a brother!' What's changed? Is it them? Is it me? Am I turning into another middle-aged white fart?"

Ray: "Another good liberal bites the dust?!"

Bruce: "I was always more liberal than you. How come you're the big liberal now?"

Ray (self-consciously): "I live in a white neighborhood. I can afford to be a liberal."

If Frank Pesci had a first choice for county executive it would have been the fourth wheel in the race, the good-natured Richard Castaldi. He was well liked for such temperate, agreeable tasks as trying to bring the United Negro College Fund to Prince George's County. The Castaldi campaign, however, had never acquired any momentum, and the withdrawal of Mr. Castaldi two months before Election Day—he cited family concerns: his stroke-disabled mother and his Alzheimer's-ridden father—was almost, but not quite, an unnoticed event.

The one thing that made it interesting and relevant was an off-color gag Mr. Castaldi had attempted in a public forum many weeks earlier. The gag, directed at Hilda Pemberton, the county council president and the object of a political roast at the linen-clothed Ploughman and Fisherman's dinner bash thrown every year by party-line Prince George's Democrats, had sealed Mr. Castaldi's fate. A bland fellow usually, plump and stiff-haired, Mr. Castaldi had handed Mrs. Pemberton a box of clear plastic wrap. "Use it on your next date, and use your imagination," he said flamboyantly. "I'm not going to go into details, but I've attached a real-live brochure from the well-respected Walker-Whitman Clinic on oral sex for women." His smile broadening, he went on to read a line of verse he attributed to Mrs. Pemberton's muse, "I'm tired of men who promise the moon, who keep going and coming, and always too soon." There were a few gulps of astonishment in the audience, and a low groan or two, but there also was plenty of hooting—*what a gas!* The general tone of the Ploughman and Fisherman's dinner had always been rather crude-jest and low-juvenile. (A spoof of Mike Miller at the same event consisted of an amateurish trick photograph: a Miller mugshot superimposed on one man with his pants pulled down and a rival politician's mugshot superimposed on a second man who is kissing the exposed rear end.) No one would mistake Mr. Castaldi's prank for grown-up comedy either, but how upset should Mrs. Pemberton have been? Did not this sort of thing go with the territory? "It was coarse. I didn't like it," said Dell Strickler. "But bad taste is what you expect at a roast." Mrs. Pemberton sat through the rest of the evening without a word, and then, after sleeping on it, she had her secretary type out a note to Mr. Castaldi. In the note, quickly passed out in the pressroom at county headquarters, the councilwoman claimed to have been embarrassed beyond words. But in explaining why she thought Mr. Castaldi was off base she inserted a claim not so self-evident, saying the bad rhyme and the toilet humor demonstrated "racial insensitivity." It was true the insult had been perpetrated by a white man against a black woman, but did that mean race was at issue? To Wayne Curry, a political ally of Mrs. Pemberton, it did. The insult fell into a category of "historic disrespect" toward black women. But Frank Pesci smelled "another attempt to trade on race for political gain." In his next column Frank lit into Mrs. Pemberton: "Politics rears its ugly head again. Wouldn't you know that Hilda would turn it into a racial issue? She is supporting Wayne Curry for County Executive. Do you see a connection?"

Sue Mills, who all through the campaign had been shy around matters of race, was not shy with this one because, as she said, "What does race have to do with it?" If anything Mrs. Pemberton's emotional injury derived from her gender, not her heritage—this was Mrs. Mills's take. *Anyway why the big ado? So Richard Castaldi's a lousy comedian? So what?*

Mr. Castaldi tried to avoid the full apology. The tack he took with Mrs. Pemberton's note was that of a guy blaming his speechwriters. "Obviously my joke missed its mark, and I apologize for that. That's it," he told a TV gang outside his office door. "If she's trying to make political hay about it by asking for me to say I'm sorry, then everybody who was roasting her at the dinner needs to say they're sorry." In no uncertain terms, however, Mrs. Pemberton notified him that a more forthright statement would be necessary to make the incident go away. Another three days of hemming and hawing and hot-spot publicity passed before at last he did apologize.

Prior to the Pemberton incident, the pollsters had the Castaldi campaign ranked about even with the Curry and Tignor campaigns. Afterward, he fell out of the running. At the point of his withdrawal from the race his support in the polls was at ten percent.

A week later he endorsed Sue Mills in front of news reporters. The endorsement was taken by some political observers to be a game-turning boost to the Mills campaign. If the small but significant Castaldi numbers could be added to the Mills numbers, she would appear to have an almost unassailable lead.

11 *Bruce and* Camilla would never marry, that was clear now, however they churned their hearts. But churn their hearts they did.

Constant scrutiny of one another's motives can cause an emotional devaluation. For Bruce and Camilla, fortunately, it seemed to make them better friends. They had arrived at a more nuanced, less dramatic interpretation of the powerful bond between them—and of their original breakup.

Camilla: "We were Romeo and Juliet."

Bruce: "We knew we were asking for trouble. But we weren't trying to shock people for the sake of shocking them. We were in love."

Camilla: "In the beginning I didn't identify Bruce as a white guy or a Jewish guy. I didn't put a label on him. I was interested in him because he was kind of artsy and intellectual and he enjoyed a good time. I felt like, 'Hey, he's my kind of guy,' and it felt perfectly natural for me to be drawn to him. It was Bruce's father who insisted on pushing the black-white thing to the forefront."

Bruce: "It wasn't just my father. We'd get these angry comments, guys coming up to us and saying it was bullshit for us to be together. Black guys as well as white guys."

Camilla: "Yes, I remember. There were these late-night parties at black fraternities where I was afraid for us to go together. My nightmare was that I'd be seen with a white man—someone I was clearly attached to—and it would cause a reaction in normal, regular black guys who'd had too much to drink, and resentments would build up to the point everybody would be stepping outside to settle things."

Bruce: "Camilla's parents weren't overly keen about us either."

Camilla: "But that didn't come out until later. I know now that my mother was hyperventilating at home, trying to stay quiet about us. But she did stay quiet. She never put pressure on us. Bruce's father was the one. His objections kept coming up. We couldn't seem to get past it."

Bruce: "He never went, 'Oh, my God, how can you go with a black woman?' But he would relate his own history of persecution, when he had to fight a line of boys because he was Jewish, and he'd say, 'A Jew already has two strikes against him. Soon as people realize you're a Jew with a black woman you'll really be in for it. You won't be welcome anywhere.' "

Camilla: "I recognize now his father was afraid Bruce would screw up his entire life. That's the part I can understand."

Bruce: "There was a grain of truth to what he was saying, but really there was no pleasing him, short of me becoming a big-shot doctor. And he figured I wasn't going to make it if I hung with Camilla. Forget that I had a three-point-eight in pre-med at a fancy private college. In his eyes I couldn't measure up to those really smart Jewish kids from New York. I wasted a lot of time in pre-med before I figured out medicine was not what I wanted for my life's work. The real problem was that he had influenced me into pre-med, so while I was at Brandeis I felt I had to live up to his ambitions."

Camilla (softly): "That wasn't the real problem. You can't be thin-blooded when you're in love. You must plunge in."

Bruce: "Why wasn't I man enough to stand up to my father? I've tortured myself for years with that question. I wasn't making my own money, which was part of it. I was a kept person. My dad was putting me through school. Being the kind of courageous individual I was at that time I basically went whining to him, 'Please, Daddy, don't stop paying for my education. I'll do what you want. I'll dump Camilla.' It was between my father and me. I let him destroy a beautiful thing. But I don't blame him anymore. If anyone is to blame, it's me. I wasn't strong enough."

Camilla: "I'm glad to hear that. The letter hurt me tremendously. I couldn't eat, I couldn't sleep, the pain was so great."

Bruce: "Nearly as soon as I sent the letter I regretted it. I had this vision of Camilla reading the letter, her face all crumpled. I felt like a total shit. It wasn't so much that I wanted to be free of her and the expectations we had for ourselves. I wanted to be free of my father and his expectations. Which is why I left and went to Florida. It turned into a fortuitous path. Otherwise, I'd be another Jewish wimp."

Camilla: "There were lots of other options besides going to Florida to hang out with blond beach girls."

Bruce: "I needed to act on the craziness that exists in all of us. Sow my wild oats."

Camilla: "I wasn't his wild oats?"

Bruce: "No. She was the woman I actually loved."

Camilla: "That's very romantic of him to say, as far down the line as we are."

Bruce: "The thing is, I didn't commit an act of sexual intercourse for more than a year, which is a long, long time when you're twenty years old."

Camilla: "I had this fantasy, oh, he's down there pining away for me. It turned out to be true."

Bruce: "I was lovelorn and morose the whole time, whereas she went on with her life."

Camilla: "First, I went through a kind of purifying anger. When Bruce left I had to face reality. I was at a feminist college, and the last thing on my mind was supposed to be marriage and children, but I had this passion for a man who felt like a life partner. I wanted to marry Bruce. We couldn't just be best friends and occasional lovers like we are now. It was a scary kind of intensity. It was consuming. We were burning out, but we couldn't pull back."

Bruce: "We'd be together in her room all weekend, then I'd cry all the way driving back to Brandeis. I couldn't bear to be apart. It was too much of an adult relationship. That's why I sent her that letter. For all the blame I've laid on my dad, I guess I was using him as an excuse. When you strip the rest away, I needed to get out. I couldn't handle it."

Camilla: "I kept trying to convince myself things could work out between us, and then the letter came. I think somewhere in the back of Bruce's mind he was looking for the one thing that would be unacceptable to me. The letter pushed all these buttons in me. On some level, conscious or not, he must have known I couldn't stay with him after I got the letter. If I was just going to be a mistress, I couldn't go on believing we had plans to get married. Maybe it worked out for the best. We might've had a lousy marriage."

Bruce: "Will she ever forgive me?"

Camilla (soothingly): "I forgave him a long time ago."

It was strange—not that the issue of race, the issue most Prince George's politicians wished to avoid, kept popping out, but that it popped out in miscellaneous and measly circumstances and soon got out of control.

Following on the Castaldi incident, one of Maryland's U.S. senators, Barbara Mikulski, a white woman of Polish stock, took it on herself to demand an apology from the Prince George's Community College president, Robert Bickford, for telling a "Polish" joke in a speech. The joke was old: An aunt and an uncle suggest names for newborn twins, "Denise" for the girl and "Denephew" for the boy. For years black Americans had heard this as a "black" joke, and Senator Mikulski, taking offense because she thought Robert Bickford was a black man trying to zing white people the way his people had been zinged, wrote a criticizing, widely disseminated letter. "I thought you, who have had to endure similar expressions of prejudice, would never engage in such activities," she lectured him. But Senator Mikulski had made her own mistaken racial assumption. Although the Prince George's Community College's student body and faculty were drawn primarily from the black meritocracy, the college president was a white man.

You had to be a believer in the world of the sublime, two white people getting into a fuss over a "black" joke told as a "white" joke. In his column, Frank Pesci had a field day. "I asume that by now Dr. Bickford has apologized to Sen. Mikulski. What next? Will Sen. Mikulski apologize to Dr. Bickford for getting his race wrong?" he wrote.

But to Richard Castaldi, his campaign now a lost cause, Frank said, "How did civil rights and ethnic pride get so far off track?"

On the bulletin board in Bea Tignor's cubbyhole office at Prince George's Community College she had thumbtacked a gem from the comic strip "Calvin and Hobbes," "The purpose of academic writing is to inflate weak ideas, obscure weak reasoning and inhibit clarity." Students liked Professor Tignor's funnybone; she was a favorite on campus. At the end of each school year she would find in her office mailbox a collection of thank-you notes. *My best class ever!* Some of the quirky schoolmarm could be found in Mrs. Tignor's approach to politics. However, she was quickly orienting herself to the tougher realities inherent in trying to make history. The black-and-white-together theme of her flyers could not be counted on to carry the election. Out on the stump she had to find a means to gain an edge over Wayne Curry. So, toward the end of the campaign, Mrs. Tignor enlivened one of her rallies with a personalized reprimand of Mr. Curry. "Wayne is a polarizer," she said. "I think his comments and his actions serve to divide people. He believes blacks will only vote for blacks and whites for whites. I'm the only candidate who can bring people together." A newspaper reporter wrote this down as Mrs. Tignor said it and double-checked it with her because it was news—mean-spirited perhaps, but perhaps healthy for the body politic. Finally, someone besides Frank Pesci was stating with direct, refreshing aggressiveness the subterranean dilemma that had run through the campaign all along.

Meanwhile, Mr. Curry, having moved into second place in the polls, was urging Mrs. Tignor to drop out: "While Bea and I are both trailing Sue, I'm the one in the position to potentially defeat Sue because I'm the stronger of us two." He was not thrown off by Mrs. Tignor's attack, nor would he discuss it, except to say it was sour grapes. His strategy was to characterize Mrs. Tignor as a candidate sadly groping for the main chance when it was already beyond reach.

Bea Tignor had never possessed the icy-cool Curry style, and in the past few weeks she had looked even unsteadier in her appearances, almost spooked. But there was a reason for it. On nine occasions she had been followed, or stalked, as people said now. Her campaign headquarters had twice been vandalized, the computers and fax machines stolen. There had been dirty-word phone calls. *Getch-u ho-ass outta here, bitch!* And one afternoon at her headquarters, while she lay in a catnapping curl on a couch next to a big picture window on which her name was broadly stenciled, someone must have been watching and signaling because the moment she woke up the driver of a gray Cadillac roared backwards over a curb and across a sidewalk and through the window. Glass exploded on the couch. "It's hard to believe these incidents are not political sabotage," Mrs. Tignor told a reporter. For his part, Mr. Curry speculated on an inside job, perhaps a fanatical fan of Mrs. Tignor trying to elicit sympathy for her. The police were investigating but had no leads. This seemed to be another situation where nothing would ever be proved, another ugliness that would raise brief comment and then be ignored.

While Mrs. Tignor continued to do her unnerved best to make a campaign out of it, the insiders now predicted the election was between Mr. Curry and Mrs. Mills, between the blackest and the whitest.

Amy Smith was free, innocent once more before the law. There would be a new trial, but in the meantime Amy had a day job ringing up luncheon meats and frozen juices at the checkout counter in a Cape Cod supermarket. Evenings she was attending school. Thomas and Elizabeth

Pickering, waiting and grinning when Amy came through the Patuxent doors with her civvies and toothbrush and a helter-skelter of legal papers, had custody of her again. Amy had no plans to contact her father and stepmother. For all practical purposes her grandparents were now her parents. In Dr. Schouten's office Amy had borne witness to the bountiful extra of a "real" home, describing in glowing terms her wish to be reunited with her grandparents: "She feels that the relationship she has with them is something she never experienced with her father and stepmother. She feels that they truly care for her and show her tremendous affection, while at the same time trusting her judgment and not treating her like a small child."

The second trial would not be on a court calendar for six months, maybe longer. For now Amy could feel optimistic. Only in her dark moments or when a letter came in the mail from Larry Polen would she worry about what it might be like to return to the Prince George's courthouse. Would she have to swear an oath and talk through all the throat-catching details? Would she be watched by twelve jurors stroking their chins in their judicial masks? For sure, she would be watched by Elbert and Daphne Jones.

Suffice it to say that the trial could not arrive fast enough for Mr. and Mrs. Jones. With consuming anticipation—night sweats, mental rages in the middle of the day—they looked forward to seeing Amy on the stand and listening to a cross-examination that might test their theory of the case. This theory was the work of Mr. Jones, who had put himself through the ordeal of playing detective in his son's killing. Good detective work involves open-mindedness and thoroughness, and what Mr. Jones lacked of the former he made up with the latter. Every detail was committed to memory, details from the police crime sheets, from the defense team's investigation, from court testimony, from the psychiatric confessional, from the private eye's report. Mr. Jones had traced and retraced every movement his son made in the days leading up to his death.

What had been on Derrick's mind at the point he left home to hook up with Amy? Whatever it was, that was the key to the case, in Mr. Jones's estimation. And what else could have been on Derrick's mind but sex? Derrick was a kid "naive in the ways of women" but hankering for manhood, as his father saw it, and Amy was his sexual transport. Crying on Derrick's shoulder, telling him how she longed to be her own woman, Amy had led him along. That Amy had, in her talks with Dr. Schouten, disavowed having been intimate with Derrick was not so odd as it seemed. Withholding sex has its charms. Amy would flirt and cause Derrick to become jealous, according to Gregory Drew, who remembered, "A friend of ours, we called him Cosi, said he had 'been with' Amy, and Derrick got pretty upset about it." On that July day, it was finally Derrick's turn to be with Amy, so Mr. Jones presumed. About five o'clock in the afternoon Derrick said good-bye to his father, "I'll be back by midnight." A friend of his, Keith Harrison, drove him to a bus stop and later recalled an odd intensity in Derrick's voice—"nervous, stuttering a little"—which the authorities chose to interpret as telltale criminal intent but which his father thought was the natural trepidation of a boy about to undergo a sexual initiation. A note in blue ink, written in Amy's hand and found on Derrick's body, had directions via bus and the subway line that took Derrick in the direction of a mall where Amy briefly held a job dishing out cups and cones of yogurt: "Get off bus at Swan Creek Road and Gable Lane. The store will be across the street. Call from High's." Amy, waiting a mile away at the Smith house, expected Derrick to call a cab, but apparently he didn't bother, instead walking the distance in the evening sun. Probably he was in no hurry. Amy's stepmother was also at home, and it made sense to arrive under cover of dark. From the looks of a jimmied ground-floor window Derrick used it to sneak in. The screen was pulled from its mooring, and Amy's seashell collection in a box of beach sand on the windowsill was disturbed, a trickle of sand spilled to the floor. According to Mrs. Smith, Amy had eaten her supper in the downstairs family room, after which she watched TV for a while and drank a soda. Police found the empty bottle on the floor. Earlier, unasked, Amy had neatened up her bedroom—a thoughtful attention for her lover? Around nightfall she showed off the bedroom to her stepmother. Mrs. Smith took a perfunctory look. Where was Derrick hiding all this time? Under Amy's bed? In the downstairs bathroom? Outside in the bushes? As Mrs. Smith headed back upstairs, Amy asked, "What makes you decide whether you take a shower in the morning or at night?" Mrs. Smith gave a blank stare and said, "It all depends on my mood."

By midnight, to follow along with Mr. Jones's theory, the Smith house would have held a stepmother asleep upstairs and two teenagers in passionate disregard downstairs. The police reported that Amy's bed was found unmade. Suppose, in their rambunctiousness, Amy and Derrick awakened Mrs. Smith, and she stole down to Amy's bedroom for a peek. Would she not have wanted to cry out and slap them till her hands burned? But that would have meant a contest between a small, fiftyish woman and two tall, physically strong near-adults. (Amy outweighed her stepmother by twenty-five pounds, and in their physical exchange at Christmas had refused to back down.) Suppose Mrs. Smith instead phoned her husband, out on patrol. Suppose he rushed home and walked in on a frantic, half-dressed Derrick coming up the downstairs steps, his Champion T-shirt and Reebok shoes tight to his chest. Imagine Derrick's reaction at finding himself in the situation of a black teenager facing an armed white police officer in the middle of the night, the peril warned against across the decades in the black households of Prince George's County. Suppose Derrick tried to scramble to safety down the steps and lost his footing and landed back first on the carpeted floor. He would have been an easy target for a man with a gun standing three or four steps above him. This was what Mr. Jones supposed, and his theory was not without supporting facts. Derrick had been shot with his T-shirt off and with his unlaced shoes left on the final step. (Does someone with murder in his heart go about in a half-naked state?) The bullet hole through Derrick's chest and up and out past his shoulder blades and into the carpet indicated the first bullet caught him while prone on the floor. There was a white unbloodied washcloth near his body, and Mr. Jones speculated that Amy meant to use the cloth to staunch Derrick's wound and that her father, perhaps with crazy words, made her drop it.

Other items found with the body, however, were less easily explained: a ski mask, an orange Playtex Living glove (the matching glove was found in the disarray of the upstairs bathroom), and a key to the Smith house tied to the drawstring of green swim trunks worn under navy blue Bermuda sweat shorts. With Mr. Jones's theory, the only way to explain the presence of these items was for them to have been planted. According to the medical examiner, Derrick may have lain on the floor for several minutes before receiving the second, fatal shot, perhaps long enough for Mr. Smith to have left the premises and acquired from somewhere an arrangement of clues.

The account of the neighbor who described Mr. Smith's car accelerating down the street at a point in the night when Mr. Smith claimed to have been asleep in bed was, to Mr. Jones's mind, the sort of testimony that might bring a jury around to seeing it his way. If you were Mr. Jones, you might believe that prior to Amy's 911 call the Smith family could have worked out a storyline, and some staging could have gone on inside the house. Someone could have tugged the ski mask over Derrick's head. Awful to think of—putting a hood over the condemned man, but it could have happened. Soon after Amy's arrest, in an interview with juvenile authorities, she told of being unable to sleep at night because Derrick's face kept appearing to her. "Derrick's face as he got shot." If you were Mr. Jones, you might believe that Amy was in the downstairs rec room, with a fallen Derrick practically at her feet, his face naked, when her father took the first shot.

If you were Mr. Jones, you might believe that a shy, sex-struck boy met his Maker because of one night of forbidden pleasure.

Among a few friends who had watched Derrick grow up, this "truth," as developed by Mr. Jones, invited fantasies of revenge. "Me, I'd like to have Dennis Smith's head delivered in a shopping bag," said a friend of the family. "It's a credit to Elbert that he still believes he can get justice at the courthouse."

While Bob Magruder spoke his piece, the bystanders had a ghostly view in the linoleum-floored, movie-clichéd relic of a gym across from the Gordon house: the young upstarts at the leather bags, a punchy old cut-man with a bucket scrubbing down a section of wood bleachers salvaged from Georgetown University, and, looking out from the knotty-pine walls, a gallery of sour-pussed strongmen of the fifties on fading-ink posters. Bob Magruder could remember some of them and feel at home. Right now the old-fashioned Magruder personality was on display, the one unafflicted by doubts. He was letting out his opinion that the boxing world had been done a disservice by a decision of the Maryland State Boxing Commission to grant eligibility to a black middleweight named Keith Holmes for a championship match in Upper Marlboro despite the fighter's arrest for a drive-by shooting. "Holmes's lawyer probably gave the commission a lot of legal talk," Bob Magruder was saying, "so they're afraid to do the right thing. What the commission should do is cancel the fight and tell Holmes, 'Sue us.' I'd rather they had to pay him a settlement if it does turn out he beats his court case. To me, it's the other kids we have to look out for. What kind of message is the commission sending our kids? You can shoot somebody out your car window and they let you be a champion? I'd never allow Holmes in our gym, not on your life. This gym is for one thing and one thing only, to build character. We turn out good citizens. We've had our problems, but nobody can say we haven't tried to clean the bad guys out of here." You might have thought the Brylcreemed Magruder, a guy with the cock's-crow swagger of someone packing cigarettes in the roll of a sleeve, was at this moment the embodiment of the old Hillcrest Heights spirit. But the men listening and nodding at him around the red-roped ring were black men. A huge ex-fighter known as "Big Mac Attack" McDonald growled his agreement, "Got to have standards. Crazy, dumb, to sanction a lowlife like that. It rubs off on all of us." The "us" he referred to were his people—not black people, but the people in the boxing life, the people at the gym, such as Bob Magruder. Which is another way of understanding the weird looks you would have caused had you brought into the gym an assumption about Bob Magruder as the trainer of young white hopes. At the gym they knew Bob Magruder for his work with the twelve black teenagers he had trained into amateur champions and with a young black man he had gotten close to a professional championship and with Lonnie Rogers, an overaged black welterweight hungry for a few extra bucks. Lonnie Rogers trusted no one more than he trusted Bob Magruder, who a few times a year set him up on fight cards so he could collect a purse without getting his brains scrambled. At the gym is where you learned the Bob Magruder credo: Everybody gets a second or a third chance, but you must be worthy. You must have a heart that is violent only when the gloves are on.

As Bob Magruder finished his little diatribe he was already yelling at one of his charges. "Five minutes on the heavy bag!" Later, after the workouts were done and he was on his way out, he said, "I love this place. If this place didn't exist, I'd have gone to the penitentiary."

(As for Keith Holmes, he would win the U.S. Boxing Association junior middleweight title, would be acquitted on all counts in the drive-by shooting and later, in 1998, while still the champion, would be arrested again and charged with assaulting a Prince George's police officer.)

On August 11, in Judge Duckett's courtroom, a lawyer for the Parole Commission announced a reversal in the case of Terrence Johnson, who was now considered to have met all the criteria of rehabilitation and was to be granted parole.

"Would Mr. Johnson care to make a statement?" Judge Duckett inquired.

The clean-cut thirty-one-year-old man rose wobbly to his feet. "I would like to first say thank you, Your Honor, for allowing me a second chance," Terrence Johnson said. Choking out a few more thank-yous, he dropped his chin to his chest. Would he say more? Would he address any feelings from the night he stopped the futures of Officers Claggett and Swart? "I'm not going to retry my case today," he proffered. "I can only beg for forgiveness. I beg God for forgiveness. It's agonizing to know you killed a man. I will suffer. I will suffer the rest of my life with that. I can only hope that the families, the Claggett family and the Swart family, will forgive me. I'm very sorry." Was this a miracle of the redeemed soul? A peephole into the transcendent heart? Terrence Johnson had said nothing like this at his trial. Why? "Because I did not think I would've been believed."

Of course, there were those who still neither believed nor forgave. "I don't buy one word of it," said Blanche Claggett, the sixty-nine-year-old matriarch of the Claggett family, when contacted by a newspaper writer. "I don't think he's changed. He's the same person. If he gets out, he'll probably do the same thing again—or something like it." And the ex-prosecutor Arthur Marshall suddenly had an angle and a justification for his campaign. Compassion for a cop-killer? "What's our priority? To give a pat on the back to the street hoodlum? Or to stand up for the officer on the beat?" Mr. Marshall said, holding forth. "When you assault a uniformed police officer, you're assaulting society itself."

There are a number of writers intent on satisfying America's appetite for true crime, and a few of them early on had attempted to contact Amy Smith to discuss the literary and film rights to her story. Elvira, as Amy's attorney, had dismissed them out of hand, telling her client they were "sleazebags and macho blood-and-guts guys." Elvira's critics at the courthouse insinuated she was holding out for the fame of a John Gregory Dunne or a Joe McGinniss. Whatever the case, big-league authors never presented themselves. Shortly after Amy's first trial, though, a Baltimore writer named Delores Wright, who had once been featured in an *Ebony* personality piece, volunteered to collaborate on a book with Amy, and Elvira passed on the offer: "I told Amy it was daunting to say things in print that you've never articulated to anyone out loud. I told her I'd tried to write about myself, and it was painful. But I thought it might serve a useful purpose for her to go public with the truth about her case." A contract was drawn up, and Delores Wright, whose one previous book featured a Patuxent inmate in a theme of godly feminism, handed it personally to Amy. Their meeting in the Patuxent visiting room had a strange hush-hush air, with the ghostwriter telling her subject not to let word of the book out on the prison grapevine lest black inmates come to resent her for enriching herself at a dead black boy's expense. Amy appeared to be game for the project, but she wanted approval from her grandparents. Elvira placed a phone call to Cape Cod in which she built up Delores Wright as "a compassionate, God-fearing women" but also applied a touch of strongarm, appealing to the Pickerings' hatred of Dennis Smith. "Why should he have the last word on the subject?" Elvira asked rhetorically. When the Pickerings were noncommittal, she followed up with a letter, penned in ballpoint on lined notebook paper:

> I truly understand that you want to guard your privacy. Unfortunately your privacy was invaded when you came to Maryland to help your granddaughter who became a public figure through this case. . . .
> Amy wants the chance to rid herself of the ghosts that haunt her

within and seeks your blessing in helping her to confront the past while she prepares for the future. Throughout the time I represented Amy she and I dealt with reality and the real possibilities of this case. We left you with your happiness of baking snacks after school, preparing for the prom and other normal high school activities. I am so glad that you had that time. However do not think that a day went by when Amy didn't think about prison.

The letter's wheedling, guilt-inducing tone repelled the Pickerings. They felt Elvira was trying to take unfair advantage, setting them against their granddaughter, and they did not understand why. Why should Elvira care if a book was published? As the losing attorney she could not expect to be the book's heroine. Of course, one motive is clear from the letter. Elvira wanted very much for Amy to purge herself—"to rid herself of the ghosts that haunt her." The truth, Elvira believed, would set free Derrick's good name. If there was a second motive, it had to do with a second book, a book that would have told Elvira's own story, which Delores Wright claimed to be willing also to write after she had leafed through two scrapbooks of Elvira's newspaper clippings. A sum of $125,000 had been proferred to Elvira, contingent, though, on actual publication. At the courthouse the book about Elvira was laughed at as a straight-faced flattery, a way to string her along until the book about Amy was done. As it worked out, neither book was written. The deal with Delores Wright fell apart because Amy, learning of her grandparents' concern about "darkening the family name," backed out. Amy wrote to Elvira of her change of mind: "A while back we discussed the possibility of me writing a book about my life, and at that time I thought it was a good idea. However, this book has been very stressful on some members of my family, and I know that no amount of money is worth the health and well-being of the people I love. So I've decided that I will not continue to pursue this book." Amy signed it, "Thank you for all your help."

Elvira scribbled a response and mailed it to Patuxent: "Thank you for letting me know your decision, which will be respected."

That was the end of it, or would have been the end of it, except for $500 of good-faith money, in the form of a cashier's check, which had been turned over by Delores Wright. Elvira had cashed the check and divided the money, half for Amy and half for herself. There was nothing untoward in a fifty-fifty split, it appeared, since the deal called for separate books, but, in the course of the investigation for Amy's appeal, Delores Wright let it slip that all the money was supposed to have gone to Amy alone.

Subpoenaed to testify at Amy's postconviction hearing, the writer, done up in a teased *Ebony*-style hairdo and dressed to the teeth, squirmed about in the witness chair, clumsily describing reasons for the come-hither, big-money, pay-later price tag she had placed on the rights to Elvira's life story—a ruse, plainly. Asked about the $500 downpayment meant for Amy, Ms. Wright admitted to having been somewhat vague about it with Elvira. "It wasn't crystal clear. There may have been room for a misunderstanding," she testified. Nonetheless, if you were so inclined, and a good many at the courthouse were, you could interpret Delores Wright's testimony as an allegation against Elvira of unethical conduct, a lawyer diverting $250 away from a client. An anonymous tipster had forwarded Ms. Wright's testimony to the Maryland Attorneys Grievance Commission, whose members held the power to lift Elvira's law license. No judgeship, perhaps no career whatsoever in the law—all for the pittance of $250? It was not believable, and yet the allegation was being kept alive by Elvira's former colleagues. They let it be known that Elvira, under siege from bill collectors, was desperate for money. "I think it's possible she knowingly took money that wasn't hers. Yes, I do," said a woman in the public defender's office. "Where there's smoke there's fire."

Another investigation of Elvira was now under way. Her finances would be gone over again. Penalties would be weighed.

"All along that's been the real agenda: get my license, get me disbarred, keep me from being a judge," Elvira said. A tossed-aside *Prince George's Journal* with its unfriendly black print stared up from her desk. "Now you know why I was kept on the stand for six hours at Amy's hearing. Now you know why I lost my composure and went into that tirade. The real purpose of that hearing wasn't to get Amy out of prison. I was the fish they wanted to fry. They were trying to build a case against me. And those women from my office were in on it." Elvira's expression, already fierce, grew fiercer. Bile and venom, fire and brimstone she would heap if she could on her "so-called friends," these weakling, ingratiating agents of hell, white women in the thrall of white male superiors—as she saw them.

In the muster room of a district police station at the kickoff to a midnight shift, a white lieutenant had informed the patrol crews to keep an eye out for gang members armed with a machine gun.

A white officer, Alphonse Gauthier, not kidding around, had asked, "Excuse me, Lieutenant, but what race are the suspects?"

"What race do you think?"

"Black?"

"Aren't they always?!"

But Officer Gauthier was not amused—he was married to a black woman and was father to a black stepdaughter—and he filed a complaint against the lieutenant, who was disciplined and ordered to pay a penalty out of his paycheck. This led to unhappiness within the white rank and file, however, and, after a review, the lieutenant was exonerated. Then in quick succession charges began to accumulate against Officer Gauthier and against J. B. Harrison, a black officer who had spoken up for him. The officers were cited for a long list of petty violations. Officer Gauthier considered his options and resigned. Officer Harrison's job was terminated.

In the polls Sue Mills was still headily exalted, but victory, if it came at all, would come with a harsh examination of her past. Indeed, this campaign was beginning to resemble Mrs. Mills's last campaign, four years earlier, when she had won reelection to the county council. Her opponent, a black man named Isaac Gourdine, had made Mrs. Mills out to be someone cartoonishly out of step with the march of history in Prince George's County, a relic, a grotesque embarrassment. In the election home stretch, Mr. Gourdine had elaborated on Mrs. Mills's past, going so far as to connect her with George Wallace. The allegations were unfair; the Sue Mills of yesteryear may have seemed indistinct from the most loathsome of the segregationists, but, in truth, she had never preached segregation, and in the days when George Wallace brought his southern exhibitionism to Prince George's County and fever for the man from Alabama ran high, she had stayed clear of him. Mr. Gourdine's tactics, however, turned voters his way, and he had come closer than anyone to defeating Mrs. Mills. The Gourdine team had had as a chief adviser Wayne Curry, the same Mr. Curry now running against Sue Mills, and it was not likely the Curry team would search high and low for a new stratagem when an effective one was easily at hand.

Wayne Curry, no militant, was a forty-three-year-old real estate lawyer and a member in good standing of the new rich. But in recent weeks, sounding a lot like Mr. Gourdine, he had taken to mentioning Mrs. Mills in the same breath as the old segregation-forever crowd. Mr. Curry would tell of dark incidents from before the civil rights movement and say this was the time that had formed Mrs. Mills. He justified his vituperations by saying voters who had not lived through those days needed the information. "A lot of people who moved here in recent years don't know Sue's history, but when they find out about it they aren't very pleased," he said in an interview. "Should it matter? I think anytime there's a history of racial hostility it's proper for it to be considered, especially in a jurisdiction that is now majority African-American. This election is a generational litmus test for Prince George's. What are we going to be when we grow up? The voters have a fairly stark contrast between the old and the new Prince George's."

Mr. Curry knew firsthand of the old days. He had grown up in the Prince George's town of Cheverly, in the fourth ward, a neighborhood then without sidewalks. Neighbors on most every side were black people. His parents, Eugene and Juliette, were college graduates with jobs in the school system—he was a shop teacher, she a secretary—who believed in reaching out to the wider world. They sought out white people of the same persuasion and crossed paths with Frank Pesci, who, with his young family, was also living in the neighborhood. The preadolescent Wayne Curry and one of the Pesci daughters became playmates. When Wayne was in the fourth grade, in 1959, the Currys enrolled him and his older brother Daryl at Tuxedo-Cheverly Elementary, where the Pesci children were students. The Curry boys had adult escorts in case of trouble from other kids, but there was none. Led by residents like the Pescis, the town of Cheverly was changing, ahead of the rest of Prince George's County. In 1961 the Curry brothers helped integrate the Cheverly Boys Club basketball team. Things went well at first, but the team's schedule put them against teams of white boys from Upper Marlboro whose parents objected to black boys running and perspiring on the same court. A lawsuit was filed—the integrated team was in violation of an equal-but-separate clause of the Prince George's Boys Club constitution—and, during the litigation, the Curry boys had to wear their jerseys inside out as "contested participants." However glorious it is to fight the good fight, it must have been an agony as well for Wayne Curry's father. The elder Mr. Curry was dead now and could not be asked, but something had eaten at him. While his own career in the school system prospered for awhile and though his sons held their heads high, he drank heavily, stuporifically, narcotically. His oldest son, part of a lonely minority again in high school, was shot six times during a dispute over a girl. Eventually his wife could stand no more. There was a divorce and more drunken binges and then three years of drying out in a veterans hospital. That, for Wayne Curry, was the "old." The "new" was a splendid house in Enterprise Estates and an even more splendid house currently under construction outside Upper Marlboro, his entry into big-spender fantasy, one of those architectural renderings that seeks to add more and more embellishments, in this case eighteen rooms, nine bathrooms (with Belgian marble detail), four fireplaces (with earthstone hearths), and a caterer's kitchen, situated on 23.7 acres of trees and hills alongside a street named for him, Waynesford Drive, in a subdivision owned by a business venture in which he was a limited partner—all of it a monument to his struggle for better-than-equal footing in White America. Win or lose this election, Wayne Curry would be living in larger quarters than Mike Miller (owner of a red-brick rambler in Clinton) or any of the other white political bosses.

When you are coming up on your twenty-year reunion the highs and lows of your school life can feel like part of an ancient world—unless you have unfinished business, such as a senior prom that was one long unhappy memory for Bruce and Camilla.

As for why the big dance had been a bust, Camilla said now, on reflection, "That was the first time I felt like we really and truly gave in to social restrictions. But I didn't feel we had a choice. For us to go to the prom and dance cheek to cheek in public? There would've been a huge scene. The music would've stopped." And Bruce said, "Physical violence was a possibility. We laugh about it now, but it was real. We could've been jumped." So Bruce had taken a white girl for his date, and Camilla went on the arm of a black friend, and the two forbidden lovers had spent the prom staring theatrically at each other, feeling like imposters.

At their twenty-year reunion things would be different. This time, even if it was just for one night, they would live the stupendous truth, all eyes on them. Bruce and Camilla were ready to mark the date on their calendar, soon as the reunion committee sent them a notification letter. The trouble was no letter had been forthcoming. Inquiring around, Bruce found out why. The reunion had been canceled!

"The committee didn't get its act together," he reported to Camilla. " There's nobody to take the lead. Unless I do it."

"Well . . .?"

"Okay, okay, I hear you."

It was rare to see Elvira at the Prince George's courthouse anymore, but there was no stopping the talk about her. Into the idlest of conversations would be introduced "the Elvira situation." According to the talk, everything had been hotsy-totsy until Elvira's arrival in Upper Marlboro. This talk was gossip-ridden, sniggering, artless. What did they mean to imply with their rumor (denied by Elvira) about Elvira leaving B.J. in a parked car while she sat for an interview in the governor's office? Clearly Elvira was no more neglectful than any other single mother with a profession. The boy loved her; he would run into her arms. No, the rumor did not seem to be about Elvira's mothering but rather about Elvira's "appalling, no-holds-barred ambition." *See the lengths to which she'll go to get ahead, even endangering the apple of her eye.* The bailiffs and attorneys and court clerks were now trying to reassess Elvira's "white" diction; her "white" wardrobe; her proper, boozy, gesture-making parties; the favors she had done for judges. Had these been the actions of someone showing ambition, or holding it in check? Yet what did they know of her upbringing? To have amusements and fancy things entirely absent! Anyone with ambition would have wanted to escape. Anyone with ambition would have been drawn into this black people's paradise where you could aspire to be, as it were, the best and the baddest. Dwight Jackson's analysis was: "She ingratiated herself. She played the consummate old-boy game. They used to tell me, 'Elvira throws a nice party.' Apparently they didn't realize she wanted to be a judge. Then when it came time to cash in, she fell from grace. You have to wonder if she wanted more power than they were willing to give her." Ambition and power—there was the rub. *Behold the unmasked lady! See her imperial face!* "Yes, I was one of them for a while," Elvira said at her new office. "They took me into their bosom, but only so they could silence me, suffocate me. They were never going to allow me to reach a position where I could bang the gavel down on one of them." As Elvira spoke, the rigidity of her body expressed an obstinacy. Meanwhile, at her old office, one of the staff attorneys had this to say: "Power went to Elvira's head. She acted like the head nurse, like the foreman. We became her minions. It was a rude awakening, her power trip, although it was probably predictable. Did you ever catch one of her performances in front of a jury?" In the courtroom, Elvira's stance was daring, her voice loud. She hogged the limelight, in the opinion of her white colleagues. (And they, reverting to their quieter culture, tried to make her look bad by overdoing the soft and feminine bit.) But if Elvira was at times obnoxious and vainglorious, at times a showboater, hadn't she poured all her heartfelt emotions into her job?

Perhaps, a friend suggested, Elvira's hatred of the courthouse society was in direct proportion to her total belief in it. With her husband gone and her first son enlisted in the army, her life was lived at the courthouse. She had pledged her faith in its orthodoxies. Didn't she still wish to be-

long? Else why would she now, under all these circumstances, be campaigning for a fifteen-year term as judge?

At the Pennsylvania farm, on the hillside where Merv and Dell with
sweat in their eyes had hacked out a clearing in the treeline, the stumps
were now suckering up. Their idea of building a house in this spot had
come up hard against the reality of a septic field (a budget-busting expense) and the long setback from the road (winter snowstorms would cut
them off from civilization, and what if an emergency vehicle had to get
in?). More than a tad rueful—a house on a hill can be an intoxicant once it
seeps into your dreams—Merv and Dell were trying to come up with Plan
B. Dell thought they might make do with an addition to the old farmhouse. An Amish carpenter suggested they site a new dwelling some paces
away, on the other side of the well pump, and connect it to the old house
by a breezeway, this to comply with local zoning laws. "How did it happen that the middle of nowhere abounds in zoning lawyers?!" Merv grum-
bled sharply, shaking his head.

Without an alternative on which they could agree, no plan went forward. As for Heather, what could she do? A kind of flat-footedness seemed
to have hold of her folks. "I don't know if they'll ever move," she said.
"Their heart isn't in it."

(Another auditorium, another forum.) What a vaudeville show! A
dead-panned, dark-suited Wayne Curry said in a disagreeable voice, "I
agree with Mrs. Mills," and Sue Mills, pumped up, glowing in a hot-pink
outfit, her hands doing a head-konking pantomime, crowed afterward, "I
love it! I love it! When Mr. Curry was going to college twenty-two years
ago I told everybody it wouldn't work. I knew in my bones it wouldn't
work. I knew it all along! Twenty-two years later he's saying what I said
from the beginning."

The three principal candidates were now all publicly in agreement with
regard to Judge Kaufman's order for school busing. They were all agreed
that busing had outlived its usefulness. This was not exactly a new development—Bea Tignor had issued a position paper several months back
calling on Judge Kaufman to lift his order, and Mr. Curry had never been a
fan of the busing plan. But, more and more in county executive forums,
Mrs. Mills was taking credit for persuading them of her position. If the fed-

eral busing order was discredited and the issue was declared null and void, so should the old political knock on her. "History has proved me right, and I shouldn't be blamed for being ahead of the times" was the line she was using with voting audiences.

Thus it came to pass that Sue Mills was able, apparently, to rid herself of the thing that had first propelled her into political orbit and ever since had dragged on her.

The lengthy desegregation proceedings in Judge Kaufman's court had taken place mainly in 1972. The case competed for attention locally with George Wallace, who four years earlier had carried Prince George's County in the Democratic presidential primary and who was expected to do as well in his second opportunity. In May, one day before the 1972 primary, a scene of him at a Laurel shopping mall that began with fingers in the air for the pleasure of his jumped-up crowd was flashed abruptly into the middle of afternoon soap operas. Viewers saw him lying on the pavement, dropped for dead. For a moment he looked like the Kennedys, or King. This was how Americans came to know Prince George's County: as the place the Wallace political juggernaut, at its northernmost edge, was stopped by Arthur Bremer's gun. Then, within months, Prince George's County received more national recognition as a result of Judge Kaufman's order. From these two events came the beginning of the big utopian change in the county that spread out from Hillcrest Heights toward the farm fields outside Upper Marlboro. The children at the front end of the change had to endure the little immemorial Grit-like tactics of other kids mean as jackals. Black students dressing in a locker room would hear the shout of white voices through a cracked gym door—"It smells like niggers in here!" In the hallways they had to run a gauntlet of fists, a game called "ping-pong." Sue Mills, in whose name such guerrilla actions were often conducted, had, as a child, attended the Prince George's "dual" school system, hopping three steps every morning up into her yellow ride to be driven from her dad's parsonage past two "black" schools so she could attend a "white" school in Oxon Hill. The logic she trotted out to oppose desegregated busing went as follows: "It's a hell of a slap in the face to tell a black child he's incapable of learning unless he's sitting next to a white child" and "What's the point of forcing kids to integrate when their natural instinct is to sort themselves out by neighborhood? Kids want to be friends with the kids who live next door."

The *Washington Post* during that time had printed several disparaging quotes about Mrs. Mills. However, on the twentieth anniversary of Judge Kaufman's order, the morning delivery boy threw onto her doorstoop a front-page, three-part *Washington Post* series in which a staff correspondent, Lisa Leff, posed the questions, "For Prince George's, the issue has come down to this: Was busing worth it? After twenty years is it still?" Ms. Leff had canvassed the data and reported this answer: "The county's schools still are not desegregated. The hoped-for gains in minority student achievement never materialized. The quality of the school system, the real issue all along, was obscured by the emphasis on quantities." Several black parents, whose children were the ones rising before dawn for the long bus rides, explained to Ms. Leff how the court order interfered with their children's education. Students who might be kept after school for tutoring must leave instead with the buses. PTA meetings, held in the evenings, drew fewer and fewer parents willing to undertake the long commute. One principal had gone so far as to offer a coupon worth one night free of homework if a student's mother or father took the time for a PTA meeting. But the real failure of the Prince George's busing program, the most comprehensive ever undertaken for the purpose of integration (with more buses than those dieseling the streets of Los Angeles), was told by the numbers. The definition of integration set out in Judge Kaufman's order was that no Prince George's school should be populated with less than ten percent or more than eighty percent of one race. But over time about 63,000 white students, more than half the total number, had transferred out of Prince George's schools. Now, in one-third of the schools, the court order could not be met, even with busing, because of the multitude of black students. At Potomac High the ratio of black students to white students, about 1 to 2 in Bruce and Camilla's graduating class, had changed to 60 to 1. There were not enough white students at Potomac High to fill a single classroom.

Even though Judge Kaufman, who retained jurisdiction of the case, had stated an unwillingness to abandon the busing program, a committee was being organized with the sole goal of superceding his solution. The chief organizer was Alvin Thornton, the political scientist on the school board and a supporter of Wayne Curry. Several of the committee members were from either the Curry or Tignor camps. That their goal was the very goal for which Mrs. Mills had taken so much abuse—a generation of *Washington Post* reporters had her pegged as the "ugly sister" of local politicians, just as they had once pegged Prince George's County the "ugly sister" of Greater Washington principalities—was sheer delight to her. It was a delight Mrs. Mills had trouble controlling. In the maplewooded county council chambers or out campaigning at a pig roast, sizzled meat stabbed by plastic forks on plastic plates, she would light into her old tormentors. Regarding the three-part *Washington Post* series: "What a spread! Seven or eight pages of newsprint, and did you see my name once? I didn't. Not once. I'm no longer of interest because they can't paint me as a villain anymore." Regarding the "conversion" of Wayne Curry and Bea Tignor: "I invented opposition to busing. But I'm glad Wayne and Bea have come around, even though their realization is twenty years late. That's okay. God forgives a sinner on his deathbed." Regarding the intransigent Judge Kaufman and a passel of unconverted NAACP activists: "It must really stick in their craw. Of course, they never cared what we thought. We were just like lab animals to them, somebody they could practice their social engineering on." Regarding the feelings now abroad in the Prince George's black community: "See, their leaders convinced them busing was the only thing that would work. They had to find out on their own their leaders were wrong. A very expensive error, $45 million a year spent on buses."

Frank Pesci had this comment: "Well, you have to say Sue did see at least one part of the future with real clarity. She saw the busing issue wasn't going to be the big disadvantage to her in this election that everyone thought. It's ironic. Busing has been a plus for her. It's the one thing that fires her up in these debates. Her opponents are the ones who are uncomfortable with it." Indeed, Mr. Curry and Mrs. Tignor, by and large, offered up only sketchy one-liners during most of the busing discussions. It was Professor Thornton who, in long letters mailed to the Prince George's newspapers, provided a fierce rebuttal to Mrs. Mills's white shiny vision of local history: "Surely, as a former member of the Board of Education when the Board massively resisted desegregation, you recall that the policy was to bus, at great financial and psychological expense, black and white children past the school nearest their home. You must recall that the Board of Education, in the context of 'Colored' and 'White' education, bused most black children from all over the county to one high school [Fairmont Heights, where Gloria began her teaching career]. Indeed, many of those children had to get bus transfers to travel the long distance to the school. . . . The freedom to choose is the principle we fought for and will never surrender." As Frank Pesci had observed, however, this debate was energizing Mrs. Mills. She was intent on having the last word. To Professor Thornton's rebuttal she delivered a counterrebuttal, defending herself by telling of her own choices. It was a point of pride with her that when Judge Kaufman's buses began to roll she had not yanked her children out of the Hillcrest Heights schools, surprising many in the NAACP. Instead, Steve and Cindy Mills graduated from Potomac High, the same as Bruce and Camilla.

Ironies were the bedevilment of Professor Thornton's committee. While the tide of popular opinion, black and white, appeared to be with his committee, the law—which is to say, the principles and legislation derived from *Brown v. Board of Education*—was not. Just a year ago a legal challenge to Judge Kaufman's order had worked its way to the U.S. Supreme Court. The challengers were several Prince George's teachers who had come to resent the racially-based job transfers handed them under the dictates of the court order. The legal filings of the teachers had been aided initially by attorneys in the Justice Department of President Reagan. The desegregation order was defended by Prince George's County legal representatives, who were obliged to do so, joined by attorneys from the NAACP. As an institution, the NAACP was in decline, but these attorneys with their scratched, worn briefcases were like the old Jews in Spielberg's movie, unwavering. And unwavering, too, was the law, at least as defined by the Supreme Court justices. Notwithstanding that eight of the nine justices were Republican appointees, they had upheld Judge Kaufman's old racial dictum.

The Reverend Bruce Haskins having accepted a calling to a larger congregation in Baltimore, the Ryland Epworth congregants were between ministers, and, to make matters worse, a dollar crisis was upon them. At a congregational meeting Merv and Dell urged everyone to face facts. "It's no good pussyfooting around this," Merv insisted. "We need an infusion of money to survive. Let's admit it. Let's announce it. We have to be willing to cry out for help."

A solicitation drive was agreed on. But for whom would the old souls of Ryland Epworth be a worthy cause? They would have to appeal to friends and family who had moved away, lost members of the church. Merv and Dell made calls to former Prince Georgians now living in Ohio and Utah and other faraway places. A mailing went out, for which Merv bought special envelopes at a giftshop of the Air and Space Museum. A hologram of the Space Shuttle flickered on the front of the envelopes. Spendthrift gimmickry, some of the old deacons said, but Merv overrode them. A gimmick was necessary to distinguish the Ryland Epworth letter from the everyday junkload of dunning letters.

Within a few weeks the solicitations had succeeded well enough, and the immediate crisis had passed. As for the next crisis, it seemed likely the congregation would not have the Stricklers to call upon. "It makes my heart sink to hear you talk of leaving us," said their friend Cheerful. "What on earth will become of us without the two of you?"

12

"This is perfect. I'm fired up!" said Bruce.

He was talking with Camilla about contacting everyone from their old racially mixed crowd at Potomac High—Yolanda Jackson and Steve Dawn and Reggie Alexander, not to mention Ray Norris, and, of course, Heather.

"I'm going to love to see the look on that woman's face when we all walk in together," Heather said. And yet in Heather's visits to Hillcrest Heights she had begun to wonder if some of the emotional effect of their reunion plot was derived from the changes she saw around her, the sense that Hillcrest Heights represented a teenage faith since misplaced.

Heather was disturbed by the changes and disturbed by her reaction to them. "All through school I had plenty of black friends. We recognized there were differences between us, but the differences weren't important. Now I get the feeling a lot of black people here want to make their culture the prevalent culture and too bad for white people," she said one day in a kind of involuntary, spontaneous confession. "There is a sense of exclusivity. It's black this, black that. At the drugstores there are shelves upon shelves of hair sheen and pic combs. The Hillcrest Heights mall is a big consumer market for black-oriented items, Air Jordans, St. Ides malt liquor. Out in the parking lot, man, there's all kinds of stuff going on around you, woofing, strutting. I guess you can say they're just expressing themselves, but these dudes are definitely staking their claim. It's their territory. You better not mess with them. Get me out of here. I'm not afraid, but it's uncomfortable. I'm not used to this. I'm in a minority, and I don't fit in.

Maybe that's the way black people used to feel in Hillcrest Heights. Maybe it's my turn to feel that way. But it's different from when I was in school. The differences are shoved in your face. You can't avoid them."

How rapt Elvira looked! At the front of the Prince George's courthouse, she looked like her old self, distinctly Elviraesque, straitlaced but burning inside, and regal, queen for the day. Her heels click-clacked on stone uneven and gritty. About a hundred onlookers, the faithful and the curious, had stolen away from their schedules to stand and watch on the grass. Elvira smiled a formal smile and waved a formal wave. No one could say she didn't know how to make a correct entrance. She came to a standstill between the smooth Ionic columns, a spot that had become a fixation for her. In the cloud-mottled sunlight of August a thick, green summer smell abounded. The TV and radio people flipped the switches on their gear, and microphones began picking up the strident and incessant cry of cicadas from overhanging trees.

On the way to this press event some of Elvira's friends had expressed bewilderment. Why invite everybody just to bring up the Amy Smith case again? It violated every canon of good judgment. But where her friends saw only further public disgrace Elvira saw opportunity. The legal disaster of the Smith case could be presented, with a turn of the mirror, as political evidence that the courthouse system "can't handle a black woman who does not toe the line." Besides, notoriety brings its own rewards. Anything to set Elvira higher in the public imagination would help with name recall on Election Day. Elvira's minister, the Reverend C. Anthony Muse, had a short speech to give, as did Linda Weatherspoon-Haithcox of the NAACP, and Delores Tucker, director of the National Political Congress of Black Women. Reverend Muse roared, "All the things they've done to Elvira, they're clearly trying to railroad her out of town. Is there a martyr effect here? Certainly there is."

Elbert and Daphne Jones were on hand, too, flanking Elvira. Much as Mr. and Mrs. Jones wanted a new trial in the Smith case, Judge Missouri's ruling was not the procedure they favored. It was not right for Judge Missouri to give in to "pressure from the system."

Elvira's supporters spoke with political purpose. Firm poses were struck; solidarity was expressed. No one faltered. It was only Elvira who, as she darted glances at the Joneses, began to lose her public face. Her voice slipped into the wrong register. "If somebody had told me 'Befriend Derrick's family and you will lose everything you worked for,' I would still have done the same thing," she said. "I wouldn't hesitate to do the same thing all over again. Mr. and Mrs. Jones are good people." Elvira began to sound strangely apolitical, low key and maternal, no longer the Elvira who loved to talk from the gut. No doubt some in the crowd figured this was a play for sympathy or figured she would spew forth in a minute. This was a woman who a few days ago, conversing with Gloria, had said, " 'Vengeance is mine,' sayeth the Lord, and we will see what vengeance God delivers." This was a woman who, behind her back, was called "Queen Elvira" for her off-with-their-heads attitude. Hard-heartedness is a quality much disliked in women, even in women wishing to be judges, and it was one of the counts against Elvira in the Smith case. But here, on the warm, dust-blown stoop, departing from her text, mouth uncertain and trembling, Elvira gasped out, "I feel I did what was right, I did what was moral. If I was wrong for feeling sorry for Mr. and Mrs. Jones, then convict me of being too nice. Convict me of being human. I'm a mother. Oh, sweet Lord, that could've been my son lying there. That could've been my boy." On a sort of stifled, tissue-muffled sob, she swayed and leaned her whole body against one of the pillars. The crowd did not know how to react, and so there was silence, except for the racket of the cicadas.

Such an unexpected turn, but Elvira's sudden personal sorrow, tender and wavering, appeared to be unfeigned. Did Freud have a term for it? Or the Good Book? Was this a heart released from servitude?

The publicity stunt had turned into something quite different.

Out there is an enclave of strangers ever on the lookout for someone else who also likes to carouse in the shower and who doesn't mind an old dog panting on the living room rug and who will drink beer straight from the bottle. Such vain imaginings go on and on, but what are the chances the two of you will ever meet? How might it happen?

On a morning when Bruce was trying to sing "Only the Lonely" in the shower at his father's house, trying to capture the words and wondering why the old song had started to play in his head, elsewhere two of his Potomac classmates were talking on the phone. They were Pat Ford, who had once lived five blocks from the Gordon house and used to wait with Bruce at the bus stop, and Angela English, an officer from the Class of 1974 who had volunteered to help Bruce with the reunion. "Guess what?" Angela said to Pat. "Bruce Gordon's back in town."

Pat's blood rose. "Oh, how's he doing?"

"He's divorced, like everybody else."

"Hey, that's great! What's his phone number?"

Pat Ford, who had never been married, lived by herself in a Washington apartment and worked as a legal secretary. She felt a desire to dial Bruce's number right off the bat but stopped herself. ("I thought 'this is silly, don't do it. He's probably got a girlfriend. He's probably engaged.' Anyway what would I say? Would he even remember me? It's not like I'm an old flame.") Once, in the eleventh grade, Bruce had asked her out, but she had said no, and they had never dated. Still, as she would say later, sitting in the Gordon house, with Bruce's head nestled impishly on her shoulder, "I wanted to see how Bruce had turned out. You know, had he lost his hair yet?" A week later Pat phoned and offered her ideas for the reunion. Bruce's tone was sweet but beleaguered. *I need another old grad with her bright ideas like a hole in the head.* He remembered her, though. "You were the one who spurned me in the eleventh grade," he said. Pat laughed, sheepishly.

Bruce and Pat saw each other later that afternoon during a gathering of the reunion committee at the Landover Mall community room. Pat was wearing a straw hat, and his hug knocked it off.

What sort of man was he not to have a better memory of this curvaceous and big-bosomed beautiful lady with a dimpled friendly face, a woman Georgia O'Keeffe would have taken to? Pat had a robust physical presence and the kind of unapologetically frank manner that can come across as too formidable, but Bruce found her "eloquent, sharp, funny." During a break the Class of 1974 crew began to exchange life histories. Pat said she had lived for a while with a man who followed orthodox Jewishness and that she herself was a convert to Judaism.

Bruce was eavesdropping. His hand went up. "You're Jewish?"

"For about ten years now."

What an eye-opener! What a daring original—a black woman who had converted! *A black Jew!*

After the meeting Bruce said to Pat, "You can hitch a ride with me. It's on my way."

"It's nowhere near your way," said Angela, giving him a hard time.

"It's only a little bit out of my way." Bruce took Pat's arm.

Pat allowed herself to be guided into his Toyota. Bruce put on his Raybans, then took them off. "Do these bother you?" he said. "I'm not trying to hide, but I've got sensitive eyes."

"No problem," she said.

He slapped the glasses back on. You doddering fool! But he was not to be denied. They stopped at Hannibal's in downtown Washington and ordered iced cappuccinos. Shyly their hands began to touch. By mutual agreement they set a date for later the same evening. For Bruce it had the feel of serendipity. ("There was a buzz the minute I saw her. I kept think-ing, wow, could she be Ms. Right?") He went home and fixed his father a generous dinner and decided on a short nap, after which he took his sec-ond shower of the day and went through the nervous doubts of prepara-tion. He fluffed up his gray curls with a hot-air dryer. He sucked in his belly. During the four or five months since his last date he had cheated on his workouts. Who cares about the indignities of middle-aged spread when you go every night to an empty bed? But tonight he tightened his belt. Dressed smartly and heavily perfumed, he met up with Pat at nine o'clock. She would confess later she had broken a date with someone else. To impress her Bruce was now driving his father's Cadillac, although, to be on the safe side, he deprecatingly introduced it as "the Yom Kippur Clipper." They went to a bar. A white man came up and gave them the once over. "You are the best-smelling couple here," the man said. Bruce and Pat sniffed each other. Breezes from Polynesia flowed from under their chins and ears. They left the bar arm in arm. Outside, pulse high, face on fire, Bruce was in a state. The alacrity of the evening, so peculiar in the dragging throes of summer, threatened to unnerve him. What mistake might he be on the verge of making this time? He went ahead anyway, rapturously aggressive. "I put a lip-lock on her," he would say afterward.

And no need to ask what had kept him in bed late the next morning. His shirt was pulled out and hung over his slacks.

There was a search on for a reliable member of the courthouse, prefer-ably a black man, to fill in the last few months of Alex Williams's term as prosecutor, and Judge Taylor was an obvious choice. For several days in the Upper Marlboro lunch spots, free meals were bet on a Taylor appoint-ment. The old upright, white-haired gentleman near to the end of his string would have liked to have tied it off with this honor. He told a few friends afterward, "It would've been a nice final bow." Nonetheless he no-tified the circuit court judges, who were charged with making the appoint-ment, that he was taking himself out of consideration. Why set himself up where Elvira could use him for a political ploy? Also, gent that Judge Tay-lor was, he did not want to cast another shadow on Alex Williams's mo-ment.

For eleven months Alex Williams's nomination for a federal judgeship had been stalled, the longest delay suffered thus far by any of President Clinton's judicial nominees. Alex Williams's record had been subjected to the soothsaying evaluation that the American Bar Association administers for the U.S. Congress, and, despite his noteworthy accomplishments in Prince George's County—first black public defender, first black prosecutor, founding partner of a law firm—he had received rough treatment. His legal writings were downgraded as "pedestrian," his legal analyses as "shallow." It was said that he had tried to "puff himself up" by overstating his courtroom experience. Overall he was found to be "unqualified." The tradition of the U.S. Senate is not to grant a judgeship to anyone with such a poor rating. Thurgood Marshall, given the same rating as Alex Williams on his nomination to the U.S. Court of Appeals, had been a noteworthy exception. What caused the senators to think twice about Mr. Marshall, and now Mr. Williams, was the matter of their race. A black nominee is ten times more likely than a white nominee to be labeled unqualified by the American Bar Association, a statistical anomaly that in recent years had begun to discomfit more than one senator. In fact, when the Williams nomination had now finally come up for a vote in the dog days of summer, the senators in attendance approved it unanimously, which spoke to the level of unease felt about the ability of a silk-stockinged review panel to render a fair and impartial understanding of prospective black judges.

These then were the reactions:

Robert Watkins, chairman of the American Bar Association's Standing Committee on the Federal Judiciary: "If they chose to confirm him, so be it."

Judge James Taylor: "The U.S. senators after due consideration did the right thing."

Alex Williams, partying with Gloria and a gang of guests: "In the past year I've received probably five thousand letters of support. How can I be bitter when I have that many friends?"

Gloria: "I'm so glad for Alex, and thank God for the U.S. Senate."

Also, from Gloria: "Tell me, do you see a similarity between what the American Bar Association tried to do to Alex and what the local powers that be are doing to Elvira?"

In Upper Marlboro a debate in the county council chambers centered on whether to prohibit the commerce of rib vendors and seafood dealers alongside Indian Head Highway. There had been complaints from the nearby subdivisions. The grill smoke and hydrocarbon-reeking generators were noxious. However, several members of the council talked nostalgically of the roadside life. "The blight of nostalgia!" said someone else. Nothing was decided.

The next day a new debate possessed the council. The use of the court-house steps by political candidates was noted with disapproval. A ban was voted into effect. No longer would Elvira be able to deploy herself in front of the old columns.

The epic legal action, the upset of the apple cart, the scattering of local customs—these bring to mind the NAACP, not the Chamber of Commerce, and for a long time the very idea of entering the business world dulled the spirit in the homes of NAACP activists. Who in the old NAACP would have cared if the Prince George's master transportation plan created barriers to road-building? Roads are the domain of subdivision developers—a white domain, pretty much. But Wayne Curry, an NAACP man of the 1990s, was keenly interested. Mr. Curry had railed against the transportation plan: "Some misguided and frankly racist people have decided if you don't have roads, you won't have more development. If you don't have more development, you won't have more new people. If you don't have more new people, you won't have any more new black people." To Mr. Curry the subdivision developers were the enemy of the white rural crowd and the friend of black professionals like himself. Thus did Mr. Curry make himself into an exemplar of the "third wave" of an upwardly mobile African-American culture. The "first wave," according to John Shipley Butler, a black professor at the University of Texas, dated back to the shopkeepers and mule-plowing farmers who received property rights after the Civil War, and the "second wave" was constituted by the kente-cloth lawyers and minister-politicians of the modern civil rights movement. Professor Butler held in warm regard the ex-slaves who had searched out the dollar but was rather uncomplimentary about Thurgood Marshall and Martin Luther King and their yen for equal rights. "A focus on rights practically forces you to think in terms of victimization," he had written, "but a focus on business forces you to look for opportunity." High time too—that was his sensible advice. A deficit in wealth has always proclaimed the separate-ness of Black America. If Black America was its own nation it would rank 35th in the world in quality of living, according to a United Nations Human Development report. White America would rank first. (Combined, they rank sixth, behind Japan, Canada, Norway, Switzerland, and Sweden.) In the part of Prince George's inhabited by Wayne Curry, the focus was un-abashedly on money. If elected, Mr. Curry would be asked to oversee a billion-dollar budget, no small piece of change and yet not of a size to faze him. Mr. Curry was a major functionary in the business world—part developer, part lawyer. The law firm in which he was a partner represented the commercial interests of several construction and retail groups. He had been chief counsel for the Prince George's hospital system. He had been a bank director. He had served as president of the Prince George's Chamber of Commerce. He referred to himself as "a businessman first, a politician second." He was not a freak, just another success story. A whole generation of black Prince Georgians, eyes on the twenty-first century, was fast with him. All three of Gloria's children were entrepreneurs—John IV, the owner of a computer firm; Gary, an executive with a telecommunications company; and Gloria Jean, a desktop publisher. Gloria was pleased by the enterprising nature of her children except for when she was troubled by it. "I don't know what to make of it in its totality. My kids don't think the way I think," she said, a small distress signal in her voice. "They are much more business-oriented than my generation. They want to own their own businesses rather than become public servants. I worry about that because we need teachers, we need police officers, we need social service workers. We even need politicians. Quality public servants are the backbone of the system. I worry about who will take our place." Not a sales pitch, just being practical: Both generations could say they had the best interests of their community in mind, yet the stronger agenda seemed to belong to the young. The Maryland Business Council had listed ten thousand "black-owned" businesses in Prince George's County, about half the total for all of Maryland, and leaders of the Black Alliance were called on more and more to be a right hand of this entrepreneurial movement. Gloria's latest cause had nothing to do with Elvira and the courthouse. No, she was rallying support for a venture headed by black businessman Carl Jones in a competition to build a stadium for the Bowie BaySox, a Baltimore Orioles minor league team relocating to Prince George's County. "That's the other side of the coin. In terms of economics, we can predict greatness for our county. One day we will have a hundred thousand successful minority businesses here." And why not? Getting ahead has always been more of a classic dream in America than getting along. Duty, social justice, public service—they can be suspect. Money substitutes for them. Money is real; it can be trusted.

Merv Strickler, during a public questioning of the county executive candidates, asked, "Do any of you have a plan to get a store like a Nordstrom's located here?" He and Dell—and Gloria, too—were on a kick to reconfigure the shopping malls of Prince George's County. For all the profit motive of the Chamber of Commerce, and for all the money burning a hole in the collective pockets of the new consumers, the malls were almost completely devoid of those retail stores associated with affluent communities. Where was Nordstrom's and Bloomingdale's? Where was Anne Taylor? *Criminy, where was Banana Republic?* Prince George's County was still the land of Marshall's and K-mart and Montgomery Ward. (Old joke: "What are the first three words a Prince George's child learns to say?" Answer: "Attention, K-mart shoppers.") The style of capitalism familiar to other American suburbs was, in many respects, missing from the Prince George's quadrant of metropolitan Washington. Frank Pesci longed for the day he could get home delivery of the daily *New York Times,* and he resented having to drive to Bethesda for veal piccata. A couple of times when he had tracked the release of Woody Allen movies, he discovered the bookers each time had passed over every single Prince George's theater; same for *The Age of Innocence.*

Here was a cause to unite such feuding parties as a Pesci and a Lawlah and a Curry. Indeed, Mr. Curry was promising to shake up the brand-name retailers: "They like to avoid a community until the average income hits $40,000. That's the threshold. But we're at $50,000. There has to be a reason we're being overlooked."

Frank: "I've called all over the place looking for answers, and nobody calls me back. Of course, it doesn't take a genius to figure out what's going on. We're victims of stereotyping, all of us, black and white. We've been red-lined by the big shots in New York. Low-brow whites or middle-brow blacks, that's how we're categorized, and it's the same difference to them."

Gloria: "Their marketing people obviously are not looking at our available disposable income. They're looking at something else. Is it racism? I don't know. What do you call it when affluent blacks are equated to blue-collar whites?"

On weekdays Bruce measured his schedule down to the minute, but on weekends all precision was lost. It was sometime late and lazy on a Sunday afternoon, after the music sounding from open-door churches had ceased and after the Baltimore Orioles radio announcers had completed their game wrap-up, when, sunglasses on, he went out the back door and down the three-tiered ramp on his way to the High's dairy store in the strip mall. This stroll to get an ice cream cone, pistachio, double dip, was pure pleasure. It had been part of his routine all through the summer. He cut around the backyard fence and crossed 23rd Place. It was a fine day.

The benevolent idleness of Sunday lay everywhere. Pat Ford was on his mind.

Bruce did not give a second thought to the black teenagers, about twenty strong, lounging in the parking lot. They had on their "uniforms," as he called them, the downward-tugged baggy shorts and pirates' decorations of knotted red bandanas over the head and gold pieces stuck on the ear, everything in appreciation of the Hollywood look that is a standard for young black men. Bruce knew their stamp, or thought he did. They were an imitation version of street kids. In less public places they presented themselves as well-scrubbed children of the suburbs. Their loose-hanging garments were top-dollar items, name clothes bought for them without them ever having to do a hand's turn probably. They were good kids dressed up as bad, a phenomenon different from Bruce's youth when the Grits wore a punk garb of thin, pastel-colored baggy "dags" and white high-top Converse "chugs" while the Collegiates made sure to distinguish themselves in their precisely groomed tight pants and fully synthetic Ban-lon shirts or collarless surfer shirts. Now, in the 1990s, there was just one look. The scholar Cornel West had written about the influence on fashion (and on music and film) rendered by the "worst-element" kids—the kitsch, dreck, and schlock of pop culture summed up in the bad dude's attitude. "Protective coloration" is what the columnist William Raspberry called it. Middle-class black kids who do not ape the ghetto run the risk of being alienated from their race.

Out among these local kids in their fashionable disguises Bruce assumed he was in safe company. But then came a frightful turn. Perhaps he was in violation of their turf, or perhaps they were besotted by the heat, or perhaps they were just being teenagers in the full stride of their season who once again wanted to prove they could lay claim to a place like nobody else. Or maybe it was something impersonal and systematic from America's long racially hurting history; maybe they wanted to orchestrate fear in this particular white man so they wouldn't be taken for granted. Something, anyway, made them decide to perform on Bruce a type of street kidnapping. They clogged around him in a shuffling, belligerent circle. Bruce had a sensation of time grinding to a halt. Later, when he talked of the incident, his mind seemed to recall each minute in slow-motion. A couple of the kids started in with taunts. "Where you going so fast, big boy? You planning to get nasty?" He wanted to think them playful, but their tone was goading. They stank of a dead and empty rage. ("I could feel this surly bad vibe. They picked on my fear. It started with a few of them, but then it was the whole bunch of them, jawing, making noise. They were swaggering, getting physical. They wanted to take something

from me, not money, more like my pride, and I was damned if I was going to yield it up.") As a teenager Bruce had read a magazine article about
advisable conduct for a white person who enters a "ghetto" environment.
Walk purposefully, be neutral and exhibit neither defiance nor fear, nothing of a personal nature. This was advice for racists, he had thought at the
time. A direct, open glance is what he believed in. But now that old advice, regurgitant, unexpectant, seemed to be prompting him. He tried to
smooth his face but thought also of a pellet-shot black woman running for
her life years ago from this very spot. A beading broke out under his arms.
He felt it career down his sides. Sweat also got in his eyes. The light
greasy spice of asphalt and burned barbecue was in his nose. Several seconds passed. The wet on his body went cold. ("It's true what they say
about being too scared to piss. I could feel my penis and testicles contract,
the cold ocean effect.") Big as Bruce is, he had never been well cast as a
victim. But being big does not keep you from suffering alone in your room
when you are afraid of the Grits for not being white enough. Now, con-
trarily, he felt a "whiteness" welling up in him. ("Was I going to be another
white guy who's turned into an object lesson? Another Reginald Denny,
pummeled and bleeding? That's what I was wondering.") Bruce was at an
impasse. If he tried to push through he was sure to touch someone's
sweat-sleeked arm, and any physical contact, it seemed clear, would bring
the situation to flash point. But doing nothing, it seemed just as clear,
would bring the situation to the same point. Danger and the suburban
landscape seemed suddenly one and indivisible. Might he actually have to
lay down his life? Well, he would refuse to beg—he was resolved to that.
He looked for weapons. Not switchblades like the Grits used to carry, but
guns. Guns were the weapon today's young men handled with instinctive,
casual skill. He could see no bulges in their outsized clothes but could not
be sure. A youth whose elongated face was made longer by a beard
moved up to speak to Bruce. "Ain't nobody in a hurry here, is there?" The
long-faced kid seemed older and rougher than the others, maybe a
washout from a gang somewhere. His worked-up expression was sullen,
contemptuous, like a two-bit dictator. He wore a T-shirt lettered with
"White Men Can't Pump." The words were voguish and modern-sounding,
but the boast itself was a reminder of the long-simmering sexual tension.
"Hey, hey, the white boy's scared," he sneered. "See the white boy turn
red." The excitement was great. The teenagers hyped each other with
more trash talk, a couple of them singing in a fake falsetto. It was the insulting casualness that finally unlocked Bruce from his trance. ("They
thought they had me in their power, and it pissed me off.") Their casualness gave his anger scope. All of a sudden he wanted to take action. ("I

started making plans. Could I bust an aerial off one of the cars in the lot and use it for a weapon?") He would lash out like a tomcat. ("I didn't envision victory. Only to go down fighting.") He raised his right hand and shoved his way through with a determined palooka authority. His arm spun two or three of the youths sideways. It was a bold, lucid act, the most lucid since he had been entrapped. The teenagers did not react, and Bruce picked up his pace. He did not look back. Behind him he heard someone yelling, "Kiss mine, man! Kiss mine!"

The mob let him go. It had been public theater for its own sake, apparently. Only the long-faced kid sauntered after Bruce. The two of them entered High's Dairy, Bruce a couple of steps ahead. But now Bruce had his confidence back. He went to the counter and ordered a double-dip cone and a pack of gum. He took stock of the situation. He bobbed on his toes and flexed his shoulders as if readying for a workout. The long-faced kid had moved to a rack near the counter and was pulling one-shave razors off the rack. He held up two fistfuls.

"I'll put them in a bag for you," said the clerk, a white woman, calling his bluff.

"Or you can put them back," Bruce said. He settled glaring eyes on the kid, as if counting every hair on his face. Bruce shifted his weight. One on one, the long-faced kid had no chance.

"Fuck you!" the kid shouted. But the razors went back onto the metal spokes of the rack.

Walking home, insides no longer quaking, Bruce breezed through the crowd. As he reached 23rd Place, one of the stragglers came over and put up a hand—a pleasant-looking kid with a Maynard G. Krebs goatee and granny glasses. "Everything cool with you?" the kid asked, being friendly, trying to salvage the situation. What Bruce read into these few words was the following: "The unspoken message was that he thought his friends were assholes. I felt he was saying, 'No wonder white people don't trust us.'" But it was a momentary respite. In bed later, doors double-locked, shades drawn, agitated again and sleepless, a belly full of twice-heated coffee, it came to Bruce there was no arrangement with fate to be had. Purity of heart did not protect anyone from bullies; the truth never made anyone free; good intentions never sent anyone to heaven; and integration was another virtuous myth.

Gloria continued to take a diplomatic approach toward the Mills campaign even as other black politicians resorted to Klan-baiting. "White robes would fit Sue Mills nicely," Elvira was heard to say. To Gloria, some-one who had had experience with the Klan, such terminology constituted overkill. Gloria would never use it. But Gloria's neutral style was laid atop an underground strategy operating through neighborhood meetings and along "phone trees." Politically tuned-in activists with allegiance to Gloria were getting out the word about Mrs. Mills to the black voting public. *Don't trust that mama's conversion—she ain't no John the Baptist!*

At what age do you no longer get teary-eyed at the singing of "We Shall Overcome"? When do you stop being the idealist who put a white arm around a black man's shoulders up on a segregated convention dais? When do you lose touch with the self who put southern waitresses in their place? When do you stop hosting jolly barbecues so full of "color" they are the talk of the neighborhood?

It was said of Merv and Dell Strickler that life itself could not wipe away their pleasure at doing the right thing. However, at least in Hillcrest Heights, their time appeared to be coming to a close. The Stricklers had been replaced in the neighborhood hierarchy by the black residents they once upon a time had welcomed in. Merv and Dell were getting old; they were out of kilter. Such is the natural progression of things and not, in their opinion, reason enough to move away. But Merv and Dell also had to factor in racial demographics. If they were no longer asked to be an of-ficer in the neighborhood association were they being shoved aside be-cause of their age—or because of their race? Did younger black residents want them off Foster Place for the sake of new homeowners who might be a better fit for the neighborhood? These were the sort of questions Merv and Dell might have put to Gloria, but the call of politics left Gloria pre-cious little time anymore for her neighbors. The Stricklers had to sort out answers as best they could, and, while they were sorting out, they could not forget the criminal factor. In America's berserk era of crime, how long could their guardian angel be trusted to keep from their person the many random essays at violent action? Merv had come home for lunch one day and found the glass window in the front door knocked through by a rock. A minute sooner, and he would have been face-to-face with the thief, loaded up with cameras and jewelry. As it was, Merv could hear the man exiting out back, flinging himself over the deck rails.

And yet, eyes twinkling, Merv would laugh about the episode. "Like they say, everything in life is timing."

• • •

Being worldly—that is to say, being a normal person well aware of the
commonness of encounters with dangerous young men on the street—
Bruce understood his experience at the strip mall was an inevitable American moment, a sixties guy embracing the fate of the sixties. He was of a
mind to forget the whole thing. Yet it was not within him to forget. He
slept badly. The incident worked on him. He began a round of calls to
friends, wishing to talk through the feeling of having been in one instant
undone, reduced again to a boy looking over his shoulder. Perhaps he
was overreacting, but something pent up in him had been released. Suddenly he saw aliens in his midst, after everything he had done to personalize and familiarize his neighborhood. Who were these little terrorists?
And what was their excuse? They had no claim to deprivation and suffering of the type that was said to cause so many kids to go wrong. They
were not victims of poverty or inferior schools nor dwellers on the wrong
side of the tracks; nor were they, presumably, part of that clinical population of child abuse, poor prenatal nutrition, high lead levels, head injuries
and so forth from whence, according to a new academic study, come the
seven percent of teenagers responsible for seventy-nine percent of the violence. The lives of these Hillcrest Heights kids, Bruce was willing to bet,
contained positive influences—the two-parent family, the African-American role models in business and politics, a basic assurance about where
their next meal was coming from. They had no excuse!

But there must be social forces to explain why young black men of
good backgrounds would turn ruffian and run roughshod through civilized society. There must be something to blame. Newspapers, magazines,
and books are stocked with periodical ruminations on this and related
racial subjects, the sort of topical sociology Bruce had left behind after college, but in the following weeks he perused the popular media. To be
young and black in America's suburbs was an agony; you were caught between the depravity of the African-American urban poor and the nervousness of the Anglo-American suburban well-to-do—this was the theory that
seemed to have seized the new sociologists. In Bruce and Camilla's
teenage days they had to dodge not only the gauntlet of Grits but also
those black classmates who sneered at her as an "Oreo" for her summers
in the south of France and her Kennedy Center box seats. Even so, peer
pressure had come a long way. Camilla would now have been expected to
join in clubbish, secret society street scenes like the one at the strip mall

because this was said to be the authentic African-American experience. She would have been expected to participate in public menace—producing what the sociologist Henry Louis Gates calls the "scary Negro." Style had become all-important. The gunplay was real, the blood real, and yet the "scary Negro" in his angel-of-death getup seemed to be laboring under the illusion he was performing for a movie audience. William Raspberry had interviewed a random number of high school counselors and was in full lament about the persuasions placed upon the good-egg black youth. Kids who said thank-you to a teacher were picked on; kids who volunteered for conflict-mediation sessions were "sissies." Mr. Raspberry had written, "Something profoundly disturbing is happening to a society when ordinary gestures of courtesy and civility become tokens of exploitable weakness—when the rules of behavior come to be set by the most debased and most hopeless elements." Add to peer pressure the natural insolence of teenagers—Bruce thought back to the Grits. Add in maleness. For men, whatever life deals them, there is always machismo, the universal experience. Add, furthermore, the fearful face put on, almost against their will, by white people on middle-class streets. Fear of the black man is as old as the colonies, and it has worn on successive generations of law-abiding black Americans. The book *Parallel Time* was just out from the black man Brent Staples, an owlish-faced, scholarly *New York Times* editorial writer who had recollected on his attempts as a graduate student to act friendly to white strangers in lakefront Chicago, calling out "Good evening" and whistling Vivaldi. For all his efforts he had received back the stares of the enemy; white men girding themselves for an assault; one white woman turning and running, as if she had seen her doom. "I did violence to them just by being," he wrote. He had begun to keep his head down, hoping to seem harmless, but then his individual goodness withered. An idea formed, and he began a perverse game he called "scatter the pigeons." He hid in the shadows until a young white couple stepped from their car toward their town house. "The two of them stood frozen as I bore down on them. I felt a surge of power: these people were mine; I could do with them as I wished. If I had been younger, with less to lose, I'd have robbed them, and it would have been easy. All I'd have to do was stand silently before them until they surrendered their money. [Instead] I thundered 'Good evening!' into their bleached-out faces and cruised away laughing. . . . [In their minds] they'd made me terrifying. Now I'd show them what terrifying could be." To be given this glimpse into the fury on the inside of the most docile-seeming of black men was to begin perhaps to get a picture of life at the strip mall. The author Richard Wright in *Native Son* (an old college text) depicted a main character, Bigger Thomas, whose wrong turns begin with a black man's mass-induced misperception of himself: "Every time you try to find a way to live, your own mind stands in the way. You know why that is? It's because others have said you were bad"—the self-fulfilling prophecy of white Americans. The killing of a white woman by Bigger Thomas is presented as an unabashed accident of race: she is unknown to him; he is the scary Negro; he kills because of her fear, and his. The only context is the happenstance of birth, to be born of the wrong parents. It is the logic of the Grits and the southern night riders. Bruce did not disagree. Undisputably, black racist evil-doing does imitate white racist evil-doing. No uniform method exists for tracking hate crimes, but the Klanwatch Project of the Southern Poverty Law Center, praised by law enforcement officials for its general awareness of the subject, was reporting that black Americans now are the culprits in perhaps 35 percent of all racially motivated violence, a category of crime which white Americans once had to themselves. In a separate essay by Richard Wright, the author explains Bigger Thomas's descent into mayhem as answering "the call of the dominant civilization." Newer writers like Henry Louis Gates were pushing the idea that a notoriously large subset of white Americans long ago established themselves as inhabitants of Thomas Hobbes's brutish "state of nature." So why shouldn't the spirit of evil also exist in some of today's young black people? Indeed, Bruce was willing to grant each of the above explanations. But, to him, they didn't follow. Especially not to 23rd and Foster Place. The young black men at the strip mall remained impenetrable, their actions inexcusable.

Some days later Bruce took his dog for a run out among the happenings of Hillcrest Heights life—women in short shorts, Bob Magruder's arriving entourage of gym rats, the hellos at Mrs. Jones's rib joint, the swoosh, swoosh of the traffic that seemed to mimic the rhythm of his heart. But now, to him, these were distractions. He blocked them out with a laboring, concentrating brain. He wanted to be prepared for trouble.

No trouble developed, and he was left alone with his thoughts. His thoughts were these: "I've been the one out here being friendly. I've been the one saying 'Good evening!' I didn't disrespect anyone. I was friendly to everyone. They want to act like assholes? They're welcome to Hillcrest Heights!"

At a corn boil Sue Mills was passing out "Sue Mills" magnets, and at a bingo hall there were donkey-shaped hand fans. At a crab feast Wayne Curry was quoted as saying, "A vote for Tignor is a vote for Mills." The pace of the campaign was picking up. Candidates were showing more of their true colors. Sue Mills gave her okay to a "specialty" leaflet for distribution at the courthouse—a leaflet that endorsed the incumbent judges and was dismissive of Elvira White as a political species apart. Mrs. Mills felt it politically advantageous to link her name to the judges, but she also freely stated her dislike of Elvira. Two years earlier, at a Montessori school attended by Elvira's son B.J. and Mrs. Mills's granddaughter Kimberly, a dispute had arisen, dividing the parents. It became a racial dispute. Elvira, as president of the board of trustees, took one side, Mrs. Mills's daughter, Cindy, the other. The meetings were emotional, draining, destructive. On the pleading of her daughter Mrs. Mills invaded one meeting. To sit incognito on a folding chair was, with her hairdo, out of the question. Anyway, Mrs. Mills was not able to sit for long. She got to her feet and began a harangue. Elvira cut her off. They argued. Their gestures were large and abrupt. From the audience there would later be comments about an "embarrassing feel," an animal-bristling, to the scene. Elvira ordered Mrs. Mills to leave, "You don't belong here. You're not a mother here." Mrs. Mills left with a strong bitterness. ("Elvira White is not nice; she's vicious. Although in the end she prevailed. She was very effective, I'll give her that, effective on a negative basis, all based on race.") The white principal resigned. The lock on the principal's office door was changed. Mrs. Mills's granddaughter transferred out of the school.

Bruce and Pat were guessing at the spices in the grill smell of marinated chicken at a friend's house. "Cajun pepper?" "Tabasco?" Out on an open pineboard deck they then held hands and gazed at the twilight sky. An orange September sun warmed them. In another hour bats would come out of the trees and swoop at unnatural angles. Blimpie, swishing his tail, glowered at their feet. Pat combed Bruce's hair with her fingers. At his prompting she smacked him on the cheek with her lips and oohed and ahhed as she wiped off the raging red smear.

Bruce swore he had not been looking for romance. "Earlier in the year, yes, I was desperate, but I'd gotten past it," he said. "My life was quiet, and the quiet felt good. Whenever I saw an interesting woman, I'd think, 'Why take the chance?' "

"Exactly," Pat said. "That was exactly my mind-set. I was tired of dating. I'd been there, I'd done it, and I was through with it. I'd wised up."

Of course, they were fooling no one, not even themselves.

"Okay, okay," said Bruce, giggling hard. "We were in a state of denial."

"Exactly," Pat said.

You might desire someone at first sight—a green teenager's version of sexual politics—and later find the right reasons brought to you by fate. Sometimes it takes just one night to be smitten; sometimes it takes the full twenty-one years.

Bruce: "My first memory of Pat is from that afternoon bus stop. We took the same bus home from Potomac. [Turning to her] When did you move to Hillcrest Heights? Eighth grade?"

Pat: "Yeah, Hillcrest Heights was the last destination for my dad. He was an army major, and I was an army brat. We lived all over the place."

Bruce: "Anyway, you made an impression on me. You were cute, nice personality, and you wore those fabulous miniskirts."

Pat (with twisted smile): "Thanks."

Bruce: "We were at the bus stop, and I asked for your number."

Pat: "Everybody was staring at us. I had this odd sensation in the pit of my stomach. I thought, 'Oh, my God. This is never going to work. You're a white guy. You're not black.' "

Bruce: "I felt displaced back then, ethnically speaking."

Pat (eyes bugging): "But our school was predominantly white!"

Bruce: "Whites don't automatically meld with other whites. Can you see me melding with a bunch of holy-roller Baptists or hard-core Catholics?"

Pat: "Okay, but . . ."

Bruce: "I related much better to you. Honestly, it felt natural to ask you out."

Pat: "Yeah, well, I was worried what everyone was going to say. There were some pretty prejudiced people at Potomac. You had all this chutzpah, but I was nervous."

Bruce: "You really told off that kid who gave you a hard time, though."

Pat: "The black kid? Yeah, he goes, 'You're nothing but an Uncle Tom.' And I got mad. I told him, 'If I'm an Uncle Tom, your mother's a whore.' And he goes, 'I guess she is.' And I go, 'Yeah, I guess she is.' "

Bruce: "I called you that evening and asked you out, and you politely declined."

Pat: "I was a free thinker, but I would've never dated a white boy. I wasn't the rebel you were. Everyone knew you were into black girls. Black girls were old hat for you."

Bruce (smiling): "Black women are the most beautiful, that's why."

Pat (in a serious vein): "To me it wasn't a positive occurrence that you were a white guy. The pressure against interracial dating was so enormous. Kids would stare you down. They'd bump into you, really harass you. I was insecure. I wanted to be accepted. I wasn't ready to live on the fringe of society. [Pause] I haven't told you this before, but when we lived in Gibbstown, New Jersey, people would call up and threaten to burn us out. Because my father was black and my mother was white. That's what set people off. My folks had this wonderful storybook romance—they met in a Long Island bar a few days before the army was to post my dad to Germany and they got married before he shipped out—but we were treated like we were from Mars. The kids on our block were hateful. They wouldn't play with me. And at this Catholic school, the mother superior said it was fine when my mom enrolled me, but then I showed up with my little ebony face and slam! There was no room for me!"

Bruce: "I had a hard time of it, too, being Jewish. Which is probably why I identified with black kids."

Pat: "I guess it was when I converted to Judaism that I started to feel natural going out with a white guy. A weird circle, huh?"

Bruce (with a breakaway joy): "My whole life is a weird circle. Fantastically weird and amazing, don't you think?"

On Route One the old Remington's bar had a new proprietress—Bonnie Aldridge, late of the public defender's office. In a honky-tonk with knotty-pine paneling and $6.99 Bud Light buckets and Kenny Rogers on the jukebox it was unlikely Bonnie would run into Elvira, which was one way to resolve a busted friendship.

For quite a while Bonnie had fretted over the end of things with her "spiritual sister," not the least because she thought she knew precisely when the end had come. She and Elvira had been at LaGuardia Airport in New York, on a jaunt to interview a wayward court witness. They were discussing one of the new investigators in the Prince George's office, a black woman who had been giving Bonnie a hard time.

"Why do you think she isn't more friendly?" Bonnie asked.

"She doesn't know how to play the game," Elvira answered.

Bonnie felt one of those twinges. "What do you mean?"

"I mean like me. I know how to get along. I'm everybody's friend."

"I thought you actually were my friend."

"You don't understand. I'm your friend, yes, but I don't feel friendly toward every white person I smile at. Black people have to pretend. That's the way the game is played."

"Game? Game? That's a cop-out! Either you like someone, or you don't."

Standing by the baggage conveyor belts Bonnie and Elvira were a spectacle of arm-waving and shouting. Bonnie kept saying, "You're right, I don't understand!" ("I was devastated.") When they got to the line for the rental car, though, they started to laugh at themselves. ("Just like that, it seemed funny.") The reality was, and they would separately attest to it, there never had been false deference or game-playing between them, not in their lunches, the shopping blowouts, the fun on the job. They had been legitimate pals. This was a believable fact because on the same evening Elvira had learned of her husband's cheating, by way of the trans-fixing "The Price Is Right" tape, she had called Bonnie and poured out her heart.

It is possible, however, that the beginning of the end of their friendship did occur at LaGuardia Airport. Doesn't a doubt wedged between two friends grow on its own? And doesn't it grow ten times faster, a hundred times faster, when the doubt is racial, when it introduces a racial hurt?

Now, two years later, relations between Bonnie and Elvira were fully lost. Bonnie called the outcome "a self-fulfilling prophecy." She sat in a booth at her bar. She wore white ankle socks and white tennis shoes. Soft-faced and pretty, eyes downcast, a melancholy turn in her mouth, she said, "I couldn't act normal around Elvira. Whatever I did—was it racial? Would Elvira take offense? Everything with her turned into black and white. All she could see was race, race, race, even though there were half a dozen other things causing her life to fall apart."

Bonnie's testimony at the hearing for Amy Smith, of course, later on had become one of those things.

The basic line about Elvira's life was generally agreed upon at the court-house, how it had been one long searing grudge against the white world, a world she distrusted with all her being, a world from which she had al-ways expected to be cast out. All those years of properly, unceasingly ex-pressing the American desire to "play the game," her work habits, the old-hat gestures, all of it was a sham. It was the Good Negro who had got-ten the star treatment, and it was the Other Negro, the Negro lapsing into woe-is-me histrionics, the Negro with African artwork on her walls, who was responsible for having the good life snatched away—so went the talk about her. Yet race did not explain everything about Elvira, as the sophis-ticates at the courthouse were glad to tell you. Race did not explain the woman who had enjoyed the trappings of the courthouse even as she op-posed its assumptions. Race did not explain her willful denial of her mis-takes and of the consequences sure to follow. It did not explain her rectitude and stubborn virtuosity and why she would not let her hair down (except at her own parties). Nor did race speak to her curious naïveté when she was reined in. "How Elvira got herself into her predicament, really, it's on her head," said a criminal lawyer who herself was looked on favorably as a possible judge someday. "She reaped what she sowed." All this character analysis was delivered by people striving to answer the question of why, in Elvira's hour of embattlement, they were staying away from her in droves. These were white people who had an image of themselves as forward thinkers, New Testament liberals who looked positively upon the changeover of Prince George's County. They had made a mistake, too, they said. They had assumed a person's work reflects a person's worth, but an attorney with good courtroom techniques does not always walk on life's right side. Fortunately, they had caught their mistake in time.

Many of the security guards and secretaries and custodians did not take part in this high-flying talk about Elvira. Their assessment was simpler. "You piss people off, what do you expect?" said a young black man who had a job sweeping floors. But people with high school diplomas are never surprised by a political trammeling. They are the true sophisticates in any courthouse.

It is in the nature of men to employ, at the very least, a minor amount of deceit in wooing a new love. But some men are more straightforward than others. Anyway, Bruce could not very well fail to tell Pat of his plans to do a head-turning entrance with Camilla on reunion night at the Ramada Inn. Everyone on the reunion committee knew about the torch he had been carrying for his first-ever love. And Pat seemed to accept the situation because she had teased Bruce, "I thought I was your first. You loved me at the bus stop before you ever went out with Camilla."

Pat's little play on his affections was unexpected. He felt a jump of happiness and a quickening desire to forgo his date with Camilla in favor of asking Pat. Twenty-four hours after writing a check that reserved a Ramada ballroom and a kingly buffet, he rang up Camilla. "I have something terrible to tell you," he said. "Well, not terrible, but here's the thing: I've met a woman—she's on the reunion committee—Pat Ford, you probably remember her. Hoo boy, I better just say it. Pat and I are getting serious."

"That's wonderful. That's wonderful!"

What other reaction could there be from the pure-souled Camilla? Besides, she had recently returned from two weeks of Dance New England Summer Camp in the Maine woods with David, the man she was seeing, and a life change was upon her as well. On her kitchen table were architectural plans laid out for a customized wood-and-glass house, five thousand square feet, and she, the unmaterialistic VISTA girl, was mooning over it. It would fit like a natural temple on two green acres she had found on the outskirts of Cambridge. She had lined up investors—one of her brothers, his girlfriend, and an obstetrician-gynecologist she knew from her clinic. They would live in the house communally with her and David. She was already banking on it.

Still, Camilla seemed adrift as to the true purpose of Bruce's call, and he felt like a heel. "Would you mind terribly if I . . . you know, on reunion night . . . ?"

"Brought Pat? Yes, by all means, bring Pat," Camilla said quickly, the second she caught on.

"You're such a mensch! And bring Dave. I'll reserve a room at the Ramada for you guys."

"Save one dance for you and me?"

"It's done. It's a deal."

13 **More delays** with Amy's case led to a dark and dumb rumbling that if Elvira in the meantime was elected a judge she might find a way to have Amy's second trial assigned to her. Such talk went against the logic of the law, of course. Elvira was automatically disqualified from ever sitting in legal judgment on a former client. Nonetheless it disturbed Amy to think of having to return to a courthouse where her ex-lawyer might be walking the halls and might appear like Banquo's ghost in the middle of her trial. Playing and replaying in Amy's sleep up in Massachusetts was a shrieking black-gowned woman. *Ye shall crawl cursed on your belly, and the fiery pit shall receive thee.* On one bad hangdog morning, Amy called down to Polen's law offices, and the thin-voiced Larry Polen explained again that Elvira would not be allowed to have any influence over a jury verdict. Beyond that, and beyond a dose of general, positive thinking, what more counsel could he give?

Larry Polen's hiring had been unusual and outside normal channels, and as someone unfamiliar with the particulars of the case, he was still boning up. The more he examined the evidence the more sobered he became about the complexity of the task before him. The central question remained: Whose theory was the most credible? Had Amy and Derrick plotted to kill her parents as the crowning conception to an intricate plan? (The police theory.) Had Amy invited Derrick to her house simply to aid and abet her in a juvenile burglary, and had Derrick invented a reason to increase the stakes to murder? (The Anne Gold-Rand theory.) Or had Amy and Derrick's only crime been one of sneakiness and lust for which Dennis Smith meted out an ultimate penalty? (The Jones family theory.) Or, perhaps, was there a more lurid and tangled truth of artful seduction and a calculated botch by Amy, then an execution and cover-up by Mr. Smith—the devil in a daughter, evil in a father? (The Elvira White theory.) Having slotted the evidence as they wanted it, most of the principals from Amy's first trial had little interest in trying for a new interpretation. It was up to Larry Polen to settle on a theory for himself, to the best advantage of his client but in accordance with the facts available to him. If he assumed the testimony of the Smiths did not fully conform to the events as they had actually occurred inside their house, as Judge Johnson concluded at the first trial, and if he assumed Amy would again not be completely forthcoming, he was left with the physical items: the nine-millimeter bullets, the spilt sand, the front-door key, a Reebok box, the pages of notebook paper. He could determine from the location of the bullets that Derrick was probably killed in a defenseless state, but what about the rest of the clues? What did they reveal about Amy and Derrick's modus operandi? Had the two teenagers, as the police believed, calculatingly set up the disarray of the seashore souvenir on the windowsill and the sand on the carpet in order to pin the blame for their crimes on a phantom—false clues meant to suggest the forced entry of an unknown intruder? If so, Amy and Derrick had done an excruciatingly inept job of it. The chunk of wood used to lock the window in place had unquestionably been removed by someone on the inside. The most sensible and most favorable interpretation of this part of the evidence, from a defense attorney's point of view, was that Derrick had felt it prudent to enter the Smith house surreptitiously, that Amy had lifted aside the wood and opened the glass for him to slide through, and that his beanpole frame had knocked the sandbox akilter. But what then about the key tied to the drawstring of his shorts? If Derrick entered through a window, he had no need of a key. Nor was it likely to have been in his possession from previous trysting because apparently there had been none. Yet why would anyone have planted a key on Derrick's body? For Mr. Smith to have done so would have served no purpose except to further implicate his daughter in a conspiracy, and would Mr. Smith have truly wished for that outcome? Perhaps the key could be interpreted as a good-faith gesture on Amy's part, a symbol by which Derrick could believe he was her man. *You gotta go in through the window this time, but the next time just come through the front door, long as it's, like, three or four in the morning.*

Aside from the key, there was the Reebok box found on the upstairs living room floor. Tucked inside was Derrick's T-shirt and, inside that, the set of sterling silverware. The silverware and the wrapping may have been placed there by Mr. Smith or his wife—it was possible to imagine the Smiths snatching the T-shirt off Amy's bedroom floor and in frantic glee staging a burglary scene for Mr. Smith's fellow officers. But the Reebok box itself was an item Derrick had brought oddly with him; it was identified by the neighbor who had given Derrick a lift to the bus stop and who remembered it cradled in his lap. Derrick also had with him a plastic Athlete's Foot shopping bag and an audio cassette of the rap album *Another Bad Creation*. The box and the bag, receptacles perhaps for stolen goods, seemed to indicate premeditation at least of a burglary, and if Derrick was a believer in the hip psychology about rap and crime, he might have taken along the cassette to get himself in the mood. It was hard to know which of the clues were to be taken at face value. How devious might the Smiths have been? In their testimony, Mr. and Mrs. Smith claimed it was Derrick who, with a gun trained on their vital spots, demanded to know the whereabouts of the silverware. After Mr. Smith surrendered the information, Derrick left their bedroom, they said, and they could hear him "just seconds later" dumping the chromium-polished, braided-neck utensils out of the dining room serving cart. Except how did he know to go to the serving cart? Mr. Smith claimed to have misdirected Derrick. He claimed to have told Derrick to look for the silverware in the dining room hutch. The Smiths, furthermore, stated that simultaneous with the clang of the silverware they heard someone else rustling about in the kitchen or hallway. A trained policeman like Mr. Smith would know these are details of the sort to appeal to other cops. Details like these do not sound made up; they layer a witness's testimony with plausibility. Yet how plausible, in fact, was this testimony? If Derrick's mission was to murder the Smiths in their bed, why would he have gone through the exercise of pretending he was a sneak thief? How much more sensible to commit the crimes in order of relevance, the murders first, the fake theft second. It was possible therefore to believe these clever details were manufactured. But why? The someone else the Smiths allegedly heard rustling about could only have been Amy. Only she coveted the set of silverware (it had been in the provenance of the Pickering family and had been passed on by Amy's grandparents to her mother), and only she could have directed Derrick to the serving cart. Thus the Smiths had to know they were damning their daughter as his accomplice.

However, even if Mr. Polen decided the Smiths had submitted bogus testimony out of absolute spite toward their daughter, he still had to consider the crumpled notes, written in longhand on ink-stained notebook paper left over from Amy's schooling and recovered from the shoe box. As with the other evidence, these notes raised more than one possibility. Either Derrick slipped these pages into his box for later disposal, or one of the Smiths had set him up. Most of the writing, according to what Amy told the police, was in her firm clear hand. On one page she had drawn a floor-plan sketch of the Smith house. The rectangle for the master bedroom she labeled "mom & dad," the square for the den "dad," for the bathroom "lav," and for her bedroom "me." Toward the bottom of the page is an addendum: her name and phone number, as if she was conspiring with someone she did not know well. (The existence of a diagram suggests another explanation for the front-door key. Perhaps Amy palmed it to Derrick in the event he preceded her to the house, in which case he could have inserted the key, scooted inside, padded barefoot down to her bedroom, and lay in wait until she came home—although this would have amounted to an extra, unnecessary risk for him.) In another section of the notes Amy dashed down directions for how to exit her neighborhood by motor vehicle, using side streets to Indian Head Highway and from there to I-95. Since neither Derrick nor Amy owned a car, their plan must have called for Derrick to steal transportation from the Smiths. In the remainder of the notes there is a back-and-forth exchange in two different handwritings. Claiming to recognize the distinctive curl in the *y*'s on the paper, Mr. Smith identified one of the correspondents as Amy, and the police all along presumed the other had to be Derrick (although no expert was ever called to match these notes with samples of his writing). If, for the sake of argument, the police theory is correct, the scene that would come to mind is of Amy and Derrick sitting somewhere in her room, maybe cross-legged on her bed, passing pen and notebook betwixt them while Mrs. Smith upstairs goes about her bedtime routine. Derrick apparently is trying to get a better idea of the layout of the house before he ventures from the bedroom, for he writes, "Is there carpet all through the house, yes, or no?" Amy circles the "yes" and adds a clarification, "Except the kitchen." It may be that Derrick then points with an inquiring finger to the sand knocked off the windowsill, for Amy writes, "About the window, they'll think I did it. I doubt if they'll say anything, but if so, I'll say we were sneaking in earlier this week, 'cause all my friends will back me up that I am always sneaking out."

But what about the following few lines of exchange? If authentic, they are a strange, shocking revelation from the mental and emotional state of the two suburban youngsters. Actually the next lines of writing appear to be more; they appear to be the incriminatory heart of the case. At the conclusion of Amy's trial Judge Johnson referred to them as "devastating."

Amy writes, "Are you still going to be able to scratch my back? Do you know what I mean?"

Derrick writes, "What do you really mean?"

"Shoot my shoulder."

"I'll shoot at you, and hopefully I will get you in the shoulder."

"What do you mean 'hopefully'? I need a definite."

"I will stand back about 25 feet and aim for your shoulder."

"You better make it or shoot again. And please not too close to the middle."

"I'll get you in the arm."

Was this then how it had happened? Were Amy and Derrick shut up in their private little hot hole, the warm moldery night pouring in, the bomp-bomp of *Another Bad Creation* sounding through their earphones, their nerves beginning to jingle-jangle, appetites ginned up? Did they visualize themselves characters in a pulp-magazine plot? Did Derrick work at getting psycho-sore at Amy's parents, or, same difference, did Amy work on him? Is it then, after all, possible to believe Mr. and Mrs. Smith's description of a tall, masked criminal positively full of hate juice who whacked open the door of their master bedroom and, who, to quote Mr. Smith, had "his voice raised up, like he was angry already."

Judge Johnson, in announcing his verdict, had said, "For two teenagers to go to this length boggles the mind," but he had concluded they "entered into an agreement, and that agreement was to murder her two parents . . . [and that] Amy Lynne Smith counseled and encouraged Mr. Derrick Jones to do this." If Larry Polen were to disabuse himself of this theory, he would have to imagine a diabolical and quivering Mr. Smith, sweaty fingers on his gun, taking the time to give himself a legal pretext for murder. He would have to imagine Mr. Smith pointing the gun at his daughter and her boyfriend and force-feeding them lines to write in a notebook and only then, Jehovah-like, striking down the infidel.

It does strain the imagination to believe either of these scenarios, and yet what might a third possibility be?

As for the lines of written dialogue, they are sophomoric and remarkably naive, but "scratch my back" is an interesting figure of speech. It is an old copper's phrase. From whose tongue other than an old copper's might such a phrase roll? Perhaps the daughter of an old copper? Or perhaps not.

Who could blame Larry Polen if, like everyone else, he felt more than a little flummoxed by the evidence?

Merv and Dell, still unsure about how to proceed with their future, continued with their trips to Penfield. On each departure from Hillcrest

Heights they now took extra precautions against criminal activity. They made sure the front door was dead-bolted. They put the house lights on a timer. A vacuum cleaner was set prominently in the middle of the living room floor, as if they were out on an errand and due back any second.

"I hate doing it, but . . ." Dell's voice trailed off.

It was a free weekend, and Bruce was able to overcome Pat's faint heart and get her into a raft on a whitewater stretch of the Shenandoah River. Out on the raging foam—too bad they had to wear life jackets— Bruce was in love with the danger. But the greenhorn Pat overextended herself and was swept halfway overboard and had to be hauled back, hair in glistening wet spirals—a "near-death experience," according to her. For the rest of the trip she then cleaved to Bruce with such a grip he thought she would drown them for sure if they went over, but, near to the finish line, when they knew they had survived, they broke into song. *Row, row, row your boat.*

The survival of the self is part of the American culture in ways that sacrifice for the common good is not. Yet a plea for a higher morality can be a powerful element, even among the cynical.

This was Bea Tignor's reaction, at least in part, to her latest standings in the polls. With a week to go before the primaries, Sue Mills had lost her lead, and, to almost everyone's surprise, the prospective voters were now choosing Mrs. Tignor's old civil rights vision. She was now the front-runner, as reported in a *Prince George's Journal* front-page story, two columns, above the fold. Mrs. Mills was now in second place and Wayne Curry in third.

However, Mrs. Tignor was not prevailing by a substantial margin. The difference in the poll percentages between the three candidates was small enough to give each a sound reason for hope.

Bruce felt like a man whose principles were being tested to the breaking point. All his life he had been in search of an abstraction called by many names but most aptly called "the melting pot." To have come home to Prince George's County and found it on his doorstep had been a stirring discovery. It had entertained Bruce and lifted his spirits to walk down the sidewalk pavilion of the strip mall and see all around the lollygagging teenagers, the old pewter-haired men in their shoeshined black tasseled loafers, the BMW set smelling of money. If racial integration was feasible on a small scale in his old neighborhood, why couldn't America go whole-sale with it? But he had been the fool. The scene at the strip mall had been revealed as a self-delusion industriously arrived at. Even while he watched, the social broth had begun to separate into unmelted parts. He found it impossible to believe anymore in his corny sentiments. What he noticed now on his walks were the burglar bars and peepholes and meshed windows dark as widow's veils. A shadow of fear and revenge had fallen on him. He was skittish, always braced for another run-in, and this skittishness had invaded his attitudes. Around any corner might lay madness. The kids at 23rd and Iverson might look easygoing, but brute force was in their hearts. He had been taken advantage of; his assessment of the next generation had proved inadequate. Now everyone was sus-pect. To become aware of a face behind the smoked glass of a cruising high-slung car or to see in the illumination of a streetlamp the shaved-dome silhouettes of men on the sidewalk was to make him abruptly sick to his stomach, and then later sick at heart. He had never thought condi-tions in Hillcrest Heights could ever again be so decisive in his life. But these hard-eyed kids with their little taunts were no different from the ones who scared him into not inviting Camilla to the senior prom. The fact is, Bruce was filled with red murder. He relished a fantasy of stomping somebody into the ground. His dark, stormy desire pressed his guts. He had come to understand the mechanism of racism.

On a Friday night, at a poker game with old friends, Bruce announced he was leaving the neighborhood.

"It's the end of the story for me in Hillcrest Heights. My animal instinct for survival is telling me to get out. I can't live like this," Bruce said to Ray Norris. Bruce and Ray were modern men with little room in their lives any-more for baring their souls, but they could still say things to each other that went straight to the point. "Are you telling me you've finally had it with your dad?" Ray asked nimbly.

"No, it has nothing to do with my dad. We're getting along the best we ever have. Which maybe is why I feel free to leave." The poker game was over for the night, and the two of them were about to cash in red, white, and blue plastic chips. "It's this other shit with these predators who hang out right across the street."

"Have they been messing with you again?"

"No, but I'm tired of being afraid. I just want to relax. I just want to hang. The reality is I'm watching each and every individual. I'm watching to see if there is hate in their eyes. It's an existence in a Roman coliseum. Who wants the life of a gladiator? That's not a life." Bruce's face was beginning to burn with anger.

"Maybe they have you confused with an old Grit."

"Believe me, these kids don't have any personal score to settle. They've never had white street kids hassle them. Their only excuse is I'm a white guy who dares to walk on their turf. That's the only reason they have. It's groundless, and it's racist."

"I wouldn't say you're a target just because you're white. I'd say it's because they're hot young badasses, and you're a middle-aged sitting duck."

Bruce laughed despite himself, but he would not be deterred. "I've tried to deny it. I've tried to say race is not the issue. But the reason I'm overly conscious of race is they started it. Everything they do is connected to race."

Bruce's outburst was one of those terrible, sad, throw-up-your-hands kind of outbursts that attend the aging of idealists, and he knew it. "Okay, you're right, there are moral ambiguities here," he said. "But I'm not talking about moral ambiguities. I'm talking about practical considerations. Like gaining some peace of mind."

In Westchester Park, a place of chromed Buicks and Pontiacs with window stickers from wintering spots like Hobe Sound and Port St. Lucie, Sue Mills was given another indication of the collapsing condition of her campaign. Thirty-five white people, formerly stalwarts in the Castaldi campaign, had gathered to meet with Mrs. Mills and Mr. Castaldi. They sat on a chintz-covered sofa and on French chairs or stood next to bric-a-brac, and, after listening to Mr. Castaldi's endorsement of Mrs. Mills, they took a straw vote. They were, to a large extent, unmoved by his endorsement. Only nine of the thirty-five held up hands for Mrs. Mills. Seven voted for Bea Tignor, six for Wayne Curry. The others in the room, although professing themselves "undecided," talked about the "high discomfort level" they felt with regard to Mrs. Mills.

"After all we've been through, and all the progress that's been made here in race relations, we can't turn back the clock," said one man.

Things had moved fast in the few weeks since Bruce and Pat hooked up. Pat was a frequent nighttime guest, and so easygoing was her conduct at the

Gordon house she and Bruce had decided to take the chance of including both his father and her father in a dinner for four. It was a cool, pleasant evening. Pat looked reassuringly American in her white blouse and a dark skirt that showed off her hips. Bruce loaded everybody onto the velvety high-riding seats of the Cadillac. The two fathers, the white man Dr. David Gordon and the black man Major Bill Ford, Ret., sat in the rear over the chassis—two men who had suffered divorces after a long period of marriage and had stumbled from the full power of a career into a restless retirement. Not only that, but like Dr. Gordon, Major Ford also had been struck down by a stroke and was trying to regain a measure of normal health. His face on one side had a sag to it. But these were topics of discussion for later. What broke the ice was Major Ford's croaked-out admission that he, too, was a worshiper of America's supreme luxury car. In the fifteen minutes it took for the troupe of four to reach a little family diner in Waldorf, the two old men managed quite a start on the subject of traveling in style.

At the diner they took a prominent table in the middle of the room, Major Ford stepping smartly on his cane. "You got to shake it," he said to his companion, and Dr. Gordon rose on his toes, clunking forward with his four-legged walker. While Pat went to freshen up in the ladies' room, Bruce told a joke about a nun who leaves a convent for a year of fornications but returns to her sisters in saintly cloth because—sex preserve us!— she has discovered she has a lesbian nature. The major busted up with laughter and threw a rascally punch at the arm of the doctor, who punched him back. *Freilich!* The two old gents were almost too rowdy. Other diners on nearby seats tried to censure them with severe sniff-nosed looks.

"Can't you punch harder than that?" Major Ford joked.

"Hell, I'm lucky I'm not a vegetable," Doc rasped back.

"My stroke got me a couple days afore last Christmas. Whole left side went dead, but it's coming back." The retired military man had been rushed in the middle of the night to the Andrews Air Force Base medical facility.

"See, you got immediate treatment, but I went a whole day before they got me to the emergency room."

"Spilled milk now. Listen, goddamnit, you got to work your arm, work your leg!"

"Been trying to. It's a bastard business. I need a new therapy."

"Screw therapy! You need inspiration!"

They clicked on like this the whole evening, working up a few last laughs.

After the meal Doc made a move to the men's room, leaving his walker at the table, and Bruce quickly jumped up to guide him.

"No, leave him alone. He can do it. He can do it!" It was an order from an army bull.

Bruce watched his father push one foot ahead of the other, huffing, pain up and down his back, but unaided—a hobbled but amazingly strong figure. The rest of the evening Doc acted all sporty and jacked up, like he had just steered his holy-rolling Caddy down the front of a parade. Or, as Bruce said later, "like he had just answered the riddle of life."

The polls were open. At one minute past seven on a September morning, Sue Mills placed a leaflet into the hands of the first voter entering Eleanor Roosevelt High School. Her entreating voice was sharp. "Remember me when you go inside," she said, by rote. With a snap of her lighter she fired up a cigarette, probably not the image her publicists wanted her to present to the public. The cigarette was puffed on between wet flaring-pink lipstick. She tapped the ash compulsively, a nervous flicking. The preoccupied, down-looking, almost disconsolate candidate went on passing out more of her literature, but only her hands seemed to be working.

About seven-thirty she saw Frank Pesci coming across the parking lot.

"How goes it?" he called out affably.

"Oh, Frank, I feel like a fool." She put an arm around his shoulders and whispered, "Frank, I'm going to lose. The last few weeks, it hasn't been there. The crowds, my people, it's like they realize we can't make it here anymore. It's a spooky feeling."

By eight in the evening democracy had finished having its day. At eight-twenty the early returns showed Sue Mills in third place, behind Bea Tignor, who was in second. Wayne Curry, who in the last hours of the campaign had secured the endorsement of the *Washington Post* and the *Prince George's Journal,* appeared to be the winner.

Local TV newscasts reported the early returns. Advisers and friends of Mrs. Mills watched with long faces, shell-shocked into silence. A black female newscaster on all-news Channel Eight, by way of commentary, referred to Mrs. Mills as someone "best known in Prince George's for her blond beehive."

"Can't they leave my hair out of it?!" said Mrs. Mills, acid on her tongue. "If they want to call me a white person, go ahead and say it. Get it off their chest. Call me whitey!"

• • •

Joy, riotous, strenuous, deafening joy, came hurling out in a lot of places. A lemon-smelling woman in a dress of bright plumage greens danced a tango on the dance floor inside the restaurant known as CJ's, where many of Gloria's precinct workers had gathered. The woman waved a yellow campaign T-shirt in the air. "Oh, yes, baby! We did it, baby! We sent Sue Mills back to Georgia!" she shouted. "Those black people who were planning to vote for her, we changed their minds. We did what we set out to do. Sue didn't get no hundred votes in our precinct." Other women, still in their yellow T-shirted costumes, left behind half-finished platefuls of food and danced and hopped with the woman in green. Grease-smeared fingers wiggled in the air. Things that were said about Mrs. Mills—"all that makeup she piles on, she looks like the undertaker already done the job on her"—elicited belly laughs from a rooting section at the tables.

The restaurant had laid in spicy chicken wings, meatballs, potato salad, rolls, green beans. "I'm starved," said Elvira, who was the only one there not celebrating. She heaped up a plate and plopped herself down, herky-jerky.

"Yeah, take a load off, girl," said someone, being friendly.

"Thanks." Elvira's weary bony little frame was pared down, bonier than ever, such a study in comparative politics when you thought of the incumbent judges fed by invitation dinners. Elvira's state of fatigue from rushing about in her off-hours was such that all expression had been wiped from her face. She had bloodshot, robot eyes, and in her rumpled "White for Judge" T-shirt and dingy black slacks she was nothing like the snappy attorney of courthouse fame. Her hair lay in matted clumps on her scalp. She ate the chicken wings with her fingers. She had no star mannerisms anymore; she was just people.

"What happened out there today?" she was asked.

"What didn't happen today?! Someone lost several boxes of my flyers. Or else they got stolen," she said with that familiar note of violation. "I've been running, running, trying to keep it all together."

The band struck up "Boogie Woogie Blues." "That brings back old times on the Eastern Shore," she said. Elvira leaned back and closed her eyes, but her tired face did not rest easily. The band leader began directing Gloria's yellow-shirted supporters through the Stroll. Elvira chose not to join in. She went out into the night heat of the mall. Wan, fuzzy, broken bits of incandescent light yellowed her face. Four doors down was Gloria's campaign office, with more big doings inside. The atmosphere was so slap-happy it was indistinguishable from the scene at the restaurant. Someone had taped together three of Gloria's campaign posters, and, flipped on their backsides and laid flat to the floor, they served as a huge scoresheet. As the precinct tallies came in by phone from a campaign flunky stationed in Upper Marlboro, two middle-aged women scrunched down on their toes and wrote the numbers with blue felt-tip pens. "Lord, Lord, look at these numbers!" one woman shouted at Elvira. "Didn't I tell you, we'd work our precincts for you, girl? Oh, yes, oh, yes!" Needing only to finish in sixth place, Elvira was in first place in two precincts, ahead of all the incumbents. In two others she was in second place. Boasting aside, however, it would be the shock of the season for Elvira to win. Once the tallies came in from subdivisions away from Gloria's stronghold, Elvira's cumulative total was bound to go down.

"I've got a slim shot," Elvira said, subdued, realistic.

Next to Gloria's name the posterboard was filling up with big scores, first places in every precinct. This produced no hip-hip-hooray, though. Winning was expected.

"Is Gloria here yet?" Elvira asked.

"In back."

Past the shrill cries of the women on their knees and past a couple dozen campaign folks hovering birdlike in the aisles and a row of cubicles and past ringing phones and desks littered with Styrofoam cups of coffee and chicken bones on disposable plates there was a back office where Gloria had stationed herself. Elvira peered in as if peering into a throne room. Gloria waved a beckoning hand. "Here comes the judge," she said with a strong smile. Every inch of Gloria was a commanding presence. She had the charged look of someone who has taken well to power.

Elvira, nervous and pent-up, soon ricocheted out of the office. "I got to get my son. He wants to be here for the excitement." An hour later she returned with Andre, her firstborn. He had flown in from Texas the previous evening. By now there was considerably more blue on the scoresheet, and doing the arithmetic in her head Elvira foresaw that the precincts in Upper Marlboro and elsewhere would deny her. The incumbents would be elected—Vincent Femia, C. Philip Nichols, Robert Mason, William Spellbring, Robert Woods, and Sylvania Woods. A white newsman came up to study the scoresheet with Elvira. He did not ask for a quote but said for general edification, "I think the problem was that you ran for judge instead of a more traditional office. A black judge who speaks her mind is a tough sell to the white psyche." Was the newsman a blockhead? Elvira let the comment pass. Perhaps he was just talking out of awkwardness.

Four of the incumbent judges had once been assistant prosecutors to Arthur Marshall. However, Mr. Marshall would not be returning to the prosecutor's office. He was a loser like Elvira. He had lost out to Jack

Johnson, one of the candidates on Gloria's slate. That Gloria had endorsed Jack Johnson instead of Dwight Jackson, her daughter's brother-in-law, had produced a few difficult times within Gloria's family, but such is the nature of politics. Anyway, Gloria had a knack for picking winners. Her campaign workers were growing excited and rowdy at the completeness of their triumph. It did not dampen their mood that Elvira White and Bea Tignor were the exceptions. Doubtless the two of them would have other opportunities.

The rest of the evening Elvira felt herself in a stupor. She showed no anger, just a head-sagging lassitude. Twenty-five-year-old Andre was saying "It's not fair" and "I'd like to know what it costs to buy an election." She put a calming hand on his shoulder. "Think of the positives," she said. "Think of how many nightmares I gave them." She stood by Andre's side, arm clutched around his waist.

"He's her man?" one of the campaign workers asked out loud.

"No, honey, he's her boy."

Elvira's public persona was so thoroughly concealing of the complexity of her private feelings that even Gloria was left to wonder sometimes about the part of Elvira that had raised two warm and affectionate children, her only darlings. At this very moment, however, the mother in her was obvious.

So was the grandmother! Andre's wife was due to give birth to a first grandchild within a few weeks!

Americans, and perhaps especially Jewish-Americans, put a lot of stock in family legacies, but what had been passed on to Bruce? After all this time he and his father had never had a man-to-man talk, and probably they never would. The most Bruce had hoped for was a lifting of the heavy-heartedness between them, and progress even on that score was probably lost, he figured, the moment he began bringing home a black woman. Which just went to show what a miracle of the gods Pat Ford was. Right from the start Pat had handled Doc Gordon in that mock-bossy, sweet-talkative manner forebearing women have for curmudgeons who might be redeemable. On her first Friday night in Hillcrest Heights, she went into the bedroom to clean up his supper tray and saw him inert and superfluous on his TV chair in front of the big box. Who did she think she was, barging in on his musty sanctum and, without a by-your-leave, inquiring about his lazy habits? When Pat did not leave Doc cut off the TV and said "I'm going for a walk," to which she said, "Good, let's go." *Feel sorry for him because he was a cripple?! Not on your life.* "Hurry up! We don't have all night!" she sang in his face. He followed her into the cooled-down air. *Pity is not good for the soul!* This was Pat's philosophy. Where did it come from? ("That's the first lesson they teach you in the self-help guidebook for black single women of the Jewish faith.") After a few weeks Doc stopped trying to hide her from the Old Settlers. Instead he became uncharacteristic in his praise of her. "By all rights she could be one of those negative people, down on society, but she isn't," he said, bragging. And he would be sure to slide in gleefully, "Did you know she's con-verted?"—the utmost family sanction. Pat's Jewishness meant more to Bruce's father than to Bruce, who was far from an orthodox man. He had once summed up his beliefs in terms of karma and the Golden Rule: "If you purge yourself of your worst instincts and try to do good, you'll enter a spiritual plane when you die. Otherwise you have to do another lap. A lot of people are coming back for another lap." He had no doubts his fa-ther would be sent back. "Maybe as a waiter, to humble him." Talking like this one evening he drew a fast objection from Pat. "Stop it, please. Your father is so proud of you. When he talks to me, it's always how you were top of your class, how you were this fantastic tennis player."

"I had one good year."

"He's trying to make up with you. Can't you meet him halfway?"

"You want me to tell him he's a paragon of good deeds?!"

"None of us is related to God on high. Okay, he did all these wrongs against you, but he's still your father."

Well, what good was there to be said of that tough, profane old Cadil-lac-driving cookie? That he had godfathered street punks and raised cheers from Bob Magruder and the other hard-fisted boys in the Quonset hut? Of course, there was more to his life's work than that, as Bruce had gradually come to see. David S. Gordon, M.D., also had stuck his neck out with his open medical shop, everybody welcome. In those antiseptic-smelling downstairs rooms he had been Albert Schweitzer, charmer of the whole community. The Gordon clinic was a comfortable, benevolent, in-tegrated place. A black woman running from the Grits had looked to Bruce's father for rescue! What did the Grits think of that? Why, they thought he'd bounce them on their ass! And what effect did this have on Bruce as a child, before he became such a know-it-all and his father such a cold fish? Bruce had played the experience over and over in his mind's eye, the woman hysterical from the gun pellets, his father's hand reaching comfortingly for her as they went to the examining table. Real bravery was like that—dull doings, but with a flurry now and then. Much of what Bruce had done from that day on, first trying to alter the world and then later incriminating himself with his high-value conscience, much of the gleam of a boy idealist surviving in his present strivings and in the acts of karmic Jewish conscience performed on his past, might be said to be set against a standard his father had already met.

Family legacies are passed on chancily, but perhaps they cannot help but be passed on—this was Bruce's new insight.

The morning after Wayne Curry's victory in the Democratic primary the lead editorial in the *Prince George's Journal* contained an apology written in response to an African-American reader who was upset over a headline from the waning days of the campaign. The headline writer, as headline writers do, had used an old cliché, "Signs Point to a White-Knuckle Finish," which the reader took to be "offensive, racist and insulting." A *Journal* editorial writer, trying to make amends, wrote, "Words may not break our bones but they most certainly can break our hearts and our spirits. . . . Those words hit a nerve for that reader. We understand that. Certain words have that effect on all of us. They can trigger feelings and emotions in us that we may have thought were long dormant. Other times, the rage is right beneath the surface, smoldering. And the offending words simply fan the flames."

Such was the defensiveness of the good white people. The black voters had put a black man in charge! No offense taken, no offense to be given!

That this was a "black" victory was not much questioned. By far, Mr. Curry had done his best in "black" precincts; Mrs. Mills had done her best in "white" precincts; and Bea Tignor, with her crossover appeal, had done well everywhere, but not well enough. Behind closed curtains the voters had been true to form. An American history of extremes, the majority once again casting their lot abruptly, instinctively, in with their own kind, had repeated itself. This was the analysis at the ready, the analysis spread about and accepted—even though it may have been off the mark.

Weeks after the election, polling experts affiliated with the University of Maryland would look at the data and see another distinction. They would ascribe the Curry victory to his age, not his race. Bea Tignor and Sue Mills were from an older generation, the generation of the Stricklers and Doc Gordon, and apparently Mrs. Tignor and Mrs. Mills had split the "old" vote between them. Slightly more than half of the old settlers, under Gloria's busy influence, had voted for Mrs. Tignor, in fact. Meanwhile, Mr. Curry had tapped deeply into his generation, the generation of Elvira White and Bruce Gordon. Of course, in Prince George's County, a generational analysis was not much of a distinction from a racial analysis because the older set was made up mainly of white people and the younger set mainly of black people.

Merv Strickler, in what is called his minister's voice, said, "Now we have the final positive result from the civil rights movement: a black person in charge of Prince George's County. Martin Luther King is shouting in the heavens above! But, but . . ." Here he was taken by a thoughtful look. "But is this the beginning of a political resegregation? We have to guard against going too far in the opposite direction. We don't want to become another Washington, with the black politicians totally in control and the white people skedaddled."

Experts infer what they will from events like this. Frank Pesci might have been hearing what he expected to hear at a dinner party, held soon after the election, in the high-tone Martins Woods subdivision. The dinner host, a retired military man, asked, "Frank, how long you going to be living in New Carrollton?"

Frank answered facetiously, "How long you going to be living in Martins Woods?"

The ex-military man said back, not in jest, "One year! At the most! We're not safe here anymore. We had a break-in last week in the middle of the day. You can't afford to go off to work and leave your wife alone anymore."

No one had counted white faces and black faces at the precinct doors, as Gloria once had, but it was Frank's hunch that white people who had fled the county prematurely may have enabled the Curry victory. In Frank's touring of the polls the white turnout had seemed low. The day after the election Jimmy V. Aluisi, the popular curly-haired, forty-eight-year-old white sheriff, phoned. Frank had known the sheriff since he was in short pants. "Godfather, Padrino," Sheriff Aluisi lamented, "I won by a lousy three thousand votes. Where were all the white people?"

Frank had a short laugh. "They were at the realtors, selling their houses."

To conduct a search at agencies that place round-the-clock caregivers in homes of the infirm is to find African-Americans who act on their own stereotypes. For instance ("between you and me, okay?"), there is a rating scale that has at the top ("we call them A-ones"), those immigrants from Africa and the Caribbean who rarely kvetch to their employers, and has at the bottom ("Z's, zeroes"), their American-born brothers and sisters who are less apt to turn in satisfactory performances. At least, this was the inside information Bruce was told as he went about trying to replace his father's current caregivers, the American-born team of Lee Dell and his girlfriend Sondra. Bruce was not about to dispute the stereotyping since he had nothing but praise for Patsy, the Guyanese woman with her foreign charm who, before moving on as his father's live-in aide, had taken courses and bettered herself. But with Lee Dell and Sondra, Bruce had experienced only consternation. Last night the scene that greeted Bruce was a quivering and sniffling Sondra, who said she had been beaten by Lee Dell for "catting around." Today, taking time off from work, Bruce had begun shopping for a fully guaranteed caregiver, an "A-one." He had imposed a deadline on himself, two weeks hence, by which date he hoped to be living outside of Hillcrest Heights.

In the evening when Bruce went into the master bedroom the moment became right to tell his father the complete extent of his decision. "I have to move, Pop," he explained. "I have to get out of here."

"You plan to get Pat to live with you?" Dr. Gordon murmured.

"Yeah, probably. I haven't asked her yet, but yeah."

"Go ahead and ask her, boy. You're not getting any younger." Bruce's father laughed hoarsely, what Bruce took to be confidential father-to-son kind of laughter.

As for the caregivers, Dr. Gordon didn't think there was any urgent need to find replacements. "I like Lee Dell and Sondra," he said. "They got a little temper on them, but I'm used to them. They're familiar now."

"You sure you want to referee the two of them?"

"Sure, sure. I checked out Lee Dell. He graduated from Potomac High. He was a decent student, above average."

Bruce left the room wondering why he had gotten so easily off the hook.

It had come to Elvira slowly what the consequences might be of her tenure at the courthouse, what price she might have to pay.

The latest difficulty had developed in the Court of Special Appeals in the case of another of her former clients, Donnell Wayne Watson, a twenty-two-year-old black man found guilty of murder and serving a twenty-five-year sentence. Due to another intervention by the public defender's office a new trial for Donnell Watson was now in the offing. A legal error had been found—improper instructions to the jury by the trial judge (coincidentally, Judge Missouri)—for which Elvira was being taken to task. The overseers on the Court of Special Appeals went out of their way to identify and rebuke Elvira for failing to object to the jury instructions. She had displayed a "degree of professional or lawyerly dereliction," they opined sharply in their ruling. Tim Maier, the courthouse reporter for the *Prince George's Journal* and no fan of Elvira's, was beginning to feel sorry for her. "For the Appellate Court to criticize her by name like that, it begins to look like there really is a conspiracy. They're going way overboard to nail her hide to the wall," he said. Dwight Jackson, who was leaving the courthouse for a prestige job with the U.S. Justice Department's Violent Crimes Section, said, "It's no consolation to Elvira, but all the trouble they're going to means she ran too good a race for judge. There's a fear she'll keep coming back, like Lazarus. They can't allow that. She has to be totally discredited."

Elvira, meanwhile, was exhibiting supreme confidence, as usual. She could afford to lose, she said; she could wait until 1996 or 1998 or even the millennium. Sooner or later she would be able to win her case before the tribunal of public opinion—this was her brag. Those who were still in her corner urged her on. Why acknowledge any limitations on what might be available to her? Why restrict herself to a judgeship? Why not aim higher? Why not run for county executive? ("Oh, that would drive them crazy. I'd get a cross burned on my lawn for sure.")

Because they did not believe Elvira would ever go quietly away, her "enemies" ("If they are trying to smote me they must be my enemies") had openly warned her to secure legal representation for herself. Elvira would have no time for a long, slow retrenchment. Every mistake or procedural lapse she had ever committed would be forwarded to the Appeals Court or the Grievance Commission or another authority. But finding an attorney willing to be associated with her was no easy matter. Several attorneys she contacted gave her the brush-off. A few told her flat-out that, in their judgment, she was finished in Prince George's County. Only by perseverance did she after a few weeks obtain the services of Terrence Johnson's lawyer, Charles Ware, who agreed to handle administrative complaints against her. But Mr. Ware told Elvira that he, too, could see she was marked for ruin, much as certain characters in a movie are.

• • •

Under the circumstances Dr. Gordon had reconstituted his interest in Delmar as his driver. But it was the same old story. The cars were badly used. Chores were left undone. Things were not where Dr. Gordon swore he left them. Then, late on the eve of Bruce's leave-taking, who but a disheveled Delmar should come snooping through the yard and go peeping up to a window, and who but Bruce should happen to be on the inside pensively studying the night. A face materializing like that, Bruce's heart skipped a beat or two. But it did not take him long to grab one of his martial arts weapons—a stick of maplewood, six feet long and bowed out in the middle—and give chase out the door. Bruce, hollering, had the long stick raised up, and a step behind came the hired supernumerary, Lee Dell, with a machete. The two of them must have seemed to Delmar like banshees from hell as he fled across the fresh-cut, cricket-hopping lawn.

Watching from the front door, Dr. Gordon yelled at Delmar, "Run, you fool. Run your ass off."

The next morning Bruce received a concession from his father, face-averted: "I should've never invited the bum back here."

"Pop, you were desperate for a ride. I understand."

But what did any of this really have to do with Delmar? What was the true relationship of a mistrusted man-about-town to any of these overexercised carry-ons? Why was he caught in the middle between a father and a son? It was a good discussion for a therapy group where this category of rivalry might be understood, but there was no time for it now because with the clouds burned off the hot gaseous sun was in charge, and Bruce's moving day was under way.

"I'll show you the attic," he said to Pat. He pulled down a staircase from the ceiling. Up above was a helter-skelter of old liquor boxes, shopping bags with record albums, water-spotted books, shoes of distant manufacture. "Junk, junk," he said. But, despite himself, he became absorbed, Hamlet-like. He held up a brass-studded briefcase. "A keeper." Never-opened mail? "Leave it." A pair of Italian shoes in their original box, leftovers from his charm-boy's wardrobe? "Nah." Ski boots? "Okay, bring them." The books were too numerous to examine, but one of them could not be resisted, *How to Raise a Jewish Child*. It was a gift his parents had received at Bruce's birth. "Oh, you better believe it. We'll need this!" Bruce gleefully angled his head, and Pat tilted back, hard-to-get flirtatious. Flinging the book into a box, Bruce descended, with Pat's arms around his neck, mock piggyback.

Down in his bedroom, as anonymous as a hotel room despite two years of habitation, he folded the silk sheets and collected his little plastic trophy from the cruise ship. Pat toted his clothes to the front door. The machete used in the chase stood against the living room wall; it was from Mexico, bought on a trip with his wife. "Leave it," Bruce said, "in case Delmar comes back."

Pat looked over the meager pile of suitcases and boxes. "Some banker you are. You ought to be a poet, living so cheap." She led him outside onto the deck, buying time before their good-bye, and they did a few boogying turns on the wood. In the process they knocked over a pot of artificial mums. Placing one of the plastic flowers between her teeth, bumping, grinding, Pat put on an exhibition, and Bruce responded with thrown kisses. Nerves, no doubt, the way they were carrying on, but any observer could see they were cuckoo about each other.

Bruce had a friend helping with the move, and the friend chimed in, "Don't let your dad catch you out here like this."

"Pop's caught us plenty of times. He doesn't care anymore," Bruce said.

"What about the neighbors?"

"He doesn't care if they're scandalized or not. He's beyond scandal."

Talking on top of each other, laughing, Bruce and Pat told a tale of being burst in upon en flagrante by the caregiver Sondra, who thereafter would move about the house with a stomp to announce herself. Still laughing, Bruce and Pat made up dumb-funny lines for a song, "Big Foot," which they sang to the tune of "Big John." Humor seemed to be on a par with sex in this relationship.

It was almost noon. Bruce sliced up a beefsteak tomato, and Pat spread mayo on bread and handed a sandwich to Dr. Gordon. "Thanks," he said. Everyone ate in the living room. There on the coffee table was the Potomac High letter Bruce had earned with the tennis team. Bruce had pulled it from a drawer the evening before. "I'll leave it for you, if you want," he said, and Dr. Gordon held up the letter in his one good hand. In this last happy month the gestures of sentiment were easier to come by between father and son. Certain words of reconciliation had been spoken, certain feelings laid bare. Dr. Gordon had said, "The way I used to feel when you were in school, it was like you were embarrassed to be my son," and Bruce had stuttered out something about being cocky and a rebel and so forth. The real words got stuck. It was difficult for them to talk with emotion, but at least they were not passing the bitter cup anymore. Now that Bruce was about to take his leave of the place where he and his father had known so much spitefulness and venomous mutterings and mutually unrecognized misery it was to Bruce's relief that they had achieved this odd, clumsy, human peace.

The driver of the moving van was out front, honking, and Dr. Gordon motioned for his old doctor's desk and chair to be placed on board. When Bruce was a boy, his father had said of the desk, "Some day this'll be yours," but after Bruce dropped his pre-med studies, Doc had kept bitter possession of it, stored in the basement, a souvenir of Bruce's failure.

"Take it. You should have it," Dr. Gordon said now with spirit. His hands were folded on his stomach.

"That is so nice of you," said Pat, who took for granted the love between a father and a son.

"You got a keeper with her." Dr. Gordon winked at his son, gloating. He got his hand working again and touched Pat on the arm. He had the glide of restored health in his movements. The doctors said he was at a peak, even if he would never walk again. He was keeping his weight under control. He was down to two hundred pounds, his best shape in thirty years.

"Next Friday night, Bruce, you two come for dinner, okay?" Dr. Gordon ordered, smiling, with no apparent thought to past fiercesome scenes.

Would Bruce be able to find the right single-chance words to say? "I love you, Pop," he managed at last. A great blast of fire came into his face. He went out with a slap at the screen door, his forehead and cheeks spattered with that red badge of courage.

One item of business was left. Bruce and Pat got into his new red all-power Taurus station wagon. (When the Toyota with his mother's personalized license plate that was an irritation to his father had been traded in for the Taurus, his father had lit into him on bad instinct—"So you're the big spender now?"—before realizing his mistake and softening his tone, "Looks nice, looks like a family car.") The Taurus went up and down the adjacent streets. The Quonset gym, their old schools, Pat's old house, the community center—all the landmarks passing by engrossed Bruce and Pat in an uncertain but determined nostalgia. "What I'll miss are the warm people around here who give out loving vibes, the people at the ribs place, the places where I shop, those people. Even the new neighbors, they turned out to be okay. At least we're waving hello," Bruce said. "But those creeps at the mall—did I tell you they hassled me again outside People's? It was last week, just a couple of them. I put on my neutral face, truly expressionless, a person in search of his Ice Bull. I didn't blink. I didn't look back. But, you know, they've won. I'm out of here." In his youth Bruce had thought of himself as a kid born wrong, a kid wishing to switch his skin. Now, as a grown man, he was again on the margins of acceptability, but, it struck him like a bolt, he had become more like an immigrant from an earlier generation, more like his father, the town Jew.

Yet who had he been all along if not the town Jew? And what of his father, who had fit into Hillcrest Heights better than he, who had mastered his situation and survived the trap that the psychoanalyst Erwin K. Koranyi writes about? The trap of waking each morning with the same unending trauma: Make the wrong move and someone will kill you. It is the experience of prisoners of war and the experience of civilians among street criminals. A far easier trauma, to read Dr. Koranyi, is to be kidnapped by a stranger in the night, a terrible thing but it probably will last a short time and be followed by rescue and a return to the bosom of friends and home. So much worse to live with shrinking heart day in and day out among semi-strangers who present you on each encounter with the possibility of a disastrous end.

"I'm so glad to be getting out of this sorry-ass fucked-up neighborhood!" Bruce said suddenly

"Don't hold it in, Bruce. Share those feelings. Let them out," Pat said, yukking gently.

They left Hillcrest Heights and began the drive to Virginia. "You know the worst thing I remember?" Bruce said. "The worst of all?! It's when I wanted to play baseball at Holy Family, and they wouldn't let me because I was a Jew. I was so young and innocent, I had no clue. I hated being an innocent."

"You're still an innocent."

"Look who's talking."

In Virginia, Bruce and Pat directed the unpacking of the van. Dr. Gordon's desk and chair were carried around back and through the patio doors of a newly purchased town house. Bruce gave a grunt of pleasure moving the desk into place. Evening was coming on by the time they were ready to relax. Bruce's dog appealed successfully to go on a walk and set a good pace down a leafy path, nose to the ground. Up ahead a landscaper had scooped out a pond to add to the communal value. It was empty of people, and, standing on the bank, Bruce and Pat could believe they were a gentleman and lady on their private estate. On the deep dark water a bull's-eye sun reflected a golden ethereal patch like heavenly warmth. Bruce and Pat stayed until the day was almost done. Blimpie splashed in the shallows, dull teeth snapping at birds. The lights of the town houses began to throw blurry streaks across the water. In the grass the last crickets of the year were trilling their armored hearts out.

14

The belly laughs came bouncing out of Pat at the sight of a photograph of Bruce, his hair done up in the bushy style of a generation ago. As for Bruce, he was experiencing a time displacement. "Don't I look like a white boy desperately trying to look black?!" he said, trying to hold his own on the laugh meter.

In an encounter with your former self it is good to see the humor. And it is good practice for your school reunion, when everybody will be poking fun while divining the lessons of growing up.

The fun for the Potomac High graduates, Class of 1974, started on the fifth floor of the Ramada Inn in New Carrollton. Bruce had rented a room for Pat and himself alongside a room for Camilla and her boyfriend Dave. Half the floor was occupied by the homecoming crowd. Pat took some of the crowd down the hall to knock on doors and shout, "Hello, anybody from Potomac?" The door to Camilla's room was ajar, and Pat burst in. "Camilla, Camilla!" Half-dressed, clothes askew on the bed, Camilla jumped up and put aside any annoyance and ran to embrace Pat. In seconds the room was full of company, including Heather. Heather had settled foursquare into middle age while Camilla was still free-dancing and jitterbugging a night or two every week. But they hugged instantly, and later they would talk here on the bed past the point of being able to hold up their heads.

But first they were led by Bruce down the elevators to a room with a portable dance floor. You could feel Bruce's need, after so much time alone with his dad, to be surrounded by the old gang, to be among fellow travelers. He was boisterous, making the rounds, sopping it up, and when he called full-throatedly to the assembly he sounded like a TV impresario. "Everybody to the front to get your picture taken." A big yowsa-yowsa grin was over his face, and you half expected him to start snapping his fingers. A hundred and fifty Potomac High alums dragged chairs onto the dance floor, forming a pyramid with the chairs for elevation. At the apex were Bruce and Pat, who else? Camilla sat front and center, with Ray Norris a couple spots over, and so on—a band of middle-aged black and white Americans with arms around shoulders. A paid photographer hit the switch on a formal portrait. The moment was high. Taking it in, Ray's wife, Nancy, said, "Can you believe this many people can get along with each other?"

They reassembled in a line for a big steaming silver-dish production of shrimp newburg, sauced scallops, medallions of beef and bacon wrapped around water chestnuts. The line was slow, and Bruce and the others put on wacky acts, everybody wishing to be young and foolish again, although there was serious talk, too. Why had the reunion of ten years ago been such a lily-white affair? "I think a very select group got invited," Heather said, looking about vainly for anyone to confront. The organizers of the tenth reunion had apparently thought it prudent to skip the twentieth. Tonight's crowd was Bruce's crowd. He had been president of the class as a sophomore. "I was a horrible president. I only did it to beef up the old extracurricular for college," he said. His reminiscing about high school was tongue in cheek and charged with teenage ginger, but there was a certain pride in his stories of racial equanimity. "Back then we were stoned quite a bit, which I think is germane. When you're feeling good you're feeling good," Bruce said to general acknowledgment. "I remember Ray and I were in this old LTD, and we pulled up alongside these brothers in another car and got to passing tokes back and forth through the windows. We could hang with them, and vice versa. They could tell we weren't Grits because we'd have Curtis Mayfield on the radio."

"It was our hair—that was the universal language," said Ray. "Plus we knew some of those guys from the football games. I loved those smorgasbords on the hilltop, eating and smoking and getting sick on Polar Bear wine and barfing in the woods. And remember Spider's Web? Our very own head shop right there at the strip mall. They sold American-flag rolling papers."

"This is politically incorrect, but I'll say it," Bruce said. "We were the wagged-out fun guys. Chicks dug us."

Ray's steady in those days was a girl, among the missing tonight, of Japanese ancestry. "We broke up when we went off to college, which relieved the hell out of my folks. They didn't think she was as bad as Bruce going out with you, Camilla, but in their opinion she was a rock around my neck."

"Why, for God's sake?" Camilla said. "As if I have to ask!"

"Probably it was her color, yeah, but I think it was related more to stuff that happened in the war. My dad had friends of his killed by the Japanese."

"Baggage, baggage!" Bruce said.

"I have to tell you about a conversation my daughter had with her friend Rose," Camilla said. "They started talking about where their ancestors came from, and my daughter says, 'My people came over on slave boats and on boats from Ireland.' It was wonderful because she has an assumption that what Americans have in common is we all came over on boats."

But who wants to jabber once the music begins? And anyway, who can hear when the deejay has the amplifiers set at a high electronic register and every song is pulsing loud and hypnotic, the bass pounding, the treble shrill?

"Can it be turned down a notch?" someone asked Bruce.

"Sorry, that's a negative!"

Camilla and Dave were first onto the dance floor, and Bruce bounded out to make a threesome, and then Pat was found. She stopped shy of the floor until Bruce drew her into the action with what has to be called charming swagger. For a good ten minutes it was the four of them cutting a rug, with a crowd around watching. Camilla took off her shoes and danced barefoot, an exuberant Caribbean effect, and did a spin of mightiest difficulty. Bruce, in cruise-ship form, did a dip in the center of the floor with Pat. The music was a flashback, his head abuzz with thoughts of black-light posters and dry-humping and the one bust-your-gut, drunken, makeout party at the Gordon house when his folks were having marriage problems and left the place unguarded. "Hey Jude" came on, and "Satisfaction," oldies to loosen one up. Bruce was full of life, and it was his party. Over the course of the reunion his unbridled style would make him the most highly prized of men, and he would get to dance solo opposite a dozen or more women while footsore husbands and boyfriends soaked up at the bar. Everyone would say later it was a bravura performance.

Meanwhile, Camilla and Heather did a calculation. It had been eight years since they had last laid eyes on each other, since that exchange of maternity clothes when Camilla was on VISTA duty. "And now we have kids who are almost adolescents," Camilla said wryly and told of a bad time her daughter had run into recently at school, saying with more wryness, "So my daughter is going to write a report about injustice."

"Just like her mother. That's what you were writing in the seventh grade, before any of the rest of us knew there was such a thing as injustice," Heather said smartly.

"Now I remember why I like you." Camilla's face brightened. "You've got the sassiest mouth for a white girl."

She yanked on Heather's hands and pulled her out into a disco number. One number was enough for Heather, and they went back to a table to murmur together conspiratorially. After a few minutes to themselves they were joined by Pat and a couple of others, and in this mixed company Heather received a startlingly easy introduction to the fears about her father and mother that were always at the back of her mind. What to do about one's parents was an eagerly seized upon topic. "My dad left Hillcrest Heights, and he's happy in Baltimore," Camilla said to Heather. "But your mom and dad? That's tougher. They're rooted. I think anybody whose folks live in a place like Hillcrest Heights has a dilemma. Should older people keep running these risks just because they're emotionally attached to their home?"

"My folks are much more wary than they used to be," Heather said. "They have more of a siege mentality."

"Who can blame them? You never know who's carrying what."

"I don't want to butt into their business, but . . ."

"I say go ahead and tell them to move." Camilla was firm.

"They're starting to wean themselves away, I think. They're at the farm more. They discovered a concert series up there, big-band music."

"Good."

"I just wish they'd hurry up and get on with it," Heather said with more passion than she probably intended.

The other topic of the evening was everyone's address and state of living. "Believe me, being out in the boonies has its drawbacks," Heather said. "But where is there a place that's perfect in every way?"

Reginald Alexander had ended up in Detroit, in a federal housing job. But who was Reginald Alexander? In an earlier incarnation Reggie played ball with Bruce and stole cherries with him and boxed at the Quonset hut and was the kid who saved him from a thrashing during junior high school. Reggie's savior role came about because Bruce proved a poor sport at the outcome of a popular vote for student council and alleged in a column for the school newspaper that his opponent, a black student named Hernandez Williams, was unfairly aided by the bloc-voting of other black students. Word was passed to Bruce: "You idiot, Hernandez is going to kill you." But the nose-bloodying scuffle that ensued on the playground was stopped by Reggie, a single black kid fending off the others.

"In hindsight," said Bruce, taking a time-out from the dance floor to bear hug Reggie and confess this tale, "Reggie shouldn't have spared me. I deserved to have my butt kicked."

"You're absolutely right, one hundred percent," said Reggie, slapping five.

Camilla was waiting to grab Bruce next. "I still want to dance with you," she said. She had been striking a figure all night in a long, flyaway skirt and an open blouse over a leotardlike bodice.

"How about right now?" The booze was working in him.

"This one's too slow."

"You've gotten so bossy."

"I was always bossy."

The deejay called for the last dance, the Electric Slide, and Bruce and Camilla hustled into line, grabbing up their other partners, but before it was over they had separated from the line onto a corner of the floor, faced off by themselves, thus creating for the sake of posterity the scene they had talked about. But it was a chaste scene, after all. They would not do anything to undermine the person the other had brought .

At midnight the motel crew moved in fast, disassembling the walls along ceiling tracks. Pat, perfectly good-humored, took Bruce up to their room, he with his lady-killer smile. The room filled up behind them. Until nearly daybreak Bruce and his soulmates would tie one on with unrepentant hilarity, and for this night at least they had no thought as to their blackness or whiteness. It was not so much a time of reckoning as a good old time. Security guards would visit the room twenty-three times. (In his foolishness Bruce kept count.)

Upon waking in the middle of the morning Bruce staggered into two more ex-classmates in the hall, a satin-slipped black woman and a touseled-hair white man who after twenty years had acted on long-suppressed lust. At that moment, to think they were all creations of Prince George's County made Bruce proud.

Officially Wayne Curry had to wait for the general election in November to become the executive-elect, but this final period of campaigning was the slack season. The general election, completing the political year, existed only to validate the primary winners. It was an early night everywhere except at Wayne Curry headquarters, where the historic ending was handled with slow relish. The lyrics to "Lean on Me" blared out. Mr. Curry called it his song. "We need to lean on each other," he said. In his victory statement Mr. Curry tried to calm the white community. "Normally the mere arrival of an African-American political majority is like a fire alarm going off, saying, 'Don't use the elevators. Use the staircase and get out!' Well, that's not what I am all about." His speech had the modest ring of a seasoned pro, and he was no less modest for letting a twittering hub of reporters know the score. "History was made tonight. This election was literally for the soul of Prince George's County."

It was indisputable. A University of Maryland political scientist, the white man Bart Landry, the next morning declared the Curry election "the coming of age politically of the black middle class in America."

The Stricklers had begun discussions with mechanical engineers about snow-stress loads for the roof of a mountainside house. At Thanksgiving they settled into a Penfield winter to test their own capacity for snow and cold. The trial run went better than expected until early one evening. While they were engrossed by the MacNeil-Lehrer show, fire escaped up the flue of a woodstove and flamed out in the kitchen rafters. Black smoke at the back of the house was their first warning. Since the house had no phone Merv drove to the local fire station, and Dell ran back and forth with half pails of water and heaved them at the ceiling, a one-woman brigade. "You better stop. You're no spring chicken," a neighbor shouted at her, but she was magnificent and saved the main house. Still, on January 13, the date of their golden anniversary and Merv's seventy-fifth birthday, they had to celebrate in a charred, torn-up kitchen, without running water. They drank from plastic jugs and washed their hands in a bowl. They drove twenty-five miles for a shower. They were reminded of days spent in Outer Mongolia and Siberia. They could not have been happier. Snow was blown under the dark spruces at the driveway. Merv was zipped up in an oversized parka, a red-faced sturdy heap of a man who weighed too much but had the look of a strong constitution, and Dell, his live-wire bride, thin as the day they married, pitched a snowball in the air.

Their return to Hillcrest Heights was dictated by a staging of *Richard III* at the Folger Theater, where they also were volunteers. Back in the fold of accustomed civilization, Dell took up her work at the hospital, and Merv became the host for a pair of Russian video-journalists, friends of his. The Pennsylvania farm again receded from immediate plans.

• • •

Winter had come down from the Alleghenies and had reached the Washington suburbs on the southern bank of the Potomac. A wood fire rustled next to a beige carpet in the quiet of Bruce and Pat's love nest— their three-story, three-bath town house with wet bar, a painting of mountain goats on a wall, ironing board leaning in a corner, a silver-framed black-and-white reprint of JFK on a book shelf, and the hits of Third World, Verge Overkill, and the Allman Brothers in a CD rack. Bruce was up and down throwing logs onto the fire. He had bought half a cord of West Virginia mixed wood for $75, an overly generous sum, but the woodcutter looked like he needed the money.

Bruce, in his new job, was bringing in the commissions. Yesterday he had set a deal for three fire trucks, with cash up front. It was a deal located in Prince George's County, through the Bowie fire department, and would use several hundred thousand dollars raised by "Las Vegas" nights. Having crossed the river, Bruce more than ever was working the northern bank, pursuing Prince George's clients. This was partly happenstance, but it was also Bruce's design to check on his father by day. They would lunch together, or Bruce would drop by and chew the fat during rush hour. He felt good about holding up his end of this bargain because he was going home every night to Pat, to an unvexed, fireplace-lounging home. They had old-married expectations about each other. On New Year's Eve they had watched a movie on the VCR and drunk beer and talked of vacations ahead, Jamaica in April, the Rocky Mountains in summer. They fell asleep before midnight and woke up on the couch at three in the morning and smooched in the New Year with the Pacific Coast. Tonight, having a casual dinner with friends, Bruce was put into a brief sulk when Pat said he reminded her of Dan Aykroyd. "But Aykroyd's a pudge!" he said in protest. It was Bruce's comfortable routine now to moan about having to shed pounds and to make only token attempts at exercise. He had no excuse either because, along with hiking paths, the town house complex came equipped with a loaded-up gym. "My excuse is that things are too close at hand. If something doesn't require a special effort I don't do it," Bruce said, not disingenuously.

Their town house was in the planned town of Reston. Stores and theaters and restaurants were in a prearranged layout at the center of Reston, a type of contemporary, convenience-conscious style that on the other side of the river would rile envious people to say, "It's okay, if you like that kind of place." But Bruce was here not to save on mileage as much as for the rules of life, which were relaxed and did not require an assessment of every stranger. Reston had an extremely short history, dating back one generation. The civil rights laws had always been in force here. Reston had never known segregation. The legacy of such a fresh American beginning was evident right next door, where lived a black husband and a white wife. Here Bruce and Pat were no oddity, an important criterion for him. He had had his fill of the darting looks of strangers on the street, the creep of voyeur's eyes, eyes of the Puritan strain of America. How many interracial lovers had been stripped of their innocence by such eyes? How many had been undercut by fears and condemnations, an elaborate system of judging at the bottom of which lies the simple fact that all Americans do not yet think of themselves as alike? But in Reston a black-and-white couple could touch each other in public and still be regular society. If it had been up to Bruce, someone would have hung a sign above the main street. *Advertise the place as a miracle, with a capital M, a place longed for and found! Hail, hail, this champion of perfect civilization!* That Bruce had once had a similar feeling about Hillcrest Heights was a minor point, he thought.

To Elvira's critics she was a respecter of nothing, no tradition, no civility, but even her critics felt she now had outdone herself by filing a federal lawsuit against the Maryland public defender's office. The lawsuit described wrongs done to her, acts of "racial discrimination." Money was requested, to compensate for a damaged career, but many at the courthouse assumed Elvira was foremost seeking revenge. "Good, let them worry. Let them twist in the wind," Elvira said. She was all fire and ice. She was like an actress who had created a role and played it so often she had become the role and the role had become her. Whatever her personality once had been, it was now, and perhaps would be permanently, the angry black woman.

Under the white light of massive chandeliers at the Vegas-style Martin's Crosswinds, where some weeks later Bob Magruder would bring his best fighters to a TV evening of boxing, a farewell party was thrown for Sue Mills and the other departing members of the county council. Gloria paid for a ticket. She knew it might prove awkward, but she wanted a public moment of good cheer, a reconciling kind of moment, with the woman who for so long had symbolized an era despised by black people. Gloria approached Sue Mills with an extended hand and a smile, not a cheap one either. "Good luck," Gloria said. "A lot of us are grateful for all the hard work you've put in, all the roads and libraries you got for us."

Mrs. Mills had on her wrist a rhinestone broad-band antique watch. As if violence was being done to her she pulled it close to her chest. "I wouldn't shake your hand if you were the last person left on earth," she said. "Not after what you did to me in this election."

"Honestly, I came here to honor you."

"You stand here in the middle of the room and tell me that?!" A number of bystanders were intently listening. "I'm the one who helped you get elected in the first place. What's your excuse for how you repaid me?"

"I see I was wrong to come. But I came only because of you."

At the precipice of an extremely unpleasant scene, Gloria exited, a model of tact and consideration—a good winner.

Long after Elvira had become disassociated from the Prince George's County courthouse she held on to a shoe box of snapshots taken at her parties, three-by-five glossies of herself with her friends from the office, plied by her liquor, playfully holding up glasses, smiling gaily, arms around each other, giving free rein to their emotions—a box of keepsakes smudged by handprints from more than one handling and yet oddly kept considering how harsh were her later memories.

While living primarily in Bruce's town house, Pat had been paying for a Washington apartment, hedging her bets, as is common in matters of the heart when someone is midway to the grave. Then, on February 1, one week after Bruce's thirty-ninth birthday, Pat ended the apartment lease and officially moved in with him, performing the equivalent of vows.

This also was the morning that Terrence Johnson spoke to a nationwide audience via a video hookup from the downtown Washington offices of Charles Ware's law firm. Mr. Johnson had been released at daybreak from the Brockridge Correctional Facility, and he had hightailed it straight to the news conference. A room had been prepared for him. Mr. Johnson presented himself to the nation in dapper coming-out duds, creased pants, ironed shirt, gray double-breasted suit, a black-and-white checked tie. His black curls were plastered down and combed to the side. "I am a liberated man," he said with hard-knock solemnity. The mask that longtime prisoners wear was tight to his skin. Did he feel he deserved his freedom? No one among the newspeople was impolitic enough to inquire, although he was asked, of course, about the shootings, an episode that by now had embraced more than half his lifetime. He expressed remorse, as he had in court, and added that he held no grudge for his lost years. "But I have no interest in stepping foot again in Prince George's County," Mr. Johnson said. The mask was coming loose, and he spread his arms joyously. "It feels so wonderful to be standing here before you. I feel like I'm floating away!" He rose and shook hands. A purist about drugs, he refused a cup of coffee. He put on a pair of black leather driving gloves that he had peeled off earlier, and a black leather overcoat. His goals were to attend law school and to work as a youth counselor, he said: "I have much to share."

Blanche Claggett had steeled herself for this day and for the inevitable phone calls from news reporters, but when the day was done only one reporter had rung up. This then was the final gall. That the murderer should become revered and the murdered ones be forgotten—this was the real crime, in Mrs. Claggett's opinion.

The subpoenas from Elvira's federal lawsuit had caught her former secretary, Ruth Jones. "Ruthie," as everyone knew her, was asked under oath about the letter she had written that later wound up in the hands of the Judicial Nominating Commission and killed off another friendship. Eleven years of friendship done in by four neatly scrawled pages? Could even a federal lawsuit resolve something like this? For the bound-up, extroverted world of Elvira White and Ruth Jones to come unraveled made no sense. All had been well, so it seemed, in their sisterhood of hearty wind-downs after work and loving toasts at parties—until a few grinning, lounging rowdies at a lockup were called "black Sambos." The events proceeding from that remark had drawn Elvira and her co-workers into a contest, who could show up the other as the worst, most revulsive racist. The day Elvira got into her tiff with Ruth Jones was the same day Elvira refused to accept Jeff Singman's letter of apology. One of the white attorneys had said to Elvira, "Fuck you! I'm going to get you, bitch!" From state headquarters arrived a quick-fix idea that soon backfired. Two Howard

University professors set up easel boards in the main conference room and wrote out words like "racial sensitivity" and "racial displacement." The entire staff was subjected to hours of grilling. *You might have college degrees and live in faux baronial houses but you're still rednecks.* This was the between-the-lines message to white staffers. They were resentful of Elvira for having to explain inner feelings in public. Elvira said later, "They blamed me. It was like how dare someone insinuate that nice white ladies might have a few prejudiced bones in their body." The friends who had paid get-well visits when Elvira was hospitalized now began to cut her dead. In the ladies' rooms they would check the stalls for Elvira's short black legs before commencing to speak among themselves. So it was, in this dark period, that on the afternoon of May 1, 1992, Elvira perched on the edge of Ruth Jones's outer-room desk and began a conversation that led to Ruth's letter.

The conversation, however, was not directly related to events in the office. The two women talked about the recent beating of Reginald Denny, the luckless white guy who stopped his truck at a Los Angeles intersection and came under the fists (and a tire iron, a brick, and a fire extinguisher) of black men feeling the rage of the Rodney King verdict and the corruption of a moment's power.

Ruth: You can't condone their violence. Two wrongs don't make a right.

Elvira: Easy for you to say. You didn't grow up like those men did, the system always against you.

This part of the conversation was what got Elvira in later trouble with the judicial commissioners who felt she had displayed a sympathy for lawbreakers and a lack of respect for legal canons. But after Elvira and Ruth finished debating the mad scene out in Los Angeles they started to personalize matters—and this was the part Ruth would remember, the part where she put to Elvira a hypothetical scene involving her daughter Kristie: "How would you feel if Kristie were driving to a movie and someone threw a rock in her car window and killed her because she has white skin?" Elvira did not give a straight answer. She wanted to know more about the motives of the rock-throwers. *Nothing personal, just thinking like a defense attorney!* But Ruth felt a true friend would have put an automatic hand to the mouth and would have said words to this effect: God forbid! If that ever happened, I'd turn prosecutor. Ruth felt wronged, as if her daughter's murder could be sanctioned because the Jones family did not belong to the African family. "You told me in so many words that you wouldn't care because [Kristie] is white," Ruth would write in her letter to Elvira. Friend to friend, mother to mother, this could not be countenanced. Three years later, dragged into Elvira's lawsuit, Ruth felt the wrong no less sharply. Face hot and crimson, she would tell Elvira's lawyer, "Elvira acted like there might be some justifiable excuse for my daughter to be killed by a mob. How could there be?!"

But what about Ruth's actions? Would a true friend commit to paper such an unsavory conversation? This was the part that had bothered Elvira, made her suspect the poison letter was created specifically to doom her judgeship, either out of spite or because Ruth had been manipulated by someone else. Why hadn't Ruth kept their fight private and tried to work it out with her at a luncheonette?

Under oath, Ruth explained how she had reached the breaking point. The reason she wrote the letter, she said, was to tell Elvira to get herself a new secretary, and, in fact, the last paragraph is a belligerent ultimatum: "I've worked with you for 11 years and have always backed you up, but this time I feel you are filled with anger. If the fact that you are 'black' and I am 'white' is causing you to have ill feelings toward me, maybe it is time to reassign you a different secretary. I'm sorry, but I can't understand your way of thinking." It was signed "Ruthie."

Yet why had the letter not produced a further communication between the two women? Ruth said now that she had wanted some contriteness from Elvira and had hoped to find it in a note or on her phone machine. ("Or in person, eye to eye.") Instead, Elvira did nothing. Ruth did the same. Her transfer papers were executed. The two of them became proficient at avoiding each other in the hallways. Difficulties of mixed origin transposed one into another. Ruth's letter was leaked to the judicial commissioners. Before giving the original to Elvira, Ruth had made a photocopy, as is in the nature of secretaries, but who had put the photocopy to nefarious use? Ruth denied it was her, and Elvira's new attorney, Erroll Brown, could not now establish the guilty party. However, as a result of Mr. Brown's discovery work, Ruth's state-trooper husband, Paul, was identified as the person who had snitched on Elvira's extracurricular law business. Paul Jones, who used to come to Elvira's parties as a working stiff—her paid barkeep (and how this arrangement worked on his head was another question left unanswered)—had taken his information to one of the staff attorneys, Dent Lynch, who relayed it up the chain of command, resulting in the official investigation that had shadowed Elvira's campaign.

There was no relevance in this discovery, needless to say, to Elvira and Ruth's woebegone friendship. In the years that had passed they had not exchanged a word. And they were now managing, through the legal comings and goings, to stay their distance—illustrating once again the extraordinary lengths to which a racial insult can be carried.

• • •

For the first time in months Bruce planned to leave Pat alone for a Saturday evening, although not entirely to her own devices. All afternoon he was agitated by an overwrought gallantry. He piled wood in the fireplace and cooked from scratch a boiling pot of matzoh ball soup and bought French champagne. "Wait up for me," he told Pat. Then, running late, he drove at high speeds to a boy's-night-out at the fights. On the card was Bob Magruder's best hope, with a name and a nickname right out of the pictures, the 130 pound Joseph ("Lightnin' Joe") Fitzpatrick, Jr., now five-and-oh as a pro. Too untested a boxer to quit daywork, Lightnin' Joe was a coppersmith by trade, pounding and riveting fancy rooftops and offbeat decorative panels for home bars, this to subsidize $240 light-skin boxing gloves. Bob Magruder had him on a fifteen-fight pace toward a shot at a belt. Tonight, Lightnin' Joe would be giving away 12 pounds against Nate Hardy, an older, thick-chested brawler from Washington known as a crowd pleaser, someone able to throw and take a lot of punches. Bob Magruder had signed for the bout despite misgivings. A big journeyman is not an ideal opponent. But there are never enough green kids to go around nowadays. Without journeymen and has-beens the fight game in America would be in even worse shape than it is. Once a respectable route out of poverty, boxing is a sport verging on extinction almost everywhere. Only in places peculiarly populated, places like Hillcrest Heights, where sassy-looking, strong-punching black guys are coupled with rough-customer white-guy trainers and mentors, is it possible to bring out standing-room crowds in an old hut of a gym. Bob Magruder could lay a big claim for keeping the sport alive locally with this radical formula of people. A few weeks ago he had been inducted into the Maryland Boxing Hall of Fame, a designee in the Lifetime Achievement category. Sugar Ray Leonard had greeted him with a crunching bear hug (Sugar Ray, who was lately talking of unretiring and getting back in the ring!). For tonight's fight an entourage from the Quonset hut had hauled themselves in Isuzu four-wheelers across the Potomac to a Virginia gym. Comingled on metal folding chairs they were a pandemonium of tattoos and turtlenecks and gold-crowned teeth and also Armani suits and nyloned legs. Bruce took his seat among them. He had paid $25 for ringside tickets.

The purses averaged $500 a boxer. "Damn, it's a hard way to make money," said Lonnie Rogers, hands taped, walking gamely off. The has-been welterweight in the Magruder stable, not much younger than his manager, had been laid out by a blow to the chin. Some minutes later a huge roar went up for Joe Fitzpatrick. "Lightnin' Joe! Lightnin' Joe!" Bruce found it interesting to note that it was a black-faced crowd, in the main, giving its heart to a white-faced kid, the fourth Fitzpatrick in a boxing lineage that had started in America with a great-grandfather in the Pennsylvania coalfields.

A tuxedoed ring announcer made the introductions, and Lightnin' Joe swung away. He had an arresting rhythm, but in the second round a punch from Nate Hardy whizzed under Joe's right arm and hurt him. He had to pussyfoot until the bell, body and face reddening and dripping sweat. Between rounds there was a careful pageantry of ring girls in skintight dresses, first a white woman, then a black woman, holding up cards to declare the next round. Meanwhile, Bob Magruder maneuvered himself into earshot of the ring judges and learned his boy was well behind on points. "You got to nail him now. Take him down," he told the kid, blotting his face with a towel. Halfway into the third, Lightnin' Joe reached out with a right and felled his opponent, another black man out cold. The Hillcrest Heights fans were overwhelmed and leaped up, arms raised. Bob Magruder did a jumping jack into the ring and danced an Irish jig.

"Congratulations, Bobby!" Bruce had his hand out as the Hillcrest Heights contingent came out between the ropes.

"How you doing? How you doing?" Bob Magruder grabbed the hand, but he had to take a moment to place Bruce. "Sonofagun! You're Doc Gordon's boy! How's Doc doing?"

Bruce smiled haltingly. But of course! It was Doc, not his son, who had made a mark in Hillcrest Heights!

"That's why I came by," Bruce said. "I wanted to thank you for taking my dad to the racetrack."

"Soon as it's spring, I'll take him again."

"Great, it means a lot to him."

A big Italian-suited man with dead-calm eyes had come up on them. "This is Boone Pultz, one of my other guys," Bob Magruder said. "Boone had the cruiserweight belt for a while, and he's looking for bigger things, maybe a fight with Riddick Bowe or George Foreman."

"I recognize you," Bruce said. "From Hillcrest Heights."

Bob Magruder's eyes were twinkling. "Bet you didn't know your dad was the doctor who delivered Boone."

Bruce had a fleeting thought as the cruiserweight strolled away, and he let it fly, "You know, I'm bigger than Boone. I wonder if I could take him?!"

• • •

Now and again the investigative phase of Elvira's racial discrimination lawsuit produced a buzz at the Prince George's courthouse. Certain papers in the files of the public defender's office had to be disclosed to Elvira, and these included a letter from Thomas and Elizabeth Pickering to Chief Public Defender Stephen Harris, dated Valentine's Day, 1994, four months prior to Amy's postconviction hearing. In the letter the Pickerings expressed their loyalty to Elvira. "We have no reason to find fault with Miss White's defense of our granddaughter," they wrote, "and we hope the matter can now be closed." The letter had been a well-kept secret throughout the appeal process, and reading it now bolstered Elvira's contention that private manipulations must have transpired to turn the Pickerings against her.

People who deal in secrecy have an advantage against someone whose life is more or less an open book. At the Prince George's public defender's office—"just to be on the safe side," as a staff attorney explained—an intensive amount of labor had gone into tabulating Elvira's public comings and goings. Altogether four chock-full boxes of materials were amassed—every news article with her name in it, every piece of her campaign literature, transcripts of her radio and TV interviews, her memos, her letters. Someone with an Instamatic camera had slipped inside Elvira's office and taken pictures of items thought to be incriminating. There was a photograph of a passage Elvira had spelled out with colored markers on eight-by-eleven paper and pinned to her office wall: "Satan, the Blood of Jesus Is Against You!" By this bit of scripture she was said to be putting the evil eye on her officemates. (An easel-size blowup of the passage would later be introduced as an official court exhibit.) But what of the sneak shutterbug? That Elvira had been spied on, even at this minor level, made her allegations of wiretap surveillance and black-bag jobs seem less farcical. Indeed, if one thing was established by Elvira's lawsuit, it was that her paranoia had a basis in fact. An informal type of conspiracy against her had existed.

But the lawsuit also led to revelations that Elvira was less happy about—for instance, a summary of the psychiatric consultations she had sought with Dr. Frances Rankin during the worst of her tumult. According to Dr. Rankin, Elvira had expressed "feelings of hopelessness and anger" and demonstrated "shifting moods." She suffered from "insomnia, bad dreams, crying at times." She felt she was being "held to a different standard." It frustrated her to have a "style that was to confront problems head-on, which had helped her through previous adversities, but now no matter what she did her work life continued to go downhill." Dr. Rankin would later testify that, as self-analysis went, Elvira had been on target. Yet for all the evidence of Elvira's strong grip on reality, her time in therapy was more grist for the gossipers, another excuse for denigrating her.

But was this all there really was to life, this endless game of wits and nerve and viciousness with the courthouse partisans?

On a cold weekend Elvira got away with B.J. to the Eastern Shore. The Mercedes had been relinquished to a repo man, so they went in the only remaining family vehicle, a Volkswagen already registering more than 100,000 miles. But, on the Shore, Elvira could pretend that no grim strokes of misfortune had befallen her. Here in old rebel territory, a haven in the nineteenth century for wayfaring graycoats and brigands, a place where white comedians in black face used to mimic, here she was still the girl who had made good. Here among her memories of hot, grueling days in the sun, the heavy smell of tomatoes going to rot, the steamy twelve-hour shifts in the canneries; or a worse alternative, the bloody work done in galoshes at chicken factories, the flapping of the birds, the overseers mean as Lucifer, and the shantytowns of unpaved streets where descendants of slaves dwelled, those docile spirits who, in Styron's phrasing, were "half drowned from birth in a kind of murky mindlessness in which there appeared not the faintest reflection of a world beyond the cabin and the field and the encompassing woods." As a toddling child, Elvira's make-believe play was picking tomatoes and scrubbing dishes. Growing up, her greatest fear lay in being stuck on the Shore, not able to get out, her creative years wasting away. But now, in their familiarity, the old places were restful. To return home felt "like I was going somewhere where I was automatically accepted." She was among family. "Oh, Lord, thank you for coming," one of her brothers said. He was in a hospital, resting comfortably but damaged by a blockage of cerebral blood vessels. Elvira sat with him, stroked his hand, bathed his forehead. He had led a life of hard knocks. When he slept, she closed her eyes into a state of simple, mind-freeing realization. *God will be waiting at the Pearly Gate.*

On her way back to Prince George's County, she felt as if the road signs were a mystery. What road was she on? Where was she heading? ("I don't know where I belong anymore. I don't really belong anywhere.") To stop her thoughts she had to turn up the angelic wailing of gospel songs issuing from the radio. That night Elvira retreated to her doll room, its every nook and cranny decorated with her gussied-up playthings of every creed and color, all the dolls she never got for Christmas on the Eastern Shore. The dear things, they might soon have to be auctioned off. The pieces of her middle-class setup were in hock to the bill collectors.

• • •

On a Friday afternoon late in winter Bruce dialed up Pat on his car phone. "See you at seven," he said. He was rushing to a business appointment after taking time out to visit his father in Hillcrest Heights.

"What? What?!" Pat shouted.

"I'm hurrying. Have to go."

"What? What?!"

Pat was trying to talk silly, as Bruce interpreted it, but later that evening he was not so sure. She was late coming home. The fired-up charcoal on the patio grill simmered to dust. Either she was mad at him for being curt on the phone, or something had gone wrong. He mulled over the route she would have taken, a walk to the Metro in downtown Washington, a subway ride, a bus ride, which should have put her at the entrance to their compound. In another half hour he started calling friends. "I've fallen way to hell. I can't think," he said. He was aware of the panic in his voice but couldn't stop it. He became frantic, beside himself. He phoned the police. No one of Pat's description had been a victim of a crime, and he was instructed by the desk clerks to wait until morning to file a missing-persons report. Their rote rationalizations and vague concern calmed him not a whit. His mind raced. Could she have had a heart attack? She had lately been exhibiting signs of dizziness. He phoned her father and her friends. They helped him call every hospital in the phone book, but there were no Jane Does in the emergency rooms. Bruce returned to the clock. All he could do, after all, was wait. The winter wind swirled the leaves on the patio. His whole body felt faint as if his air was cut off. The mortal crisis of his new existence was upon him.

Four hours late, Pat arrived home. On the walk to the subway she had run into someone who wanted to tell her about a job opportunity, and she had been intrigued. On the spur of the moment they had gone out for a beer and supper. She had not thought to inform Bruce.

Was he disturbed and upset? He was overjoyed. He put both arms around her. He knew now what his moment of panic had been. A leap of happiness! "You're my million-dollar baby. I can't lose you."

His solicitousness amazed her—how marvelous to have someone worry with such gravity over a minor delay, a little mixup, to be treated like you were seventeen again. Later Pat would say, "I don't know if anyone's ever been that concerned about me." There was a whir in her throat. That Bruce should suffer such agonies of love pleased them both.

• • •

In retirement Sue Mills had been trigger-happy with a hot-glue gun. An assembly of her Christmas wreaths were hung on the exterior brick of the Mills home. It was a U-shaped structure with two grand wings, a customized design in a neighborhood of aluminum siding and aboveground pools. Her husband and their son-in-law had done much of the construction work, she the trimming. There was not a subdued note around the place. A large golden eagle was nailed to the front of a two-car garage. Among ground hollies and Alberta spruces, a toga-clad figurine stood in a pink fountain, disconnected for the winter. Indoors, on a tiled foyer, there was a turquoise duplicate, bubbling noisily. A choke of vivid turquoise dye was also on display in the carpet, the blown-glass lamps, the accessory pillows. Hummel elves had been collected behind glass in walnut-veneer cabinets. A flowery ballerina centerpiece occupied a sheened dining room table.

Sue Mills sat in an easy chair, cigarette in hand. She was encased in tie-dyed purple skintight leggings and a blue silk blouse, the blue imprinted with a world map. As of yesterday, she and her husband were set to attend a $125-a-plate gala at the Washington Hilton for Newt Gingrich's political action committee. Rush Limbaugh would be there bashing Democrats. Mrs. Mills had been told to expect a level of VIP treatment. "They might announce my name from the podium," she said, teasing herself about her fate. The diehards from her campaign, who wanted her to switch affiliation to the Republican Party, thought she could muster a comeback the next time around, perhaps run for Congress, but she was through with elections. "Nope, never again. I have said adieu."

Lansdale Sasscer had appointed Sue Mills to her first political job, clerk of the county elections office, and until now she had never known defeat. "It was a shock, quite a shock, because I'd gotten such a good reception door to door, and my poll numbers were good the whole time, at least until the last couple of weeks," she said. "But, when I look back now, I see I had no chance. Wayne Curry had a cadre of voters, hard voters, the young, black professionals, very aggressive. If Jesus Christ had run instead of me, they still would've voted for Wayne." She was not in the mood for any analysis of greater range. The fact that she had lost the votes of a fair number of people like the Stricklers, and a fair number of young, white professionals, did not interest her, although it did remind her of her son and the dream his death had cost. "If Steve hadn't died, I firmly believe you'd be talking to him right now," she said. At age eight Steve had fashioned a crayoned sign for his mother and posted it in the front lawn. A photograph of her tow-headed boy, hammer in hand, was the only memento from her political life that "I really care to keep."

As for her future, she was considering either talk-show radio or real estate sales.

On the Saturday before Wayne Curry's swearing-in, the oldest Pesci son, Jimmy, came by the house in New Carrollton and popped a question, "Dad, when are you and Mom going to get out of Prince George's? Please, think about it!"

"No, no, not you, too! Not my own son!"

Yet the idea was not pulled from thin air. Just last week burglars had again shaken up the neighborhood. A family asleep upstairs, three cars parked out front: The burglars had to know someone was home. Such a bold crime makes people think of buying a gun. It made Frank think of buying one, he, a crusader for gun control. ("How would I do it? I'd have to buy it under a pseudonym.") It was the kind of crime that played into the hands of the realty agents who were working the neighborhood, actively seeking out older white homeowners willing to sell to younger black purchasers. Their system was to check the registry of deeds for houses last on the market twenty or thirty years ago, houses likely to belong to white settlers. Then the agents would hit the phones. Frank had received more than one call. He worked his reporter's angle with them, probing their motives, putting them on the defensive, until they hung up. But their system was finding plenty of marks. Within the past few months the agents had transacted more than a dozen changes of ownership from white to black.

To someone on the outside seeing only the moving vans, someone not looking sharply, it would have been simply money and real estate, not the withdrawal of friends and neighbors, not a new society imposed on the shaded streets of New Carrollton. Frank's yearlong attempt to get a handle on the next stage of white flight thus had come home. One of his old crowd, state senator Thomas O'Reilly, had retired from the legislature and moved out, as had two other friends who had once been prideful of civil rights—"two guys liberal to their toes." They acted sheepish when Frank questioned them. "Oh, Frank, why don't you just forget about Prince George's? Don't be such a stickler for principle. Come on, get out while the getting's good"—this was what they more or less said to him. ("These are not loud and angry Mr. and Mrs. Joe Sixpacks like in the seventies, but educated couples of civic stature. They look me in the eye and say, 'We're not kicking or screaming. We're just getting out, going where we're still valued.' There are plenty of excuses: children grown up, the country air, and the safety issue, always the safety issue. But no one brings up the fact a black political class has gained control over Prince George's. No one talks about that. We're too civilized.") However, the senior Pescis were staying put. Not only that, but Frank was engaged in organizing a town meeting to warn the real estate agents about the laws on "steering" and block-busting. In addition, he was willing still to say in his column what few other people were willing to say. "A person doesn't need a Ph.D. in sociology to notice that, at least in my neighborhood, when white home-owners sell their homes, they are almost invariably shown exclusively by the Realtor to black potential buyers," he wrote. "It appears Realtors have determined the New Carrollton market has demographically *tipped*."

Eventually, Frank's random and anecdotal evidence would be confirmed by the demographer George Grier. He would find that black residents, who had accounted for fifty-one percent of the Prince George's population in 1990 and fifty-four percent at the time of Mr. Curry's election in 1994, would account for sixty-two percent as of 1997—and white residents would account for a correspondingly smaller percentage. In the Grier survey, financed by businesses and private foundations, the profile of the typical newcomer would have a familiar look—unmarried, younger than thirty-five, college-educated, with an annual income of $35,000 or better—that closely approximated the look in the Marlow Heights gym and on the sidewalks of Hillcrest Heights.

Gloria had an encounter with a white woman who had declared her fealty to Prince George's for forty years but was now readying to leave.

"Don't sell," Gloria said. "Don't."

But the woman was adamant, and then the conversation took an interesting turn.

"Where will you go?" Gloria asked.

"I can go anywhere."

It came to Gloria: "That's a white woman speaking. Only black people think, where can I go? Where will I be accepted?"

A caseworker had a suspicion when she came across the name of Edrena White just moved off the waiting list and into a nursing home in Bowie. Might Edrena be the mother of the notorious Elvira? So she was, and Elvira was ecstatic to be able to relocate her widowed mother from a dreary old folks' home always smelling of mildew to a first-class place with spotless, ammonia-scrubbed floors. Black people slept in only five of the

230 beds in this new nursing home, another measure of its exclusiveness, and, in the normal course of assignments, Edrena White had been given a white roommate. Might this be a problem? The caseworker, knowing of Elvira's reputation, anticipated it would be. The director of the home was alerted, and she quickly signed paperwork to have Elvira's mother reassigned to a room with a black roommate. This then was the background for the scene that followed: a loud, angry Elvira on her feet gesticulating in the director's well-groomed office. The caseworker had anticipated too much. "No, no, absolutely not," Elvira shouted. "Do not move my mother to another room."

Elvira's reasons? Her mother, suffering from Alzheimer's and easily confused, had learned to navigate from her room to the cafeteria and did not want to learn a new route. "And she likes her roommate. She likes this white lady. They're both little itty-bitty old ladies. They get along. Please let well enough alone."

Set aside, as Amy Smith awaited her new judgment hour, all the theories and endless speculations about revenge and cover-up. Set aside, too, the questions of guilt pertaining to Derrick Jones and Dennis Smith. What were the facts about Amy, the lone accused defendant?

Elvira had a copy of the original file stashed at her house, and lately, at night, after lights-out for B.J., she was sorting through it. (The 911 tape was missing, misplaced somewhere, but all the other material pieces of evidence were in the file.) Reading, remembering, it all came back to Elvira.

A robbery that went awry—presumably this was how Larry Polen would present Amy's case to a jury. It was the scenario Anne Gold-Rand had pressed upon Elvira, the scenario she had rejected but, according to Judge Missouri's ruling, should have utilized. However, did the robbery angle make sense? If all Amy wanted was her late mother's silverware she herself could have staged a break-in at any time, without witnesses and without a co-conspirator. Why involve Derrick? And why involve Derrick with her parents present in the house? It did not take a clairvoyant to see that Amy must have been planning more than the theft of knives and forks. By all the known evidence, this was an evening about a black boyfriend, and about hatred. A month earlier Amy had called a former boyfriend, Anthony Harding, and asked if he would obtain a gun for her. "First I didn't take it seriously, then after a while I did," Anthony Harding testified. Why the gun? "So she could kill her parents." How likely was it, therefore, that in the next few weeks Amy's rage grew stronger and stronger? How likely

was it that the idea of murder seeped into her heart until the need for it became visceral? The fact was, during a later abbreviated confessional in Dr.
Schouten's book-lined office, Amy had admitted discussing patricide and
matricide with Derrick on the evening in question, although she claimed it
was Derrick who had introduced this criminal element. "Amy reported that
Derrick offered to get rid of her parents, and at that time she agreed to allow him to do so," according to Dr. Schouten. But was Derrick a killer at
heart? Or, as Derrick's parents believed, was it merely Amy's girl-smelling
bed that drew him to the Smith house. Of course, sex can be traded for
murder. It happens in bad movies all the time. Might Amy have worked her
powers of persuasion on Derrick, coming at him with a prove-to-me-
you're-my-man pout? Might she have heated him up to do her bidding?
Was it in this context that the notes found later in Derrick's pocket came to
be written? Were they fearful their whispering would be overheard by
Amy's stepmother, and is this why they laid out their plan in stealth on a
pad of school parchment? Perhaps, needing to supply the police with an
alternative culprit and motive for Mr. and Mrs. Smith's killings, the two
young conspirators came up with the idea of a thief who breaks in and
steals silverware. But to their movie-educated minds a robbery might not
have been sufficient. More pretense was needed. Hence their insane script-
like dialogue. *Scratch my back? What do you mean? Shoot my shoulder,
and, please, not too close to the middle.* But what happens next? Is the plan
interrupted? Does Mr. Smith catch them half in the sack (sex before murder) and shoot Derrick as he tries to escape? Or does Derrick go through
with the plan and take the gun from Mr. Smith's holster and proceed to the
master bedroom? In Amy's version, as recorded by Dr. Schouten, she is
downstairs and Derrick is upstairs when she hears the sounds of scuffling
and her father's sobs: "Amy knew what was going on and realized it was a
terrible mistake, that she did not want anyone harmed, and suddenly realized it was too late." Derrick has taken the game too far; she is horror-
stricken—that is her version. According to Mrs. Smith's testimony,
however, Amy is a stone-cool customer when she runs up the stairs and
sees father and boyfriend punching and grabbing each other. "What's going on?" Amy asks, very calmly, without astonishment, so it seems to Mrs.
Smith, who is beseeching her, "Call nine-one-one! Call nine-one-one!"
Amy's stepmother is temporarily spared knowledge of Amy's relationship
with the masked intruder ("I thought she was coming to our rescue!"), although Mrs. Smith does take notice that Amy is dressed in khaki shorts and
a khaki top instead of pajamas. As for Amy, she is speechless. Her father is
foiling the plan. Does she dare lay her hands on the gun and do the dirty
deed herself? No, she is no gun moll. With a panting breath, which her

stepmother thinks is from the sight of the mayhem, Amy goes to the kitchen phone and dials the police operator. Within minutes Derrick is dead, and the police are at the door. Mary Jo Elam, a friend of the family who knew Mr. Smith as "Smitty," is one of the responding officers, and she sits Amy down at the dining room table. By now the heavy drama of killing and dying is deep into the girl's veins, as Officer Elam will testify, "Amy was pretty quiet and pretty distraught. Her eyes were very red. She was shaking her head back and forth, or had her head in her hands most of the time, obviously in a very distressed state."

They are joined by Officer Jeffrey Gray, and a conversation follows:

Amy: "Who was it that got shot downstairs?"

Officer Elam: "We don't know yet. He has a mask on."

Amy: "Is it a man or a boy?"

Officer Elam: "There is no way to determine yet."

Amy: "If it was someone I know, then it's all my fault."

Sobbing, Amy lowers her face flush to the table, unable to endure more conversation, but she is moved to say over and over in a hysterical monotone, "It's all my fault, it's all my fault."

Here is what seems to be a different confession, this one spontaneous and repentant, and yet not pure either but bent to a set of qualifiers. Amy is not panicked. Nor is she quite resigned to her fate; she is careful not to give away a full statement of the facts. Her words are open to more than one interpretation. Amy might be operating out of a shrewd instinct and might be trying to say something like "Oh God, I hope the intruder lying dead on the floor isn't one of those sex-crazed black boys from school, you know, the type capable of trying to win my favor by gunning down my parents." Prosecutor Beverly Woodard will later argue that the true dark in Amy's soul is shown by her evasive bitch-conniving in the conversation with Officer Elam: "Amy knows that as a result of her involvement there is a young man who is now lying in the rec room who is deceased. If you plan a murder, and the person you planned it with is dead on the bottom stairs, the first thing you want to do is divert attention from yourself. So you say to a police officer, 'Is it a man or a boy?' That is, 'I obviously don't know what's going on, but if it's someone I know, could I be implicated?' Amy was trying to cover her tracks. She's not going to sit there and say, 'I know who the dead man is. I saw him when he came in. He was in my room, and I know what is going on.' Instead she's trying to shift the focus." But doesn't Amy's twisting and hedging show also the torture in her soul? Isn't it evidence of a collision inside her of two separate spheres of her life, the criminal accessory and the whimpering penitent? Should she not be granted at least the benefit of mixed emotions?

"Yes, sure, I do grant her that," said Elvira, when she was done review-ing the file and had put away again the transcripts and autopsy reports and pictures of the corpse ("A gruesome sight, I couldn't look at them"). Elvira was now discussing what she might say to news reporters if asked to com-ment on Amy's second trial. "Those of us involved in the first trial, on both sides, we all agreed Amy was a very mixed-up young lady."

People in conflict with themselves—Amy Lynne Smith was not the first one on that list.

If race doesn't exist as a biological category should it exist as a social category? Or should we add even more categories and thus diminish their importance?

What if the official U.S. Census added a category for Americans of mixed racial backgrounds? The concept held the promise of something new in race relations. It was a debate that might have rocked the outside world if it had not been conducted in near privacy during the middle 1990s on Capitol Hill under the auspices of unsung members of the U.S. House Subcommittee on Census, Statistics and Postal Personnel. After pro-tracted consideration, the idea of a specific multiracial category was re-jected, but the Census forms for the year 2000 were revised to permit Americans of mixed race to list themselves in more than one of the famil-iar racial classifications—"Caucasian" *and* "African-American." Thus was legalized the small rebellion of such "race mixers" as Pat Ford's mother, who used to check off both the "white" and "nonwhite" boxes on Pat's school enrollment forms. As a reform, it was less than radical, but the de-bate itself suggested the beginning of a radical process. If ever the gov-ernment-sanctioned system of racial coding is to be abolished, the American citizenry must be informed of its whys and wherefores. The cit-izenry must be informed that, since 1930, the "one-drop" rule has ob-tained: to possess a single drop of African blood is to be a person of color, a designation with legal origins in early Supreme Court rulings and in later Jim Crow laws and in the Klan ideology about the "mongrelization" of the races. For a while after World War II there was strong sentiment in Amer-ica to do away with racial coding. The Nazis, with brutal clarity, had re-minded the world how it can be exploited for evil. Institutions where Americans of Jewish ancestry held sway, such as the ACLU and the New Jersey state legislature, went on record in favor of "All-American" birth cer-tificates and "All-American" Census forms. (Not so long before, Semitic Jews had constituted a "race" even in America. The American Jews who then lived in ghettoes and flourished in the sport of boxing used to wear the six-pointed star on their trunks much as black fighters today wear African colors.) Within the NAACP the idea of taking race out of official government forms was considered good and necessary headway toward integration. To eliminate racial categories was to eliminate the very foundation of racism. Gloria Lawlah, whose grandmother on her father's side was half German, grew up in an NAACP atmosphere of *e pluribus unum*. "I believe in integrated marriages, all that stuff, because that's the only way you can ever break it down," she once commented. "I love it when I go into a school and see black and white kids with arms around each other, flirting, courting, or just being silly." Yet by the 1960s the full power of the civil rights movement gave rise to leaders wishing to influence history with their blackness, and they found typecasting by race useful. Black was beautiful; white genes were a contamination. Sperm from slaveholders had bleached out the blood lines, stolen the African shine, stolen purity, made black people more American. A checkoff box on a piece of paper made them African-Americans. The one-drop rule! In the service of black sovereignty racial labels acquired a newfound value. But labeling also took on another purpose, broader and better. It enabled the people charged with enforcing the civil rights laws to do their job. Indeed, without labeling, there would be no measure of the success or failure of the laws, no way to determine, for instance, the level of African-American employment on the Prince George's police force in 1978 (six percent) and the level a quarter century later (forty-three percent). Equal voting rights and school desegregation and fair housing laws depend for their integrity on the racial classifications of the U.S. Census. "It's another conundrum," Gloria said. "There's no other way to make sure the laws are working, and integration won't work without the laws."

Spring held forth for the opening day of Amy's second trial, the wild wisteria broken out in blue-purple in treetops along old farm roads on the way to Upper Marlboro. Around eight-thirty the sun shone through an overhanging mist, and the courthouse was revealed like the developing colors of a Polaroid picture, every hard line explicit. Up the brick walkway strolled Amy, twenty years old now, soft in the face and unshackled, though in the tow of her grandparents. The Pickerings marched straight on while Amy took little glances toward the pansies in the six-by-six timber boxes and toward a memorial of World War I dogfaces with a weather-beaten title in bronze: "The Right Will Prevail."

Upstairs there was a momentary wait outside the courtroom door, and someone asked about Amy's recent months of freedom in Massachusetts.

Mr. Pickering, all severity, replied, "She got her GED, and now she's taking night classes at the local college. Amy's been a perfect granddaughter. Couldn't ask for anyone more perfect."

"Except when she hogs the cordless phone," his wife interrupted, too brightly.

Mr. Pickering began examining the door. There was a cancer in him, and six months hence he would have to go under the knife and submit to radiation.

"I want to finish school, and help take care of my grandparents," Amy put in. "After college, who knows?" The free-spinning world was waiting for her to get on. At Patuxent she had pushed herself forward as a petitioner of inmate grievances, and in one of her letters to Judge Johnson she had drawn a quiescent smile-face next to her signature and predicted in her girlish hand, "I might come through all of this and end up a lawyer!" Amy's hopes were jailhouse hopes, dreamily conceived and upstaging, but in a positive vein. Lawyering was the one field of specialization she knew. She even had a jailhouse plan for how she might pay the expenses of law school. A Boston movie producer had been in touch and was dangling round-number sums for the rights to her story.

A bailiff opened the door, and once inside Amy whispered loudly, "Oh, God, I don't want to see Elvira." But no one from the public defender's office was present, none of the women who at Amy's first trial had backed each other up and created a sense of collusion and cooperation that passed for intimacy. As Amy looked around, the only faces recognizable from the first trial were Elbert and Daphne Jones. They sat opposite her, on the aisle, self-appointed jurors, eyes riveted.

Reporters kept a watch for Dennis Smith, who had taken early retirement after twenty-three years as a police officer and moved himself and his wife to a life of obscurity and church-sponsored activities in Florida. One rumor had it that Mr. Smith had flown in the night before and was secreted in a room upstairs, prepared to be called to the witness stand and arrayed again as the star prosecution witness (although people who had seen him recently in Florida wondered if he was up to it, saying he looked like an old man burdened with disease). According to a second rumor, Dennis Smith had remained in Florida because his testimony was no longer required. His daughter was going to plead guilty!

Amy's case number was at the top of the docket, assigned to circuit court judge Thomas Smith, who appeared to look askance at her attire of blue jeans and a green knitted sweater. Larry Polen hastened to apologize.

"Amy does not wish to imply any disrespect with the way she's dressed, but she wanted to be ready for her return to custody."

So the arrow was stopped on rumor number two. Amy had accepted a plea bargain: guilty on two counts—conpiracy to commit robbery with a deadly weapon and use of a handgun in the commission of a violent crime. Without dithering Judge Smith read off the charges and turned to Amy. "Are you pleading guilty because you are guilty as charged, and for no other reason?"

"Yes," she replied, no emotion, no hint of being scared or shamefaced, just stating a fact.

Amy had the option to say more. Following the first trial Elvira had gotten Amy to say, "I'm sorry that a young man, my friend, is not here today; he is not with his parents. I carry that all the time and will for the rest of my life." But in this courtroom Amy silently accepted her sentence, keeping her eyes down. Larry Polen then inquired of the judge if she might have a few additional hours with her grandparents. They wished to talk to her one last time on the outside, to try to adjust to her turnabout decision in favor of surrender. A last visit was an odd but human request, and Judge Smith talked it through in open court before saying no. Amy kissed her grandparents, both about to turn seventy-four. She rubbed the knuckles on her hands. Larry Polen explained to her, "You'll go to a detention center, and then to a transfer point. You probably won't make it to Patuxent till tomorrow." The bailiff cuffed Amy's hands. She gave a gigantic heave of impatience, as if she was anxious to get on with the locked gates and doors.

Elbert and Daphne Jones watched Amy go off in her jailhouse outfit, white face sullenly sealed, leaving Larry Polen to be quizzed by reporters.

"I know Amy's friends and grandparents are disappointed," he said, standing alone with his embarrassment. "They thought I'd be a white knight and charge in and get her off. It doesn't work that way in real life."

"It was your recommendation she plead out?"

"My recommendation, her decision. She didn't want to face her father in these circumstances. I don't think he wanted to face her either. It would've been psychologically hard on everyone. But he was planning to testify. We learned he was going to do it. It was off that intelligence that Amy decided to give up her right to a trial."

"You felt her father's testimony couldn't be overcome?"

"That, plus the notes from Derrick's pocket. The notes tied Amy to a conspiracy."

"In other words, you didn't feel Amy could've testified to a version of events absolving her of guilt."

"Like I said, the plea was her decision."

In one dimension the story had reached a conclusion, but in another it never would. For standing off to the side were the Joneses.

As Mr. Polen walked off, Mr. Jones, with his wife limply next to him, said, "We're probably more disappointed than anybody that there wasn't a second trial. We were hoping this time we'd hear the truth."

"What truth are you referring to?"

"That our son was killed because Dennis Smith lost control. He couldn't stand the white-black thing with his daughter."

Most of the questioning was carried out by Pat Lawson-Muse, a five o'clock news anchor at Channel Four and the wife of Reverend Muse, elected to the state legislature on Gloria's slate. That afternoon Mrs. Lawson-Muse would lead her telecast with Mr. Jones's allegations of a murderer still at large. "I'm going to the prosecutor's office. I'm hoping he might file charges in our son's death, despite the late date," Mr. Jones would be pictured saying, even as everyone knew better.

The same week that Amy pleaded guilty a retrial was held for Donnell Wayne Watson, the other of Elvira's former clients whose conviction had been overturned. The public defender's office provided a new attorney for the Watson retrial, but a jury again convicted him of murder, for shooting into the middle of a street argument and killing Conchita "Boobie" Campbell, a fourteen-year-old black girl who had tried to be a peacemaker. The two cases in which Elvira was said to have failed her clients were thereby settled, with no essential change in circumstance. In the Watson case the judge reinstituted a sentence of twenty-five years, and although Amy's sentence was reduced to five years of prison time in exchange for her guilty plea, it was likely she could have secured the same reduction more than a year ago unilaterally from Judge Johnson.

So what had been the point of putting Elvira through the fire?

In the Allegheny foothills, at a rickety roadside stand run by an aproned woman, Merv and Dell bought sun-ripened tomatoes and Silver Queen in the husk. It was nearly suppertime when they reached the farm. For all their chopping away at the undergrowth, the house still sat in obscurity, screened from the road by a row of giant green spruce three generations old. The shade underneath was brown with dropped needles. High in the boughs chipmunks were stripping off cones. Merv and Dell carried their groceries into the house through the mudroom door. The Penfield habit is to leave front doors unlocked, the nineteenth century quietly alive on the mountaintop. The Stricklers examined their house. There were no signs of disturbance by hunters or lovestruck teenagers. Everything was as they had left it. After supper, and after the PBS NewsHour, they read back issues of magazines. A good night's rest came on soft, concaved mattresses over limp springs with night air pouring through screened windows. The hooting of wild turkeys broke into the quiet. Awake at first light, they watched deer browse behind the house. In a field of oats were trails of flattened stalks where the gobblers and hens had fed overnight. Merv and Dell's morning task was to tidy up the family graves in a fenced-in cemetery of leaning sandstone markers, next to a narrow road. The plot was open to the sun; the last of the shade trees had toppled in a storm. Long-dead relatives on Dell's side were buried here, and Heather's older brother, Todd. A keyboard player on the jazz circuit, an organist for the Washington Bullets and Washington Capitals, a popular tutor of inner-city kids, Todd had been afflicted from birth with an angioneurotic edema which, when it kicked in, caused severe swelling in his throat. While Merv and Dell were gone from Hillcrest Heights one weekend, he suffered a reaction and died before he could get to his medication, kept in a bathroom cabinet. Heather had to be called away from her freshman year at Georgetown. ("It was so sudden, like a thunderbolt.") Camilla and Bruce interrupted their studies and romantic difficulties to attend the funeral. Now, at this stage of summer, the graves were overgrown with a high stubble of chicory and wild grasses. Merv and Dell toiled with a push mower until, overheated, they had to stop. When the time came this half acre of country solitude would be their final resting place, too, busy with life though they were at present. They finished the work and went back to the farmhouse to catnap; they were awake and puttering around when they heard the noise of an engine pull strongly through the spruce and quit. Heather had motored up with the grandchildren from Green Bank, leaving Mike to fend for himself a few days. Everyone washed their hands with well water in an enameled pan and pulled up chairs for Dell's corn on the cob and roasted chicken. Merv talked of writing a book about his life's experiences, although not before he was done assisting on a video documentary set in a previously mysterious Soviet gulag. Video projects were his latest fascination. Lacking neither flair nor connections, Merv had been the first American to obtain an on-camera interview with Oleg Kalugin, the former KGB general. Heather, the copy editor and linguist, listened with absorption to her father. In the back of her mind was a series of children's books about machines and mechanics she dreamed of writing, and she spoke haltingly of the idea as perhaps too whimsical. "No, no, follow your heart," Dell encouraged her. Dell passed around a one-page drawing of a west-facing house with the sunset wall comprised mainly of glass. "Let me show where the foundation is staked out," Merv said, and everyone, licking fingers from the finished feast, went out to inspect the site. It was a stone's throw from the old house, and the view through the glass would behold a sloping meadow and a jut of trees. There was also to be a gazebo—why stint on themselves? The housewarming, set for the following summer, awaited more signs of progress, though. A true sign would be blueprints. A true sign would be a bulldozer's big claw scraping and leveling. With good-natured exasperation, Heather said, "I'll believe it when I see it."

Elbert Jones was making small talk with a journalist who had come to Enterprise Estates to borrow briefly a photograph of Derrick. The Joneses kept no reminders of their son in the living quarters. "It hurts too much, my wife just breaks down," Mr. Jones said as he hunted in a bedroom closet for a tied-up cardboard box. Finding it he lifted out a snapshot, taken at Mrs. Jones's office Christmas party when Derrick was eleven. Mrs. Jones had been the photographer. In the picture Derrick is playing with a baby in a corner. His face is ecstatic, a bubbling ear-to-ear grin—"that was his trademark, that smile."

There came a time later in the year when Bruce traveled by himself to Boston on business but elected not to inform Camilla of his visit. Rather, he caught the first plane back home to Pat. So grown-up did he feel these days that he was committing acts of maturity all the time. Bruce lived with a warm, companionable woman, and they might marry. His hair was shot full of gray, but he felt youthful and potent. One-liners from romantic novels came into his head. He would introduce Pat everywhere by saying, "I'd like you to meet the best thing in my life." It was light, lavish talk they could smile over, but it carried the emphasis he wanted in his life. He had come to appreciate Pat's habituation to easy nights at home. Bruce would grill on the patio, and she would vacuum the beige carpet. They would sit by the fire. They might go to the gym. Bruce's ex-wife had left the United States for her native Mexico in order to marry a restaurateur, and in the process had lost track of Bruce's tai kwon do certification papers, an infuriating provocation in the ordinary press of life, but in his present condition he gave it no further thought and instead mailed his ex-wife a wedding card. The coming into his life of Pat, he felt, was the true magical event. He wanted to love her with every card in the deck. Let there be finality and fulfillment! During his younger profligate days of swanning around he had adopted what he called a "U.N. approach" to women, African-American, Caribbean-American, Hispanic, African-Hispanic, even the tang of the truly forbidden, a woman of Arabic descent. ("As a Jew I was really proud of her.") But what was a checklist compared to the real thing? And Pat was very real—he had not gone off his nut. "There's more than a thrilling, erotic bond between us," he said of Pat. "I love her. I'm committed. I realize finding true happiness is the stuff of fantasy, but I've found it. I see a woman who might be with me through to the end, through to rheumatism and a sentimental Florida condo. I get this secret little pleasure when she comes up the steps. She's black! She's Jewish! But that isn't what matters. It's who she is, she, herself." It was not a social statement he was making, not a metaphor. He literally meant it. He was not fooling around anymore. He longed for nothing more than for Pat to be the one. His friends, Camilla included, were rooting for them. It was possible to believe, while watching Bruce and Pat kick off their shoes and throw West Virginia wood on the fire, that theirs would be a love story to end with a kiss.

15　　*The elections* of 1996 approached. Various advisers to Parris Glendening, the past Prince
George's county executive and the present governor of Maryland, thought he could use his power
to end the "embarrassments" back home caused
by a single hell-bent attorney who had filed papers again to run for judge.
In November Mr. Glendening appointed attorney Michelle D. Hotten as
the first black woman judge on the Prince George's circuit court. ("In a
way, this amounts to a victory for Elvira, even though she herself doesn't
share in the reward," said newspaperman Tim Maier.) Next Mr. Glendening formulated a set of terms to offer directly to Elvira. She would be allowed to work again in her chosen land, although not in Upper Marlboro
and not in the public defender's office, but rather in a prosecutorial position on a special drug detail in Greenbelt. Also, a lump sum of $4,900
would go toward her unpaid bills, the Grievance Commission's pending
investigation of her would "go away," and all other scrutiny of her past
dealings would likewise disappear. In turn, Elvira would "make it right"
with the courthouse establishment by withdrawing from further action her
federal lawsuit and her judge's candidacy.

The first hint of the deal was communicated by phone the morning of
January 5, just hours before the deadline by which Prince George's candidates were to finalize their intentions for the primary. Elvira was at home,
sick in bed. It was her minister on the line, Reverend Muse.

"Can you meet with the governor?" he asked.

"Okay, when?"

"Today. This morning."

All at once Elvira's guard went up. Something in the urgency of the invitation made Elvira remember that by the end of the day her name on the ballot would be official. "Reverend, I can't go to a meeting," she said. "I had the killer flu yesterday. I'm weak as sin. I can't go anywhere."

Within the hour there was another call, this time from Gloria. "We must meet. Where can we do it?"

"I'm not leaving my house."

Soon after midday Elvira watched a shiny black car pull into her driveway. It was a Black Alliance delegation: the serious-looking Gloria, trailed closely by Reverend Muse and Bucky Trotter, the state legislator to whom, back at the beginning, Elvira had spilled the beans about Jeff Singman. The three emissaries had planned in advance how they would present the governor's offer. The major share of summarizing it in the right neutral declamatory phraseology fell to Gloria. If anyone had the credibility to negotiate between Elvira and the governor, it was Gloria, who had put herself out for both of them. (Gloria's history with Mr. Glendening dated back to 1986 when, as a reform candidate struggling in a race for county executive, he had come to her for assistance. The endorsement party she threw for him could easily have been a bust but instead became a rousing turning point in the election.) Elvira greeted Gloria and the others and listened to a full recitation, head in a meditative pose. At the mention of a $4,900 payment she had to interrupt, tart-tongued and lucid as ever, "Is that what the good governor is paying for black wenches these days?!" (Elvira had her own history with Mr. Glendening. Years ago at the University of Maryland, where he was then teaching political science, she had been his graduate fellow—one of her many lucky and strategic relationships that were now played out.) When Gloria was done explaining the governor's terms, Elvira said, "You want me to settle for this?"

"It's your choice, your life."

"I might be willing to go halfway. But this isn't halfway. It's nowhere near halfway."

"Think of what's best. For you, for B.J."

Elvira stood up, shakily. "Before I tell you my decision, I need to know if you'll support me regardless of what I decide."

Gloria was confounded it had come to this. Elvira might truly have had an unbounded future, if not for her attitude. (What might you term this attitude? Harvard sociologist Orlando Patterson has termed it "the outrage of liberation." Freedoms won through the civil rights movement allow the unchained person to express almost perpetual indignation at injustices still felt and observed—a phenomenon occurring mainly in the younger generations.) Neutrally, Gloria said, "Whatever you decide is up to you. I'm not here to leverage you."

"But will you support me?" Elvira asked again.

"Yes, all right, yes."

"Then my answer is no. Tell the governor no deal. I have no intention of bowing and scraping and kissing the hem of anyone's garments."

Was this the pride of the lioness? The anger of the wounded she-wolf? Or was Elvira bent now only on quixotic folly?

A harsh literary postscript would end the Terrence Johnson case two years and twenty-six days after he was released into a society of well-meaning friends who later said they wished they had tried to get to know him better.

In the intervening period Terrence Johnson enrolled at the University of the District of Columbia Law School on a $7,000 scholarship. Church parishioners donated to his education an additional $10,000. An admirer permitted him to live rent-free in a Washington apartment. He became the owner of a $25,000 Toyota Celica through a bank note co-signed by Charles Ware. With Mr. Ware he negotiated unsuccessfully for book and movie deals. He frequented nightclubs. The sport of boxing became an avid interest. He was cautioned by Mr. Ware about his "accelerated living." At the same time he followed through on commitments made to public-interest groups. He volunteered as a mentor for tough-luck kids and gave of his time at homeless shelters. Old pals from his Prince George's neighborhood who came to him for legal advice were well briefed. He attended organizing meetings of the Million Man March. He spoke before a panel of Congress regarding his views on juvenile delinquency. In an interview with a *Washington Post* reporter he described thinking of his former prison masters as "my mom and dad." When his law school marks fell below straight A's he grew angry with himself. Toward the end of 1996, when his admirer returned from a trip abroad, he lost his rent-free apartment and had to come up with security deposit and first and last month's rent. He lost his scholarship, too, when his patron suffered a reversal in fortune. He was named the defendant in a paternity suit filed by a woman whose marriage proposal he rejected. That same week he picked a fistfight with an opponent in a pickup basketball game. Upon learning his father was undergoing tests for prostate cancer, he began to drink excessively. He appeared more and more chimerical to his friends and sank farther into debt. Unable to pay his tuition, he dropped out of school, abandoning his announced ambition to be the first convicted killer ever admitted to the Maryland bar. Three weeks later, on the day of his thirty-fourth birthday, police radios crackled with a robbery-in-progress call from a branch of NationsBank. Responding officers chased Terrence Johnson and his brother, Darryl, both dressed in tan trench coats and black knit caps, into an alley behind a Sheraton Hotel. Terrence Johnson paused to look directly at the officers and then swiftly pointed and fired his gun, killing himself with a shot to the head. He died unaware of a surprise birthday party that had been in the works to cheer him up.

According to outward appearances, Elvira had passed through her angry phase into a quieter stage of life.

With Amy Smith returned to prison, Elvira felt vindicated. She had said all along that Amy's case was just the sad-excuse means for punishing an uppity Negro and was of no interest in and of itself to the courthouse crowd. Of everyone involved, Elvira believed, she was the one who had cared the most about the right outcome.

And had things come out right? Had God's design been served?

What a question to ask of those in this self-obsessed, tuned-out society who might still have eyes and ears for moral distinctions. Here was a case of great ambiguity from the real world. Here morality and immorality had taken on meaning; they were no longer abstract, no longer something for theologians to debate. A boy was dead, his name put to shame. His parents were lost in bitterness. His girlfriend was incarcerated. Her parents were on the hoof in Florida. But why not play God for a minute? Consider what is known of these people. Did they actually deserve better? Did any of them occupy a moral position higher than the fate that had befallen them? Of course, Mr. and Mrs. Jones did not deserve to be left with a big empty house when they had done everything America asked and committed no crime or mortal sin. But theirs was the simple answer. For the others it was much harder to track justice over the long haul of the case. There were too many incomplete spaces in the record. Even Elvira, much as she believed she knew who deserved damnation, would have liked to have known more. There was no legal need to go through it all again and analyze the facts ten times over, as her friends accused her of wanting to do, but at night sometimes her mind acted up. She couldn't sleep, and she would poke into corners of the house looking for the 911 tape. While it wasn't new evidence, or even physical evidence by forensic precepts, therein might lie some spark of overlooked truth if only she could find it.

Lost things do have a way of turning up, and several months after Amy was transported to Patuxent, as Elvira rearranged a bookshelf, her hand touched on the plastic cassette. She held the tape at arm's length and flexed her small bicep. It had been more than two years since she last listened to it. She slipped it into her son's boom box and sat down. Amy's voice came out of the box with the shrieking hurt of some animal, "We have a prowler in our house, and he's tried to kill my parents." To listen to the lying gave Elvira the creeps. Could Amy's mind have worked so shrewdly and intuitively that she could turn this quickly against her boyfriend? Or was she speaking lines scripted by her father? The tape spun on—more shrieking and then nonchalance, Amy waxing hot and cold. Next the dispatcher's recording device picked up the sound of a shot and Amy's hurry-scurry and a line that had to be spontaneous:"Dad, here, do you need this?" Returning to the phone, Amy repeated the lie, "Somebody broke in." The phone was handed to Mrs. Smith, who, with uneven breathing, announced the shooting of Derrick. In the interim Amy must have gone far enough downstairs to see Derrick's body, for when it was her turn to talk again to the dispatcher, she was heard to say, "He's dead. . . . He was trying to kill us." The dispatcher asked to speak with Mr. Smith, who, huffing, puffing, also said, with what sounded like anguish, "- He's dead." The dispatcher asked about the location of the bullet wounds, and Mr. Smith replied, "In the back, and in the front." Elvira, hearing everything as if it was real and immediate, wanted to shout, "You bastard, you cold-blooded bastard," for this was still her strong belief. The tape was near to the finish. Elvira could hear the ringing of the doorbell and could hear Mr. Smith give the phone to his wife so he could open up for the police. Listening half-interestedly now, Elvira heard Mr. Smith shout out greetings. "Hey, how you doing? He's dead. I shot him." In a trice all anguish in Mr. Smith's voice had vanished. He sounded abruptly hearty, full of locker room pep. Elvira jerked up. How had she missed this the first time around? She was convinced now that the 911 phone call was hokum through and through, all of it until this last snag of conversation, when Mr. Smith let his true pernicious self out of the bag. If only the tape could bear witness in a courtroom again, Elvira thought, although she knew it never would. Jack Johnson, the new state's attorney, had rejected with gentlemanly firmness a request from the unmollified Jones family for criminal charges against Dennis Smith. The case was closed for good. Elvira had the option of playing the tape for friends, to let them listen and judge for themselves, and in coming weeks she exercised this option. But the tone of a man's voice was no more proof than anything else in the case.

• • •

The outsiders who had tried to figure out the Smith case, journalists and court investigators, agreed it was a case about revenge—either a rebellious daughter and her boyfriend guilty of trying to even a score against her parents, or a father guilty of staging a murder and cover-up to teach his daughter a lesson for making a mockery of his values. Revenge by one generation, or revenge by the other, or perhaps—perhaps this was the only fair and just analysis of the evidence—it was revenge by both.

The neutral parties who had examined the facts believed the only way to make sense of them was to accept that the two wholly different scenarios were both basically true. It was possible to argue that all the participants, or at least three of them, were guilty of crimes: Amy Smith for conspiring to commit murder, Derrick Jones for agreeing to be her instrument of destruction, and Dennis Smith for converting their plot to his own. Indeed, the crimes may have been conceived years ago with the death of Amy's mother. To dream of vengeance, blood calling for blood, and then to be in a position to do something about it—it can be momentarily irresistible, and a moment is all it takes to set in motion "homicidal potential." Did the sweet-natured Derrick make the moment possible? Did his unthinking, sex-driven yearnings help Amy get up the gumption? So it seems. Neither Derrick nor Amy may have been a killer in isolation, but the combination of the two, living for the present, as teenagers do, far beyond what Socrates advised, apparently fell into a terrible rage, never guessing at the long-term consequences for themselves, and not understanding either that they would be too unskilled and unwitting for so cold-blooded a scheme. Beverly Woodard, in her closing argument at Amy's trial, gave Derrick credit for lacking the killer instinct: "It might be that in Derrick's heart it was hard for him to carry out the murder, and that is why he told Marialena Smith, 'You stab your husband, you do it.'" What a struggle against conscience might have gone on inside Derrick. And, at some point before he died, he must have wondered at the run-in with fate that brought him into the middle of this peculiarly destructive white family. Amy, waiting in her bedroom, might have endured her own battle with conscience, and she must have wondered about the meaning of the first explosion of her father's gun, must have wondered whose hand was holding the weapon. Added up, her actions throughout the evening were as contradictory as the winds, and years afterward she had yet to confront on the record any of the details of her now-acknowledged guilt, save for what was reported by Dr. Schouten: "Amy is sorry Derrick Jones is dead but is extremely glad her parents are alive. She realized, almost too late, that she wanted no one to die but just 'wanted to get out.' " As for the final act of the evening, the white cop in possession of the nine-millimeter gun, the black youth prostrate, this had to be a racial showdown if ever there was one. And yet if Derrick Jones had been a white boy would Mr. Smith have stayed his finger on the trigger? Probably even he could not say. What could be said is that Mr. Smith had had the wherewithal to put two slugs in Derrick, and perhaps it is unnecessary, for purposes of right or wrong, to speculate further.

The phone call for Bruce came from a wilderness section of suburban Boston out near Walden Pond—Camilla's million-dollar house, where her rules kept shoed feet off the big wooden ballroom floors. She and her children and David were moved in, along with her brother and his girlfriend, and Camilla had planted two burlapped-balled fruit trees into the front yard, one for each of the kids. "I seem to be putting down roots," she said to Bruce. "Which is maybe why I'm thinking of making this huge change in my life. A new job!"

But what earthly reason could propel Camilla out of her safe affluent in-the-shadow-of-Harvard medical practice? "I would be working for a corporation that sells medical services," she explained, "but before I say yes I was hoping you could get me a rundown on this corporation, since you're Mr. Business World."

A corporation? "Sure, I'll do it," Bruce said obligingly. But this was not your average corporation. It was one that sold services to the Massachusetts prison system. Camilla was to be a prison medical director on call every day to stickup artists and drug hustlers and all the woeful street-slick trash of society. "Oh, wow! Are you the right person for this job?" Bruce said, thinking of Camilla who, just out of medical school, had left a job at Washington, D.C., General because of night sirens bringing her the ruined bodies of black people her own age.

"I don't know," she replied, butterflies in her stomach.

But a few weeks later Camilla placed a follow-up call to Bruce with her answer: "Crazy or not, I took the plunge. It's constant pressure. And I have nothing in common with the inmates. Except they're real people, human beings, and this is a job where you do more than write prescriptions for bodily ills. I'm part of their lives. It's a strange kind of kinship, more like being a doctor in the old sense of doctoring. It's person-to-person. I come home completely exhausted, and completely exhilarated!"

So Camilla was proceeding on the power of good intentions to find a wonderfully contradictory niche—like Bruce, like everybody else who still had good intentions. Congratulations were all that were in order, plus some news of Bruce's own from the neighborhood. The Gordon house, overly commodious for Bruce's father, was up for sale. An old folks' home under a canopy of oaks would be Doc's new residence, a place he had picked out across the Potomac, in Reston of all places, approximately two miles from Bruce and Pat's town house—which had taken them by pleasant surprise.

At her dining table, shoes kicked off, Elvira fussed over a Texas-post-marked envelope containing an eight-by-ten glossy of her grandson, nine months old. The studio photograph, fitted into a gold frame, did not look right on the teakettle wallpaper in the kitchen area, nor next to her living room paintings of corn-rowed, nappy-haired Negro children that dated from the forties. So Elvira set it atop a wood cabinet. "I did a stupid thing when I was sixteen, too," she said in a passing reference to Amy Smith. "I got myself in trouble with a boy. But something good came of it."

Elvira had a visitor in her house, a writer. Up from a basement Xerox machine (the printing press for Elvira's campaign) sauntered B.J., un-dressed to his waist in the stifling, exhausting air. He held a copy of his latest novella, superhero stuff. At his mother's bidding, shyly, he turned it over. Lovingly she rubbed his close-cropped head. "Really, I'm blessed. I'm very blessed. Nobody can take away my boys!" she exclaimed. Here, near Indian Head Highway, in her subdivision of backyard gazebos and slatted pineboard fences, the courthouse was miles away. Placid-looking cement lions guarded Elvira's front walk. The lions and the bright fescue lawn patterned with blue-green sedum crowns brought her peace. How at peace she looked today, no strains showing! She changed from zippered dress into gardening clothes, and out onto a deck and down wooden steps she went to rip ragweeds with bare hands from her vegetable garden, in keeping with a new frenzy of homebodiness. To sustain a garden while under threat of eviction was Elvira's accomplishment for the summer. She had spaded in two rows of seedling Early Girls and Beefsteaks. Living off dashes of limestone and manure, the tomatoes would soon be ready for picking—her girlhood job resuscitated. At summer's end she would be giving away grocery bags of red slicers. Kneeling, she shut her eyes to the yellow-flowering plants tied to stakes, to summer flies sparkling round a dead upside-down beetle, and filled her nostrils with the pungent tomato smell, the whiff of clay. A garden, where the mind can clear itself. Several months ago Elvira had submitted herself to another review by members of the Judicial Nominating Commission, and, once again, the judgment had gone against her. No matter, her name would be in the next round of elections. There had never been any shallowness to her ambitions. People who dig for gold specks in caves or who in high-heeled abstinence eschew sweet pleasures to compete for Miss Universe have ambitions on this order. The girl on the Eastern Shore, snatching time in the fields to read and improve herself with two-dollar words, her ornery get-up-and-go, was the raw material of storybook America. Elvira's whole approach to life was raw material. But the color of her skin is what elevated her story, made her part of a larger, multitudinous saga of black Americans born into changing times. From the time she left the Eastern Shore she was aware of leading a life for history, of being someone whose birthright was not her own but was subordinate to the Negro Experience. She had felt sometimes like a soldier dispatched on a daredevil's mission, but she knew there were many others who would have loved to be in her place. She was the subject of boosterism whenever anyone from the outside arrived at the Prince George's courthouse with inquiries about the state of race relations. Later, in her waning days, she would say with heavy sarcasm, "I'm the showpiece. When you come in you get to see me. Isn't that special?" No doubt there had been a measure of tokenism in the visits from out-of-town dignitaries and in the feature stories about her printed in the local papers, and yet, without ever fully believing in her role, she had thrown herself into it. Having been declared a star, she had acted like one. High moments were an occasion for melodrama. She took matters into her own hands. She became a familiar of sitting judges and high-ranking politicians. She was *it*. (Give her credit, though. There was tangible proof of her worth: "I won more cases than any of them. They were second-stringers.") Her adversaries she regarded essentially as fools. She was famous for saying aloud in a hallway, "I don't have any trouble telling someone, 'You're a pompous, arrogant ass, and it's not my fault you were brought up that way.' " Elvira the Magnificent! What is more magnificent than the American ascension of "a tiny sass-mouthed, pitch-black Negro lady" (to quote a friend of hers)? With the investiture of racial stardom, however, you are required never to make a mistake. Therefore Elvira's starring days were over.

She had an intuition herself of a different future. "Most of the time my law license feels like dead weight," she informed her visitor. "If God granted me one wish, I'd like to spend the rest of my life as a teacher. I'd like to counsel kids. And if my church needed a pro bono lawyer, I'd be happy to do that. But I could give up the courtroom life, I really could."

The sun beat hotly on her skin. The white, glossy sky glared without au-

gury of rain, no current of air. Uncoiling a green hose, she adjusted the noz-
zle and aimed it first at her bare toes and then in an arc over the garden.
She aimed it higher, and water fell on her T-shirt and shorts, an outfit concealing a political swashbuckler who would always wish to strike blows for
the good guys but whose desire for passionate absolutes and an eye for an
eye had ebbed. The greeting on her phone machine had been switched recently to a salutation from the Gospels, "Judge not, lest ye be judged."

Did this include Amy, who, having undergone further psychological
counseling, was due to receive an early parole from Patuxent?

"I feel sorry for her, that's all I feel. Even after she gets out of prison she
will have to live with herself."

How about the Smiths?

"Their punishment is between them and their Maker." Biblical homilies
had become everyday language to her.

The women at the courthouse?

"If you're asking about forgiveness, that's for the Lord. But I feel I understand them a little better, understand what they did. Like Bonnie
Aldridge—I heard she was on the verge of tears when she was testifying
against me. They had a gun at her head. She had to look out for the security of her family—her son-in-law has a job in the public defender's office,
and her daughter is a deputy sheriff." So the mascara-ringed betrayer on
the witness stand, blinking, telling the world of Elvira's pet use of "white
bitch," was, after all, a person under duress.

Might Elvira withdraw her lawsuit?

"I would be willing to accept a quiet settlement. No trial. Let them keep
their good names, if that's what they want."

A Christian view of the world in all its pious simplicity believes in just
deserts for everyone, believes in retributions and vindications, and in a
public vanquishing of the armies of the night. This was the animal righteousness, the fighting creature in Elvira, always rising up, and to put it
down was to go against the force of her nature. She tried to explain how a
change had come upon her but was unable to give it expression, this
woman so rarely at a loss for words. Finally she said, "I've proved who I
am, what I'm made of. I don't have a single thing left to prove, not a
thing." There was about her the beatific quality of one who has passed
through the valley and come out alive, a survivor's appreciation for life.
She repeated, as though to hypnotize herself, "I've been blessed, I've been
so blessed." Perhaps this was how God meant to profit her for having survived, to cleanse her mortal soul. Perhaps retributions really were for
Judgment Day, perhaps vindications were too high voltage. Anyway, who
is truly innocent?

The visitor looked at his watch. "Time to shove off."

"No wait," she said, dropping the hose and letting it flail on the lawn. "Please, you have to read what B.J. wrote about the Eastern Shore."

Bounding up the deck stairs she called out, musically, "B.J., show this man your essay." She chanced a smile.

The essay was sure to deal with Elvira's recent return to the Eastern Shore when, on the occasion of the twenty-fifth reunion of her high school class, she had encountered two racially segregated events, in two different locations, with two different schedules, which must have seemed a strange phenomenon to her son. However, B.J. had not written of his mother's reunion. "Naw, not that," B.J. interjected with a serious smile. He added, quick and infallible, guessing at the tired old question bound to follow, "I don't usually write about race relations."

The poverty of the Eastern Shore, a rusted-out truck with axles on cinder blocks, the unpainted boxy houses, rotting cigarettes on dirt sidewalks—these were the things that had attracted B.J.'s writerly interest. These were things unnatural and fascinatingly poetic for a thirteen-year-old boy living in Prince George's County who, on his last birthday, had been treated to a ride in a rented limousine and had posed for pictures, a schoolboy-prince, nonchalant on the wide, plush seats, making wise with his birthday guests, black boys and white boys alike.

"Black and white doesn't matter to B.J. He doesn't think in those terms," Elvira said. "Thank the Lord."

She clasped her hands to her chest, as a supplicant might, or a diva, and looked fixedly at her visitor. "Tell me honestly, do you think I'm a racist?" In the burning brown agates of her eyes there might have been defiance. *Don't cross me with an answer.* But hasn't anyone who can ask this question come a long ways down the road of discovery? And it did sound like her authentic voice.

It might be tempting to leave Elvira here, in this contemplative moment, a woman in gardening clothes who once upon a time had resolved to rid herself of the fields of her youth, who had gone from black-power salutes to backpatting dinner parties and to an assertive, unapologetic one-woman courthouse parade and, now, some thirty years later, to a tomato-loaded backyard. Who would not wish to remember her as wiser and happier, a Persephone up from the underworld, calm in her soul?

Would that life could be so tidy. Over the next two years Elvira's career in Prince George's County entered its final period of dissolution, a dragged-out ending. In the 1996 primary campaign she was deserted by

Gloria, and the voting public for a second time denied her election to the circuit court. That same year, on July 18, she was fired from her defender's job. "I have lost all confidence in your integrity and ability," Chief Defender Stephen Harris wrote in his letter of notification. At her home that evening, as she showed the letter to a visitor, her hand trembled, and she impulsively extracted a wood-and-brass plaque from a drawer. It had been presented to her three years earlier by Mr. Harris as a marker of her years of "dedicated service." With a dishcloth she rubbed the stenciled words. "I want to know how he's going to explain this plaque to a jury," she said defiantly. Rather than settle her lawsuit Elvira chose a two-week trial at the new federal courthouse, in a cornfielded, country-taverned section of Prince George's County. A public airing had become important again to her, to allay suspicions that the whole affair was a figment of her making. The lead attorney for the state of Maryland, a tall, white assistant attorney general named Lawrence Fletcher-Hill, waxed in his opening oration, "Is this a tragedy? Yes, in a way, it is tragic. Elvira White had everything she ever wanted and then lost it. But is racial prejudice the reason? Or did she lay these traps for herself?" On the witness stand Elvira testified for the better part of two days. She handled herself with restraint, living down her reputation for the theatrical. During the defensive phase of the trial Amy Smith took the oath and gave testimony against Elvira. The jurors deliberated for two days before returning to the box and with brittle, perplexed looks declaring themselves deadlocked, unable, like so many others who had listened to Elvira's story, to reach a common understanding of it. Judge Peter Messitte subsequently dismissed the lawsuit, and there was no second trial. During the course of the litigation a bank foreclosed first on Elvira's investment property and then on her white-brick colonial. She had to situate herself and B.J. in temporary quarters in the town of Clinton. She had achieved an everlasting kind of fame but was without prospects. No offers from Prince George's law firms were forthcoming. Such events might have broken an average person, and Elvira did not have an easy time of it. ("I keep having to apologize to B.J. for yelling at him. Because he's the one I take it out on.") She had lived a life that did not bother for second takes, and now the world of the Prince George's courthouse, the world she had pictured long ago on the Eastern Shore ("it was something I'd dreamed of since I was seven"), was not anymore where she wanted to be. The jury's nonverdict, the foreclosures, the lowly processing of want ads—one of these, finally, was her truthful moment, for she said now, "I was merely passing through." By the autumn of 1997 her intention was to find a new start someplace out of state, to be closer to B.J., sent off to a boarding school in North Carolina, and closer to Andre, now in Louisiana.

Painstakingly she filled out work applications for jobs in the South. Up her alley, she thought, might be a position for college instructor or guidance counselor or schoolteacher.

Was she bitter? She professed not to be. Her dolls had been saved from the auction block, and she was filling her open hours with handicrafts—creating dollhouses with balsa and acrylic paints and stitching satin pillows for a granddaughter who was on the way.

Merv and Dell's lives, meanwhile, went forward at their home on Foster Place with the potted amaryllis, the big rocking chair, and the harps. They bid hello to a new pastor at Ryland Epworth and for a period of time, doing their utmost to give him a hand, they devoted five evenings a week plus Sunday mornings at the church. In addition, they kept to the rest of their volunteerism, including, for Merv, three trips to Russia to help on a documentary film. In the summer of 1996 he fractured a leg and was laid up. A cane was now his sidekick, even after recovery. One day, out for a walk along Foster Place, he watched a flatbed truck pull up to a house recently purchased by Gloria's mother-in-law. The truck was delivering a readymade pavilion. Merv called to Dell, and they slowly ventured over.

"Come on, come on, don't be shy. Nose around all you like! You're family!" shouted Gloria, who came forward to meet them. She bade them inspect the pavilion. "You like it? We're going to throw some fantastic parties. Don't worry, we'll carry on the Strickler tradition!"

Everyone took it for granted the Stricklers would depart the neighborhood, and yet, with the year 1997 drawing to a close, their plans went unrealized. No contracting bids were solicited in Penfield, no bulldozer was moving any earth. "Next year, I think it'll be next year," Heather heard once again. She and Mike themselves had relocated, to a 120-acre farm near his old job and her new one as a schoolteacher, but it remained to be seen if a final impetus for Merv and Dell's leave-taking would ever materialize. It was a family joke. Heather was able to make light of the subject, in fact. The prospect of her parents biding more of their time in Hillcrest Heights no longer dismayed her. A good daughter comes to understand it is no easy matter to leave behind the landmarks of four decades of preeminent good citizenship—a stand of trees in a slight ravine once marked for razing but fought for by her parents, a library on a corner lot, and so on, not the least of which were the genteel friends who remarked every chance they got how the Stricklers would be sorely missed.

• • •

The red was high in Bruce's face, alarming Pat until she determined it was from elation. Bruce's regular excursions to the Towering Oaks rest home were becoming quite the elixir for both him and his father. On visiting days Dr. Gordon would set up a monitoring post close by a window and watch keenly for Bruce's red Taurus wagon to arrive in the parking lot. Then again Doc was suddenly keen on everything. At the rest home he had a calling again. The czar of grouches had been transformed into a Valentino, thrilling the widows with his dotty old blarney. Like father like son, except Bruce was intent on proposing marriage to Pat, and today he had let his father in on his intentions. With nary a word of caution the old man had given his blessing.

About Bruce, Dr. Gordon said now, "Well, he's done his own thing and kept his head up."

And he said also, "Bruce doesn't care what the world thinks of him, but so what? He's got the right to do what he pleases!"

Meanwhile, Bruce said to Pat: "For the first time in my life I can picture Pop attending my wedding, sitting right up front in the first row, and me being glad he's there."

To tease him, Pat said back, "Your wedding? Who you planning to marry?"

The exchange of vows between Bruce Gordon and Patricia Ford would take many months to come to fruition because Bruce's talk with his father was only a beginning. Other members of both families had to be brought in on the discussion. There was a discerning kind of skepticism from relatives who were in favor of a formal and legal union but thought the prospective bride and groom should take a vow of permanent birth control. ("Don't even think of having a child. It's such a cross for the child to bear.") These relatives had to be listened to and tolerated and made to believe there is no preordained curse on "mixed" children. ("Look how well Pat turned out.") Fortunately, Pat's father already had approved of Bruce as a potential son-in-law. ("Pat needs someone who can make her laugh.") Major Ford also was looking forward to more old-goat times with Dr. Gordon—funny how the two of them had hit it off. But then another situation was created by one of Bruce's out-of-town cousins, who had announced his own wedding. This seemed the perfect chance for Bruce to introduce Pat to the extended family, but, after making ready, plane tickets purchased, credit-card numbers phoned in for hotel reservations, party clothes dry-cleaned, what should happen but the invitation arrived with

Pat's name left off. "You go. I don't need to go," Pat said generously, but Bruce would not hear of it and phoned his cousin and made an issue of it. "I'm not attending without Pat. My day-to-day is more important than your once-in-a-blue-moon," he decreed. So they stayed home. "Just when you think you've gotten past all the bullshit, you get smacked in the face with this kind of deal," Bruce said.

It was not possible, of course, to find any family, or any room crowded randomly with people, in which there are no forms of racial snobbery. This was still planet earth in a day and age preceding full enlightenment. "Forbidden lovers" might still be printed in the tabloids over Bruce and Pat's wedding photo. Certain people still spoke of the union of a white man and a black woman as "the original sin," it being a well-established fact that scholarly research, or even a political theory, is less useful than folklore for understanding race relations. Bruce was not so pie-eyed in love he failed to notice the looks devoid of civil recognition brought down at business dinners he and Pat attended or the insults of a man who accosted them with whiskey breath at another wedding, the matrimonial ceremony apparently having inflamed the drunkard's passion for pure breeding.

Where on earth can you feel truly confident of a welcome? Only with people you love. And love is the only course of life where advancement really matters. Love: It was the recurring word. Love can be a wizardly experience, striking like an arrow from Mount Olympus. Hadn't blind circumstance brought eager and starry-eyed Bruce and Pat together? Wasn't the future Mrs. Bruce Gordon more substantial than a dozen treatises on racial harmony?

In the early months of 1997, Bruce and Pat began to shop for a house. They found one near a lake, with a ramp leading to a side door, well-suited to Bruce's father. Before negotiations could get under way, however, Doc suffered another stroke. He lingered a week before dying on the morning of March 28. Bruce and Pat sat with him all that week, and while Dr. Gordon was still in a cognitive state Bruce stood by his side and declared, "You were a good father, and I love you." The old man smiled and heaved back his head like a bear about to roar. Services were held in Hillcrest Heights, graveside. Bob Magruder spoke emotionally about the old family doctor who once had helped young pugilists make honest men of themselves. Soon afterward Bruce and Pat decided to attempt to have children immediately upon marrying—they had been up in the air about this. A traditional saying of Jewish nuptials took place on October 26 in a rented structure of rough lumber and open timbers. Bruce and Pat were in svelte form from a crash course in the gym. All through the evening couples of differing colors danced together. The newlyweds kissed several times to the banging of silverware. The highlight toast of the evening was delivered by Bruce's brother Leon, who said, "The first time I saw Pat with Bruce, I said to myself, 'Two peas in a pod.' " That drew a big laugh, and Leon went on. "It looked like love at first sight. So I said to Bruce, 'Hey, maybe it's time to tie the knot one more time.' Well, I've stayed close to these two lovers, and it's worked out to the max. I don't like long speeches, and I'm not going to go on and on, but I want to say, 'Here's to Brother Bruce and Sister Pat.' "

Afterword

You can make a movie come out any way you want but not real life. None of the principals in this book knew, at the beginning, that what would transpire would be ruin and death but also unexpected happiness and a reckoning or two to bring peace at the end of the day. Ahead for all of these folks, of course, lie more unknown changes. Not that their success or failure affects the outside world in any way; their experiences speak for themselves; all else is vanity. Yet their dealings with each other in matters of race relations are also America's dealings. Put another way, this look into their lives may have value for us if we can understand and learn. Am I speaking of moral boundaries? Probably, but preaching is not quite my intention. Suppose a child is born into the marriage of the new Mr. and Mrs. Gordon. What might they say to this child, under the category of Personal Statement—Practical Lessons Learned and Humble Philosophies Understood from Life's Watertank of Unclear Moralities and Spiritual Vacancies? What might I say, or you?

A host of Americans who came of age in the 1960s and 1970s tried to organize their lives on a civil rights model, a high and righteous aspiration in the vein of ancient Greek zealotry. But all those who expect to lead an exceptional life will naturally set themselves up for disappointment. One way to look at Prince George's County is as a cynical hoodwinking: how civilized things looked on the surface, how venomous and miserable they were underneath, another bum steer—the story of race relations in America a quarter century after the civil rights movement. We can say Elvira lost herself in a place that sprang from the sinister soul of slavery. The taunts and insults of yesteryear rang in the ears. The motives of white people were suspect. As for Bruce, some hoodlums spoiled it for him. Live on the edge of a big city, and you can feel the excitement of the dream at work, but you also risk coming face to face with the stereotype of young, black, and dangerous. You can be enveloped by a fear that is indifferent to statistical persuasion. You do not care that white Americans murder other white Americans at 5.6 times the rate that black Americans murder white Americans. You give no regard to social historian David Shipler's little dig, "If fear were logical, whites would be more afraid of other whites than of blacks."

Logical? Very little about debate over race relations in America is logical or rational or clearly rendered. It is overly opinionated. At present the pessimists are in charge. University of Michigan demographers report that 194 of America's 232 metropolitan areas, examined block by block, were demonstrably less segregated in 1990 than in 1980; this is back-page news. We are ready to say "it's over," as to the allure of integration. We feel people can't be forced to buy the package. No social organizing can change the character of humankind. Man's character is his fate (more Greek wisdom), and no wonder our fate is so gray and lackluster. People may act out of a larger, rather idealistic attraction to the good, but for all our best intentions we are possessed by human weaknesses. The heart dreams, but our own eyes and mouths and weak knees mock the dream.

Harold Cruse, who authored *Plural but Equal* and *The Crisis of the Negro Intellectual,* posits the argument for pessimism this way: "No point in us crusading under that banner [of integration]. It's not a question of integration being right or wrong. The issue is that sociologically, psychologically, biologically and racially it is not going to happen. Never mind that we have more integration than forty years ago, more civil rights. Integration is humanly impossible because groups do not disappear." Truth be told, I am someone who is inclined to agree with Harold Cruse. Black Americans and white Americans do seem to be two different groups, each devoid of the studied, documentary knowledge that passes down in families and communities because the other group is not of our family or community. There are too many gaps, not enough common experiences. To grow up white is a privilege. The Harvard Law Review was able to find eighty-three pages worth of legal opinion establishing "Whiteness as Property," the material value of white skin. To grow up black involves hauling extra weight. Most black Americans cannot help but carry a memory of a long hurt—what Shelby Steele calls their "enemy-memory." To huddle in a basement during a bombing raid is to be unnerved for a lifetime, even after a peace treaty is signed. The calamity of segregation, and worse, the master-slave ordeal, lasted for so long. What has been an overall state of affairs for three hundred years is damnably hard to overcome.

And yet I refuse to give up on my young man's optimism. The challenge is to find an intellectual basis for it. I guess I would start by citing America's love affair with migrations. America is all flux and turnovers. Prince George's County is as good an example as any. Close on the heels of the arrival of a major African-American population comes now the next demographic transition. At Prince George's Community College there now are Korean characters written in chalk on buildings to help Korean émigrés who have yet to master English. There is an even bigger immigrant influx of people one generation removed from the Philippine Islands, and one of the most popular vote-getters on Gloria's slate was a Filipino-American politician. The genes of the whole world reside within America's boundaries, which is a fairly positive starting place for integration. As for ethnic pride, every rising group in America has tried to hang onto an old identity, but eventually that obsession fades. The group is integrated into the base culture—cars, guns, TV, sports, and, more often than not, the fine precepts of idealism. In addition, physical proximity leads to a level of better interaction. For every bad experience you have with members of another group, there are plenty of good experiences. Not so long ago black Americans had to work in a subjugative state as farm laborers or janitors or maids to be in daily contact with white Americans. The better off they were the less they saw of their white counterparts. Now America is alive with the likes of Pat and Camilla and Gloria who, whatever their gripes about white people, are on a social par with them and enjoy their company.

Then there is intermarriage, an American fashion of incomparable worth. From group to group, the elders have always frowned on forsaking your own kind, but the young have always won out. Black and white Americans are already "twined by blood" (in novelist Myra McLarey's phrase). Will marriage follow, in relevant proportions? I have no way of knowing, but don't you think this is America's best hope, bothersome and nervous-making though it may prove through several generations?

In the interim, what else can bring us together? We have consensus on slavery, illegal discrimination, enforced segregation—we're against them. We believe in equality under the law. Is that foundation enough for friendships, for caring about each other? Or do you have doubts about the reconciling power of legally mandated rules of behavior? The essential truth at this stage of human development is we don't have a consistent, worked-out code, legal or otherwise, that deals with all race-related situations—which may be a sign of progress. Come to think of it, a dry-eyed discussion of race relations may miss the point. Much of race relations lies in the zone of the emotional, which is to say the unknown. I cannot know your inner feelings; you may not even know them. Acceptance has to come from the heart, a heart willing to be exploratory. "A sentimental view of humankind is more practical. The races cannot comingle successfully unless every man, woman, and child accepts the shortcomings of every other man, woman, and child," to quote Bruce. Bringing white and black people together on the same plane is an abstract concept, and what undermines abstract concepts is that nothing occurs in the abstract: not murder, nor friendship, nor sex, nor love. When Bruce left Hillcrest Heights he knew his personal situation was symbolic of nothing; it was merely personal. Life is made up of people, their dreams and realities, all singular, and, in the end, the personal is the most we should be expected to achieve. Sentimentality may propel you toward the corny proposition that racial separatism will be solved by the goodwill of individuals, but what else has ever worked? Down in the ranks of ordinary people in an ordinary life, you must do what you can. You have to fight for the never-automatic good deeds. No matter how lowly you perform, you must get involved. Not to be involved is Dietrich Bonhoeffer's "cheap grace."

To continue with this line of thought, rights and wrongs do not occur in the abstract either. One thing may be a right thing to do and another a wrong thing, but life is hostile to anyone who believes there is a right-thinking and wrong-thinking crowd. Rights and wrongs can be ascribed only to individuals, not to a people. No group of people is an indistinguishable whole, presumed guilty of this or that. An elemental observation, yes, and nobody was born yesterday. The trouble is we go around acting like we were; the simplest realities elude us.

Fear is not logical. Memories are imperfect. Experience cuts both ways. It undermines our idealism, but it should also teach us to be less dogmatic. By middle age everyone's record is morally questionable. The world has too many irreducible ambiguities, and it is our nature to botch everything we set our hand to, which falls under the category of the Imperfectibility of the Human Race. So let's give each other a break. No one is entitled to forget and start over entirely from scratch, all mistakes canceled, shedding the old life like old skin. But most of us do get more than one chance. We all deserve a second look. The past traps you. Isn't there a proverb about living life in the present?

Dr. King's famously called-upon line about judging people by the content of their character is a high and righteous challenge, but it is also an almost unavoidable part of daily life. Once you get past caring about the gravity of big concerns, "You have to figure out how to share the toothpaste," as Bruce said after Pat had moved in. Not much of a grand scheme, not a major statement, but you can tell a lot about a person's character in the moments of choice that come along every day. Whether to pick up a hitchhiker? Whether to try to protect the name of a dead boy's family? Whether to give medical assistance to a stranger at the door? Prosaic happenings, without great rhetorical color. The Lord lays them before us. The rest is up to yoy and me. Our actions in these moments determine our collected condition. As long as there are good people the struggle will go on. Not that any of us wish to rely on Nietzsche in his German superiority (Great Philosophers 101 from that party school where Bruce never once sipped champagne), but wasn't that Nietzsche's point? A dream unfulfilled might be a dream deferred, a dream still waiting to happen. "The trick is to live long enough, and get lucky," to quote Bruce again.

What might an era of full enlightenment be like? Uppermost will be moral primacy. But there must also be hope, the odd, unquenchable instinct that allows me to sign off with Bruce and Pat happily married and with the rest of the people I met still involved in the real world, none of them above it all, everyone worthy of our best wishes.

Acknowledgments

I am indebted to everyone who shared so honestly the inner dealings of their lives, reproduced here, as best I could. The thoughts, feelings, and observations of these grand-spirited people inform this book, and by their generosity we are made privy to the conduct of racial doings, some quite personal but all, on some level, dauntingly universal. I thank each of them for their cooperation over the past five and a half years.

Like every writer I need support and advice, and I got it over the duration of this book from my wife, Diana Kohn; my agent, Kathy Robbins; my editor, Dominick Anfuso; and also Alice Mayhew, Ana DeBevoise, and Victoria Meyer of the Simon & Schuster family—as well, among many comrades, from David Weir, Paul Hendrickson, Mark Hertsgaard, Mark Cohen, Denny May, and the late Angus Mackenzie. Finally, I want to make special mention of Takoma Park, Maryland, the town where I live and a community of unsurpassed friendships.

February 1998

Index

About the Author

Howard Kohn is the author of the acclaimed *Who Killed Karen Silkwood?*, the story of a nuclear technician whose martyrlike death became the basis of a Meryl Streep movie, and *The Last Farmer,* a family memoir that was a finalist for the Pulitzer Prize in General Nonfiction. Mr. Kohn was a senior editor and a Washington bureau chief for *Rolling Stone* and at the Center for Investigative Reporting. IIis work has appcarcd in thc *New York Timcs Magazine,* the *Los Angeles Times Magazine, Reader's Digest, Esquire, Mother Jones,* and other periodicals. He lives with his wife, Diana, and their two children, Jennifer and Gregory, in Takoma Park, Maryland.